Willa Cather
and Her Critics

WILLA CATHER

Portrait by Leon Bakst, dated 1923. Reproduced by
permission of the Board of the Omaha Public Library.

Willa Cather and Her Critics

Edited by

JAMES SCHROETER

CORNELL UNIVERSITY PRESS

ITHACA, NEW YORK

CORNELL UNIVERSITY PRESS

First published 1967
Second printing 1968

Library of Congress Catalog Card Number: 67–13043

PRINTED IN THE UNITED STATES OF AMERICA
BY VALLEY OFFSET, INC.
BOUND BY VAIL-BALLOU PRESS, INC.

To Joan

Acknowledgments

I WOULD like to express my thanks, first of all, to James E. Miller. This book germinated in a conversation with him several years ago. My thanks also to Virginia Faulkner, who knows an immense amount about Willa Cather, and who gave me corrective criticism. My thanks, lastly, to Henry Knepler, who gave me tactical support.

J. S.

Chicago, Illinois
April 1966

Contents

Introduction

MORE than a half century has passed since Willa Cather began
to achieve national stature as a novelist with the publication, in
1913, of *O Pioneers!* As it grew clearer that her mark on American
literature was likely to be permanent, there began to accumulate
a body of criticism, gossip, reviews, praise, learned explication—the written comment of all kinds that any successful writer
attracts. For the most part, this accumulated comment of a half
century is a detritus of the trivial and uninteresting—workaday
newspaper reviews, repetitious paragraphs in literary histories,
anecdote, pedantry. But it also includes sensitive criticism, accurate scholarship, revealing insight. Most of these materials, good
and bad, made their appearance in some fairly humble way—as
an article in a magazine, as part of a classroom lecture, as a newspaper review. Some of the best comment, especially that written
by people who later gained fame, found its way into books. The
essays by Trilling, Rebecca West, E. K. Brown, and Whipple, and
the reviews by Edmund Wilson were all published years ago in
books, and some have since been reprinted. But much of the best
commentary has been neglected, and none of it has been brought
together in the form that seems to me to be most clearly called for
—that is, as part of the corpus of Willa Cather criticism. This
book is an attempt to remedy that deficiency—to sort out the best
criticism, and to give it a place of permanence.

But I have tried to do more than merely gather together good
essays about Willa Cather. I have also tried to gather representative criticism. Ten years ago when, in preparation for my doctoral
dissertation, I was laboriously reading through hundreds of pieces

of criticism about Willa Cather, it occurred to me that they fell
into categories. Partly the categories were merely those of fashionable vocabulary—made by the difference between the critical jar-
gons of, say, the twenties and the thirties. But they reflected other
differences, too: shifts in Willa Cather's work; the temperaments,
tastes, and sensibilities of individual critics; conflicting notions
about the purposes and values of literature, and about the nature
of criticism. It has not seemed necessary to refer these differences
to ultimate sources. This book aims to shed light on Willa Cather,
and only secondarily on American criticism. But I have thought
it valuable to disentangle certain local assumptions and attitudes
employed by groups of critics, especially when these have been
important enough to color the criticism of a decade. The chapters
into which I have divided the pieces of criticism represent my
notion of what the significant categories are; and my introductions
to these chapters are an attempt to set forth as briefly as possible
the relevant critical and cultural factors that explain why a group
of critics makes the assumptions and takes the attitudes that it
does.

The sophisticated reader hardly needs to be warned against
taking such labels and categories solemnly. Obviously some of the
essays I have put in one chapter could easily go in another. The
labels I have used are at times arbitrary. My introductory points
are debatable rather than definitive. These are, I believe, the
faults of classifying literary materials; and they are likely to be
especially noticeable when the materials classified are complex.
Bad essays can be grouped definitely, but good ones do not want
to be confined in a pigeonhole. I have tried to include good essays,
and have been drawn to those that resist classification. My grouping of them is intended to be only suggestive.

I would have liked to come out with a book that could be read
straight through with interest. I would have preferred that the
reader be told no more than once that Willa Cather moved to
Nebraska in the 1880's, that *O Pioneers!* was published in 1913.
But I also wanted to include whole critical pieces rather than frag-
ments. The two aims—to have whole essays and to avoid repetition—refused to be reconciled. As a result, there remains more

irksome repetition than I like. The justification is that the critics in the following pages are interested in using facts rather than in simply presenting them. It is true that the facts they use are sometimes the same facts, but the uses of them are different.

I have had in mind, while editing this book, the close student of Willa Cather, who may need a compendium of the important critical statements, or a detailed and exact record of the growth of her critical reputation. But I hope the book will be of interest also to the nonprofessional—to those who are not committed to the historical study of American literature, or who may have no special devotion to Willa Cather. In the late 1920's Willa Cather was generally considered one of America's two or three best living writers.[1] This judgment, shared by a good many writers, scholars, and critics of the time, may not have been correct. Almost no one today would agree that it was. But the pendulum, it seems to me, has swung too far. There has been no Willa Cather revival in the sense that there has been a Fitzgerald revival, a Sherwood Anderson revival, and a Nathanael West revival. Her work, never noisy or self-assertive, has attracted fewer and fewer champions in recent years. I hope the concert of critical voices in this book will help to bring about a more intelligent and enthusiastic audience for Willa Cather's work, and, by showing the ways it has been responded to for a period of fifty years, suggest what possibilities exist for responding to it today.

[1] According to a survey conducted in 1929 by John Stalnaker and Fred Eggan, Willa Cather was ranked first in "general literary merit," Edith Wharton second.

Willa Cather
and Her Critics

I

"AMERICA'S COMING-OF-AGE"
CRITICISM: EARLY VIEWS

THE decade that saw the publication of Willa Cather's early novels—*O Pioneers!* (1913), *The Song of the Lark* (1915), *My Antonia* (1918)—was, like many literary periods, a time of struggle between a new order and a dying one. The American literary tone, insofar as we can claim to have had one at the time of World War I, was still largely set by the dying order—by Eastern-based editors and reviewers of the stamp of Hamilton Wright Mabie, editor of *Outlook*; Richard Watson Gilder, editor of *The Century*; Frederick Taber Cooper, reviewer for the *Bookman*; or Harold Bell Wright and William Lyon Phelps. This tone was characterized by heavy attempts at refinement, uncritical loyalty to the prevailing business ethic, a narrowly Protestant, Anglo-Saxon viewpoint, a naive delight in stories with a "well-made" plot—in fact by most of the ideals which Shaw satirized at that time under the names "middle-class morality" and "Romance" in *Pygmalion*. It is a dreary task for a modern reader to dig into Phelps's literary column in *Scribner's* or Wright's *When a Man's a Man*, but unless he does so he is likely to miss entirely one of the two poles between which our literary and cultural life was poised, and to miss much of the significance of the opposite pole—that is, critics such as Randolph Bourne, H. L. Mencken, Van Wyck Brooks, Ezra Pound, and Waldo Frank, who were attacking the puerilities of American culture at the time of World War I, and calling for "America's Coming-of-Age."

This second group, the critics representing the new literary movement, had little that could be called a program, but they were united by a restless dissatisfaction with the state of American letters. Mencken, Bourne, and Brooks, for instance, were struck at every turn by glaring cultural incongruities—by what Brooks called "high brow" versus "low brow" culture; by the tiny fringe of "high civilization" in Boston versus the "stockyards civilization" of Chicago, the one entirely unaware of the other; by the Emersonian phrases used in public by preachers, professors, and politicians versus the crudely pragmatic purposes to which the phrases were put; by a European theater producing an Ibsen, Shaw, or Yeats versus a New York theater producing a Clyde Fitch or Langdon Mitchell.

However different the tone of Brooks's sometimes preachy polemics from Mencken's wickedly raucous invective, both were fueled by the spectacle of a debased and divided cultural life, and a desire to prod it into significance.

They waged war on common enemies—on "Puritanism," "ethical idealism," the suppression of "passion," academic stultification, the geographic provincialism that stood Boston and the East coast at the center of the world and ignored the rising giant of the Middle West. They tried to prepare the way for a new kind of literature, the literature Bourne and Brooks referred to rather mystically as a "literature of youth," reflecting the realities of contemporary American life and speech. Perhaps above everything else they objected to a certain staleness in the literary air and simply wanted to open the window, to hear a genuinely new accent and view a wider scene.

No American novelist, except possibly Dreiser, better answered the hopes of these new critics than Willa Cather. Her "prairie" novels peopled the American fictional scene with representatives of the immigrant tide which, although one of the important forces in American life at that time, was ignored in literature very much as sex and bad breath were ignored: Hungarians, Mexicans, Bohemians, Scandinavians, Germans, Russians—such as Harsanyi of *The Song of the Lark,* Spanish Johnny, the Shimerdas, Thea Kronborg and Alexandra Bergson, Wunsch, Pavel, and Peter. Her use of the Nebraska scene, which was still referred to in the Eastern magazines in 1913 as "the Great Steppes" or "the American desert," helped shift the geographical center of the literature toward the heart of the continent, where Mencken and Brooks thought it belonged. Even her diction came as an answer to a hope. It had "distinction," as Bourne commented, rather than the "crudity" of David Graham Phillips or Dreiser; but at the same time it was a genuine American speech. (Elizabeth Moorhead tells of how Isabelle McClung in 1918 reading the manuscript copy of *My Ántonia,* balked at the title of one section—"The Hired Girls." "But that's what they were," Willa Cather answered. "Where I lived in the West we didn't talk about 'servants' or 'maids': if we needed help and could afford it we hired 'girls.'") Most important of all, though, the morality of these prairies novels, the sense of values behind them, was in its way a triumphant negation of "ethical idealism" or "Puritanism," although Willa Cather would has hesitated to use any of these labels to describe what she was doing. "The old moral molds are broken," wrote Bourne in reviewing *My Ántonia,* "and she writes what we can wholly understand."

It is hardly surprising that the genteel response to Willa Cather between 1910 and about 1920 was to ignore, undervalue, trivialize and misunderstand her. The comment one is likely to meet in the pages of the *Outlook,* the *Bookman,* the *North American Review* —that *My Ántonia* is an excellent "guidebook" to the state of Nebraska, that Miss Cather does a fine job in *The Song of the Lark* of painting Thea Kronborg's unfortunate "Scandinavian racial inheritance"—is much the sort of meaningless praise the reviewer doled out to any other book of the day that crossed his desk. It is hardly surprising either that almost the only intelligent appreciation of Willa Cather came from the Coming-of-Age camp—from Bourne, Mencken, H. W. Boynton, and such journals as the recently founded *New Republic,* the revitalized *Nation,* and Mencken's delightfully irreverent *Smart Set.*

What is surprising, however, is that all the enthusiasm and intelligence of the Coming-of-Age movement produced, in the last analysis, so small a residue of permanent criticism. Mencken's forte, and Bourne's too, was attack rather than defense, criticism in the sense of denigration rather than in the sense of appreciation. They lacked the habit of praise. It is a significant fact that *My Antonia*, which Bourne greeted with the words "Here at last is an American novel, redolent of the Western prairie, that our most irritated and exacting preconceptions can be content with," and which Mencken called flatly "the best piece of fiction ever done by a woman in America," was used by both critics in their columns simply as an object lesson to lambaste another novel appearing at the same time by William Allen White, as though they could not be bothered with merely a good novel when a bad one was at hand.

The real significance of the Coming-of-Age criticism was extrinsic, and probably lies in the influence it had on the following decade. As late as 1926 Hemingway was still chafing at the bonds of Mencken's literary influence; whole passages of *The Sun Also Rises* consist of jibes directed at Mencken. Ten years earlier bright undergraduates like Edmund Wilson and F. Scott Fitzgerald read the new issues of the *Smart Set* in much the way their followers were to read the *New Yorker*; it was the school in which they formed their tastes, snobberies, and sense of humor. In other words, Mencken and the others were what was alive in the decade, and it would be hard to overestimate their influence on the taste of the twenties.

Mencken wrote only one appreciative essay on Willa Cather, printed in the *Borzoi* in 1920. It is simply a comic polemic against the "New England" school in the style of John Macy, to which he appends the appreciative sections of three of the reviews reprinted here. Considerably younger than Mencken, Brooks, or Bourne, Carl Van Doren was not strictly speaking a Coming-of-Age critic. But he was influenced by them when he wrote his essay on Willa Cather in 1921, and this shows in a number of ways: his denigration of Sarah Orne Jewett and her New England lack of vitality, for instance, and his celebration of the "passion" that blows through Willa Cather like a "free, wholesome . . . wind." These evaluations now seem quaintly dated or irrelevant, but Van Doren's essay was the first serious evaluation of Willa Cather published in America, and stands as a kind of codification of the Coming-of-Age attitudes.

H. L. MENCKEN

Four Reviews

THE SONG OF THE LARK

There is nothing new in the story that Willa Sibert Cather tells in *The Song of the Lark*; it is, in fact, merely one more version, with few changes, of the ancient fable of Cinderella, probably the oldest of the world's love stories and surely the most steadily popular. Thea Kronborg begins as a Methodist preacher's daughter in a little town in Colorado, and ends as Sieglinde at the Metropolitan Opera House, with a packed house "roaring" at her and bombarding her with "a greeting that was almost savage in its fierceness." As for Fairy Princes, there are no less than three of them, the first a Galahad in the sooty overalls of a freight conductor, the second a small town doctor with a disagreeable wife, and the third Mr. Fred Ottenburg, the *Bierkronprinz*.

But if the tale is thus conventional in its outlines, it is full of novelty and ingenuity in its details. . . . Miss Cather, indeed, here steps definitely into the small class of American novelists who are seriously to be reckoned with. Her *Alexander's Bridge* was full of promise, and her *O Pioneers!* showed the beginnings of fulfillment. In *The Song of the Lark* she is already happily at ease, a competent journeyman. I have read no late novel, in fact, with a greater sense of intellectual stimulation. Especially in the first half, it is alive with sharp bits of observation, sly touches of humor, gestures of that gentle pity which is the fruit of understanding. Miss Cather not only has a desire to write; she also has something to say. . . . Our scriveners are forever mistaking the *cacoethes*

Reprinted from the *Smart Set*, January, 1916.

scribendi for a theory of beauty and a rule of life. But not this one. From her book comes the notion that she has thought things out, that she is never at a loss, that her mind is plentifully stored.

MY ÁNTONIA

Two new novels, *My Ántonia*, by Willa Sibert Cather (Houghton-Mifflin) , and *In the Heart of a Fool*, by William Allen White (MacMillan) , bear out in different ways some of the doctrines displayed in the earlier sections of this article.[1] Miss Cather's book shows an earnest striving toward that free and dignified self-expression, that high artistic conscience, that civilized point of view, which Dr. Brooks dreams of as at once the cause and effect of his fabulous "luminosity."[2] Mr. White's shows the viewpoint of a chautauqua spell-binder and the manner of a Methodist evangelist. It is, indeed, a novel so intolerably mawkish and maudlin, so shallow and childish, so vapid and priggish, that its accumulated badness almost passes belief. . . .

It is needless to add that Dr. White is a member of the American Academy of Arts and Letters. Nor is it necessary to hint that Miss Cather is not. Invading the same Middle West that engages the Kansas tear-squeezer and academician, and dealing with almost the same people, she comes forward with a novel that is everything that his is not—sound, delicate, penetrating, brilliant, charming. I do not push the comparison for the mere sake of the antithesis. Miss Cather is a craftsman whom I have often praised in this place, and with increasing joy. Her work for ten years past has shown a steady and rapid improvement in both matter and manner. She has arrived at last at such a command of the mere devices of writing that the uses she makes of them are all concealed—her style has lost self-consciousness; her feeling for form has become instinctive. And she has got such a grip upon her materials—upon the people she sets before us and the background she displays behind

Reprinted from the *Smart Set*, February, 1919.

[1] The "doctrines" are the "Coming-of-Age" doctrines set forth by Van Wyck Brooks.—ED.

[2] The "luminosity" apparently refers to a quote from Brooks: "We shall become a luminous people, dwelling in the light and sharing our light."—ED.

them—that both take on an extraordinary reality. I know of no novel that makes the remote folk of the western prairies more real than *My Ántonia* makes them, and I know of none that makes them seem better worth knowing. Beneath the swathings of balder-dash, the surface of numbskullery and illusion, the tawdry stuff of Middle Western Kultur, she discovers human beings embattled against fate and the gods, and into her picture of their dull struggle she gets a spirit that is genuinely heroic, and a pathos that is genuinely moving. It is not as they see themselves that she depicts them, but as they actually are. To representation she adds something more. There is not only the story of poor peasants, flung by fortune into lonely, inhospitable wilds; there is the eternal tragedy of man.

My Ántonia is the best American novel since *The Rise of David Levinsky*, as *In the Heart of a Fool* is probably one of the worst. There is something in it to lift depression. If such things can be done in America, then perhaps Dr. Brooks, if he lives to be eighty-five, may yet get a glimpse of his luminosity.

YOUTH AND THE BRIGHT MEDUSA

The book [*Youth and the Bright Medusa*] is made up of eight stories, and all of them deal with artists. It is Miss Cather's peculiar virtue that she represents the artist in terms of his own thinking— that she does not look *at* him through a peep-hole in the studio door, but looks *with* him at the life that he is so important and yet so isolated and lonely a part of. One finds in every line of her writing a sure-footed and civilized culture; it gives her an odd air of foreignness, particularly when she discusses music, which is often. Six of her eight stories deal with musicians. One of them, "Coming, Aphrodite!" was published in this great moral periodical last August. Another, "Scandal," was published in the *Century* during the spring to the envious rage of Dr. Nathan who read it with vast admiration and cursed God that it had escaped these refined pages. Four others are reprinted from *The Troll Garden,* a volume first published fifteen years ago. These early stories are excellent, particularly "The Sculptor's Funeral," but Miss Cather

Reprinted from the *Smart Set,* December, 1920.

has learned a great deal since she wrote them. Her grasp upon character is firmer than it was; she writes with much more ease and grace; above all, she has mastered the delicate and difficult art of evoking the feelings. A touch of the maudlin lingers in "Paul's Case" and in "A Death in the Desert." It is wholly absent from "Coming, Aphrodite!" and "Scandal," as it is from *My Antonia*. These last, indeed, show utterly competent workmanship in every line. They are stories that lift themselves completely above the level of current American fiction, even of good fiction. They are the work of a woman who, after a long apprenticeship, has got herself into the front rank of American novelists, and is still young enough to have her best writing ahead of her. I call *My Antonia* to your attention once more. It is the finest thing of its sort ever done in America.

ONE OF OURS

Willa Cather's *One of Ours* divides itself very neatly into two halves, one of which deserves to rank almost with *My Antonia*, and the other of which drops precipitately to the level of a serial in the *Ladies Home Journal*. It is the first half that is the good one. Here Miss Cather sets herself a scene that she knows most intimately and addresses herself to the interpretation of characters that have both her sympathy and understanding. The scene is the prairieland of Nebraska; the characters are the emerging peasants of that region—no longer the pathetic clods that their fathers were, and yet but half rescued from mud, and loneliness, and Methodist demonology. Her protagonist is one who has gone a bit further along the upward path than most of the folks about him—young Claude Wheeler, son of old Nat, the land-hog. Claude's mother was a school-teacher, and if the dour religion of the steppes had not paralyzed her faculties in youth, might have developed into a primeval Carol Kennicott. As it is, she can only hand on the somewhat smudgy torch to Claude himself—and it is his effort to find his way through the gloom by its light that makes the story. Defeat and disaster are inevitable. The folks of Frankfort are not

Reprinted from the *Smart Set*, October, 1922.

stupid, but beyond a certain point their imaginations will not go. Claude, fired by a year at the State University, tries to pass that point, and finds all that he knows of human society in a conspiracy against him—his father, his brothers, the girl he falls in love with, even his poor old mother. He yields bit by bit. His father fastens him relentlessly to the soil; his wife binds him in the chains of Christian Endeavor; his mother can only look on and sigh. . . .

Then comes the war and deliverance. The hinds of that remote farmland are easy victims of the prevailing propaganda. They see every event of the two years of the struggle in the terms set first by the Associated Press and the *Saturday Evening Post*. Comes 1917, and they begin flocking to the recruiting officers, or falling cheerfully upon the patriotic business of badgering their German neighbors. Claude is one of the first to volunteer, and presently finds himself on the way to France. Months of hope and squalor in the mud, and his regiment goes forward. A brush or two and he is a veteran. Then, one morning, a German bullet fetches him in the heart. . . . He has found the solution to the riddle of his life in his soldier's death. A strange fish out of Frankfort, Nebraska, his world misunderstanding and by his world misunderstood, he has come to his heroic destiny in this far-flung trench. It was the brilliant end, no doubt, of many another such groping and uncomfortable man. War is the enemy of the fat and happy, but it is kind to the lonesome. It brings them into kinship with their kind, it fills them with a sense of high usefulness—and it obliterates the benign illusion at last in a swift, humane and workmanlike manner.

What spoils the story is simply that a year or so ago a young soldier named John Dos Passos printed a novel called *Three Soldiers*. Until *Three Soldiers* is forgotten and fancy achieves its inevitable victory over fact, no war story can be written in the United States without challenging comparison with it—and no story that is less meticulously true will stand up to it. At one blast it disposed of oceans of romance and blather. It changed the whole tone of American opinion about the war; it even challenged the recollections of actual veterans of the war. They saw, no doubt, substantially what Dos Passos saw, but it took his bold realism to disentangle their recollections from the prevailing buncombe and sentimentality. Unluckily for Miss Cather, she seems to have read *Three Soldiers* inattentively, if at all. The war she depicts has its thrills and even its touches of plausibility, but at bottom it is fought out not in France but on a Hollywood movie-lot. Its American soldiers are idealists engaged upon a crusade to put down sin; its Germans are imbeciles who charge machine-guns six-deep, in the manner of the war dispatches of the New York *Tribune*. There is a lyrical non-sensicality in it that often glows half pathetic; it is precious near the war of the standard model of lady novelist.

Which Miss Cather surely is not. When she walks ground that she knows, her footstep is infinitely light and sure. Nothing could exceed the skill with which she washes in that lush and yet desolate Nebraska landscape—the fat farms with their wood-lots of cotton-wood, the villages with their grain elevators and church-spires, the long burning lines of straight railroad track. Nor is there any other American novelist who better comprehends the soul of the American farmer-folk—their slow, dogged battle with the soil that once threatened to make mere animals of them, their slavery to the forms . . . of a barbaric theology, their heroic struggle to educate and emancipate their children, their shy reaching out for beauty. To this profound knowledge, Miss Cather adds a very great technical expertness. She knows how to manage a situation, how to present a character, how to get poetry into the commonplace. I give you an example from *One of Ours*. In one chapter, Claude visits a German family named Ehrlich, and one of the other guests is a remote cousin of the house, a celebrated opera-singer. She is there but a day or two and we see her for but a few moments, but when she passes on she remains almost as vivid as Claude himself. It is excellent writing, and there is a lot more of it in the first half of the book. But in the second half good writing is not sufficient to conceal the underlying unreality. It is a picture of the war, both as idea and spectacle, that belongs to Coningsby Dawson and 1915, not to John Dos Passos and 1922.

CARL VAN DOREN

"Willa Cather"

When Willa Cather dedicated her first novel, *O Pioneers!*, to
the memory of Sarah Orne Jewett, she pointed out a link of natural
piety binding her to a literary ancestor now rarely credited with
descendants so robust. The link holds even yet in respect to the
clear outlines and fresh colors and simple devices of Miss Cather's
art; in respect to the body and range of her work it never really
held. The thin, fine gentility which Miss Jewett celebrates is no
further away from the rich vigor of Miss Cather's pioneers than is
the kindly sentiment of the older woman from the native passion
of the younger. Miss Jewett wrote of the shadows of memorable
events. Once upon a time, her stories all remind us, there was an
heroic cast to New England. In Miss Jewett's time only the echoes
of those Homeric days made any noise in the world—at least for
her ears and the ears of most of her literary contemporaries. Un-
mindful of the roar of industrial New England she kept to the
milder regions of her section and wrote elegies upon the epigones.

In Miss Cather's quarter of the country there were still heroes
during the days she has written about, still pioneers. The sod and
swamps of her Nebraska prairies defy the hands of labor almost
as obstinately as did the stones and forests of old New England.
Her Americans, like all the Agamemnons back of Miss Jewett's
world, are fresh from Europe, locked in a mortal conflict with nature. If now and then the older among them grow faint at remem-

From *Contemporary American Novelists: 1900–1920* (New York, 1922),
copyright 1922 and renewed 1949, and reprinted by permission of the estate
of Carl Van Doren. The essay in a somewhat different form was originally
printed in the *Nation*, 1921.

bering Bohemia or France or Scandinavia, this is not the predominant mood of their communities. They ride powerfully forward on a wave of confident energy, as if human life had more dawns than sunsets in it. For the most part her pioneers are unreflective creatures, driven by some inner force which they do not comprehend: they are, that is perhaps no more than to say, primitive and epic in their dispositions.

Is it by virtue of a literary descent from the New England school that Miss Cather depends so frequently upon women as protagonists? Alexandra Bergson in *O Pioneers!*, Thea Kronborg in *The Song of the Lark*, Ántonia Shimerda in *My Ántonia*—around these as girls and women the actions primarily revolve. It is not, however, as other Helens or Gudruns that they affect their universes; they are not the darlings of heroes but heroes themselves. Alexandra drags her dull brothers after her and establishes the family fortunes; Ántonia, less positive and more pathetic, still holds the center of her retired stage by her rich, warm, deep goodness; Thea, a genius in her own right, outgrows her Colorado birthplace and becomes a famous singer with all the fierce energy of a pioneer who happens to be an instinctive artist rather than an instinctive manager, like Alexandra, or an instinctive mother, like Ántonia. And is it because women are here protagonists that neither wars, as among the ancients, nor machines, as among the moderns, promote the principal activities of the characters? Less the actions than the moods of these novels have the epic air. Narrow as Miss Cather's scene may be, she fills it with a spaciousness and candor of personality that quite transcends the gnarled eccentricity and timid inhibitions of the local colorists. Passion blows through her chosen characters like a free, wholesome, if often devastating wind; it does not, as with Miss Jewett and her contemporaries, lurk in furtive corners or hide itself altogether. And as these passions are most commonly the passions of home-keeping women, they lie nearer to the core of human existence than if they arose out of the complexities of a wider region.

Something more than Miss Cather's own experience first upon the frontier and then among artists and musicians has held her almost entirely to those two worlds as the favored realms of her imagination. In them, rather than in bourgeois conditions, she finds the theme most congenial to her interest and to her powers. That theme is the struggle of some elect individual to outgrow the restrictions laid upon him—or more frequently her—by numbing circumstances. The early, somewhat inconsequential *Alexander's Bridge* touches this theme, though Bartley Alexander, like the bridge he is building, fails under the strain, largely by reason of a flawed simplicity and a divided energy. Pioneers and artists, in Miss Cather's understanding of their natures, are practically equals in single-mindedness; at least they work much by themselves, contending with definite though ruthless obstacles and looking forward, if they win, to a freedom which cannot be achieved in the routine of crowded communities. To become too much involved, for her characters, is to lose their quality. There is Marie Tovesky, in *O Pioneers!*, whom nothing more preventable than her beauty and gaiety drags into a confused status and so on to catastrophe. Ántonia, tricked into a false relation by her scoundrel lover, and Alexandra, nagged at by her stodgy family because her suitor is poor, suffer temporary eclipses from which only their superb health of character finally extricates them. Thea Kronborg, troubled by the swarming sensations of her first year in Chicago, has to find her true self again in that marvelous desert canyon in Arizona where hot sun and bright, cold water and dim memories of the cliff-dwelling Ancient People detach her from the stupid faces which have haunted and unnerved her.

Miss Cather would not belong to her generation if she did not resent the trespasses which the world regularly commits upon pioneers and artists. For all the superb vitality of her frontier, it faces—and she knows it faces—the degradation of its wild freedom and beauty by clumsy towns, obese vulgarity, the uniform of a monotonous standardization. Her heroic days endure but a brief period before extinction comes. Then her high-hearted pioneers survive half as curiosities in a new order; and their spirits, transmitted to the artists who are their legitimate successors, take up the old struggle in a new guise. In the short story called "The

Sculptor's Funeral" she lifts her voice in swift anger and in "A Gold Slipper" she lowers it to satirical contempt against the dull souls who either misread distinction or crassly overlook it.

At such moments she enlists in the crusade against dulness which has recently succeeded the hereditary crusade of American literature against wickedness. But from too complete an absorption in that transient war she is saved by the same strength which has lifted her above the more trivial concerns of local color. The older school uncritically delighted in all the village singularities it could discover; the newer school no less uncritically condemns and ridicules all the village conventionalities. Miss Cather has seldom swung far either to the right or to the left in this controversy. She has, apparently, few revenges to take upon the communities in which she lived during her expanding youth. An eye bent too relentlessly upon dulness could have found it in Alexandra Bergson, with her slow, unimaginative thrift; or in Ántonia Shimerda, who is a "hired girl" during the days of her tenderest beauty and the hard-worked mother of many children on a distant farm to the end of the story. Miss Cather, almost alone among her peers in this decade, understands that human character for its own sake has a claim upon human interest, surprisingly irrespective of the moral or intellectual qualities which of course condition and shape it.

"Her secret?" says Harsanyi of Thea Kronborg in *The Song of the Lark*. "It is every artist's secret . . . passion. It is an open secret, and perfectly safe. Like heroism, it is inimitable in cheap materials." In these words Miss Cather furnishes an admirable commentary upon the strong yet subtle art which she herself practises. Fiction habitually strives to reproduce passion and heroism and in all but chosen instances falls below the realities because it has not truly comprehended them or because it tries to copy them in cheap materials. It is not Miss Cather's lucid intelligence alone, though that too is indispensable, which has kept her from these ordinary blunders of the novelist: she herself has the energy which enables her to feel passion and the honesty which enables her to reproduce it. Something of the large tolerance which she must have felt in Whitman before she borrowed from him the title of *O Pioneers!* breathes in all her work. Like him she has tasted the savor of abounding health; like him she has exulted in the sense of vast distances, the rapture of the green earth rolling through space, the consciousness of past and future striking hands in the radiant present; like him she enjoys "powerful uneducated persons" both as the means to a higher type and as ends honorable in themselves. At the same time she does not let herself run on in the ungirt dithyrambs of Whitman or into his followers' glorification of sheer bulk and impetus. Taste and intelligence hold her passion in hand. It is her distinction that she combines the merits of those oddly matched progenitors, Miss Jewett and Walt Whitman: she has the delicate tact to paint what she sees with clean, quiet strokes; and she has the strength to look past casual surfaces to the passionate center of her characters.

The passion of the artist, the heroism of the pioneer—these are the human qualities Miss Cather knows best. Compared with her artists the artists of most of her contemporaries seem imitated in cheap materials. They suffer, they rebel, they gesticulate, they pose, they fail through success, they succeed through failure; but only now and then do they have the breathing, authentic reality of Miss Cather's painters and musicians. Musicians she knows best among artists—perhaps has been most interested in them and has associated most with them because of the heroic vitality which a virtuoso must have to achieve any real eminence. The poet may languish over verses in his garret, the painter or sculptor over work conceived and executed in a shy privacy; but the great singer must be an athlete and an actor, training for months and years for the sake of a few hours of triumph before a throbbing audience. It is, therefore, not upon the revolt of Thea Kronborg from her Colorado village that Miss Cather lays her chief stress but upon the girl's hard, unspeculative, dæmonic integrity. She lifts herself from alien conditions hardly knowing what she does, almost as a powerful animal shoulders its instinctive way through scratching underbrush to food and water. Thea may be checked and delayed by all sorts of human complications but her deeper nature never loses the sense of its proper direction. Ambition with her is hardly more than the passion of self-preservation in a potent spirit.

→ That Miss Cather no less truly understands the quieter attri-

butes of heroism is made evident by the career of Ántonia Shimerda—of Miss Cather's heroines the most appealing. Ántonia exhibits the ordinary instincts of self-preservation hardly at all. She
is gentle and confiding; service to others is the very breath of her
being. Yet so deep and strong is the current of motherhood which
runs in her that it extricates her from the level of mediocrity as
passion itself might fail to do. Goodness, so often negative and an-
noying, amounts in her to an heroic effluence which imparts the
glory of reality to all it touches. "She lent herself to immemorial
human attitudes which we recognize as universal and true. . . .
She had only to stand in the orchard, to put her hand on a little
crab tree and look up at the apples, to make you feel the goodness
of planting and tending and harvesting at last. . . . She was a
rich mine of life, like the founders of early races." It is not easy
even to say things so illuminating about a human being; it is all
but impossible to create one with such sympathetic art that words
like these at the end confirm and interpret an impression already
made.

My Ántonia, following O Pioneers! and The Song of the Lark,
holds out a promise for future development that the work of but
two or three other established American novelists holds out. Miss
Cather's recent volume of short stories Youth and the Bright Medusa, striking though it is, represents, it may be hoped, but an interlude in her brilliant progress. Such passion as hers only rests
itself in brief tales and satire; then it properly takes wing again
to larger regions of the imagination. Vigorous as it is, its further
course cannot easily be foreseen; it has not the kind of promise
that can be discounted by confident expectations. Her art, however,
to judge it by its past career, can be expected to move in the direction of firmer structure and clearer outline. After all she has written but three novels and it is not to be wondered at that they all
have about them certain of the graceful angularities of an art not
yet complete. O Pioneers! contains really two stories; The Song
of the Lark, though Miss Cather cut away an entire section at the
end, does not maintain itself throughout at the full pitch of interest; the introduction to My Ántonia is largely superfluous. Having
freed herself from the bondage of "plot" as she has freed herself

from an inheritance of the softer sentiments, Miss Cather has learned that the ultimate interest of fiction inheres in character. It is a question whether she can ever reach the highest point of which she shows signs of being capable unless she makes up her mind that it is as important to find the precise form for the representation of a memorable character as it is to find the precise word for the expression of a memorable idea. At present she pleads that if she must sacrifice something she would rather it were form than reality. If she desires sufficiently she can have both.

II

DISTANCE, TONE, AND POINT
OF VIEW: THE ARTISTIC PROBLEM

THE Coming-of-Age criticism was in its origins more like a moral crusade than a school of literary criticism, an assimilative and democratic literary equivalent of Jane Addam's sociological "uplift." To be sure, Mencken, Bourne, and Brooks paid tribute to superior craftsmanship and style, and Bourne especially knew how to discriminate shrewdly between fine and shoddy artistry. But they all basically regarded fine artistry as secondary or suspect, and put their literary discriminations in the service of their cultural reform. Later in the twenties their movement died partly of its own success; it depended on an opposition which no longer existed. It was absorbed by a criticism which transformed and ultimately reversed the earlier emphasis—which played down cultural values by simply accepting them, and placed considerations of craft, method, and form squarely in the center.

In addition to its Coming-of-Age origins, the aesthetic criticism of the twenties had a number of other antecedents, including the chilly formulations of T. S. Eliot, who wanted to keep biography, economics, sociology, and politics out of criticism, much in the way a chemist wants to keep his laboratory free of dirt. Eliot's criticism had no immediate, popular consequences; it made its impact at the universities. But the gap between the university and the

Sunday review was never narrower than in the twenties. The reviewers who dominatd the scene were likely to be educated amateurs—Edmund Wilson is the supreme example—or men like Joseph Wood Krutch, H. S. Canby, Stuart Sherman, Carl Van Doren, T. K. Whipple, Robert Morss Lovett, and Ludwig Lewisohn, professors with one foot in the classroom and the other in the newspaper and magazine columns. Their reviews, along with an increasingly large number written by practicing poets, novelists, and playwrights, threw out the old critical terms of the preceding decade—"literature of youth," "veritism," "sentimentality," "realism"—and replaced them with a drier, cleaner set of words: "point of view," "technique," "irony," "surprise," "pattern." A review of a Willa Cather novel in 1926 begins with the words: "There is perhaps no more difficult technical decision in writing a novel than the position of the narrator. Is he to be the author directly, or a third person within the book?" It is inconceivable that a review written ten years earlier would have begun in that way.

It is always hard to say whether criticism leads or follows the books it criticizes. The Coming-of-Age criticism probably led, and surely imagined it did so. But the aestheticism of the twenties seems to have followed. The decade was a dazzlingly rich, productive, and inventive one in nearly every literary form—in poetry, in the novel, and even in drama. Our maturation in fiction can be measured by comparing a Hemingway short story of 1925 with even the best short fiction of 1915; by comparing Fitzgerald's handling of point of view in *The Great Gatsby* with his handling of it in *This Side of Paradise*; or most simply by comparing Faulkner's technique in *The Sound and the Fury* with that of any American novel written before that time. Criticism was trying, not always successfully, to get ahead or simply abreast of that kind of thing.

Willa Cather did not consider herself a part of any school or movement of experimentation. On the contrary, she increasingly fell into the habit in the twenties of regarding herself as radically removed from her time. But without question the decade of the twenties is her period of novelistic ferment. Her experiments are not so spectacular as those of E. E. Cummings or John Dos Passos, but in their quiet way they are of a similar kind, nearly as radical, and perhaps more diverse. *A Lost Lady* (1923) is, among other things, an experiment in point of view, rewritten three times before Miss Cather found the right balance between the objectivity of her third-person narration and the intimacy of her controlled limitation of perspective to the mind of a young boy. This was hardly a "new" achievement, of course; Henry James had done the same thing successfully forty years earlier. But Willa Cather's next novel, *The Professor's House* (1925), essayed an experiment of a more daring kind. It consisted of deliberately risking a disastrous break in the middle of the book by inserting there a long piece of writing with no apparent narrative relationship to parts one and three; and of making this "intrusion," her most beautifully sustained piece of prose up to that time, an oblique and ironic commentary on the rest of the book. *My Mortal Enemy* (1926) made in some ways a still more daring experiment, and one of a completely different kind, although it resembles Edith Wharton's earlier *Ethan Frome*. Like *Ethan Frome*, it embodies a theme, a story, and a chronological span that would, if developed according to normal novelistic techniques, make for a longer-than-average novel. Instead the book is pared ruthlessly to the bone. But whereas *Ethan Frome* makes a completed picture, rather like a long short story, *My Mortal Enemy* reaches outside the canvas, almost as if Miss Cather were testing in practice the critical notions she had put forth in 1922 in "The Novel Démeublé": "Whatever is felt upon the page without being specifically named there— that, one might say, is created. It is the inexplicable presence of the thing not named, of the overtone divined by the ear but not heard by it, the verbal mood, the emotional aura of the fact of the thing or the deed, that gives high quality to the novel. . . ."

But it is the last novel of the decade, *Death Comes for the Archbishop*, the one that seems most stodgily conventional, that is surely the most experimental. There is no other novel like it in American literature. The author throws out all the ordinary sources of appeal—plot and story, surprise, characterization in the usual sense of the term, social criticism and the play of ideas, wit, a striking diction or manner, a "new" subject. Instead of these, the author takes what may be the slightest resource at the writer's command —simply what might be called "scene," the power of evoking with words the feel of a place—and elevates this to the unifying principle of the book. In a sense this completes the technique of *The Professor's House* by expanding the "intrusion" and omitting the narrative frame altogether; but the author said the idea came to her while she was studying a fresco by Puvis de Chavannes, and like the fresco the book is a series of static pictures done "without accent." The Southwest is, so to speak, the canvas, and everything else—the character sketches, the stories and legends—are conceived of as elements to be subordinated to the background.

Many of the reviews and critiques of Willa Cather written in the twenties and after attempt in some way to follow these experiments in composition, tone, and point of view. For instance, Edmund Wilson's adverse criticism of both *One of Ours* and *A Lost Lady* rests on his dislike of Jamesian use of "reflectors" and "observers," his criticism being that she uses this method to evade the problem of getting "inside" her characters in the way James Joyce and D. H. Lawrence succeed in doing. Rebecca West uses quite a different set of terms, what she calls "Puritanism" versus "Classicism," to draw the same contrast between Lawrence and Cather, although her preference is entirely reversed. She prefers Cather staying outside to Lawrence's constantly trying to get inside. Krutch's distinction between "Nordic" and "Celtic," although derived independently, boils down to something similar to Rebecca West's "Puritanism" and "Classicism"; it is a distinction which speaks to the question of method, distance, and—broadly put—point of view.

The reason for the extraordinary interest in point of view may be partially that critics of the twenties were infatuated with this kind of analysis, and imagined they had discovered it, as is quite clear from the books of the time dealing in a theoretical way with the novel—for instance, Percy Lubbock's *The Craft of Fiction* (1929), Joseph Warren Beach's *The Outlook for American Prose* (1924), and *The Twentieth Century Novel* (1932), which play with point of view like a new toy. But it is also because questions about point of view, distance, and tone get at what was vital in Willa Cather's work of this her most important period.

EDMUND WILSON

"Two Novels of Willa Cather"

ONE OF OURS

Can H. L. Mencken have been mistaken when he decided that Willa Cather was a great novelist? I have not read *My Ántonia*—which is said to be her best book—but I have not been able to find anything in her last two that seemed to bear out this description. Miss Cather's new novel—*One of Ours*—seems to me a pretty flat failure. She has taken what might, if it had been better handled, have provided a very interesting theme—the career of an imaginative Nebraska boy, who, though charged with the energy for great achievements, is balked and imprisoned first by the necessity of running his father's farm, and then by his marriage with a pious and prosaic Prohibition worker; but whose noble and romantic impulses are finally freed by the war. The publishers hint that Claude Wheeler is a symbol of the national character, and one can see that Miss Cather has aimed to make her people American types: the money-making farmer father, jocular and lacking in intelligence; the sympathetic religious mother; the son made wretched by passions which are outlawed among his neighbors and for which he can find no fit objects, which he is finally obliged to extinguish in the dubious crusade of the war. And this theme might indeed have served for a tragedy of national significance. But I feel, in the case of this book as I did with her collection of short stories, *Youth and the Bright Medusa*, that it has cost Miss Cather too much effort

Reprinted from *The Shores of Light* (New York, 1952) by permission of Edmund Wilson. The two pieces were originally published as reviews, the first in 1922 and the second in 1924.

to summon her people from the void and that, even when she
has got them before us, they appear less like human beings, or
even the phantoms of human beings, than like pale unfeatured sil-
houettes, pasted on cardboard backs and, skillfully but a little me-
chanically, put through the paces of puppets. Even in incidents
that might be convincing—as in the first night of Claude Wheeler's
wedding trip, when his new bride coldly tells him she is ill and requests him not to share her stateroom—the emotions of the hero
are not created: we do not *experience* the frustration of Claude
when his wife will not return his love, and in the latter part of the
book, where Miss Cather has imposed on herself the special handi-
cap of having to imagine her hero in relation to the ordeal of the
war, we feel that she has told us with commendable accuracy almost everything about the engagements she describes except the
thing that is vital to the novel—what they did to the soul of Claude.

Admirers of Willa Cather will declare that this kind of criticism
is based on a misunderstanding; that her method is not to get inside her characters—as Dostoevsky does, for example—and depict
their emotions directly, but rather, in the manner of Turgenev,
to tell you how people behave and to let the inner blaze of their
glory or grief shine through the simple recital. But the reader, in
either case, must demand that the characters come to life. In this
novel, they never do. Flaubert, by a single phrase—a notation of
some commonplace object—can convey all the poignance of human
desire, the pathos of human defeat; his description of some homely
scene will close with a dying fall that reminds one of great verse
or music. But Miss Cather never finds this phrase.

Let it be counted to her for righteousness, however, that, like
Flaubert, she has devoted her life to her art; that—even though
her colors are faint and the characters she animates shadowy—she
understands how fine work should be done. She knows that in a
decent novel every word should be in its place and every figure
in its right perspective, that every incident should be presented
with its appropriate economy of detail. If *One of Ours* only had
more vitality, it might figure as a standard and a stimulus, as, for
the limited number of people who have read it, James Joyce's *Ulysses* has done. It might serve to shame the "younger novelists" from

their sloppiness and their facility; but, as it is, they can evade the moral of Willa Cather's example by complaining that her books are dull. And, unfortunately, one cannot deny it.

A LOST LADY

Willa Cather's new novel—*A Lost Lady*—does something to atone for *One of Ours*. Miss Cather seems to suffer from a disability like that of Henry James: it is almost impossible for her to describe an emotion or an action except at secondhand. When Henry James, in *The Wings of the Dove*, wants to present his heroine, Milly Theale, who is supposed to be dying for lack of love, he abandons the direct record of her psychological processes as soon as the situation becomes acute, and allows the reader to watch her only through the eyes of the fortune-hunter Merton Densher, and when the relation between Milly and Densher begins to be really dramatic, he sidesteps it altogether and passes on the culmination of the tragedy to the insight of a second observer who talks with Densher after Milly's death. I am aware of the aesthetic advantages on which Henry James insisted in favor of this use of reflectors, but I am inclined to believe he arrived at it by way of his limitations. It had always been his tendency to admit us to only so much of the drama of his more daring and sophisticated protagonists as might have been observed or guessed at by some timid or inexperienced person who happened to be looking on. If the most satisfactory of James's novels is perhaps *What Maisie Knew*, it is because here the person who is looking on and whose consciousness is to be laid before us is not even a grown-up person, but merely a little girl, who in consequence makes a minimum demand for experience or adult emotion on the part of the author himself. *One of Ours*, for a converse reason, was one of Miss Cather's least satisfactory performances: she had to deal directly with the problem of rendering not only the cramping of the passions and aspirations of a young Middle Westerner on a farm, but also his eventual self-realization as a soldier in the war.

In *A Lost Lady*, however, Miss Cather falls back on the indirect method of James—who was a great artist, as novelists go, for all his not infrequent incapacity to fill in with adequate color the beautiful line and composition of his pictures; and she achieves something of James's success. Here her problem is to present the vicissitudes of a young and attractive woman, with a vigorous capacity for life, in the course of her marriage, during the pioneering period after the Civil War, with an elderly contractor of the "railroad aristocracy," who has brought her from California to live somewhere between Omaha and Denver. For this purpose, she invents another of those limpid and sensitive young men to whom she has always been rather addicted and makes him the Jamesian glass through which we are to look at her heroine. It is significant that on the only two important occasions when the author tries to show us something that was not directly witnessed by young Niel Herbert, she strikes, in the first case—the brief scene between the lady and her lover that takes place in the house at night—perhaps the only false melodramatic note to be found in the whole story (" 'Be careful,' she murmured as she approached him, 'I have a distinct impression that there is someone on the enclosed stairway. . . . Ah, but kittens have claws, these days!' ") ; and in the second—the expedition in the sleigh—is able to save the situation only by introducing a subsidiary limpid young man whose function is to witness phenomena unmanageable for the first.

In any case, *A Lost Lady* is a charming sketch performed with exceptional skill. Willa Cather is, in fact, one of the only writers who has been able to bring any real distinction to the life of the Middle West. Other writers have more enthusiasm or animation or color or humor, but Miss Cather is perhaps unique in her art of imposing a patina on that meager and sprawling scene. There are exquisite pages of landscape in *A Lost Lady*, and the portrait of the veteran railroad man is surely one of the most sensitive and accurate that has ever been put into a novel of the best type of old-fashioned American of the post-Civil War period—a type greatly preferable, I grant Miss Cather, in its straightness and simplicity and honor, for all its cultural limitations, to the sharpers who superseded it.

Not, however, that Willa Cather sentimentalizes the Middle West or represents it as spiritually richer than it is—as Mr. Vachel Lindsay, for example, seems to do. There run through Miss

Cather's work two currents of profound feeling—one for the beauty of those lives lived out between the sky and the prairie; the other—most touchingly in *A Wagner Concert,* my favorite among her short stories, and now in certain scenes of *A Lost Lady* —for the pathos of the human spirit making the effort to send down its roots and to flower in that barren soil.

SINCLAIR LEWIS

"A Hamlet of the Plains"

Moments of beauty which reveal not an American West of obvious heroisms but the actual grain-brightened, wind-sharpened land of today; moments out of serene October afternoons and eager April mornings and cold-grasping winter nights; all of them as tenderly remembered as the hedges of "A Shropshire Lad." A portrait of a farm boy, whom the publisher in his rather vociferous jacket note has reasonably called "a young Hamlet of the prairie." A decidedly interesting chronicle of the boy's marriage to a determined young female who loved the souls of the missionized Chinese, but who disdained to love the splendid flesh of the Nebraska farmer. A question as to the value of modernizing, of the motors, phonographs, cameras, farm machines for which the farmers trade their . . . wheat, and their contentment. A picture —scarce sketched before—of the new and mechanical type farming. . . . Half a dozen brilliant "minor characters": Mahailey, the mountaineer woman; Mrs. Wheeler's shy beauty; Wheeler, the farm pioneer, curious about everything . . . ; a German family [which] retains the musical love of its lost home. The courage to be tender and perfectly simple, to let the reader suppose, if he so desire, that the author lacks all understanding of the hard, varnished, cosmopolitan cleverness which is the note of the hour.

These admirable discoveries are to be made in Miss Willa Cather's novel *One of Ours*. Miss Cather ranks with Mrs. Wharton, Mr. Tarkington and Mr. Hergesheimer and a few others as one

Reprinted from the New York *Evening Post*, September 16, 1922, by permission of the New York *Post* Corporation.

of the American talents which are not merely agreeable but worth the most exact study, and a new book by her is an event to be reported intently.

Yet her name is, even after . . . *My Antonia* and *O Pioneers!* scarce known to the general. Many a woman's club, which is fervent in its knowledge of all the novelists who seize attention by sneering, by describing frocks or by fictionalizing handbooks of psychoanalysis has never heard of this quieter competence. Her style is so deftly a part of her theme that to the uncomprehending, to the seekers after verbal glass jewels, she is not perceivable as a "stylist" at all. But to the more discerning Miss Cather is a phenomenon to be explained excitedly, both as a pure artist and as an interpreter. Particularly is that true at present, during the discussions of the so-called "Middle Western group," whose grouping lies in the fact that they [were born] within a couple of thousand miles of one another. Of the . . . fabulous Middle West not even Mr. Hamlin Garland has given a more valid and beautiful expression than has Miss Cather.

Because of these tokens of significance all sophisticated readers have prayed that the new novel, *One of Ours*, might be the book which would at last bring to her the public acclamation which she has never courted, yet without which, perhaps, she would never be quite content. Is *One of Ours* that book? Probably not. There is ground for fearing that, despite many excellencies, it is inferior to others of her novels. It is indeed a book which, had it come from an experimenting youngster, would stir the most stimulating hope. And in any case it is one of the books of the year which one must recommend, which must be read. Yet from Miss Cather it is disappointing. The penalty of her talent is that she must be judged not by the tenderly paternal standards which one grants to clever children, but by the stern . . . code befitting her caste.

The most important defect is that, having set the Enid problem, she evades it. Here is young Claude Wheeler, for all his indecisiveness a person of fine perceptions, valiant desires, and a thoroughly normal body, married to a bloodless, evangelical prig who very much knows what she doesn't want. The scene of Enid's casual cruelty on the wedding night is dramatic without affectation—a rare thing in domestic chronicles. And here are two possible and natural sources of complication: the young woman whom Claude should have chosen and the itinerant minister who fawns on Enid. In all of this, even without the conceivable external complications, there is infinitude of possible interest. But Miss Cather throws it away. With Claude's relations to Enid left all unresolved, the author sends Claude off to war. She might as well have pushed him down a well. Such things do happen; people with problems fairly explosive with vexatious interest do go off to war—and do fall down wells—but the error is to believe they thereby become more dramatic.

The whole introduction of the great war is doubtful; it is a matter to be debated. It is fairly good journalism, but from Miss Cather one demands more than good journalism. Where she makes the collapse of a pig pen important, she makes the great war casual. In the war Claude is so heroic, so pure, so clever, so noble that no one can believe in him. Except for the arousing scene on the army transport, with influenza stalking, her whole view of the war seems second-hand and—for her—second rate.

It is a common belief that when the mountain portentously gives birth to a mouse the affair is ridiculous. In the arts the opposite is clearly true. It would be absurd for an active mouse to take the time to produce a lumpish mountain. In Flaubert, his provincial housewife is more significant than Salambo. The Dutch pictures of old women and cheeses are not less but more heroic and enduring than the eighteenth-century canvases massing a dozen gods, a hundred generals, and a plainful of bleeding soldiers.

In the world of the artist it is the little, immediate, comprehensible things—jacks, knives or kisses, bath sponges or children's wails—which illuminate and fix the human spectacle: and for the would-be-painter of our Western world, a Sears-Roebuck catalogue is (to one who knows how to choose and who has his inspiration from living life) a more valuable reference book than a library of economics, poetry, and the lives of the saints. This axiom Miss Cather knows: she has lived by it not only in her prairie novels but in the sketches of that golden book, *Youth and the Bright*

Medusa, in which the artist's gas stove and the cabman's hat are paths to everlasting beauty. In *One of Ours* that truth does guide the first part of the book, but she disastrously loses it in a romance of violinists gallantly turned soldiers, of self-sacrificing sergeants, sallies at midnight, and all the commonplaces of ordinary war novels. . . . Lt. Claude Wheeler could not have been purer if he had been depicted by that sweet singer of lice and mud, Mr. Coningsby Dawson.

It may well be that Claude was suggested by some actual, some very fine person who was tragically lost in the war. It may be that because in this book Miss Cather's own emotion is the greater she rouses the less emotion in the reader. Certainly there is no intentional cheapening of her work to tickle the banal reader. But it is hard duty of the artist to slay his own desire for his eternally selfish characters; to be most cool when his own emotion is most fiery; and in the death of Claude Wheeler there is far less beauty than in the small-town burial of the sculptor in *Youth and the Bright Medusa.*

As to the story of *One of Ours,* it is excellently natural. It concerns the unfolding of a youngster who, more by his own inability to explain himself to his father's coarse incomprehension than by any tricky complication of fate, is torn from his career and a chance to discover what he wants to do with his life, and sent back to farm work, which—for him if not for his mates—is a prison. The war gives him an escape which is closed by his death.

Miss Cather does not seem to be quite certain what does happen to him. At times she is as undecisive as her own hero. There might be, in his losing all in what seemed to be the freedom of the war, a noble irony like the irony of the brooding Hardy. Perhaps there is meant to be. But it does not come through to the reader.

One of Ours is a book which must be read. It is a book to which it would be an insult to give facile and unbalanced praise. It is a book for discussion. And one reviewer, at least, will rejoice if he be convinced by more competent discriminations that *One of Ours* is not only as good as he thinks but incomparably better. There are books which it is a joy to attack; lying books, mawkish books, pretentious dull books; the books which stir a regrettable but natural spirit of deviltry, a desire to torture the authors, and a desire to keep people from reading them. *One of Ours* is quite the opposite. It makes the reader . . . hope more for its success than for the authority of his own judgment.

T. K. WHIPPLE

"Willa Cather"

To the query whether it is possible for an artist to exist in the United States, the best answer would be: Go read Miss Cather. Her chief importance is neither historical nor social, but literary. True, she has done her part in the recording of American life; she has played, though not often, the rôle of critic of society; no doubt she and her work are products of the United States, in so far as any art and any artist must be affected by environment. Yet primarily it is as an artist that she is of interest. However one may estimate her achievement, no one, I think, will deny that fact. That her art has undergone development, that it was not born full grown, that it has been evolved in spite of difficulties both internal and external, all only serve to lend additional significance to her present position. Because, whatever may once have been the case, she is not now tied up in social influences, not "bogged and mired" in American conditions, because she has worked herself free from entanglements, she makes clearer what current literature has to reveal concerning the present United States: she shows that the American writer need have no peculiar or invidious relation to American life.

Miss Cather has been somewhat slow in bringing to fulfillment her talents and her purposes, and her progress has followed a zig-zag course. Her intention and her conception of her art have altered more than once. She began her career while still an under-

Reprinted from *Spokesmen* (Berkeley, 1963) by permission of the University of California Press. The essay originally appeared in the New York *Evening Post*, December 8, 1923, and in its present revised form in *Spokesmen* (New York, 1928).

graduate at the University of Nebraska; during her first three years, she wrote sketches of the immigrants whom she had known during her girlhood on the prairies, with the wish merely, it appears, to note down her observations and perhaps to defend people whom she thought misjudged. Not until her senior year, she has said, did she become interested in the art of writing for its own sake: "In those days, no one seemed so wonderful as Henry James; for me, he was the perfect writer." The reader of *Alexander's Bridge* is prepared to learn of this early enthusiasm, which indeed has left its traces in Miss Cather's later work as well; according to Miss Cather herself.

In *Alexander's Bridge* I was still more preoccupied with trying to write well than with anything else. It takes a great deal of experience to become natural. A painter or writer must learn to distinguish what is his own from that which he admires. . . . What I always want to do is to make the writing count for less and less and the people for more. I am trying to cut out all analysis, observation, description, even the picture-making quality, in order to make things and people tell their own story simply by juxtaposition, without any persuasion or explanation on my part. . . . Mere cleverness must go. I'd like the writing to be so lost in the object that it doesn't exist for the reader.

If her work is considered in connection with the preceding statement, which was made while Miss Cather was writing *One of Ours,* three stages are clearly perceptible in her development, in the first of which her object was to set down facts as accurately as possible, and in the second of which she busied herself with mastering her technique. The third stage may seem a return to the first, yet wrongly; for in it she is engaged primarily not in the faithful reproduction of an exernal reality but in telling a story—in creation, that is, not in imitation. And with *The Professor's House,* perhaps one may say, a fourth stage supervened, in which additional subtler motives of interpretation as well as presentation are at work. At any rate, since her student days her main interest has been not in mimicking actuality but in practicing one of the fine arts. In spite of all she may have said about being natural, it is obvious that so far from abandoning art in favor of a return to nature,

she has simply altered her conception of art. Ever since her discovery of Henry James she has been the conscious artist, most of
all in her efforts to conceal her art. And this shift in her views on
writing has been accompanied by a corresponding change of emphasis in her choice of themes and in her treatment of her material.

The point that during the third stage of her progress, the stage
to which belong all her novels from *O Pioneers!* to *A Lost Lady*,
Miss Cather was first of all a creative artist, must be stressed, because many reviewers assumed that she was producing a sort of
combined guide book and history of Nebraska. They insisted that
My Ántonia has "historical value for its minute and colorful depiction of life on the Nebraska prairies and in the Nebraska towns
about 1885," that Miss Cather's volumes contain "a clear picture
of the life of pioneers," that she "evidently studied this immigrant
life close at hand," and that she has "reproduced it almost with
the fidelity of a kodak picture or a graphonola record." No doubt
her work has this anthropological interest; and no doubt, furthermore, those who thought of her chiefly as a recorder have this justification, that even after reaching maturity she has seemed at times
so to regard herself. Her interest in the peculiarities of Nebraskan life has obviously been intense, and she has sometimes dwelt
on them for their own sake. *O Pioneers!* is dedicated to the memory of Sarah Orne Jewett, "in whose beautiful and delicate work
there is the perfection that endures," and Miss Cather has been
much influenced by Miss Jewett, to whom she is indebted for
friendly counsel as to the proper practice of her art. Possibly at one
time she hoped to do for Nebraska what Miss Jewett had done for
Maine; *O Pioneers!* is full of scenes which have no other end in
view than verisimilitude, than local color, quaint and picturesque.
Even *My Ántonia*, though it shows marked advance, is still profuse
in detail and minute in observation; it too contains many idyllic
genre pictures which are their own excuse for being. But in *One
of Ours* the background, though extensively developed, is kept in
its place; and in *A Lost Lady* the setting is made altogether sub-
servient to the theme, which is in nowise peculiar to a locality.

Yet Miss Cather was not an old-fashioned local colorist even when she wrote *O Pioneers!*; its appeal is not mainly to the curiosity which likes to see how people live in strange places, but to universal emotions. It draws from wells of feeling at which Miss Jewett never dipped, though it lacks Miss Jewett's "perfection that endures." Alexandra's struggle with the soil, though it could occur only in a new country, is epic, not quaint, in quality; and Emil's tragic love, which holds the center throughout the second part, is a subject unrestricted as to time and place. *O Pioneers!* is distinguished chiefly for a sense of essential human nature and above all of tragic passion. Alexandra might have been—is, almost—a classic heroine. The weakness of the novel is not that it is limited in range, but that it is not focused. The author's aim is scattering, her interest divided among two themes and a desire to tell the world about immigrant life in Nebraska.

In *My Ántonia* the irrelevancies have been enormously reduced; the background is almost all required for the presentation of the subject, the portrait of Ántonia, upon which all attention is concentrated. And Ántonia herself, so far from being peculiar to an age or a region, has the quality of the immemorial. *A Lost Lady* has attained classic severity; the development away from snap-shot photography and from uncertainty of aim is complete. Mrs. Forrester's career would have been different in details only, not in essentials, in another setting, under the Ancien Régime or in Ancient Rome; no one even thought of dismissing her as a painstaking study of a Nebraskan type. Although in choosing the indirect method of narration Miss Cather returned to the example of Henry James, she has achieved, in her subordination of all detail, in her clarity and unity and order, in the apparent ease which shows her mastery, in her restraint and finish, a rigorous perfection of form for which there is no word but classic.

With *A Lost Lady*, Miss Cather arrived at what can only be called perfection in her art. Since then, her gain, which has been marked, has been not in her mastery of form—in which further gain was hardly possible—so much as in the substance of her novels. The change, to put it briefly, has been that she has penetrated farther into the mysterious depths of personality. *A Lost Lady*, I think, shows more of this penetration than its predecessors, but is surpassed in this respect by *The Professor's House*, *My Mortal Enemy*, and *Death Comes for the Archbishop*. These books have all a complexity and an inscrutability of which there is none in the earlier novels, and only a trace in *A Lost Lady*. The theme, or at least the chief theme, of Godfrey St. Peter's story, is a strange sinking or regression of desire and of energy, of the love of life, which almost causes his death before he sees the necessity of learning to "live without delight"; and this state of mind is linked on the one hand with the difficulties that attend a newly acquired prosperity and on the other with a psychological return to his youth, partly to his own childhood, to the primitive that he had been as a boy, but still more to his youth in imaginatively sharing the experience, primitive like his own, of Tom Outland. Again, Myra Henshawe, who asks: "Why must I die like this, alone with my mortal enemy?" raises questions as difficult as does St. Peter: Miss Cather entered into those intricate secrets of the heart which are insoluble. And in *Death Comes for the Archbishop*, if these mysteries are more lightly touched upon, they are none the less present.

To speak thus of these books, however, is no doubt to give one who has not read them a false impression. They are not in the usual sense of the term "psychological novels," or novels dealing with psychological problems: Miss Cather does not dissect and explain her people; she presents them, but more, so to speak, from the inside—presents not only their surfaces but their most hidden recesses. This presentation is perhaps less simple and direct, and is accomplished somewhat more by use of implication and symbol, and is more colored or shot through with interpretation —but she is still making "things and people tell their own story." Furthermore, the aspect of the stories upon which I have been dwelling is only one among many: these are novels which are conspicuous for their many-sided richness and fullness, for their commingling of many interests. In particular, *Death Comes for the Archbishop* is a portrait of a whole country and of a whole era and a whole society, as well as of individuals and their interrelations. Finally, one thing certain about these recent books is that they mark Miss Cather's total emancipation from Nebraska.

As her conception of her art has deepened, then, her artistic power has correspondingly grown, and not in her management of form alone: especially she has strengthened that particular power which is all-important to the novelist, power in the delineation of character, power by virtue of her words to make people live in her pages. The change, in a word, is that she has become increasingly objective. Perhaps it is because our knowledge of actual people is derived solely from the outside, from seeing and hearing them, that the objective treatment is so superior to the analytical, that in novels the characters are dissipated, vaporized, by explanation and dissection; however that may be, it is certain that as Miss Cather has restricted herself to showing us her people, they have taken on a firmer reality. In *O Pioneers!* there is much description and elucidation of character; in *My Ántonia* comparatively little, the people being so solidly set before us that little is needed; and in the later novels there is practically none. If in these it is true that we know the characters from within as well as from without, and if these stories are psychological in the sense that the main events take place in the mind only, yet these events are exhibited rather than explained.

Her insistence on objectivity no doubt explains Miss Cather's success in the biography and portrait-painting to which she is inclined in preference to drama. The reader can fully visualize the appearance of her people; he knows what they look like, as well as what they think and feel. They are independent and three-dimensional, made of substantial flesh and blood, entirely projected. Their pictures and their natures are depicted by a multitude of minute touches, none of which in itself seems of much moment. Of this the early chapters of *One of Ours* afford excellent illustrations—work to which justice has not been done because the second half of the book is disappointing. Miss Cather brings Claude himself, his family, and his associates visibly before us and gives us an intimate knowledge of their personalities by infinitesimal but graphic detail. This cannot be illustrated by quotation; without the context, the fact that "Claude muttered something to himself, twisting his chin about over his collar as if he had a bridle-bit in his mouth" looks insignificant; yet in its place that sentence contains all of Claude Wheeler. It is subtle, strong, and penetrating. Such portraiture is the result of insight and imagination, as well as of observation.

Being primarily a biographer concerned with transmitting a sense of the personalities of her people, Miss Cather is comparatively indifferent to action, whether narrative or dramatic. She eschews exciting incident, and she is sparing of those scenes and deeds in which character is elicited and crystallized and made permanently memorable. True, as Stevenson says, "this is the highest and hardest thing to do in words; the thing which, once accomplished, equally delights the schoolboy and the sage"; yet the novelist who foregoes the appeal of the big scene, in which character and emotion at their utmost come to a crisis in physical action, is foregoing the strongest appeal which literature commands. It is the height of fiction, and I doubt whether any story-teller who lacks it can attain greatness. It is not altogether absent even from Miss Cather's earlier books—witness the snowstorm in *One of Ours* and the scene with the long-distance telephone in *A Lost Lady*—but for the most part until lately her scenes have tended rather to idyllic picture than to dramatic crisis or stirring action.

Not that excitement is absent from her earlier novels, but that it is commonly obtained in them by other means than the dramatic, by means similar to those she employs in her characterization, by the use, that is, of details and minutiæ. Sidney Howard has well said of her: "To treat the small facts and the microscopic phenomena of every-day as significant of the dominant energies and emotions of living, this pretty generally is the woman's method of novel-writing." So Miss Cather has imparted her thrills, by means of the subtly significant. In *A Lost Lady*, Neil overhears the murmur of two voices, a man's and a woman's, or Captain Forrester picks up a letter written by his wife and comments on the handwriting—such are the exciting crises of the story. It is such incidents, commonly two or three to a novel, that give intensity to Miss Cather's work. Her most recent writing, to be sure, may indicate some development on Miss Cather's part, for in Tom Outland's story and still more in some of the episodes of *Death Comes for the Archbishop* there is more narrative interest, and in *My Mortal Enemy,* there is tenser drama—there is more in all three of these of what Stevenson called "the highest and hardest thing to do in words"—than in any of the preceding volumes. Yet even if she is learning to sustain a longer lift and sweep, I should say that she still stirs the reader chiefly by means of the detail charged with meaning, the implication which creates a brief flash and a sharp, poignant instant.

If in her method of characterization and in her handling of intense crises Miss Cather is feminine, she is not peculiarly so in all her qualities. Nothing is more striking than the vein of hardness, as of iron or flint, that runs through her world. Sometimes it is harsh, even brutal. No other trait of hers is more impressive than her sense of fact, her clearness of eyesight and honesty of mind. Yet her hardness is not incompatible with sensitiveness; those who confound strength with crudity will get no comfort from her. Her work is refined and fastidious; these qualities, however, come not from squeamishness, not from shrinking, timorous *noli me tangere* which vitiates much American writing, but from disciplined taste and controlled force. In *A Lost Lady* she has achieved an exquisite delicacy without fragility, and in *The Professor's House* she has carved a set of Chinese filigree boxes, one within another, out of a substance as firm as ivory; it would be difficult to find two stories at once more subtle and more powerful than *My Mortal Enemy* and *Death Comes for the Archbishop.* Hers is the delicacy and the refinement of mastery, not of weakness; her uncommon union of fineness and strength more than anything else distinguishes her among her contemporaries.

Oddly enough, it looks as if Miss Cather's truth of feeling were at least in part an acquired trait, self-imposed and self-cultivated. That she has avoided a dangerous pitfall there is evidence in her earlier work, particularly in *O Pioneers!* The chapters leading up to Frank Shabata's murder of his wife and Emil are admirable in their austerity, the most moving in the book; and then, at the very climax, is found this passage:

But the stained, slippery grass, the darkened mulberries, told only half the story. Above Marie and Emil, two white butterflies from Frank's alfalfa-field were fluttering in and out among the interlacing shadows; diving and soaring, now close together, now far apart; and in the long grass by the fence the last wild roses of the year opened their pink hearts to die.

The butterflies are bad enough, but the roses surely are unforgivable. All one can say is that such roses open their pink hearts with less and less frequency in her later books and have long since become extinct; they are only a sign of a tendency which Miss Cather has conquered, but of one, nevertheless, which she has had to conquer. Downright sentimentality, it is true, is rare even in her first writing, but a tender sensibility and a wistful mood of reverie are not uncommon in her prose, and are dominant in her verse, *April Twilights,* of which the title is itself symptomatic, and in which prettiness of sentiment is general. These poems show how easily Miss Cather might have gone off on the sentimental track, had she not known better; they show to what extent the unsentimental tone of her novels is due to conscious elimination and restraint. Miss Cather's taste has not always been faultless.

Many signs—her not infrequent sentiment and rare sentimentality, her original difficulty in focusing her subject, her early inclination to irrelevancies, her initial preoccupation with local color, avoidance of big scenes, dramatic crises, and stirring action, and infrequent communication of emotion, and then by implication—all point to a central limitation in Miss Cather. Hers is an extraordinarily conscious art, and in the beginning one chiefly of conscious exclusion. Her original deficiency, I hazard, was in the high pressure and the intense heat of imagination which fuse material and burn out impurities. Surely a writer who is sufficiently possessed by his theme does not have to lop off irrelevancies, to be always on his guard. He finds appropriate expression, with difficulty perhaps, but instinctively; his expression may sometimes be inadequate, but it cannot be false. Such intensity of conception I suggest that Miss Cather has had to acquire, The completed work was not at first the crystallization of the conception; if it had been, she would not have been tempted to digress or to strike false notes. Her unity she attained, not under compulsion of an inner force, but by careful pruning off of excrescences. Her earlier novels seem not to have grown from a germ but to have been put together. They look as if she were afraid of letting herself go, as if reticence were her only defense, and she had need to be watchful. This defect was hinted by Francis Hackett:

It is her admirable gift to discern certain excellent themes and to treat them with fastidiousness and sympathy. It is apparently the paucity of her gift that she does so deliberately, with her inspiration perfectly in hand. . . . She burns illuminatingly and steadily, but mainly because she is sane and capable.

Her signal skill in her self-management is a token of her extraordinary tact and taste. She has developed a remarkably keen critical sense, and has subjected herself to the strictest sort of discipline. The result is even better than one would have thought possible: all adages to the contrary notwithstanding, she has added several cubits to her stature. One no sooner thinks that he detects her limitations than she triumphantly outgrows them, until at last one learns to look forward expectantly to unpredictable improvement, believing that Miss Cather is capable of anything—or everything.

Her style is a case in point. Until her later writing seldom was there emotional tension or lift in her language, seldom did it rise to a dramatic pitch and communicate strong feeling directly. Within its range, however, it was marked by a quiet, unobtrusive competence and on occasion by what Randolph Bourne called a "golden charm." As another critic remarked: "Her style has distinction, not manner"; simple, easy, lucid, and smooth, it has always had finish and beauty of texture—the texture of broadcloth, rather than of silk or of homespun. Yet when a reviewer wrote, in the London *Athenæum*: "Her real shortcoming is that she is at present quite without a 'style': placed beside any European model of imaginative prose she is dowdy and rough, wanting in rhythm and distinction," he was not indulging merely in the absurd blundering common to English discussion of American books; he was justified to the extent only that Miss Cather's way of writing is inconspicuous, as she wishes it to be, and in a sense impersonal. It stands outside the English tradition; its polish is not that shiny gloss imparted by the *eloquentia* which Englishmen have learned from French and Latin. Her style is her own natural mode of expression painstakingly cultivated, and it constitutes a perfectly modulated instrument which can attain to surprising range of compass and volume.

Nowhere does Miss Cather manifest her power over words more successfully than in her description, especially of nature. I trust she will never manage, if she still desires, to eliminate "the picture-making quality," and suppress such passages as this:

There were no clouds, the sun was going down in a limpid, gold-washed sky. Just as the lower edge of the red disc rested on the high fields against the horizon, a great black figure suddenly appeared on the face of the sun. We sprang to our feet, straining our eyes toward it. In a moment we realized what it was. On some upland farm, a plough had been left standing in the field. The sun was sinking just behind it. Magnified across the distance by the horizontal light, it stood out against the sun, was exactly contained within the circle of the disc; the handles, the tongue, the share—black against the molten red. There it was, heroic in size, a picture-writing on the sun.

For sheer sustained beauty of description I know nothing that surpasses the account of the Blue Mesa in *The Professor's House* —far too lovely and too cumulative to injure by quotation. Here, unless it is the pictorial element in *Death Comes for the Archbishop*, is the final triumph of a gift in which Miss Cather has always been eminent, of evoking concrete sensuous imagery, an ability which lends full-bodied solidity as well as beauty to her work. Not only is she thoroughly alive herself to the appeals of the senses, but she is able to impart her impressions with added glamour. As in Hardy's novels, though less obviously, the setting which she so creates plays an integral part in her stories, as in *The Professor's House* always behind the figure of St. Peter, as well as of Tom Outland, stands the huge purplish mass of the Blue Mesa, and as in *Death Comes for the Archbishop* the land is independently and for its own sake as interesting and as important as any of the persons. The way in which the farm traps Claude in *One of Ours* is plain enough; and in *O Pioneers!* and *My Ántonia* the rôle is yet more evident: the land becomes a great antagonist in the dramatic conflict. The plains and prairies, friendly or hostile, are always present—often terrible but always beautiful, most terrible and most beautiful in winter. The sense of space which they add is all important in lending an effect of greatness to the novels, an epic scope which would have been denied by a more restricted background.

In all the novels from *O Pioneers!* to *One of Ours,* the human life which is set in this country is closely related to it either by sympathy or by contrast. Among Miss Cather's protagonists, the women have a peculiar kinship with the land: they are simple, primeval, robust with a strain of hardness, heroic. Alexandra is a heroine of the Sagas, Thea Kronborg in *The Song of the Lark* has the integrity of a single driving force, Ántonia is elemental motherhood. Much of the quality of these figures is in this picture of Ántonia:

She lent herself to immemorial human attitudes which we recognize by instinct as universal and true. . . . She was a battered woman now, not a lovely girl; but she still had that something which fires the imagination, could still stop one's breath for a moment by a look or gesture that somehow revealed the meaning in common things. She had only to stand in the orchard, to put her hand on a little crab tree and look up at the apples, to make you feel the goodness of planting and tending and harvesting at last. . . . It was no wonder that her sons stood tall and straight. She was a rich mine of life, like the founders of early races.

The only adequate comment on this is Carl Van Doren's:

> It is not easy even to say things so illuminating about a human being; it is all but impossible to create one with such sympathetic art that words like these at the end confirm and interpret an impression already made.

On the other hand, the young men in the early books, including Claude Wheeler of *One of Ours* and Neil Herbert of *A Lost Lady,* are antipathetic to the environment; they are sensitive, artistic, idealistic, deficient in force if not weaklings, fitted to thrive in favorable conditions but unable to conquer difficulties. A more complicated social picture is presented by *One of Ours, A Lost Lady,* and their successors, a wider range and greater diversity of character, and less typical, more sharply individualized portraits. The Wheeler household and Claude's friends, Mrs. Forrester and her husband, the old railroad pioneer, Professor St. Peter and all his family and in-laws, Tom Outland and Rodney Blake, even the seamstress Augusta; above all, Myra and Oswald Henshawe, and not only the Bishop and his friend, but the minor characters such as Señora Olivares—they have the variety and the separate uniqueness of life itself. Humanly speaking, Miss Cather's world is not made to fit a plan or theory and it is growing constantly richer in its multiplicity.

Yet her favorite theme persists throughout: the conflict of the superior individual with an unworthy society. And since this society is her version of the world in which she has lived—of the West primarily, and incidentally of the United States—it may be taken to embody implicitly her conception of American life. Her view is that the pioneers in general were folk largely endowed with creative power and imagination, but that the second generation, except for a few artists who have inherited the spirit of the fathers, has degenerated and succumbed to the tyranny of ease and money and things. Usually she sets off society against the background of natural grandeur. I cannot agree with Van Doren that she has few revenges to take on her environment. On the contrary, her scarification of it, repeated again and again, is as vitriolic as that of any contemporary. The American community, whether family or town or neighborhood, is always the villain of the piece. It is the foe of life; it is worse than sterile—deadly, poisonous, adverse to human growth, hostile to every humane quality. She shows us communities of people who are little and petty but withal complacent and self-satisfied, who are intolerant and contemptuous of what differs from themselves, who are tightly bound by conventionality—not the sort that springs from free, deliberate approval of conventions, but the sort that has its source in cowardice, stupidity, or indolence—of people who hate whatever does not jibe with their twopenny ha'penny aims, who hate everything genuine and human—genuine thought, or religion, or righteousness, or beauty—everything that means being genuinely alive, everything that shows true mind or feeling or imagination. In consequence, the living individual is not only of necessity isolated and cut off from sustaining human relationships, but thwarted and frustrated so far as possible. There is no social life save among peripheral settlements of foreigners. No wonder Miss Cather's characters find more sustenance in the companionship of the prairies than of their neighbors; the prairies are better company.

For such folk as her Nebraskan protagonists, placed in such a natural and human world as theirs, life is bound to have a tragic aspect, for it is bound to involve a needless waste of human possibilities. Whether their undertakings end in success or in failure, the waste, and therefore the tragic element, is there: if they fail, as Ántonia and Mrs. Forrester do in part, and as Claude does wholly so far as his struggle with his surroundings is concerned, they are thrown away because their world is not worthy of them; if, like Alexandra and Thea, they succeed, it is at a great cost in suffering and in a sort of hardening of the spiritual arteries.

Yet the upshot of Miss Cather's tragedy is not a meaningless futility, for there is compensation in the very fineness which separates her characters from their neighbors. Theirs is not a tragedy of frustration, for even at the worst they have been true to themselves and maintained their own integrity. Besides, one infers from Miss Cather's work, the only real failure is indifference, tepidity, timidity, the fear which shrinks from encountering experience and possible unhappiness, for the reason that to have lived so, without passion and without valor, is not to have lived at all. To have cared intensely about anything, even if one has not gained it, is to have lived not altogether in vain; mere living, living as ardently, as wholeheartedly as possible, is an end that justifies itself. Miss Cather always tacitly champions the poetic temper and the life of realization against practicality. The quarrel between the two furnishes the theme of *The Song of the Lark* and of *One of Ours,* and is prominent in *O Pioneers!* and *My Antonia,* as well as in most of her short stories. All her chief characters have the poetic point of view, and are forced by their viewpoint into conflict with their families and neighbors.

Miss Cather sees the faults of American life clearly enough; that, unlike some contemporaries, she does not take refuge in sheer denunciation, nor accept it as the only possible life, nor inveigh against the useless senselessness of all life, is an indication of her poise. If she is not ready with remedies, beyond illustrating what she holds to be the proper point of view, it is because she is too much occupied with making the most of her world to fret over causes and cures. She writes without the rancor of disillusionment because she has perfect balance. She has a sanity and a wholeness which prevent her from being one-sided. For example, she does not exalt the body with contempt for the mind, nor does she go to the other extreme: though she knows that passion is rooted in physical vigor, she sees the man or woman as one piece, alive in both body and spirit, with therefore a strong vein of sensuality which may find its proper outlet, as Ántonia's does in motherhood, but which may prove calamitous as it does to Mrs. Forrester. This sense of personal completeness may account for her preference for robust if simple types, and for her liking for the primitive, evident in *The Professor's House* and elsewhere, on the ground that modern civilization has entailed the loss of elements essential to an entire human development.

The shrewdest criticism yet made of Miss Cather is that she represents "the triumph of mind over Nebraska." Not only has she found matter for literature—which in itself speaks highly for her keen scent and her avidity for experience—but she has converted that matter into the universal forms of art. If the victory was not bloodless, if it left its scars, if some of her books suffer in comparison with those of writers who have grown in a more fertile society, yet they are richer and more varied than those of any other living American novelist—they are opulence itself compared with those, say, of Sherwood Anderson. The marvel is that she has been able to achieve so much, to discern so much humanity in the flat and vacant land she pictures, with its teeming soil and human dearth. She has worked this wonder by having the strength to give herself to her native environment and to extract what juices and sustenance it afforded. By not dwelling on the aspects of her world which had nothing to offer, by leaving what she disliked in the background, she has managed to find a surprising amount of nutriment for her imagination—sensuous and emotional experience, and a considerable acquaintance with human nature, among isolated individuals, which goes far in the stories of Nebraska to atone for the absence of any healthily functioning social complex. And even the latter makes its appearance in the later novels which signalize her graduation from Nebraska.

Her triumph over Nebraska implies that Miss Cather has also conquered the Nebraska in herself. At this self-conquest we can only guess; but that poise, that disciplined taste and unfailing tact, that clear integrity of thought and feeling of hers are not products of any western farm or village, nor of any state university. From the first no doubt they were latent possibilities; but since a child can scarcely help assuming the point of view that surrounds it, the development of these possibilities must have cost a struggle. Perhaps the ten years after college during which she wrote little were her period in the chrysalis when the transformation took place. At any rate, she has finally emerged showing no marks of undernourishment or of that warping to which a practical and puritanical society subjects its members. She has been able to go ahead and do the best of which she was capable—an achievement so rare in American literature as to verge on the miraculous. Had she been born into any happier clime or age, I doubt whether, save for rendering more abundant social relationships, she would have done notably better. Though she began by largely subordinating herself to her subject-matter, she has ended complete mistress of the situation and produced books which enlist interest not as social documents but as fine art. She proves that the rule that American writers must be partially incapacitated by their environment has conspicuous exceptions—and she also proves the rule that they succeed in spite of their environment.

JOSEPH WOOD KRUTCH

Reviews of Four Novels

"THE LADY AS ARTIST"

A Lost Lady

Since American criticism is as tolerant as it is, only her own artistic conscience can explain the fact that Miss Cather has slowly
and surely perfected herself in her craft. Easily pleased in general
we are; we praise one writer for his interesting story, another for
his satirical keenness, another for his philosophy, and still another
for his realistic detail, without crying out much in protest when
the defects are as glaring as the virtues. Obviously, Miss Cather
has had her own counsel of perfection which has made her not so
easily pleased. She has not been content to be praised justly for
the vividness and freshness of the sketches which made up *My
Ántonia* nor for the adroitness in the handling of plot which
she exhibited in the stories composing *Youth and the Bright
Medusa.* Instead, she has constantly struggled to achieve that synthesis of qualities which alone can make a novel really fine, and in
A Lost Lady, short and slight as it is, she has achieved it. There
would be no excuse for calling it a great novel—it is not that; but
there would be equally little excuse for not recognizing the fact
that it is that very rare thing in contemporary literature, a nearly
perfect one. Miss Cather has come to the point where she can do
the two or three things at once which a novelist must do. She can
evoke by a few characteristic touches and by subtle suggestion a

Reprinted from the *Nation,* November 28, 1923, by permission of the
Nation.

scene and a society without producing merely a "document"; she can present a character without writing a psychological treatise; she can point a moral without writing a sermon; and hence she is a novelist.

Memory is in a very true sense the mother of her muse, for in her youth she gathered a remarkable wealth of impressions, but instead of "pouring forth" this material in the approved contemporary fashion she has brooded upon it and formed it until her picture has both composition and meaning. Thus in the new book she has evoked again an epoch of the West, the epoch which she loves, when the land had been settled by "great-hearted adventurers who were unpractical to the point of magnificence" but had not yet passed from the hands of the pioneers into the hands of the swarm of exploiters and business men who came to "develop the country" with railroad, with factory, and with the hosts of thrifty hard-headed farmers who destroyed the "princely carelessness of the pioneer" and made the land populous and hence competitive and hence mean. But at the same time she has given us an original character completely integrated with the scene and a subtle problem in morals or aesthetics.

Miss Cather has been praised, and adequately praised, so many times during the last few years for her pictures of a civilization just past that in the case of the present book a fresher task will offer itself if the critic will turn from that aspect of her work and ask himself what she means by her story and what it reveals of the things to which her soul is most loyal. This lady, lost not upon the plains but lost to "ladyhood," who seemed in her big and gracious house an embodiment of the delicacies and refinements of a civilization which, save in her, had not yet reached the plains, but who was spotted within by a secret and unworthy passion—what does she mean to Miss Cather and what is the nature of her guilt? To the romantic boy through whose eyes we see her she is simply the problem as old as the time when women first were fair and false, but to Miss Cather, I think, the guilt is not moral but aesthetic, and aesthetic in a very particular way. The lady, though she did not write nor paint nor act nor sing, was essentially an artist. She was consciously a lady, and she had devoted her vitality to the creation of a person who was more than a person, who was The Lady as a type and as a work of art, so that when she failed she failed as an artist. In a completer civilization she might have found lovers worthy of her who would not have spoiled her creation but she failed because she was not artist enough to refuse to do at all what she could not do worthily. Her life on the frontier with her aging husband would have been dreary enough, and any mere private person might have been forgiven for seeking diversion wherever he could find it, but the artist must sacrifice himself for his work. The lost lady was guilty and lost because she put her own happiness before her art and betrayed her ideal to snatch at the joy of life.

When *One of Ours* was published many critics went into sackcloth and wept for a talented writer who seemed to have given her allegiance to a vulgar ideal, but *A Lost Lady* will serve to set fears at rest. It makes clearer than any of her previous books has done the essentially aristocratic character of Miss Cather's sympathies and explains her choice of subjects. The artists and the pioneers whom she has always written about are united in their spirit of high adventure, in the romantic impracticability of their aims, and in their success in the creation of comely and rounded types —hence her interest. It is obvious that Miss Cather looks not only at her own craft but at life as well from the standpoint of one to whom fitness is all.

"SECOND BEST"

The Professor's House

There is nothing which reveals more clearly the most characteristic defect of modern fiction than the fact that the theme—even the chief substance—of most contemporary novels is easily reduced to abstract intellectual terms; and there is nothing that indicates more clearly the nature of Miss Willa Cather's peculiar excellence than the fact that the intention of her works generally

Reprinted from the *Nation,* September 23, 1925, by permission of the *Nation.*

defies any such attempt at restatement. It is not merely that one would find it difficult to say what *My Ántonia* proves, but that it would be almost equally difficult either to define the author's attitude or to describe the effect produced; and even when, as in *A Lost Lady*, there is unmistakably a theme, it remains as in solution, never crystallizing into an entity separate from the story which embodies it. The quality of the emotion aroused is perfectly distinct; toward the lady in question we have an attitude different from that inspired by any other person; but from the author we get no hint how we may analyze the subtle guilt of her heroine or how we may formulate our charge against her.

Miss Cather begins, one is led to suspect, not with an intellectual conviction which is to be translated into characters and incidents but with an emotional reaction which she endeavors to recapture in her works; and she completes the whole creative process without ever having, herself, imperiled the fresh richness of the emotion by subjecting it to analysis. Some incident observed in life or recalled to memory appears in her imagination surrounded by an aura of feeling. It reverberates through her mind, awaking complicated echoes and making many strings vibrate with sympathetic overtones from which a haunting chord of music, soft but intricate and new, is born. As an artist her task is not to resolve this chord into its constituents nor to describe the strings from which it comes, but so to reproduce the various elements of her apperception as to transfer it bodily to the mind of her reader. She is not one of those who, knowing our stops, plays what melody she will upon them, but one whose skill consists in her ability to reconstruct a situation by which she herself has been moved.

Being essentially an intuitive artist she is at some times markedly more successful than at others, and her new novel is not among her best. Its method is characteristically hers, for though the theme is fairly distinct it never degenerates into a thesis; her story of a scholar whose faith in life fails him when he sees how fortuitous wealth destroys the spiritual integrity of his family is never made, as most contemporary writers would have made it, "an indictment of commercialism"; and, being always rather elegiac than argumentative or bitter in tone, its effects are purely artistic ones. Yet in spite of many fine touches it does not live up to the promise of the earlier pages. Fragmentary and inconclusive, it starts off in several different directions but never quite arrives at any of the proposed destinations.

The initial mistake was, I think, the elaboration of the character whose story constitutes the second of the three parts into which the novel is divided. Miss Cather has wished to multiply the incidents which produce in the professor his dominant mood —the result of a conviction that while achievement is good its rewards, whether reaped by those to whom they are due or by others, are invariably evil. For this purpose she invents a young student who turns up at the university and carelessly presents the professor with some priceless Indian pottery which he had discovered in the West. Later he invents a vague but wonderful gas, rushes away to be killed in the war, and leaves it to the professor's bright son-in-law to commercialize the invention. In a fashion this young hero runs away with the story. He is glamorous, he has adventures, and he furnishes the reflection about which the whole book turns: "Fellows like Outland don't carry much luggage, yet one of the things you know them by is their sumptuous generosity—and when they are gone, all you can say of them is that they departed leaving princely gifts." Yet he has no business to dwarf as he does the professor, for he is not made one-tenth so interesting nor is he by any means so richly conceived. The professor's household was, I would be willing to wager, the observed or remembered situation with which the book started. It is the fact which appeared to the author with that aura of feeling of which I have spoken, and Outland is largely as invention. He is merely a hero, almost an abstraction; he has attributes but he has no character; and he is only very superficially convincing. Put beside Outland even the casually indicated Marcellus, the active son-in-law, and the former pales to a shadow.

In "The Professor's House" there is much that is very beautiful —passages which only Miss Cather could have written. Taken as a whole, however, the book is a disappointment to those who know how good her best work can be.

"THE MODEST METHOD OF WILLA CATHER"

My Mortal Enemy

A characteristic contemporary novel which lies open before me begins: "The door opened and the sunlight sprang into the hall like a great blond beast." Miss Cather, on the other hand, commences thus: "I first met Myra Henshaw when I was fifteen." Where the first would capture the attention by violent assault, the other asks only with classic courtesy for the loan of one's ears; and this beginning is characteristic of a certain modesty of method in which half the charm of Miss Cather's stories lies.

In a penetrating essay, "The Novel Démeublé," she has herself made a plea for a type of fiction less elaborate in its mechanics than the conventional novel, and she has put her preaching into practice by scrupulously avoiding in her best work any machinery more elaborate than her tale required; yet the modesty of which I speak is something beyond that—something which inheres in the very fact that her stories are frankly stories, events retained in the mind of, and recounted by, a definite person. At a time when novelists are seeking above all else "immediacy" of presentation and are employing not seldom fantastic means to attain it, she has sought no such illusion, has made no effort so to dramatize her narrative as to make it the equivalent of a contemporaneous experience. Events are seen frankly through the haze of distance; the thing immediately present is not these events themselves but the mind in which they are recollected; and the effect is, therefore, not the vividness and the harshness of drama but something almost elegiac in its softness. The knowledge of the narrator is both mellow and imperfect; he gropes, reflects, and tries (after the manner of a human, far from omniscient, spectator) to piece together the bits of his information and to extract from it as much as he can of its secret meaning. What we get is not that sense of present action for which novelists more commonly seek but rather a mood—the reverberations of wonder, of interest, and of pity

Reprinted from the *Nation*, November 10, 1926, by permission of the *Nation*.

which have lingered after many years in a sensitive, resonant temper.

Told in a different fashion the story of *My Mortal Enemy* might be almost lurid. Its central character, a somewhat spectacular woman who made in her youth a sacrifice of wealth for love and then found herself throughout life unable to maintain the high mood which would make of such sacrifice a success, is all but flamboyant. Yet told as Miss Cather tells it the effect is not of storm and stress but rather of a quiet and brooding sadness, because its center is the mind of the narrator. She has known the woman when she was still the heroine of a village legend, still a symbol of the love and youth that triumph over difficulty; she has seen her at intervals during the years that follow; and she has gradually divined how things stand, how what began as high romance has ended in the sordid impasse to which a wife who insists upon luxuries beyond her husband's income leads both him and herself. To the girl who tells the story, Myra was more than merely an acquaintance, she was one of those from whom life could be learned. In her she had hoped to see romance justified, young faith encouraged; but from her she heard instead: "People can be lovers and enemies at the same time, you know. We were:—A man and woman drawn apart from that long embrace, and see what they have done to each other. Perhaps I can't forgive him for the harm I did him. Perhaps that's it. In age we lose everything; even the power to love." And it was not, we feel, that Myra was worse than most; only that high resolution is an affair of minutes, life an affair of years. Only things founded in selfishness and prudence last it out—hence the *lachrymae rerum* for which there is no help.

This method of Miss Cather's—and she has never, I think, been entirely successful except when adhering to it—has its obvious limitations. It does not stir deep passions and it is, as Nietzsche would have said, to the last degree Apollonian. The mood is a minor mood, brooding and faintly melancholic, with an eye turned always backward. But in the midst of our strident literature its graceful ease has a charm not easy to overestimate. Whenever

Miss Cather evokes memory there comes with it a lingering fragrance.

"THE PATHOS OF DISTANCE"

Death Comes for the Archbishop

In one of his literary essays Havelock Ellis drew a useful distinction between what he called the Nordic and the Celtic treatments of the past. The uninstructed reader of Homer might, he pointed out, very reasonably suppose that the poet was contemporary with the events which he described, whereas in the case of any Celtic epic it is always perfectly evident that the author is dealing with things which, for him as well as for the reader, are remotely picturesque. The Greeks, in other words, preferred to treat the past as though it were present because they were interested in a dramatic immediacy, but the Celts deliberately evoked the pathos of distance because that pathos was to them the essence of poetry.

Now I am by no means certain that this distinction upon the basis of race is valid; perhaps it would be safer to speak merely of the heroic and the elegiac moods; but certainly the distinction itself is of fundamental importance and it is, moreover, the one which serves better than any other to define the particular quality of Miss Cather's work. Though she is absorbed in what would be to another the heroic past of our continent, her mood is that which Ellis would call the Celtic. She has upon occasion evoked her own memories, and one would expect to find in them the softness of remembered things, but even when her stories are rather documented than recalled she manages to invest documents with the wistful remoteness of recollected experience and to make past things vivid, less because they are present in the heat and sweat of actuality than because some softened memory of them seems to be. Not Calliope nor Melpomene is her muse but rather she

Reprinted from the *Nation*, October 12, 1927, by permission of the *Nation*.

who was called the mother of them all, and she is always at her best when that fact is most clearly recognized.

Certainly her newest story—concerned with the life of a missionary bishop to the newly annexed territory of New Mexico—would be in the hands of another something quite different from that which she has made it. These were stirring, adventurous times; many writers might feel that they could be recaptured only in some exciting and dramatic narrative; but Miss Cather softens the epic until it becomes an elegy. In recounting the lives of her characters she chooses by preference their moments of calm reflection; when she wishes to throw the long tradition of the priesthood into relief against the primitive background of the new land, she seizes upon some contrast that is deep without being violent; and she sees everything as one sees it when one broods or dreams over the past. The tumult and the fighting reach us but dimly. What we get is the sense of something far off and beautiful —the picturesqueness and the fragrance of the past more than the past itself, pictures softened by time and appearing suddenly from nowhere.

In a garden overlooking Rome, a cardinal drinks his wine and discusses the appointment of a new bishop for a vague and distant see. That bishop, come all the way from the Great Lakes, struggles with the paganism of his priests, rides miles over the desert to perform a belated marriage ceremony over the Mexicans whose children he has baptized, or dreams of the cathedral which shall some day rise in the savage land; but at night he cooks himself a soup with "nearly a thousand years of history" in it and in the sense of these vanished contrasts lies the effect of the book.

After supper was over and the toasts had been drunk, the boy Pablo was called in to play for the company while the gentlemen smoked. The banjo always remained a foreign instrument to Father Latour; he found it more than a little savage. When this strange yellow boy played it, there was softness and languor in the wire strings—but there was also a kind of madness; the recklessness, the call of wild countries which all these men had felt and followed in one way or another. Through clouds of cigar smoke, the scout and the soldiers, the Mexican *rancheros,* and the priests, sat silently watching the bent head and crouching shoulders of the banjo player, and his see-sawing yellow hand, which sometimes lost all form and became a mere whirl of matter in motion, like a patch of sandstorm.

Even when Miss Cather strives most consciously to give to her books a narrative movement there is likely to be something static or picture-like about her best effects, and when she falters it is usually in the effort to carry the reader from one to the other of the moments which rise like memories before her. In the present instance she has nothing that could properly be called a plot, but she is wisely content to accept the fact and to depend upon the continuous presence of beauty rather than upon any movement to hold the interest of the reader. When things are recalled in the mood of elegy there is no suspense and they do not take place one after the other because, all things being merely past, there is no time but one. And so it is in the case of *Death Comes for the Archbishop*. It is a book to be read slowly, to be savored from paragraph to paragraph, and it is quite the most nearly perfect thing which its author has done since *A Lost Lady*.

REBECCA WEST

"The Classic Artist"

The most sensuous of writers, Willa Cather builds her imagined world almost as solidly as our five senses build the universe around us. This account of the activities of a French priest who was given a diocese in the southwest during the late forties, impresses one first of all by its amazing sensory achievements. She has within herself a sensitivity that constantly presents her with a body of material which would overwhelm most of us, so that we would give up all idea of transmitting it and would sink into a state of passivity; and she has also a quality of mountain-pony sturdiness that makes her push on unfatigued under her load and give an accurate account of every part of it. So it is that one is not quite sure whether it is one of the earlier pages in *Death Comes for the Archbishop* or a desert in central New Mexico, that is heaped up with small conical hills, red as brickdust, a landscape of which the human aspect is thirst and confusion of the retina at seeing the earth itself veritably presenting such re-duplications of an image as one could conceive only as consequences of a visual disorder. When the young bishop on his mule finds this thirst smouldering up to flame in his throat and his confusion whirling faster and faster into vertigo, he blots out his own pain in meditating on the Passion of our Lord; he does not deny to consciousness that it is in a state of suffering, but leads it inward from the surface of being where it feebly feels itself contending with innumerable

From *The Strange Necessity* (New York, 1928), copyright 1927, 1955 by Rebecca West. Reprinted by permission of The Viking Press, Inc. The essay originally was published in the New York *Herald Tribune,* September 11, 1927.

purposeless irritations to a place within the heart where suffering is held to have been proved of greater value than anything else in the world, the one coin sufficient to buy man's salvation; this, perhaps the most delicate legerdemain man has ever practised on his senses, falls into our comprehension as lightly as a snowflake into the hand, because of her complete mastery of every phase of the process. But she becomes committed to no degree of complication as her special field. A page later she writes of the moment when the priest and his horses come on water, in language simple as if she were writing a book for boys, in language exquisitely appropriate for the expression of a joy that must have been intensest in the youth of races.

Great is her accomplishment. That feat of making a composition out of the juxtaposition of different states of being, which Velasquez was so fond of practising, when he showed the tapestry-makers working in shadow and some of their fellows working behind them in shadows honeycombed with golden motes, and others still further back working in the white wine of full sunlight, is a diversion of hers also. She can suggest how in this land of carnelian hills that become lavender in storm, of deserts striped with such strangeness as ochre-yellow waves of petrified sand, of mesas behind which stand cloud mesas as if here Nature had altered her accustomed order and the sky took reflections as the waters do elsewhere, of beauty on which a quality of prodigiousness is perpetually present like a powerful condiment, the Bishop and his boyhood friend would find refreshment in going back in memory to the cobbled streets of Clermont, where ivy that is cool to the touch and wet about the roots tumbles over garden walls and horse-chestnuts spread a wide shade which is scarcely needed, and simple families do explicable things and eat good food and love one another. Perfectly conveyed is the difference in palpability between things seen and things remembered; as perfectly as those other differences in palpability which became apparent to the senses of the Archbishop as death approached him. Then the countryside of Auvergne became a place too wet, too cultivated, too human; the air above it seemed to have something of the heaviness of sweat. The air that can only be breathed on land which has not yet been committed to human purposes, the light, dry air of the desert, is more suited to one who is now committed to them as little as it. He has now the excess of experience which comes to old age; since no more action is required from him. There is no particular reason why his attention should be focused on the present, so as he lies in his bed in the study in Santa Fé where he had begun his work forty years before, all the events of his life exist contemporaneously in his head; his childish days in Clermont and on the coast of the Mediterranean, his youth in the seminary at Rome, his travels among the deserts and the mesas, the Mexicans and the Indians. That is well enough but it could not go on. He longs, and one can feel the trouble in the old man's head as he wishes it, for this free wind that has never been weighed down by the effluvia of human effort to blow away his soul out into its sphere of freedom.

The book, it may be seen, though clear as a dewdrop, is not superficial. The author is inspired to her best because she is working on a theme that is peculiarly sympathetic to her. When Father Vaillant goes to administer the sacraments to the faithful on the ranchero of Manuel Lujon he bustles into the kitchen and with scarcely less care than he bestows on preparations for the holy office he rescues the leg of mutton that is destined for his dinner and cooks it himself, so that when he carves it at table a "delicate stream of pink juice" follows the knife. It is an incident which Miss Cather relates with a great deal of sisterly feeling; and it is, of course, a beautiful symbol of the effective synthesis which inspires the Roman Catholic Church to its highest activities. That Church has never doubted that sense is a synthesis of the senses; and it has never doubted that man must take the universe sensibly. The people, the suffering generations, deprived of material for the enjoyment of the senses, cry out for saints who shall sanctify their own fates by being holy and choosing it as the most suitable medium for their holiness, who court suffering, who deprive their senses of all material enjoyment. But behind them watches the Church to see that they avail themselves of this hungry sainthood only as one does of some powerful opiate, in small doses and not habitually. Not for long were the faithful to be allowed to abuse

or miscall the body which has been given them as the instrument
with which they must perform their task of living. Those who
claimed supersensual ecstasies were—as one may read in the life
of St. Teresa—exposed to the investigations of persons who com-
ported themselves like Inspectors of Nuisances. While it is untrue
to say that Protestantism invented or even specially stimulated
Puritanism—the type of mind which tries to satisfy an innate
sense of guilt by the coarser forms of expiation is naturally attracted to whatever the current religion may be and emerges
equally under Catholicism or Paganism or Islamism or any other
formulated faith—it is true to say that Catholicism has always
suppressed with extreme rigour such heresies as led to unwhole-
some abstinences becoming the general practice. The Cathari,
for example, were persecuted because although their ascetic teach-
ings might have led to individual sinlessness they would have
wiped out the community, and there would have been so many
happy villages the fewer. It would almost seem sometimes as if
the Church burned heretics because it was afraid that if it did not
man would burn his soup.

And soup, as the Roman Catholic Church knows, as Miss Cather
knows, is a matter of the first importance. "When one comes to
think of it," said the Bishop, sitting over a meal prepared by
Father Vaillant on one of their early days at Santa Fé, when they
were gloomily discussing the possibility of maintaining a French
propriety of diet in a country so basely ignorant that it knew nothing of the lettuce, "soup like this is not the work of one man. It is
the result of a constantly refined tradition. There are nearly a
thousand years of history in this soup. . . ." Doubtless he would,
if pressed, have admitted that while the introduction of good
soup and lettuce was not the object of his labours in his diocese,
they would at least afford a test of success. It was with no sense
of trivial declension from his activities that, at the end of his life,
he chose for the country estate of his retirement land on which he
had seen an apricot-tree with "two trunks, each of them thicker
than a man's body," which was glorious with great golden fruit of
superb flavour, and because of that indication of suitability
planted orchards of pears and apples, cherries and apricots there

from which he furnishes young trees for his priests to plant where-
ever they went, for their own eating and to encourage the Mexicans to add fruit to their starchy diet. In all his intermediate activities he has never really gone far from the earth that grows let-
tuces and apricots. There is a chapter relating to the rebellious
Father Martinez, in which Miss Cather with a blacksmith's muscle
has lifted into a compendious form a prodigious deal of reading about the problem the Church has had to face in its efforts to
secure priests lion-like enough to maintain the faith on the raw
edges of civilization against the paganism of lawless men and yet
lamblike enough to remain in loyal subjection to authority seated
half the world away; it too is a demonstration of sense founded on
a fusion of the senses. The Bishop, although fastidious to almost
the point of squeamishness, tolerates this priest who rides at
the head of a cavalcade of Mexicans and Indians like their rob-
ber chief, whose corridor walks are perpetually painted with a
shadow-show of servant maids fleeing before young men whose
origin seems to be indicated by the tart disputations at the sup-
per-table concerning the celibacy of the clergy, whose past is
stained with bloodshed arising out of lecherous desire for certain
lands, as hot as the lands themselves. In spite of all this the Bishop
does not deprive him of his parish. He looks around and marks the
theatrical fervour of the landscape of "the flaming cactus and the
gaudily decorated altars," of the gestures with which the women
flung shawls on the pathway before him and the men snatched his
hand to kiss the episcopal ring; and perceives as in complete keeping with that world this passionate and devout scoundrel who
gives his virility to the chanting of the Mass as he gave it to murder, to the enrichment of his church with vestment and shining
vessels as to the complication of his domesticity with amorous-
ness. It is as if he tasted a *chili con carne,* judged it just as
the Mexicans who were going to eat it would like it, and out of
regard for the harmonies of life smoothed from his face all signs
of what his French palate thought of the high seasoning. Though
this may be an affair of importance, it is still an affair of the senses.

But there is more to life than this. St. Teresa was greater than
her investigators. The community that chose to die might know

more in the moment when it went out to death than the neighbouring unperverted community might know when it came into supper. It is inconceivable that man was born of woman to suffer more forms of agony than there are kinds of flowers simply in order that he should make good soup. That complaint might be made against Miss Cather herself, for her own absorption in sense and the senses. She arranges with mastery such phenomena of life as the human organism can easily collect through the most ancient and most perfected mechanisms of body and mind. But must not such an art, admirable as it is, be counted as inferior to an art which accepts no such limitations, which deals with the phenomena of life collected by the human organism with such difficulty that to the overstrained consciousness they appear only as vague intimations, and the effort of obtaining them develops new mechanisms? Ought not art that tries to make humanity superhuman be esteemed above art that leaves humanity exactly as it is? One is reminded constantly of that issue while one is reading *Death Comes for the Archbishop* by its similarity in material to some of the recent work of Mr. D. H. Lawrence. Both come face to face with the Indian and find there is no face there but an unclimbable cliff, giving no foothold, like the side of a mesa; but each takes it so differently. "The Bishop," says Miss Cather, of a certain conversation by a camp fire, "seldom questioned Jacinto about his thoughts or beliefs. He didn't think it polite, and he believed it to be useless. There was no way in which he could transfer his own memories of European civilization into the Indian mind, and he was quite willing to believe that behind Jacinto there was a long tradition, a story of experience, which no language could translate to him. A chill came with the darkness. . . ." and so on. There is no attempt to fit the key into the lock. That door will not open. But Mr. Lawrence cries out in his last book of essays, "The consciousness of one branch of humanity is the annihilation of the consciousness of another branch. . . . We can understand the consciousness of the Indian only in terms of the death of our consciousness." There is nothing here to say he will not try it. Indeed, the querulousness of it suggests a tired, brave man becoming aware of an imperative call to further adventures. There may be necessary a re-entrance to the darkness of the womb, another fretful birth. He will do it!

The difference in their daring is powerfully suggested by a certain chapter of this book named "Stone Lips." The Bishop and his Indian guide are on the desert when a snowstorm breaks and covers the land with a white blindness. The Indian makes the Bishop leave the mules and clamber over rocks and fallen trees to a cliff in which there is a cave that has an opening sinister enough in itself, with rounded edges like lips. It is large, shows signs of being used for ceremonial purposes, and is clean and swept; but it is icy-cold and full of a slight but loathsome odour. There is a hole in the wall about the size of a watermelon. This the Indian guide fills up with a mixture of stones, wood, earth and snow. Then he builds a fire, and the odour disappears. There is, however, a humming as of bees, which puzzles the Bishop till the guide takes him to a part of the cave where there is a crack in the floor through which sounds the roaring of an underground river. The Bishop drops off to sleep, but wakes up and finds the boy mounting guard over the hole in the wall, listening as though to hear if anything were stirring behind the patch of plaster. The episode owes its accent, of course, to the proximity of the cave to the pueblo of Pecos, which was reputed to keep a giant serpent out in the mountains for use in its religious festivals. Miss Cather passes through this experience responding sensitively and powerfully to its splendid portentousness, but she stays with the Bishop the whole time. Mr. Lawrence, on the other hand, would have been through the hole in the wall after the snake. He would have been through the crack in the floor after the river. Irritably and with partial failure, but also with greater success than any previous aspirant, he would have tried to become the whole caboodle. Does not such transcendental courage, does not such ambition to extend consciousness beyond its present limits and elevate man above himself, entitle his art to be ranked as more important than that of Miss Cather?

To ask that question is our disposition to-day. It is the core of contemporary resentment against the classics. But one must suspect it. It leads to such odd preferences on the part of the young:

for example, to the exaltation of James Joyce over Marcel Proust, although *A La Recherche du Temps Perdu* is like a beautiful hand with long fingers reaching out to pluck a perfect fruit, without error, for the accurate eye knows well it is growing just there on the branch, while *Ulysses* is the fumbling of a horned hand in darkness after a doubted jewel. Such a judgment leaves out of account that though a jewel is more precious than a fruit, grace also is one of the ultimate values, a chief accelerator of our journey towards the stars. It should, like all occasions when we find ourselves rejecting non-toxic pleasantness, make us examine ourselves carefully to see if we are not the latest victims to the endemic disease of Puritanism, to this compulsion to satisfy an innate sense of guilt by the coarser forms of expiation. There is, after all, no real reason to suppose that there is less Puritan impulse in humanity than there ever was, since the origin and control of such infantile fantasies as the sense of guilt has hardly yet begun to be worked upon; and it would be peculiarly apt at this moment to express itself in the sphere of art. The Church no longer takes care of it among the literate, for during the last century they either ceased to go to church at all or have transferred it to some faith which does not pander to those lownesses; but they found a new and disguised channel for the old impulse in reformist politics. That again has been denied them, for the war has damped political enthusiasms just as the biological advances of the nineteenth century damped religious fervour. The weaker spirits are scared by the evidence that social change may involve serious hardship and have scuttled back to Toryism; the stronger spirits who can bear to envisage hardship are just as paralyzed by their doubt whether there is any economic system yet invented which is certain to justify by success the inconveniences of change. There has happened therefore a curious reversal of the position in regard to the gratification of the Puritan and counter-Puritan impulses in the last century. The young men who were Puritans in politics were anti-Puritans in literature. They were willing to die for the independence of Poland or the Manchester Fenians; and they relaxed their tension by voluptuous reading in Swinburne. Nowadays the corresponding young men gratify their

voluptuousness by an almost complete acquiescence in the political and economic *status quo,* an unremorseful acceptance of
whatever benefits it may bring them personally; and they placate
their Puritanism by demanding of literature that never shall
it sit down to weave beauty out of the material which humanity
has already been able to collect with its limited powers, that perpetually it must be up and marching on through the briars towards some extension of human knowledge and power.

It is characteristically Puritan, this demand that the present
should be annihilated. The church-goers of the breed insisted
that we should have no pleasures in this world but should devote
ourselves to preparation for the next. The political sphere made
the same demand in many veiled forms, which one may perceive,
in the phrase constantly used in propagandist literature that it
is the duty of each generation to sacrifice itself for the sake of future generations. That is, of course, pernicious. It makes man try
to live according to another rhythm than that of the heart within
him, which has its systole and its diastole. It deftly extracts all
meaning out of life, which, if it were but an eternal climbing of
steep steps, sanity would refuse to live. And æsthetically it is the
very deuce, for in rejecting classical art it rejects the real sanction
of the revolutionary art it pretends to defend. When Willa Cather
describes in terms acceptable to a Catholic Missionary Society the
two young priests stealing away secretly from Clermont to avoid
saying good-bye to their devoted families, who would have been
too greatly distressed by the loss of their sons, she is not as explicit as Mr. Lawrence would be in his statement that in this separation a creature as little Christian as a snake was trying to
slough its skin, that a force as hidden from the sun as an underground river was trying to separate itself from its source. But by
proving exhaustively what joy a man can have and what beauty
he can make by using such materials and such mechanism as he
already has, she proves Mr. Lawrence's efforts to add to their number worth while. Since man can work thus with his discoveries,
how good it is that there should be discoveries! There is nothing
here which denotes rejection of any statement of life fuller than
her own. Her work has not that air of claiming to cover all the

ground which gives the later novels of Henry James the feeling of pretentiousness and futility which amazingly co-exists with the extremes of subtlety and beauty and which is perhaps due to his attempt to account for all the actions and thoughts of his characters by motives established well in the forefront of consciousness. She is indeed deeply sympathetic to what the order of artist who is different from herself is trying to do, as can be seen in her occasional presentation of incidents that would be beautifully grist to their mill: as in the enchanting story of the El Greco painting of a St. Francis in meditation, which was begged from a Valencian nobleman by a hairy Franciscan priest from New Mexico for his mission church, who forced the gift by his cry, "You refuse me this picture because it is a good picture. It is too good for God, but it is not too good for you"; and was at the pillaging of the mission church either burned or taken to some pueblo. How we can imagine that part of the spirit of El Greco which was in that picture, crying out while flames made it the bright heart of an opening flower of massacre, or while the smoke of the adobe dwelling discolours and stripes it like a flagellation, *"It is just as I thought!"* And how like the anguished accents of Mr. Lawrence's work sounds that imagined cry. Willa Cather is not unaware of these fissures in the solid ground of life, but to be aware of them is not her task. Hers is it to move on the sunlit face of the earth, with the gracious amplitude of Ceres, bidding the soil yield richly, that the other kind of artist, who is like Persephone and must spend half of his days in the world under the world, may be refreshed on emergence.

E. K. BROWN

"Willa Cather"

Before the year [1946] ends, Willa Cather will be seventy. Lately her fiction has been of less concern to critics than it was ten years ago, and even then was of less concern than in the second and third decades of the century. It is among the gross abuses of much recent American criticism—I mean, of the criticism which mirrors the time, has influence, is widely quoted, and passes into anthologies—to discuss books primarily as illustrations or turning points of social and aesthetic tendencies, rather than as entities delightful and significant in themselves, made so by a beauty of craftsmanship and depth of vision. A well-read critic will find it very easy, even if he has little or no perception of depth and beauty, to discuss a book in the current fashion; he has no need to find his way into the core of the book, to discover its inmost principle, the source of its unity, warmth, and color; instead he may pontificate upon qualities he has known in a hundred other books, and about whose worth he has long ago made up his mind and closed it.

It is by no means easy to relate Miss Cather's fiction to the vogue of technical stunts and of psychoanalytical explorations which distinguished the nineteen-twenties, and it is scarcely easier to relate it to the ill-digested massive sociological inquiries which bloated so much of the fiction of the nineteen-thirties. There are relations. It was amid the technical enthusiasms of the twenties that Miss Cather developed a new method of narration and a new

Reprinted from the *Yale Review,* 1946, by permission of the *Yale Review* and Mrs. E. K. Brown.

use of setting, shaking off all the heavinesses and dulnesses of the traditional novel as she had formerly conceived it and as most of her contemporaries continued to practise it. Her fiction, too, has its sociology: she broke off her history of the decay of the small Mid-Western town just where Sinclair Lewis began his. Between *A Lost Lady* and *Main Street* there are many threads of relationship, and there are almost as many between *One of Ours* and *Babbitt*. No novelist has seen with a more discerning eye the role the railroad plays in the social and ethical life of the Western town. Still, the fullest understanding of such relationships would carry one but a very small distance towards the rare essence of Miss Cather's fiction. This may be apprehended not by the critic who is forever remembering what her contemporaries have been thinking and devising, but only if one will forget the characteristics of the historical moment in which she happened to write and look long and directly at what she actually has written. Before the historical moment is wholly left behind there is, however, one fact to be noted—her strong, conscious, and rapidly increasing aversion from it.

Ten years ago, in the prefatory note to *Not Under Forty*, Miss Cather remarked that "the world broke in two in 1922 or thereabouts," confessed that she was among those who had remained on the far side of the chasm, and warned all under forty that the expressions of her mind could scarcely interest them. 1922 is the year of *Ulysses* and *The Waste Land,* and in method and temper these works are a world apart from the serenity and lucidity of her fiction. But her estrangement from the modern world, particularly the modern American world, is much more than literary. When she spoke of 1922 I doubt that she was primarily remembering Joyce or T. S. Eliot; indeed, I should not be surprised to hear that she was not thinking of them at all. She was certainly thinking much more painfully of changes closer to the actual fabric of living in America. In her memorial portrait of Mrs. James T. Fields, the widow of the great Boston publisher, she evokes the old house in Charles Street, where she had so often sat at tea with the tireless hostess and Sarah Orne Jewett, amid so many relics of what was most distinguished in English and American

arts and letters and song in the last century, and where conversation continued to have that fusion of fragrance with substance
which was a mark of the older time when people could still linger
like Dr. Johnson and have their talk out, and when into that talk
they distilled suggestions of their deepest thoughts and most considered feelings. That house in Charles Street has, she says, given
way to a garage. "Perhaps," she suggests, "the garage and all it
stands for represent the only real development and have altogether taken the place of things formerly cherished on that
spot." The garage is her real enemy, not *Ulysses*. In "Coming,
Aphrodite!" a short story written not long before 1922, and expressing with delicate truth what Greenwich Village was like
when it was the true home of poetry and art, there is a deeply felt
picture of Washington Square in the spring, the grass "blindingly
green," the fountain alive again after its winter arrest, and
through the Arch a vista of "the young poplars with their bright
sticky leaves, and the Brevoort glistening in its spring coat of
paint, and shining horses and carriages," and marring all, the
portent of "an automobile, misshapen and sullen, like an ugly
threat in a stream of things that were bright and beautiful and
alive."

In 1922 Miss Cather must have been at work upon *A Lost Lady*,
which came out in the following year. In it and in *One of Ours*,
which actually appeared in 1922, the ruling mood is one new to
her fiction. She had always been critical of that aspect of American life for which the garage was to be so bountiful a fulfilment,
although it was not until she wrote these novels that she went in
fear of it. Standardized, money-minded, complacently respectable
folk, devoted to mechanical things, or spiritual things mechan-
ically apprehended, had always fared ill in her fiction. In one of
the most biting of her short stories, "A Gold Slipper," she had
exhibited lightly but firmly the core of emptiness in a pillar of
Pittsburgh (a city she knew well from her years of reporting and
teaching), a coal-dealer, member of the Presbytery of the First
Church, and despiser of all living things. In his premature old
age he goes to his office every week-end because there is no other
place in the whole round of his life that interests him, and turns

over his will and his insurance policies. He had laid his finger
upon reality only once, when a great singer, out of devilment,
left a gold slipper in his Pullman when she withdrew after a futile conversation to her drawing room. He had made nothing of
her at the time except that she was a nuisance and that he was
glad to have told her some brief home truths about herself and
her art, but after a while he was pleased that he had not thrown
the slipper away, and could turn it over in his hands between
readings of the will and the policies. "The Black Hawk boys,"
Miss Cather wrote in *My Ántonia*, "looked forward to marrying
the Black Hawk girls, and living in a brand-new little house, with
best chairs that must not be sat upon and hand-painted china that
must not be used." But this contemptible half-dead world of the
prairie town was no real danger to heroic or distinguished character; the vigorous, beautiful, dynamic Scandinavian and Slavic
girls from the surrounding farms had the future in their keeping;
if they had a rough time so long as they served in the town, one
made a fortune in the Klondike, another as the leading *couturière*
in San Francisco; and Ántonia herself, the finest of all, had a dozen
magnificent children, and ruled over a vast and fertile farm. The
townsfolk of Black Hawk were impotent creatures, and in the end
they did not matter. In *The Song of the Lark*, the same confidence
appeared. Thea Kronborg appreciated that the characteristic
townsfolk of Moonstone were her natural enemies; she accepted,
while she was still young, as the inevitable lot of great talent, that
she should find disapproval and envy among even her own
brothers and sisters. But Moonstone could not delay her in her
course; it could irritate and grieve her, but that was all. Toward
1922, Miss Cather came to feel that such confidence was misplaced. Black Hawk and Moonstone and pillars of the Presbytery
of the First Church in Pittsburgh were much more powerful than
she had supposed; it was they who determined the future. In *One
of Ours* she fights the new and appalling conviction, and there is
a roughness in the texture of the novel. In *A Lost Lady* she has
the perception under control: the shaping idea which imparts
so admirable a unity to the book, and allows it to be written with
such a tension of restrained resentment and regret, is the contrast

between a dying way of life which is spacious and noble and a new way which is petty and crude. The figure that primarily represents the old way has a grandeur that had not been within her reach before, a poetic beauty. In old Captain Forrester Archbishop Latour is already implicit.

A Lost Lady is one of the books on which Miss Cather's survival will depend, by which it will be assured. For all their vigor and truth, the earlier novels suffer from what Henry James criticised in Arnold Bennett and the other realistic novelists of the first decade of the century, an excess of saturation in material detail, a failure to make the figure in the carpet the true centre. In her essay on "The Novel Démeublé" Miss Cather is as critical of saturation as James had been. The novelist, she says, is to suggest rather than to state, is to aim primarily at that kind of effect which is given by a bare stage and a handful of characters coming into impacts which disclose nothing but their essential selves. *A Lost Lady* is the first of her novels to be wholly uncluttered. In *My Ántonia* she had adopted the relaxed form of the memoir, and in introducing it had emphasized how casually the memoir grew, how capriciously it took its dimensions. The memoir is supposed to be Jim Burden's; he is a busy New York lawyer, but still a Nebraskan in spirit, who has occupied himself at long intervals over many years during long trips by train in evoking Ántonia and his own youth, now one aspect, now another. "I didn't take time to arrange it," he says in the introductory note, "I simply wrote down pretty much all that her name recalls to me. I suppose that it hasn't any form." *My Ántonia* is not at all the insufferably garrulous book to which these warnings point; but material details do heap together in it, and for whole chapters the figure in the carpet is partly obscured and by the reader forgotten. The structure of *The Song of the Lark* is perfectly conventional; in this respect, even in its radically revised form, it does not differ from a Dreiser novel. Thea Kronborg's states of mind, the slow and difficult development of her great voice along with her growth, harsh and rough, as a great personality, are at the centre of the book; but they do not strictly govern the choice of material, and they do not always mesh with the incidents in the narrative. It is a massive work, and it communicates an impression of perfect truth, but it is somewhat cluttered; it lags, especially in the urban chapters; the controlling idea does not always control. With *O Pioneers!* the case is not very different.

In comparison with these novels, so massive, so firmly stamped with material truth, *A Lost Lady* seems very slight, even attenuated. But in essential substance, it is richer than any of Miss Cather's books that preceded and, in force of feeling as well as in the exhibition of the figure in its particular carpet, vastly their superior. It was Ántonia's greatness that she could "leave images in the mind that did not fade—that grew stronger with time." It is a large part of her creator's greatness to do the same. *Shadows on the Rock* was to be a sequence of such memorable images; they are already beautifully strong and frequent in *A Lost Lady*. When I took up the novel recently it was ten years since I had read it, but I could turn at once to a number of the images which had kept all their original strength during that time and had also gathered a depth of increasing meaning. The chief of these images is in the second part of the seventh chapter. Young Niel Herbert goes through the fields near Sweet Water in the summer dawn to pick a bouquet of roses and lay it outside the shuttered French windows of Mrs. Forrester's bedroom. "As he bent to place the flowers on the sill, he heard from within a woman's soft laughter; impatient, indulgent, teasing, eager. Then another laugh, very different, a man's. And it was fat and lazy,—ended in something like a yawn." In an instant, the gleaming candor of the dawn and of the boy's innocent idealism is blotted out. The style has not yet acquired the full beauty of surface which makes every page of the historical novels a radiant thing; it has not yet the glow or the firmness of contour; but only the shortcoming in style —a merely relative shortcoming, for Miss Cather was already writing as well as any contemporary novelist—prevents one from saying that this half-chapter could go unchanged into *Madame Bovary*, which is one of her principal admirations as it must be with anyone who cherishes the art of fiction without being the victim of sectarian prejudice. *A Lost Lady* is full of symbolic images abounding with suggestion and with beauty. In place of the elaborate descriptions of the earlier novels—one could find his way in the dark from the depot at Moonstone to the Kronborg parsonage, and then out by the sandhills and by the grove of the Kohlers—stand such golden moments arrested forever in their force and beauty.

Yet *A Lost Lady* is not of Miss Cather's very best. It has a grave intellectual weakness, a weakness of vision. Her pioneers will not quite bear the weight she assigns to them. The tone in which she always refers to Captain Forrester's powerful friends who travel back and forth on the Burlington in their private cars and break the trip at Sweet Water—railroad-builders, financiers, founders of great department stores like Marshall Field—arouses some uneasiness. It is a simple thing to grant that men in the habit of great affairs, men for whom the breaking of new ground is the breath of life, "great-hearted adventurers," are of another and higher kind than small-town shysters, vulgarians, and gossips. But Miss Cather presses us to do much more than grant this; she asks us to believe that as a group, by definition, her builders and founders have a spiritual breadth, a heroic wisdom, for which it is difficult indeed to extort our assent. One cannot long escape the feeling that she has built them up somewhat artificially out of a need to annihilate the petty present. In *One of Ours* the hero, Claude Wheeler, remarks that "no battlefield or shattered country was ever as ugly as this world would be if men like his brother Bayliss controlled it altogether." It is easy to agree, and Bayliss is of the same gross stuff as Ivy Peters, the shyster and gossip who rules the last phase of *A Lost Lady*. Still, the countervailing characters in these novels—those who represent the splendors of the Western past, and must do so for there is no other past except the almost unknown aboriginal for the area these novels picture—are not grand enough for their role. Even Captain Forrester, impressive as he is by his silences, his fixities, his genial calm, is not quite grand enough.

The hunger for a glorious past in the West appeared early in Miss Cather's writing, and is its deepest emotional motive. There is a curiously moving chapter in *My Ántonia* where the Scandinavian and Slavic girls ask to hear the tale of Coronado and his search for the Seven Golden Cities, and find in the thought that the Spanish adventurers have been in Nebraska the source of a new radiance in the wheat fields and the sunset. This is a reworking of a beautiful sketch, "The Enchanted Bluff," still uncollected. In *The Song of the Lark* the most formative of all Thea Kronborg's experiences, far more significant than any contact she ever had with a person—the experience which lent wings to her spirit and so to her voice—was a summer in Arizona when she lay every day at the mouth of one of the caves in a village of the "ancient people," the Cliff-Dwellers. To be from the West would no longer mean to her being from Moonstone; it would mean being from the region of the builders of those caves. "The Cliff-Dwellers had lengthened her past. She had older and higher obligations." She grew to meet them. In *The Professor's House*, the small Mid-Western college town with its petty professorial rivalries and the bright superficialities of academic families suddenly vanishes. In the most melodramatic strangeness of structure in all Miss Cather's fiction, the long narrative from Tom Outland's notebook breaks in upon the pace of life in the town, with its tale of the mesas. Tom Outland had taken from the Indians of the Southwest just what Thea Kronborg had taken: "I had read of filial piety in the Latin poets," he wrote, "and I knew that was what I felt for this place." The old Indian civilization turns to ridicule the new house which has been built, with its elaborate bathrooms and, of course, its garage, from the prize money the professor received for the many-volumed work on the Spanish adventurers, which was the best part of his life. He finds that he does not care to move into his new house: the bleak old house, with the creaking stairs leading to the uncomfortable attic where the great feat of imaginative reconstruction had taken place, is far more akin to his spirit. It is not so absurdly unlike what the Cliff-Dwellers had made.

The old Southwest had ruled in Miss Cather's imagination since the time of her earliest novels; but she had shied away from it in the conviction that it was eminently a subject for a Catholic to realize. In the end, she could not be content with using it merely as a background. In *Death Comes for the Archbishop* it is the core of the work. Here Indian villages, the exploits of the Spanish adventurers and missionaries, the coming of a new layer of high civilization with the French priests, and the small but true contribution of the best of the great-hearted adventurers of Anglo-Saxon blood, men like Kit Carson, are set before us as on a frieze. *Death Comes for the Archbishop* is her great book, the most beautiful achievement of her imagination; in it at last her craftsmanship and her vision are in relation, and that relation is complete. The length of her unconscious preparation to write it had served her well indeed.

Miss Cather had always understood that a person's relation to a place might be as valuable to him, and as decisive in his growth or retardation, as any relation he might have with other persons. What happens in one place could not have taken from Moonstone or from Chicago what the villages of the Cliff-Dwellers gave her. But in the earlier novels the landscape did not impinge upon the reader with the vitality that distinguishes it in *Death Comes for the Archbishop*. Much to his own surprise, Archbishop Latour decides against returning to his native Auvergne to pass the years of his retirement and preparation for death. The ties of his family, the promise of fine architecture on every side, and of the scholarly associations of which through his long years in Santa Fe he had been deprived, were, he found, less powerful than the atmosphere of New Mexico. When he wakens in the early morning at Santa Fe, the southwestern air communicates to him a conviction of eternal youth, of energy, of ever-possible spiritual growth. A response of this kind might have been a part of *My Ántonia* or of *The Song of the Lark*, but at the time when she wrote these novels Miss Cather could not have found such language as she uses in conveying the quality of the atmosphere at Santa Fe. "His first consciousness was a sense of the light dry wind blowing in through the windows, with the fragrance of hot sun and sage-brush and sweet clover. . . . Something soft and wild and free that whispered to the ear on the pillow, lightened the heart, softly, softly picked the lock, slid the bolts, and released the spirit of man into the wind, into the blue and gold, into the morning, into the morning!" Her craftsmanship in language, her sense of a true economy, her command of rhythms individual without being eccentric, had never before reached such a delicate sureness. It is the language which makes the impressions of the New Mexico landscape superior to any presentation of setting in the early books. She had borne the memories of this landscape in her mind for a long time, and at last she had the words to convey them in simple, perfect strength.

The same sure delicacy marks her maniuplation of character and incident, a richer material than she had ever before worked in, more varied, more intense, and at times more heroic. The deliberate and often ponderous movement in the earlier narratives is now replaced by a movement wonderfully quick and light, beautifully appropriate to the atmosphere. In the structure what might easily have become solid masses, comparable with long reaches in the earlier novels, is broken up by brief tales inset with an apparent casualness which recalls the ingenuous narrative manner of Cervantes or Smollett. Everything in *Death Comes for the Archbishop* is from the past, but it is not all from the same past, and in this lies much of the great formal beauty and almost as much of the great emotional effect of the novel. The framework belongs to the mid-nineteenth century when two priests from a quiet town in Auvergne who had worked not too happily along the Ohio, set out to revive the Catholic faith and discipline in the Southwest. In their missionary travels throughout the immense diocese they made fragmentary acquaintance with a far older past —the sixteenth century when the Spanish Franciscans first entered the region coming up from the see of Durango, and the slightly later time when their successors, isolated and often degenerate, gave individual twists to the gospel and the priestly estate. It is in the tales of this older past, picked up by the French priests in their wanderings, that Miss Cather's narrative art is most remarkable. She was always an admirable writer of short stories, and shortly after the appearance of *Death Comes for the Archbishop* her mastery of shorter media came to its height in the *nouvelles* of *Obscure Destinies*, particularly in the moving "Old Mrs. Harris." Her manner in the tales inset in *Death Comes for the Archbishop* is even more accomplished. It is the manner appropriate to the older and better kind of hagiography, simple, concrete, unemphatic, concentrated. The tale of the bold and evil friar who ruled on the crag at Acoma is among the perfect short narratives, suggestive, swimming in the atmosphere of the time and the place, without a touch of false exaggeration or falser complexity. At every turn in the story, the setting is alive, almost overpoweringly sensible. The friar and his clerical guests at dinner and the servant whom he kills say next to nothing, but we catch them in their characterizing attitudes and know them as human beings. The height of Miss Cather's success is in the pages which follow the death and evoke a silence and immobility as thick and ominous as Conrad with his more lavish methods could suggest. With the simplest of means, which are also the most difficult, she has accomplished a triumph.

The method of *Death Comes for the Archbishop* was used again, with minor changes, in *Shadows on the Rock*. In a letter to Wilbur L. Cross, Miss Cather defined with a preciseness unusual for her in speaking of her own work the subtle effect at which she aimed in her novel of French Canada at the end of the seventeenth century. "I . . . tried to develop it into a prose composition not too conclusive, not too definite: a series of pictures remembered rather than experienced; a kind of thinking, a mental complexion inherited, left over from the past, lacking in robustness, and full of pious resignation." The Indians and Spaniards who had given such vigorous color to *Death Comes for the Archbishop* have no equivalent in the later novel. Nor has it the peculiar depth given to *Death Comes for the Archbishop* by the inset tales of a remoter past.

Shadows on the Rock is a novel of the north. The great rock of Quebec in all its grayness is the eternal antagonist supported by the endless Canadian winter and the untouched wastes. But on the rock, stronger than its strength, the spirit of European civilization preserves its precarious life: this is a novel of survivals, a series of pictures illustrating the will of a highly civilized people to preserve its civilization. To maintain French cookery through the six or seven frozen months—not to subsist on frozen meat or coarse fare, but to have vegetables growing in the cellar and fowls laid away in lard—becomes not only significant but in its way heroic. On uncommonly cold nights little Cécile Auclair, taking her dead mother's place as head of the household before she was in her teens, would throw off the covers and stir her chilly legs to cover the parsley. Her father would call out: *"Qu'est-ce que tu fais, petite?"* The sleepy voice would reply: *"Papa, j'ai peur pour le persil."* It had not frozen in her mother's time, it should not freeze in hers. Euclide Auclair's household, a particle of Louis XIV's Paris accidentally transported to Quebec, is cherished by not only those who live in it but all sorts of people, even by Monseigneur Laval, because they find in the food and the furniture and in the spirit of the critical enlightened apothecary something that appeals to their nostalgia and promises the continuance in the colony of what they admired in the distant and at times incredible capital. The light cheerful quality of the Auclairs, father and daughter, is beautifully balanced by such grim figures as Laval with his terrifying features, his formidable language, and his immense disappointments, and Jeanne Le Ber, recluse of Montreal, won for a religious life by no less a person than the Venerable Marguerite Bourgeoys. Laval comes before us ringing the cathedral bell at every hour all through the long night before All Souls', a punctual reminder to all on the rock of the force by which it is ruled and linked with Europe. The recluse, living in her bare rooms inset in the cathedral, worn to nothing by her devotions, is an evidence that in French Canada God is already served as He had been in the deserts of Egypt in the early centuries of Christianity, that the great cold of the Montreal winter cannot alter in one iota the creed the French had planted with the lilies. Light and dark shadows are so juxtaposed that in the novel as a whole there is an image of life in its variety and promise.

It is far too little to say of *Shadows on the Rock* that it is the best novel drawn from the rich material of Canadian history. Beside it William Kirby's *Golden Dog* is clumsy and external, Charles G. D. Roberts's *Forge in the Forest* conventional, and Gilbert Parker's *Seats of the Mighty* merely facile. Nor would any historical novels written by French Canadians sustain a comparison with Miss Cather's craftsmanship and vision. Still, if *Shadows on the*

Rock is perfect in the beauty of structure and style, if the author's sense of relevance is unfailing, if the mood of nostalgic charm is perfectly conveyed, it is a novel with but little dramatic incident, and the personages are figures in a legend rather than living characters. These are indeed but shadows! The shortcomings in drama and in vitality of character are quite deliberate, the *coloring* in the sequence of pictures is intentionally faint, for the book was to be an equivalent in prose of a fresco by Puvis de Chavannes. No more graceful book has been accomplished in our time.

Shadows on the Rock was followed by a collection of three *nouvelles, Obscure Destinies.* From the appearance of *One of Ours,* Miss Cather had avoided the massiveness of the full-length novel; in everything she has written since the crucial year 1922 the literal dimensions have been relatively brief, and the method has been that of the tale or *nouvelle,* or of the short novel with shorter works inset. Nowhere does her discrimination show more finely than in *Obscure Destinies* or in *My Mortal Enemy,* that somewhat earlier work in which the same method was tried out. In the *nouvelle* she finds sufficient space to work in the symbols and pictures on which she has come more and more to depend, and to allow an occasional incident to flow into a dramatic scene, and yet has no need to make of a character a complex personality. In "Old Mrs. Harris," she exhibits in their essence the powers that in her later years she has most wished to exercise, the power of picture, the power of symbol, the power of structure, the power of style. In it also her vision of the aged, defeated, lonely, and unhappy comes to its clearest and most moving expression.

What Miss Cather has published since the appearance of *Obscure Destinies* in 1932—it has been remarkably little—has revealed no new kinds of power or charm, nor has it ever quite matched the work of the preceding decade, which will more and more be recognized as the time in which her craftsmanship and her vision attained their height. *Lucy Gayheart,* in which she returned to her own Middle West, is slight, not as *A Lost Lady* is slight but with the slightness of minor work, although the last part is, for feeling and form, comparable with almost anything in *A Lost Lady. Sapphira and the Slave Girl,* more nearly a successor to

the historical novels, evokes Virginia before the Civil War, the
Virginia of which she heard tales when she was growing up near
Winchester, in a series of quiet pictures which have the charm
but not the depth of those in *Death Comes for the Archbishop* or
Shadows on the Rock. It came out six years ago, and since then
Miss Cather has been silent.

While she is still among us, although her work must be nearly
over, if the time for a formal and considered estimate has perhaps not yet arrived, we may yet see her fiction in sufficient perspective to tell her on the occasion of her seventieth anniversary
something of what her craftsmanship and vision mean to us. What
we have gained by her craftsmanship is, above all, a beautiful
lightening of the novel form. From George Eliot's time down to
ours, the load upon the novel form has been steadily increasing
until in works such as *The Financier* and *The World of William Clissold*—to choose examples from novelists who have recently died—the form broke beneath the stress. I suppose that for
popular fiction of a semi-serious sort, and for fiction which aspires
to distinction without fully attaining it, the characteristic formula
during the past fifteen years or so has been the memoir of a
crowded life, abounding in rather crude sexual experience and
with somewhat hasty reflections on education, industry, and the
social system, and coming to a climax in a melodramatic ethical
regeneration or else in an equally melodramatic recognition of
life's futility. Examples of such fiction, written for the day, or at
best for the decade, will be in everyone's mind. In most of them,
character and story are mere props and are handled with an almost unbelievable clumsiness; structure and tone are scarcely considered; and in style the model appears to be the manner of the
more lively foreign correspondents. Against such a degradation
of the art of fiction to mere journalism, Miss Cather's craftsmanship stands out with an alien definiteness and firmness of beauty.

Her vision is of essences. In her earlier novels the essential subject, a state of mind or of feeling, was enveloped in the massiveness of the conventional modern realist novel. It was there, but it
was muffled. Then Miss Cather saw that if she abandoned the
devices of massive realism, if she depended upon picture and sym-

bol and style, she could disengage her essential subject, and make it tell upon the reader with a greater directness and power, help it to remain uncluttered in his mind. The things that pass, the things that merely adhere to states of mind and feeling, she began to use with a severe economy. Her fiction became a kind of symbolism, with the depths and suggestions that belong to symbolist art, and with the devotion to a music of style and structure for which the great literary symbolists strove, Pater and Moore and the later James. Over their work hers has the advantage that her vision was never eccentric, disproportioned, or perverse. What she cares for in humanity and in nature many sensitive and cultivated people have cared for in every time. There could be not better assurance that her fiction will endure and that some of the novels and tales will interpret us to a later day. At seventy, it may be a satisfaction to her that she has written not for the day or the decade but for the long future, and that in a time when most of those works which usurp the leading places in our book reviews will have nothing to say, *My Ántonia* (despite its passages of excessive detail), *A Lost Lady, Death Comes for the Archbishop, Shadows on the Rock,* and *Obscure Destinies* will be the sources of pleasure and the subjects of thought.

Meanwhile her contemporaries may ask, like little Oliver, for more—more of that firm and radiant prose, of the pictures and the symbols, of the light quick movement, of the essences which are central to all civilization and will outlast even the garage.

DAVID DAICHES

"The Short Stories"

Willa Cather's . . . collection of short stories . . . *Obscure
Destinies* . . . contained three stories: "Neighbour[1] Rosicky"
(written in 1928 and first published, like so many of her stories, in
a magazine), "Old Mrs. Harris," and "Two Friends," both written in 1931. In these stories she is handling themes which for the
most part she had already left behind in her novels. She is drawing on her Nebraska memories and other recollections of her childhood, and the richness of texture and clear emotional pattern
which the autobiographical impulse gave to *O Pioneers!* and *My
Ántonia* are to be found here also. She is no longer writing about
artists: there is something inbred about writers choosing fellow
artists as themes, and Willa Cather seems eventually to have realized this. Nor do we find here the note of self-conscious belliger-
ence about the status of the artist that dominates her early work.
These stories are essentially studies in the quality of country living in the American Midwest and West, done with an affectionate
interest in the human characters involved and a lyrical sense of the
natural background.

"Neighbour Rosicky" is a character sketch projected through
the arrangement of symbolic incidents. The last years of this wise
and kindly old Czech farmer in Nebraska are described so as to
develop a sense of what such a life stood for in terms of a satisfactory adjustment to the demands both of nature and of one's fellow

From *Willa Cather* (Ithaca, 1951), copyright, 1951, by Cornell University.
Used by permission of the Cornell University Press.
[1] Miss Cather seems always to have used the British "—our" spelling in this
and similar words.

men. Its earthiness almost neutralizes the incipient sentimentality, and the relation of the action to its context in agricultural life gives the story an elemental quality that is lacking in the thinner accounts of the artist's life that we find in *Youth and the Bright Medusa*. The story opens with Rosicky in the doctor's office, being told to take things easy because he has a weak heart, and it ends with his death after he has ignored the doctor's advice by raking thistles out of an alfalfa field. Between these limits Miss Cather manages to present all that was significant in the man's whole life and, in addition, to handle a specific theme—the old man's relation to his city-bred daughter-in-law—so as to focus the larger meanings. One of the most obvious pieces of "Americana" among Miss Cather's stories, "Neighbour Rosicky" has appealed to conventional taste in a way that her more original work has sometimes failed to do.

The second story, "Old Mrs. Harris," is the longest and most substantial in the book. It is the study of a southern family who have moved to a small town in the West and find that the pattern of family living they bring with them is misunderstood and resented by their new neighbors. Old Mrs. Harris has left her comfortable southern home to follow the fortunes of her married daughter: she regards it her duty, as an old woman, to do all she can to enable the younger generation to live in as carefree a manner as possible, and that point of view is accepted as a complete matter of course by her daughter Victoria, who allows her mother to act the part of family drudge (as it seems to the neighbors) without any awareness of doing wrong. The nature and results of this situation are explored in the story with considerable cunning and with most effective deployment of incident.

We first see Mrs. Harris through the eyes of Mrs. David Rosen, a intelligent and well-educated Jewish woman whose husband "didn't mind keeping a clothing-store in a little Western town, so long as he had a great deal of time to read philosophy." The Rosens represent a standard of culture and of cultured living unique in the little town of Skyline, though we are not told this about them until later on in the story. Mrs. Rosen has long planned to call on Mrs. Harris some time when she can find her alone, but has hitherto been prevented by Victoria's arrangements. This time she sees Victoria leave, then runs over with a pot of coffee and some coffee cake to ask Mrs. Harris to join her in her afternoon coffee. The result disconcerts her: Grandma Harris does not respond. "Receiving a visitor alone, unsupervised by her daughter, having cake and coffee that should properly be saved for Victoria, was all so irregular that Mrs. Harris could not enjoy it. Mrs. Rosen doubted if she tasted the cake as she swallowed it, —certainly she ate it without relish, as a hollow form." Willa Cather pauses at this point to describe the "hideous, cluttered room" in which they were sitting—a room which particularly offended Mrs. Rosen, who "liked order and comeliness so much":

A walnut table stood against a blind window, piled high with old magazines and tattered books, and children's caps and coats. There was a wash-stand (two wash-stands, if you counted the oilcloth-covered box as one). A corner of the room was curtained off with some black-and-red-striped cotton goods, for a clothes closet. In another corner was the wooden lounge with a thin mattress and a red calico spread which was Grandma's bed. Beside it was her wooden rocking-chair, and the little splint-bottom chair with the legs sawed short on which her darning-basket usually stood, but which Mrs. Rosen was now using for a tea-table.

The picking out of these details at this point in the story shows that awareness of the need to build up the emotional tone of a narrative by the proper distribution of symbolic objects—an awareness which Willa Cather displays so effectively in her mature work.

As the two ladies talk, the cat comes in, and Mrs. Rosen notices how affectionately Mrs. Harris handles it; then the grandchildren come home from school, and an atmosphere of cheerful affection breaks in, quite different from anything that Mrs. Rosen's preconceptions about Mrs. Harris' function in the family might have led her to expect. Just after Mrs. Rosen leaves, Victoria (Mrs. Templeton) comes home, and what follows is equally illuminating:

Mrs. Templeton stopped by the picket fence to smile at the children playing in the back yard,—and it was a real smile, she was glad to see them. She called Ronald over to the fence to give him a kiss. He was hot and sticky.

"Was your teacher nice today? Now run in and ask Grandma to wash your face and put a clean waist on you."

Grandma does all the dirty work; yet Victoria is not the spoilt and selfish woman one might suppose, Grandma does not in the least regard herself as ill-used, and everybody in the family is courteous and well-behaved. Having so far seen the Harris family only through Mrs. Rosen's eyes, we are still puzzled by the seeming contradictions in this state of affairs. In the second section of the story, which now begins, Miss Cather adroitly shifts the point of view and gives us a direct description of the Harrises at home.

This second section concentrates on Mrs. Harris, and while it emphasizes her weariness and scant physical comforts, it also shows the other side:

She did not regret her decision; indeed, there had been no decision. Victoria had never once thought it possible that Ma should not go wherever she and the children went, and Mrs. Harris had never thought it possible. Of course she regretted Tennessee, though she would never admit it to Mrs. Rosen:—the old neighbours, the yard and garden she had worked in all her life, the apple trees she had planted, the lilac arbour, tall enough to walk in, which she had clipped and shaped so many years.

Old women, Mrs. Harris believed, "were tied to the chariot of young life, and had to go where it went, because they were needed." She did not regard her lot as requiring pity. And as for Victoria—"if Victoria once suspected Mrs. Rosen's indignation, it would be all over. She would freeze her neighbour out, and that friendly voice, that quick pleasant chatter with the little foreign twist, would thenceforth be heard only at a distance, in the alleyway or across the fence. Victoria had a good heart, but she was terribly proud and could not bear the least criticism."

The third section introduces Vickie, Mrs. Harris' eldest grandchild, Victoria's daughter. She is working for a scholarship and comes into the Rosens' house to read and to receive encouragement in her educational ambitions. This gives a new turn to the story, providing an element of plot (hitherto we have had mostly the static situation and the character sketch) which is to be used to throw new light on the situation already presented and to project the story structurally to a satisfactory conclusion. We leave Vickie reading in the parlor while Miss Cather focuses on Mrs. Rosen and tells in retrospect the story of her relations with Victoria Templeton. This kind of handling of chronology—describing the present situation, then back to the past to show in some degree how it developed, then to the present again to show something new, then some more illumination from the past—can be irritating and confusing in inexpert hands; but Willa Cather knows what she is doing. It is a kind of mystery story, the mystery to be solved being the true character of Grandma Harris and her relation to her family. Mrs. Rosen tries to play the detective, but, as in all good mystery stories, it is not the official detective who solves the mystery. No individual, in fact, solves it, unless it be the reader, who, presented with the growing complexity of the situation, eventually sees a pattern rich enough to contain all the disparate elements. The movement back and forth in time helps to enrich the pattern until we can see in it all that we need to see.

The fourth section of the story brings Victoria into a social context in order to exhibit the other side of her nature (nurtured for society, she is seen at her best in relation to people outside her own family) and to show some of her fellow townspeople, resenting this fact in her upbringing and her behavior, exhibiting their malice. There is a conflict between the mores bred by southern standards of gentility and the rough democracy of a bustling little western town. Miss Cather takes no sides; she deploys her material cunningly, and lets the situation explain itself.

In the fifth section we are back with Mrs. Harris, exploring her background and the circumstances of her earlier life. The previous history of the Templetons is then fully related; it is shown how unsuccessful projects of Mr. Templeton's had finally landed them in this little western town, what a blind alley such a situation was for them, and how they strove to keep up the old life in increasingly discouraging circumstances. The brightest part of the picture is Mrs. Harris' relations with her grandchildren; here something of the old southern clan sense, the sense of the organic unity of the family, is preserved:

Sometimes, in the morning, if her feet ached more than usual, Mrs. Harris felt a little low. . . . She would hang up her towel with a sigh and go into the kitchen, feeling that it was hard to make a start. But the moment she heard the children running down the uncarpeted back stairs, she forgot to be low. Indeed, she ceased to be an individual, an old woman with aching feet; she became part of a group, became a relationship. She was drunk up into their freshness when they burst in upon her, telling her about their dreams, explaining their troubles with buttons and shoe-laces and underwear shrunk too small. The tired, solitary old woman Grandmother had been at daybreak vanished; suddenly the morning seemed as important to her as it did to the children, and the mornings ahead stretched out sunshiny, important.

The death of the cat and the reactions to this event of the various members of the Templeton family throw new light both on Mrs. Harris and her daughter. We have been prepared for the symbolic use of the cat by the first section, when the animal's appearance brought out more warmth from Mrs. Harris than any other single incident. Mrs. Harris' fierce resentment of her daughter's suggestion that the dead cat be thrown out on the trash pile and her conspiracy with her grandchildren to give it decent burial reveal that after all there were some basic differences between mother and daughter; yet Victoria's surprising gentleness with the children when she learns that they have deceived her at once prevents us from making too facile an interpretation of this difference. The clues to the solution of the mystery are strewn ever more thickly, but by this time it is ceasing to be a special mystery on its own and is becoming recognizable as part of the larger mystery of personality, of human nature, of life itself.

The concluding sections of the story are taken up with Vickie's attempt to win a competitive scholarship to the University of Michigan. She is successful but learns soon after that the scholarship would only pay part of her expenses; she would have to provide three hundred dollars more herself. This Mr. Templeton professes himself unable to do: he tells Vickie kindly but firmly that he just has not got the money. A crisis ensues. The problem is solved privately by Mrs. Harris, who, emerging for the first time as an independent individual, arranges with the Rosens for a loan to Vickie of the necessary money. In that final interview between Mrs. Harris and Mrs. Rosen (deliberately and instructively contrasted with that first interview with which the story opens), each sees and appreciates the other more clearly, and Mrs. Harris, now that she is acting as an individual and determining her own relation to her granddaughter, can at last understand and respond to Mrs. Rosen's affection.

Meanwhile confusion is reigning in the Templeton household. Victoria discovers that she is pregnant again and is depressed and hopeless. Mr. Templeton goes off on a business trip. Mrs. Harris, having risen to her great moment, takes to her bed in what she knows is her last illness. Vickie learns the good news, unaware whom she has to thank for it. Grandma is left alone with the younger grandchildren, the two twins, with whom she has achieved a perfect relationship. That night she loses consciousness and never regains it.

The pattern is not complete yet; Victoria and Vickie are left *in medias res*. But patterns which involve different generations are never complete; all the author has to do is to show them as sufficiently rich to illustrate the continuity of the design and the relevance of what at first appear to be isolated elements. "Old Mrs. Harris," the longest and most originally constructed of Willa Cather's short stories, is her most successful attempt to achieve this kind of pattern on this scale.

"Two Friends," the final story in *Obscure Destinies,* is a much slighter affair. It is cast in the form of a reminiscence and tells the story of two friends who lived "in a little wooden town in a shallow Kansas river valley." One was a banker and one was a big cattleman, and in spite of differences in background and temperament there was a deep affection between them. They spent every summer evening sitting side by side on two armchairs on the wooden sidewalk outside the banker's store and talked together. The flavor and quality of their talk and of their personalities are presented through anecdotal retrospect, and a tone of easy informality pervades the narrative. As usual, Miss Cather picks out the significant detail in describing the background, building up the atmosphere through the proper use of symbolic properties.

The narrator (a youngster at the time of these events) reveals himself only occasionally and in such a way as to provide a nostalgic tone to the reminiscence. "I liked to listen to those two because theirs was the only 'conversation' one could hear about the streets." "I suppose there were moonless nights, and dark ones with but a silver shaving and pale stars in the sky, just as in the spring. But I remember them all as flooded by the rich indolence of a full moon, or a half-moon set in uncertain blue."

The sketch ends with an account of how the two friends moved apart. Dillon was in Chicago at the time when the Democratic convention first nominated William Jennings Bryan, and he came back full of enthusiasm for the great orator. Trueman, who regarded Bryan as a "great windbag," could not conceal his contempt, and thus Bryan drove the two friends apart. When Trueman, believing that Dillon's enthusiastic harangues in support of Bryan were "no way for a banker to talk," at last withdrew his account from Dillon's bank, the rift was complete. For the narrator, nothing was the same in that small Kansas town again.

Dillon died suddenly soon afterwards, and Trueman departed for San Francisco. The personal note is sounded most strongly in the conclusion:

The breaking-up of that friendship between two men who scarcely noticed my existence was a real loss to me, and has ever since been a regret. More than once, in Southern countries where there is a smell of dust and dryness in the air and the nights are intense, I have come upon a stretch of dusty white road drinking up the moonlight beside a blind wall, and have felt a sudden sadness. Perhaps it was not until the next morning that I knew why,—and then only because I had dreamed of Mr. Dillon or Mr. Trueman in my sleep. When that old scar is occasionally touched by chance, it rouses the old uneasiness; the feeling of something broken that could so easily have been mended; of something delightful that was senselessly wasted, of a truth that was accidentally distorted—one of the truths we want to keep.

The story is slight enough, but it has tone and atmosphere, both achieved in a manner characteristic of Willa Cather.

III

PERSONAL VIEWS, IMPRESSIONS, AND REMINISCENCES

THERE is no shortage of biographical treatments of Willa Cather. Three book-length studies appeared in 1953 alone: E. S. Sergeant's book, which contains critical evaluation but is mainly biographical; E. K. Brown's critical-biography; and Edith Lewis' memoir. Yet despite the fact that these books are responsible, full, and largely accurate, and despite the fact that their subject was, in the words of several commentators, a woman of remarkably "clear cut" opinions and "simple" manners, Willa Cather the personality remains strangely out of focus.

Partly this may be because Miss Cather, like Sherwood Anderson and a great many other writers, was a poser, who deliberately constructed an imaginative or dramatized public image. When she was young she gave her birth date as 1873. Later, she altered this to 1875. Sometime during the thirties she moved it up to 1876, the date that became embedded—until James Shively detected the falsification—in *Who's Who* and half a dozen literary histories. She changed the economic picture of her early upbringing in somewhat the same way: at one time, trying to give a kind of Horatio Alger interest to the story of her success, she commented untruthfully on the way she was compelled to work to put herself through school; at another time, trying to give a different picture, she referred grandly to her parent's "ranch" in Nebraska. But whereas Sherwood Anderson's poses were childishly transparent and easily pierced by his biographers, Miss Cather's seem still to impose on those who write of her life.

No doubt one of the reasons is the greater intelligence and modesty of the pose, but the most important reason is the wall she quite deliberately started to build between herself and the public as early as the twenties, when she found herself a famous writer. This took the form of a forthright and decisively negative posture, the decisiveness being a means by which she could limit her public contacts and simplify her casual human relationships. She rather brusquely said "no" when she was asked to endorse anything, write reviews, speak in public, or answer reporters. All but close friends were later to notice what seemed to be a certain distance, coldness, or hauteur in her manner. That this stemmed from a desire for privacy and a fear of having it intruded upon is clear from the fact that she burned her most personal correspondence before her death, and put testamentary restrictions on her survivors of a kind that discouraged publication of facts about her life.

Those who knew her best have never and probably will never write about her in a tone of intimacy. It seems safe to predict that no biography of Willa Cather in the latest biographical style can ever be produced—that is, the kind of enormously detailed and intimate account written by Mark Schorer on Sinclair Lewis or more recently by W. A. Swanberg on Theodore Dreiser, novelists who seem to have deliberately left every conceivable kind of clue for their future biographers. Almost certainly Willa Cather would have regarded such a biography as monstrous. Yet it is hard to think of an author who has given more of an excuse for one—whose characteristic imaginative mode is so urgently tied to biographical impulse. Memory was the material for her best work, and behind the apparently cool, well-formed, and humorless surfaces of her prose is a constantly fleeing glimpse of a richly complex but elusive personal statement.

To get a reasonably complete picture of Willa Cather one must go to a number of different sources: to the memoirs of Edith Lewis, who knew her intimately during the twenties, thirties and forties;

to *The World of Willa Cather* by Mildred Bennett, a Nebraskan who spent much of a lifetime doggedly searching out the people and places that appear in the stories and novels, and who has done the most complete job of identifying the real-life models on which Willa Cather's fictional people and places were based; to *Willa Cather* by E. S. Sergeant, who knew Miss Cather fairly intimately in the early years, and wrote about her candidly. The excerpts that follow are in no sense an attempt to present such a complete picture. They are, rather, glimpses and impressions by people who knew her or talked with her at different periods in her life, and whose concern was with the person as well as with the books. They range from the intimate impressions of Elizabeth Sergeant, who enjoyed a warmly spontaneous friendship with Miss Cather until Miss Sergeant published a biographical account of Willa Cather in 1927, to the impressions of Louise Bogan, who was given the difficult job of interviewing Willa Cather in 1931, at a time when Miss Cather had already become guarded toward people she did not know well.

Leon Edel's essay, "The Paradox of Success," is not included in this chapter because it is not a reminiscence or personal impression. But it is a first-rate example of what might be called the biographical mode of criticism—and indeed was written partly to exemplify the power of this approach in revealing significant literary patterns.

ELIZABETH MOORHEAD

"The Novelist"

The May number of *McClure's Magazine*[1] fell into my hands. I
read a short story called "Paul's Case" by Willa Sibert Cather, a
writer unknown to me. It caught my attention with the very first
paragraph. I had been trying to write short stories, had even succeeded in getting a few published, but, in spite of kind words from
such editors as Richard Watson Gilder and Henry Mills Alden, I
suspected that they were manufactured articles without a spark of
true fire. At least I had learnt enough from my own struggles to
know a good story when I saw one.

"Paul's Case" was good from every point of view. Original, a
vivid character study of a boy who would be considered today a
subject for a psychiatrist. It was well written—imagery, rhythm of
phrase. Moreover, the story had caught the very tone of Pittsburgh
as I knew it. My people didn't live on Cordelia Street, our lives
were transposed to another key from that of Paul's family, but the
feel was the same—stuffiness, subservience to routine, and a fixed
unalterable set of proprieties and beliefs. A safe practical hum-
drum life, never a flash of colour or flame to brighten the drabness of our days. So it seemed to me then, in my ignorance, that
Pittsburgh of more than forty years ago. I knew how Paul felt. I

Reprinted from *These Too Were Here: Louise Homer and Willa Cather*
(Pittsburgh, 1950) by permission of the University of Pittsburgh Press. As
is clear from the essay, Elizabeth Moorhead (Elizabeth Vermorcken) knew
Willa Cather from the early Pittsburgh years before Miss Cather moved
to New York. But the two never wholly lost sight of one another, and the
reminiscence is based partly on other contacts over the years.
[1] May of 1905—ED.

had a sneaking sympathy with him, wretched creature that he was. I, too, had tried to escape, but was always inexorably remanded to the place of my birth.

The woman who had written this story must know Pittsburgh well, might even be here at this time. As soon as I was settled at home I began making enquiries and soon discovered that she was indeed living in my own neighbourhood, a member of a certain well-known judge's household. So I sent her a note at once, telling her of my special interest in "Paul's Case" and boldly suggesting that I should like to meet her. A reply came promptly. She thanked me in her turn and asked me to come to tea the following Sunday afternoon.

At the appointed hour I set out to climb the poplar-shaded Murray Hill Avenue. It was quite a pull to the top of the hill where the Judge's house stood high on a sort of ridge. Steps led up to the front porch, a bank thickly planted with honeysuckle sloped down to the cross street on the other side. It was a warm bright day, the honeysuckle was in bloom and a light breeze wafted its fragrance to me as I rang the doorbell, a fragrance that ever since brings back memories of that unexpectedly pleasant summer.

The door was opened by a young woman, apparently a daughter of the house. As she stood there framed by the doorway, a shining figure in her white dress against a background of interior gloom, I thought she was the most beautiful girl I had ever seen. She gave me a friendly welcome, then quickly disappeared after ushering me into the little parlour, typical room of a hostess, cool, impersonal. Blinds were drawn against the afternoon sunlight.

Out of the dimness the author of "Paul's Case" came forward. She was young. Short, rather stocky in build, she had a marked directness of aspect. You saw at once that here was a person who couldn't easily be diverted from her chosen course. "Pretty" would indeed be a trivial word to describe a face that showed so much strength of character as hers, yet she was distinctly good-looking, with a clear rosy skin, eyes of light grey and hair a dark brown brushed back from a low forehead—an odd and charming contrast in colour. They were observant eyes, nothing escaped them. Altogether a fine healthy specimen of young womanhood. She looked me straight in the face as she greeted me, and I felt her absolute frankness and honesty. She would never say anything she didn't mean; indeed, at times her speech would become a little hesitant, stumbling, in her search for the precise words to express her meaning. She was incapable of affectation or pretence, I saw that.

Preliminaries over, we sat down at a dainty tea table. The kettle was already boiling, Miss Cather made tea, and we chatted for an hour or more about certain writers of the day, and life in Pittsburgh as we both saw it. We parted, agreeing to meet again. This talk was indeed a refreshing experience to me, and I left the Judge's house feeling that my native town held unexpected possibilities of pleasure, after all.

Gradually I learnt the circumstances of Miss Cather's life in Pittsburgh. After her graduation from the University of Nebraska she left her home at Red Cloud in that state and came here to earn her living. That was the prime necessity. Why she chose Pittsburgh I never heard her say, but I have been told that she was attracted by the art exhibitions and concerts to be found in this city even then. She succeeded in getting a good position as literary and dramatic critic on one of our evening papers and her writing attracted the attention of Judge McClung's daughter, Isabelle. It happened that Isabelle, imaginative and outgoing, had become impatient with the narrow round of social life and, being of an independent nature, had begun to make excursions into other less conventional realms. On one such occasion she had encountered Willa Cather, a reporter on her job, in the dressing-room of an actress they both admired. At once strong liking sprang up between them which ripened into friendship and resulted in Isabelle's offering the lonely young writer a temporary home under her father's roof. To be a member of a comfortable household with congenial and stimulating companionship was a happy change for Willa Cather, after the dreariness of a boarding-house room. She showed her appreciation in the dedication of her book, *The Song of the Lark*:

To Isabelle McClung
On uplands,
At morning,
The world was young, the winds were free;
A garden fair,
In that blue desert air,
Its guest invited me to be.

At the time of our meeting Miss Cather had left the newspaper and become the head of the English department of the Allegheny High School. She had long hours, making an early start from Murray Hill and getting back at five, sometimes six o'clock. She could claim only Saturdays and Sundays for her own work, not always that if there were many student themes to read. Isabelle had fitted up a corner in the attic where she could write undisturbed.

The two young women would forsake the family group soon after dinner, and evening after evening would go upstairs to the bedroom they shared to read together in quiet. This room was at the back of the house and its wide low window gave on a downward slope across gardens and shaded streets towards the Monongahela river and green hills rising beyond. There were no close neighbours to destroy their sense of privacy. Here the friends spent many happy and fruitful hours. They devoured the novels of Tolstoi, Turgenev, Balzac, and Flaubert. Both read French easily. Willa had an intense admiration for the work of Flaubert as she tells us in her delightful essay, "A Chance Meeting," in the collection entitled *Not Under Forty*. She set Flaubert's objectivity, restraint, and rhythmic sense far above the unmeasured outpourings of Balzac. And she was naturally deeply impressed by the great Russian realists.

My acquaintance with these two young women changed that whole summer for me. Much as we love the old familiar faces we get a special delight, a quickening, from new friendships. This association brought me into close touch with the world of letters, for Willa Cather was steadily writing and publishing. We met often, either at my home or at the Judge's. There was always some pleasant plan to look forward to. I discovered at once that Isabelle was distinctly an individual in her own right, quite apart from the reflected glow of Willa Cather: beautiful to look upon, large of mind and heart, entirely frank and simple with natural dignity of manner. Not an artist in the sense of producing she could identify herself wholly with the artist's efforts and hopes and aims. She had an infallible instinct for all the arts. She never mistook the second-best for the best. She became for Willa Cather what every writer needs most, the helping friend.

She didn't always accept without question. When Willa was writing *My Antonia,* destined to be her first great success, Isabelle, while reading the manuscript, balked at the title of one of its sections: *"The Hired Girls".* But the author was stubborn. "That's what they were," she said. "Where I lived in the West we didn't talk about 'servants' or 'maids'; if we needed help and could afford it we hired 'girls'." As to whether this caption might put off a fastidious reader—which was what Isabelle feared—Miss Cather cared not at all. It was her purpose to tell things as they are.

Isabelle started the custom of giving Sunday afternoon teas for her neighbours and special friends. These informal affairs became very popular; one was sure of good tea and good talk. Sometimes the little "parlour"—a larger room across the hall was kept for the Judge's use—would be crowded but Isabelle was a born hostess, equal to any emergency; she would open doors, bring in more chairs, redistribute her guests. The faculty of the departments of drama and music at Carnegie Tech, including the Professor of course, Italians from the Dante Alighieri Society of which Isabelle was an active member, supplied a cosmopolitan and artistic element to these regional gatherings—yes, decidedly Pittsburgh was broadening, showing signs of breaking away from the fixed social order. Willa, though the chief attraction, sometimes declined to appear. She would be at her desk in the attic, leagues away from us all in that rich world of imagination which Isabelle always understood and protected.

Sunday afternoons should be kept for her own work. McClure, Phillips and Company had already published a collection of short stories, "Paul's Case" being one of them, under the title, *The Troll Garden.* Encouraged, she must let nothing interfere.

For nine years she lived among us, going faithfully to the newspaper office, then to the Allegheny High School, writing in the intervals, unknown and unapplauded except by a few.

The inevitable break came. It was an exciting event indeed when S. S. McClure, who had been a mere name, a sort of far-off benignant deity, descended in the flesh upon Pittsburgh. He was invited to dine at the Judge's house. Slim, sandy-haired, with very bright blue eyes, he was evidently of a sanguine mercurial temperament. He easily dominated the conversation at table, telling amusing anecdotes of his many hasty trips to Europe on the trail of one author or another. Once, landing in New York, he had gone straight from the boat to his office, had found a bundle of manuscript on his desk tied up to be returned, had opened and read—and here he was in Pittsburgh to see the author in person.

We waited eagerly to learn the upshot of his private talk with Willa Cather. It proved to be the offer of a position on the staff of his magazine. She accepted, resigned from the Allegheny High School at the end of the term, and left Pittsburgh for New York. From that time she travelled steadily upward in her profession, doing the immediate task as she had always done in order to live, reserving as much time and strength as possible for writing. Now and then unwelcome tasks were forced upon her; she did her best, only stipulating that her name should never appear in connection with any article that didn't represent what she wanted to do, that wasn't truly hers.

Eventually she left *McClure's Magazine,* after having been made assistant editor, and was able to devote herself wholeheartedly to her own special art—the interpretation through fiction of those shapes and scenes that "teased her mind," to use her own words. She never went back to Pittsburgh; there was no reason for going there after Isabelle's somewhat unconventional marriage to Jan Hambourg, violinist, and their departure to live abroad. The little intimate group of a few years earlier was broken up. Willa Cather had taken an apartment on Bank Street in Greenwich Village and there I often saw her.

Chance brought us together in other places, too. She was spend-

ing a summer in Boston on a magazine assignment when I happened to be at a certain hotel on the Massachusetts coast, not far
away. On her invitation I went to town to see her in her little apartment. I remember how she spread the cloth on a table in her study
window, and as we sat over a good lunch sent up from downstairs
she told me about the distasteful task she was engaged in. She was
gathering material about the life of Mary Baker Eddy for magazine purposes. Every morning she would start off early, travel to
some little New England village where the famous woman had
lived, talk to people who had known her, had come back to her
desk, tired out, with a variety of confused impressions and a
mass of notes to be sorted and arranged. A wearisome job for one
whose chief interest was the art of fiction.

On another more felicitous occasion we met in London. My
mother and I were stopping at a hotel in the Westminster quarter,
not much frequented by Americans, and we asked Willa to dine
with us there. She came into the lounge where we were sitting,
about eight o'clock, flushed with pleasure over an unexpected—I
can hardly call it encounter, apparition rather. A glimpse of the
great writer who had stirred her youthful enthusiasm, who had
influenced her, probably more than anyone else. She was walking
from her lodgings through the long June twilight and as she
crossed the square in front of Westminster Abbey she suddenly
saw a tall rather heavy figure which seemed familiar to her from
photographs. Yes, it was Henry James himself. There he stood on
one of the islets in the square, oblivious to all the people going and
coming, hands crossed behind his back, head uptilted, gazing intently at the towers of the Abbey.

But his young admirer shook her head and sighed. "No use in
that," she murmured to herself, "You'll never make it."

She was right. Though Henry James had become a naturalized
British subject during World War I, only a year before his death,
he left directions that his ashes should be brought back to America
to lie among his own people.

One morning I telephoned her, while she was still living at
Bank Street, in a mood of excitement. Her address was not in the

book; she avoided interruptions and casual chitchat and gave her number to only a few friends. But I felt justified on this occasion.

"Louise Homer has just sent me two tickets for the opera tonight," I said. "It's *Tristan*. Will you go?"

Back came the reply, succinct, final.

"If you had two tickets for heaven I wouldn't go!"

I laughed and rang off. I could easily get someone else. Willa Cather was too wise to explain, make excuses; she knew that things done, things said, things written, must stand. They can't be retracted. Some people were inclined to be hurt by her disposition to hold herself a little aloof, to reject their friendly overtures, but I understood. She was hard at work on a book and couldn't spare an atom of time and energy for anything else, not even for the music she so much loved. What she says in her admirable essay on "Miss Jewett" is entirely true of herself: "If he (the writer) achieves anything noble, anything enduring, it must be by giving himself absolutely to his material." It is this complete immersion in her subject that gives life to her humblest characters— that family in "Old Mrs. Harris," for example, commonplace people, pulling apart though united, doing nothing extraordinary, yet living and moving before our eyes, more real than many of the actual figures that surround us every day. Like Walter Pater she believed in the "removal of surplusage" and in *A Lost Lady* she succeeded triumphantly in bringing a woman to life with the minimum of detail.

"Artistic growth is, more than it is anything else, a refining of the sense of truthfulness. The stupid believe that to be truthful is easy; only the artist, the great artist, knows how difficult it is." So Willa Cather wrote in *The Song of the Lark,* a book which, though never a favourite of hers, shows fully her conception of the true artist's dedicated life. Her Thea Kronborg was a singer, not a writer, one who knew that every art demands singleness of aim if one strives after excellence rather than material success. Willa Cather had made a few uncertain experiments at first before she found her own field in the great Middle West where she had spent her childhood among its pioneers. Her statement about Miss

Jewett's *Pointed Fir* sketches is equally applicable to her own books: "They melt into the land and the life of the land until they are not stories at all, but life itself." With *My Antonia,* a masterpiece, she brought the Muse into her country. In all her books she makes us feel her intense love of life itself—"life hurrying past us and running away, too strong to stop, too sweet to lose," her understanding of its inconspicuous phases, her deep compassion for those who are thwarted in the eternal human quest. Love and pity shine out from the pages of *Death Comes for the Archbishop.* Through the hard patient discipline of work she achieved beauty of style: a simplicity and clarity that are the perfection of art, brushed lightly with poetry, so lightly that you know it only because scenes and passages linger in your mind like strains of music. Who can forget Mr. Shimerda kneeling before the Christmas tree? Young Niel Herbert in the cloudless summer dawn, gathering wild roses for his *Lost Lady?* Or old Sada before the altar of the Lady Chapel on a pale December night?

Willa Cather's affections were strong and loyal for places as well as people. Wherever she planted herself her roots plunged deep. She was not by nature a traveller; she went to Europe when occasion required, but it was never with undiluted joy, she said. There were always too many things and people at home that she hated to leave. She loved her Bank Street apartment and had made it cosy and cheerful in spite of the evidences of study and hard work. A pleasant meeting-place, that bright book-lined sitting-room where she received her friends once a week after working-hours.

Above the old-fashioned marble mantelpiece hung a copy of a portrait of George Sand, black and white, I think, but the medium I have forgotten. Looking at those strongly-marked features I used to wonder why Willa Cather had chosen this particular novelist to preside over her hearthstone. Naturally she couldn't fail to recognize the great Frenchwoman's genius, her fertility and imaginative power, but she was far from adopting George Sand's method and style. Willa's objectivity, avoidance of dramatic crises, restraint and finish, seemed to have nothing in common with her predecessor's exuberance and self-revelation. Perhaps a secret kinship may be found in a sentence from one of George Sand's letters to Mazzini: "I am, and always have been, artist before everything else. . . . Art belongs to all countries and to all time, and its special good is to live on when all else seems to be dying."

Leaving Bank Street was a hard pull for Willa Cather. She came back to New York after the summer and put all her goods into storage. Subway construction had made Bank Street impossible; there was a station almost under Number Five, her beloved habitation. She transferred herself for the time being to a quiet hotel near Washington Square before her removal to an apartment on Park Avenue.

One day she invited me to lunch with her there. We went up to her study for a brief talk after luncheon in the hotel dining-room. She was by no means lacking in the usual feminine instincts; she showed me a jacket of beautiful brocade which a friend had brought her from Paris, shook it out and fingered it with obvious pleasure. She seemed to prefer these long loose jackets to the tight-fitting corsages the rest of us wore, probably because they gave her a sense of freedom.

She had an appointment at three o'clock with her lawyer whom she had engaged to prevent the use of any of her books or any part of them, for the screen. One of the big Hollywood companies was dangling a tempting offer before her for her latest success, *Death Comes for the Archbishop*; though she had flatly refused to consider it she was afraid she might be circumvented unless she had legal protection for that and her other work. Great-hearted pioneers, rolling prairies, red sand-hills of the desert spotted with juniper, rocky mesas under a boundless sky—how could she subject all these, the very fabric of her life, to mangling and distortion for the sake of money? She was not to be bought.

Especially she wanted to protect the *Archbishop*. She had finished that book at Jaffrey, her lovely summer asylum in New Hampshire under the shadow of Monadnock. "I wish to God I was doing anything so pleasant now!" she lamented. "You ought really to send me a letter of condolence at having lost such an absorbing form of life forever. For there was a peculiar joyful happy mood about this one. It gave me so much pleasure day by day." She hoped that her friends would turn up and comfort her a little;

to lose Bank Street and the *Archbishop* within a few months of each other was almost too much to bear.

I walked away with her and we parted at the Washington Arch. As I watched her sturdy independent figure disappear around a corner I was convinced that she had the inner sense of wholeness, of complete self-realization, which is the artist's best reward.

Throughout her writing Willa Cather shows her deep understanding of the spirit of youth, its desire, aspiration, even its despair. Those country girls in *My Antonia,* close to the earth, ploughing and harvesting, barefoot through the long grass—"If there were no girls like them in the world there would be no poetry." And Claude Wheeler, surely one of her most sympathetic characters—a restless, dissatisfied boy, hating the life of the farm, wanting he didn't quite know what. Certain critics have dismissed one of her later novels as being thin and sentimental, but to my mind *Lucy Gayheart* is beautiful from the first paragraph to the last, not only for its wistful twilight mood and compactness of structure but because Lucy is the incarnation of youth itself—her joy in living, saluting the first star of evening, running in pursuit of something she knew but couldn't grasp, in the sun, in the breeze, a "fugitive gleam."—Oh, that spirit of youth, if once you have had it with all its expectancy, wonder and desire, you can never lose it. It will waken again and again, be with you until the end.

I tried to tell Willa Cather how I felt about this book but couldn't find the right words. She was very matter-of-fact. She had intended to show youth's tendency to hero-worship which somehow "seems a little ridiculous," she said, "though it is a natural feeling in all ardent young people." The first part of that book was really written for the last: the overgenerous nature leaves with us memories more vivid than any professional achievement could ever leave. To me, the slim figure of Lucy is as charming as it was to the great singer when he looked out of his studio window and saw her little red feather moving along the street.

Willa Cather was not influenced by criticism; through trial and error she had found her field and was aware of her limitations as well as her possibilities. She was always grateful for praise. She resented the sort of criticism that is based on careless reading and lack of understanding and was especially annoyed by the outcry against *One of Ours,* which had absorbed all her energy and determined every action for so long that she hardly knew where to turn after it was finished. Pacifists came at her "like a swarm of hornets." It was disconcerting to have Claude regarded as a glorification of war when he was so clearly a farmer boy, neither very old nor very wise, escaping from the dreary round of struggle for gain by fighting for an ideal. Couldn't her critics see that she was trying to treat war without any attempt at literalness as if it were some war back in history, that she was solely concerned with its effect upon one boy? Claude "died believing his country better than it is and France better than any country can ever be. And those were beautiful beliefs to die with. Perhaps it was as well to see that vision, and then to see no more."

When I came back to America in 1940 I told Willa Cather how much I had enjoyed keeping in touch with her by reading her books during my long exile in Italy. It was almost with a sense of discovery. How glad I was to find something unspoiled by the push and turmoil of our age!

"I am very pleased at what you tell me," she answered, "—that some of my books have stood up under a re-reading many years after. I am always glad to hear a good word for *The Professor's House,* which has been, I suspect, the least popular of the books you mention. To most people, I think, it is just 'another story.' But to me it was an interesting experiment. I really got the idea from a Dutch painting: a rich warm interior—and through an open window the sea, blue, very much alive, with a light wind on the water. I tried to use the Blue Mesa in that particular way, but most people seem to think it was a very faulty kind of structure."

As for me, I have always found Godfrey St. Peter a more interesting person than Tom Outland about whom the novel is built—the most interesting, indeed, of any of Willa Cather's men. A scholar absorbed in his job without being in the least pedantic, humorous, elusive, and provocative. He fell out of love with his beautiful wife —a not uncommon circumstance in well-ordered families even here and now—and it isn't surprising that he wanted to break away whenever he could from the intimacy and trivialities of domestic life. "He had never learned to live without delight."

Besides its story and the engaging character of the Professor himself this book is a convincing picture of the demoralizing effect of inherited wealth upon those who have done nothing to earn or deserve it. With all her lucidity Willa Cather consistently avoided moralistic and explanatory tags. There are her people, set before you; they live, speak, and act. She leaves the reader free to discover the inner meaning of the whole. There is an undercurrent in all her books not always discerned on a first reading.

She was truly sympathetic with my difficulties and losses in fleeing out of Italy. "I am afraid you will never again see the books you left there—no, nor the city in which you left them. I once heard Sir James Jeans say that, next to man's longing for personal immortality was his wish that his world should go on just as he had known it. Surely we are singularly unfortunate, since we lose not only our dearest friends, but see the world we loved brutally smashed to pieces—absolutely wiped out."

I was in a nostalgic mood and my mind travelled back to the peaceful time of our first meeting. She, too, liked to think of her Pittsburgh days when everyone was happy and well, and when the world seemed to be going forward instead of backward.

"Yes, indeed, I do remember the day you came up Murray Hill because you had read 'Paul's Case.' What a happy group of friends used to meet there in those days! And how few of them are left. And how little of the world they loved is left. If only we had been born in the year eighteen fifty, we would have had all the best things of four civilizations, and none of the horrors. Would never have known of, or dreamed of the horrors."

ELIZABETH SERGEANT

Excerpts from
Willa Cather: A Memoir

JUNE, 1913

Willa Cather fascinated me because she carried with her a creative force of which she was aware, yet largely uninformed. As in
an iceberg, the greater part of her load was submerged. That of
course made her masterful, and somewhat alarming. She moved
in her own powerful, inflexible direction, impervious to many
aspects of life that to others might be significant. She knew when
she was in motion, at least, and when she was jostled and churned
up from below by meeting, usually through memory, a figure she
could not deny. Then she paused, gazed, apprehended her fullest
inwardly and communicated in a story what she saw and felt.

I have seen her many times, in this state of mental-emotional passion about a new character. But never more excitingly—to go back,
far back again—than when I landed in New York in late June of
1913, from my pilgrimage to France, and paid her a little visit in
her home at Number Five Bank Street.

The late June day I am recalling some forty years back, was as
hot and dense as New York's summer days can well be. *O Pioneers!*
had been out but a few weeks. As the boat eased into her slip,
and we passengers, packed along the rail on the lower deck, looked
down on a sea of waiting faces, blobs of white, crimson or brown,

like patches of paint on a Pissaro canvas, one blob came to life for me. It was oval, rosy-cheeked, and so vernal and joyous under a hat nodding with red poppies and blue cornflowers that my heart already alight, burst into speech:

"How are the reviews?" I called.

Willa heard me, searched for my face along the row, flushed, waved and answered:

"Splendid, splendid!"

Next I see her in her green linen and myself in my new Paris clothes sitting on my trunks, surrounded by the multifarious luggage one carried in those old days, waiting for the customs inspector.

Willa, in her sweeping exhilarated way, was discussing her reviews—how they in the West said she had been right about the *country;* and that was what she cared about. She had not wanted her readers to think about her, the author, she'd wanted the writing to stand alone. Did it? Still needing reassurance? I countered, unbelieving.

But she was irked by the Inspector, scattering on the dirty dock gloves, frocks, scarves, from Paris and Avignon, books of Provençal poetry inscribed with many flourishes in purple ink, canvases and drawings by the *Fauve*—which she began at once to study with interest, since they represented a new way of *seeing.*

Willa could interpose a marble-hard wall between herself and whomever or whatever she wanted to ignore—in this case the Inspector. As I have a more passive and adaptable attitude in my dealings with the world, I was soon trying to placate them both. How we got to Number Five Bank Street, along the burning dirty waterside, clanging with trucks, I don't know. Letters, those deceptive strands of connection between friends, had moved quietly back and forth for some nine months—now the provocative living woman jogged my elbow. How close may one come to the throbbing, smoking flanks of Pegasus, without danger from a flying hoof?

I heard the word "Fremstad" which had already appeared in her letters. Fremstad, Fremstad, wonderful Fremstad . . . Nothing, nothing, Willa murmured in the cab—still quite unaware of my Provençal daze, my whirling head—could equal the bliss of entering into the very skin of another human being. Did I not agree? And if this skin were Scandinavian—then what?

But now the taxi had drawn up to a plain brick house with white trimmings in a quiet corner of Greenwich Village. Willa put her hand on my arm.

I must have noticed, she said, how reluctant she had been to have me come to the halfway houses she had enforcedly occupied so far. Place meant so much to her. She so hoped I'd like her home behind that row of windows on the second floor above the street, facing south—she wanted to live there the rest of her life!

Here is a sanctuary, here is a temple, her voice implied: should I take off my shoes at the front door? When it was opened by an exuberant maid out poured a heavy-spicy perfume of summer flowers. My first impression of Bank Street was a sensuous one. Rightly so, for Willa's work was carried on, at any season, within a fragile screen of hovering flower-scents, and gay petals.

Later, I was to know her apartment in winter, by the smell of orange blossoms, camellias, violets, freesias. I was to see it in spring, when jonquils and narcissus stood on the table, and lilac and dogwood branched on the mantel. Now as I told her, it was as if the waxy syringa, and the purple iris of the South Berwick garden had migrated to Bank Street.

Willa stood reticent, confident, as I gazed about me. Everything in the rooms but the flowers was simple, plain, all but Spartan. There was space, and the good windows and marble fireplace asserted their lines. In this walled stronghold of her very self, a plain desk, a small writing table with a typewriter, and a tidy sheaf of manuscript were central.

There was no piano—I had imagined one. Bookcases nicely filled, but not overflowing. There were no heirlooms to entangle the Muse's attention, no armchairs so comfortable that she would pause to sink into one, no magazines, no "causes" hidden in the corners. Willa had cleared the decks and sanded them down.

She just stood there watching my face, and we did not need to exchange a word. Then I was pushed along, still in my own daze of Provençal sunshine, to a bedroom. Miss Lewis, whom I barely knew at this time, was away; there was room for a guest.

The next two or three days were a blend of excellent meals, little neighborhood walks and above all—talk! About the Southwest, about Provence, about her last and her next book, and how books came to pass at all.

When a friend cares to offer hospitality in the spirit of Ceres, one does not forget the meals, especially the first ones. I still see the bounteous gesture of Willa's arm, well-rounded, white, pouring a dry Burgundy she had found for me. She had also hunted through the Jefferson Market for perfect leaf lettuce—*la salade classique* as a French friend called it. Willa's dressing, mixed at the table, was compounded of light French olive oil and of the richest wine vinegar, with a dash of tarragon. She insisted on the tarragon.

We were (or I was) drinking to *O Pioneers!* and Willa rose suddenly in her resolute way and laid at my place a little brown book. It had a half-tone frontispiece of a handsome Swedish girl, and on the flyleaf an inscription I still cherish.

"To Elsie Sergeant, the first friend of this book."

A little later I was reading it again, and also a sheaf of reviews she had laid on my pillow. I had not been wrong about *O Pioneers!* She also retired to rest with the yellow novels I'd brought her—*La Porte Étroite,* for instance—who was this fellow Gide?

China tea, hot and smoky, the kind used by Mrs. Fields, at four; and dinner at six-thirty for the sake of the maid. Dinner with Willa always had an aspect of formality. She wore that night one of her Liberty dresses of thin silk from London, to which some Czech embroiderer had added charming patterns. As for my Avignon dress with its lace fichu and sprigs of flowers, she said she would put it in a story.

She asked me many questions about the wild man from a Provençal vineyard, a *petit bourgeois* by birth, who had got to painting in this new and startling way. In later life, nothing interested her less than what the French call *le mouvement,* in poetry or novels. The *avant-garde* . . . But in 1913, the story of *le sauvage,* as his mother called him, and above all, his new way of painting, piqued her interest.

I had told Willa that the artist's parents had opposed his study of painting until he ran away and shipped as a sailor. That act of rebellion had made his family allow him to study at the Beaux Arts, but soon he had military service to do, and he had begun to paint in his head, for lack of any other chance. When he got out of the Army he found he was a Cubist, *malgré lui*—he'd never heard of Cubism before he started practising it. But the Cubists had a formula and that had alienated him.

So he threw away Cubism, and started hunting for his own style. You can't paint la Provence as if it were la Touraine—at bottom it's harsh, desert, has etched lines, nothing fluid or vague—spatial. . . . I showed Willa the abstract drawings mostly on the back of menus . . . and she mused.

"You'd better write a book on Cubism," Willa joked. "But what if you have to marry the Cubist?"

I reminded her that she had not married any of her Southwest characters, not even the one who seemed a replica of a statue in the Naples Museum.

Willa looked reflective, and rather pleased with me.

As for the *sauvage,* she said—

She had wanted my understanding of her turning to the wrong side of the railroad tracks in Winslow, to discover those singing Mexicans who had come up from the South, from *Madre Mexicana,* from Spain before that, bringing to the desert that old courtesy, and that equally old folk music that binds the human race together.

Is it the fate of the creative writer, I asked (and here we were getting to the crux of our talk) to use the stuff of intense personal human experience for art only? Must a novelist—especially a female—go around saying I'm only a mirror? And never crossing the street without seeing herself do it? In living itself—even with a high objective like hers, didn't one get entangled—even in full professional swing—have human duties to perform, faiths and ties to fulfill? Could one let all private and personal experience be burned in the fires of *art?*

Then Willa got up and wandered about the room. To be free, to work at her table—that *was* all in all. What could be more beautiful, if you had it in you, than to be the wife of a farmer and raise a big family in Nebraska? There were fates and fates but one could not live them all. Some would call hers servitude but she called it liberation! Miss Jewett, too, had turned away from marriage.

I had been waiting to ask Willa how, in *O Pioneers!* the two-part pastoral, as she had first discussed it, grew out of those two separate stories: the Swedish story she'd had on her desk for some time, and the fiery Bohemian story which had come to her on the edge of a wheatfield in Red Cloud on her return from the Southwest trip a ycar ago—and which she thought of at first as a complete narrative.

She said she could only describe this coming together of the two elements that made the book as a sudden inner explosion and enlightenment. She had experienced it before only in the conception of a poem. Now she would hope always for similar experience in creating a novel, for the explosion seemed to bring with it the inevitable shape that is not plotted but designs itself. She now believed that the least possible tinkering with the form—*revealed* from within, the better.

Next morning after breakfast with red raspberries in their prime, Willa invited me to share the little meander through the Village streets she took for domestic ends before settling down for her two-hour stint of work.

It was fun to market with her, for she enjoyed turning country-woman, and frowning over a housekeeper's list; selecting items of her predeliction, like fresh plump chickens and mellow fruits, and ripe French Camembert, and using her brisk, reliable humor with tradespeople. She found them more real and interesting than conventional people with smooth surfaces and punctilious manners. We paused to buy from a great crony of hers, an old Italian in a blue cotton cap, with stubbled chin and obtrusive tooth. Willa compared him to a correct young man who happened to pass, wearing a hard straw hat with a black band. Surely that one sold bonds on Wall Street, and no doubt his mother had had his teeth straightened! Mouths should be left as nature made them—mouths were individual as ears, or eyes, (her Western brothers, she said parenthetically, wore to her annoyance, only Arrow collars and Stetson hats) but the dentists insisted on deadly conformity.

Since *O Pioneers!* had come out, letters inviting her to join this or that group were arriving just in this little space of time. Perish all social clubs for women! Perish all these altruistic organizations!

When Willa talked of what she hated, her whole personality changed. Her chin hardened, her shoulders pushed forward, and one felt that the rigors of her life had made her tough or touchy. Her emotional nature was disciplined on the surface; but not far below burned a fiery furnace. When the wrong kind of person —for her—approached her with seeming kindness, an uncontrollable antagonism flashed out.

SPRING, 1916

In the spring of 1916, I had the first inkling that Willa had a new story in mind. I never asked questions—she was the initiator of any communication about an unborn or unfinished work.

She had not been able to forget that, in these war days, the youth of Europe, its finest flower, was dying. Perhaps our American youth had also been designed for sacrifice—by now we feared so. But a growing vital work, with Willa, usually took precedence, even in her thoughts, over the life around her.

She had come in for tea at a small apartment facing south on a garden, in the East Sixties where I was living. As it was not far from Central Park, she arrived flushed and alert from one of her swift wintry walks. I think of her as always wearing red-brown fur in winter in those years; it made her hair shine, and she had the warmth, charm, assurance, and fullness of being that allied her, despite her individual direction, with *the* American woman in her forties. She said more than once to me that nobody under forty could ever really believe in either death or degeneration. She herself carried that physical nonchalance right on through her fifties.

While I boiled the kettle Willa sat down with Henry James's *Notes on Novelists* which lay on my writing table; turned to the passage where he says that the originator has one law and the reporter, however philosophic, another. "So that the two laws can with no sort of harmony and congruity make one household."

Willa was amused by James's elaborate, subtle phrases—a bit impatiently amused by now. But with this comment she fully agreed: she had not altogether banished the reporter in her last book. Now she aimed at a more frugal, parsimonious form and technique.

She then suddenly leaned over—and this is something I remembered clearly when *My Antonia* came into my hands, at last, in 1918—and set an old Sicilian apothecary jar of mine, filled with orange-brown flowers of scented stock, in the middle of a bare, round, antique table.

"I want my new heroine to be like this—like a rare object in the middle of a table, which one may examine from all sides."

She moved the lamp so that light streamed brightly down on my Taormina jar, with its glazed orange and blue design.

"I want her to stand out—like this—like this—because she *is* the story."

Saying this her fervent, enthusiastic voice faltered and her eyes filled with tears.

Someone you knew in your childhood, I ventured.

She nodded, but did not say more.

So I sometimes wondered, later, whether she was thinking of Ántonia or Mrs. Forrester. Often she thought about her heroines for years before they appeared in a book.

Another day, of the same period, when we were walking in the Park together, past skaters on the icy pond, under brilliant blue skies, she told me of a major change in her personal life—this rather drily, rather bluntly.

Her friend, Isabelle McClung, whom I knew to be an animating force, was getting married. This, after first youth, one did not expect or foresee. But it had happened. Judge McClung, by then an old man, had died in the fall; 1180 Murray Hill Avenue would cease to be—and of course I knew that, even since she'd had a home in Bank Street, she had spent some months of every year writing in Pittsburgh, where Isabelle had always protected and quickened her work in her perfect way.

Isabelle was a musical amateur, and she had married music too: Jan Hambourg was a gifted and scholarly violinist, known on two continents for his concerts with two musician brothers, a violinist and a cellist. The three brothers had an old Russian father who was also a musical scholar, and a family home in Toronto. Isabelle and Jan would not desert American shores during the war. But Willa felt they might end up in Europe.

Her face—I saw how bleak it was, how vacant her eyes. All her natural exuberance had drained away.

MARCH, 1925

Sometimes Willa and I met by chance, at a literary gathering in New York: the one I best remember is a dinner given by Robert Frost's friends—about forty of them—in honor of his fiftieth birthday: March 26, 1925. It was celebrated in an old banquet room, a bit of shabby provincial France, at the Brevoort Hotel. The whole occasion had the charming innocence and sincerity of the unpublicity days. That retiring faun R.F., who still tried for invisibility when he met the world, had brought Poetry with him. The Frost family clump, at the head table, Elinor with her rich fairness and Puritan line, Robert tossing his head back, Lesley and Irma were themselves the early New England spring personified.

No doubt it is with the aid of the old program of the evening that I remember some of the other faces—Carl and Irita Van Doren, Mark and Dorothy Van Doren, Elinor Wylie, Sara Teasdale, Jean and Louis Untermeyer, Ridgely Torrence, Dorothy Canfield Fisher. . . . I vaguely see them. But what I really remember is Willa's large, impressive head, emerging from some rich low-necked gown with a touch of red that greatly became her. She had spent the previous summer in France and I had not seen her for some time.

Her neck, if bare, set this head with its springing bronze hair, which never greyed or curled, in just proportion. The hair was always done at the back of her neck in an unfashionable bun. Her lovely oval face brimmed with affection, her blue eyes gazed upon the hero of the evening as if he were a distant prospect, much admired. Like the *Mesa Encantada,* with a cloud mesa above it—so Willa had felicitously described it—imitating it and mirroring it in the intense blue above.

A reflection of Frost as he then was, before his hair was so snowy and blowing and his skin so rosy pink and sand-brown from the Florida sun, comes into the portrait I wrote shortly after this dinner. I saw his skin grey as a granite wall, a pasture wall. Or in another light, colored as Carrara marble, with mauve and golden shadows.

In his seventies, Robert Frost's head has the weight and balance of one of those Roman senatorial heads that used to line our Bryn Mawr academic corridors. But the half-century Frost of the Brevoort dinner insisted, sculpturally, on the Greek mode. "A good Greek out of New England," as I wrote at the time. Perhaps a good subject for Skopas who, to the calm, still features of the classic day, added musing eyes, deeply hollowed, and shadows of modern man's unrest.

Aroldo du Chêne, an Italian sculptor who lived at my home, 415 East Fifty-first Street on the ground floor, had seen Frost rather more romantically. But, as du Chêne said, Frost's countenance was changeful, moody. One could not hold him to the sculptural line. Shrewd satiric wrinkles would break his cheeks; malice, wit and blue flame would fly toward the fool who ventured to make a "still" out of life, to freeze a tempest—what words did he use?

Many times that evening did I regret having committed myself to trying to capture in words the imponderable essence of the two unique writers, two first-rate specimens, who preferred the shade to the sun, who did not at all fit into the collective American literary pattern or care to do so; yet had already so deeply affected the American professors and their students; the critics; the elite among readers.

They had certain things in common—there were likenesses in their differences. Frost had never thrown off the effect of having been born in San Francisco in a rough-and-tumble age. Nor Willa Cather the starkness of her migration at the age of nine from a soft green valley to wild red earth. To both, the hardness of the basic struggle for existence was a long memory that purified their approach to the life of the artist. The usual trappings and self-indulgences seemed to them both effete. Both thought of themselves, if I were to believe them, as "roughnecks" who had more or less happened into fame. Both liked a rather bare and timeless world. Both were suspicious of their own emotional, singing side, and imposed on it an elegant and sober line.

Frost had told me how uncertain he was, how floundering in direction as a youth. All he knew was that he "cared to write a little poem"—and to marry Elinor. Willa, far more confident, unencumbered and self-impelled, had early decided to be a writer. But, like Frost, she had turned from one thing to another to make her way—to journalism, teaching, to editorial work. Both of them had come into their first significant recognition in their late thirties. Yet in the life and work of both one could discern an absolute sureness and continuity of literary development.

"Frost," I said in my portrait, "had stuck with piety to the clarification of his own tone of voice, his own form and matter." With Willa it was the same: every novel must be a meeting between the life line and the line of personal development, must be a personal discovery. And they had in common their passionate dependence on the world of nature. They were rocks, they were trees. In common, too, they held valiantly, like a banner, their debt to the masters of the past.

"First heard the voice from a printed page in a Virgilian Eclogue and Hamlet," Frost wrote in my copy of *Selected Poems*. "Influenced by what I have supposed *Piers Plowman* to be. Never read it."

The last quip points up a divergence. Willa could be caustic at her own expense, sometimes savagely angry. But she did not make light of herself. Where R.F., with his glinting humor, wandered along, speculating about what the answer was, Willa seemed to move by will-power and was far more apt to think she knew.

But neither of them ever disappointed me, said I to myself, as I took my coat from the little old, sad French valet, in the lobby of the Brevoort. For the two were parting and Willa was offering Frost, as her birthday present, her recently published selection of the works of Sarah Orne Jewett, the Mayflower edition. In the preface she had compared *The Country of the Pointed Firs* to the tuft of meadow flowers spared by the reaper in Frost's fine poem. She said to Mr. Frost (as he has told me):

"Your success is one of my chief interests."

After this I observed Frost—with someone tugging at his overcoat—hatless, wild-looking, done forever with pretty speeches, frantically herding his family out into the dark night. Willa, on the contrary, stood with stiffly regimented air, waiting for her furs, and bearing coldly with some bold critic who had tagged after her and edged up to her.

She never had the least little bit of small talk, not an iota of ease or light friendliness with a stranger who seemed intrusive. What I thought I heard Willa say, on this occasion, to the gentleman she did not at all encourage to see her to her taxi, was that the Brevoort cuisine was not what it had been: all the best French chefs had been called to the colors in 1914, and had never returned.

LOUISE BOGAN

"American-Classic"

When, on June 16 of this year, Princeton University awarded a degree of Doctor of Letters to Willa Cather, it awarded an honorary degree to a woman for the first time in its history, Princeton University may well have experienced, on that day, the excitement and perturbation which naturally follow after any break with tradition. Miss Cather, make no mistake, took the whole thing as a matter of course. She is no stranger to the degree of Litt. D. The Universities of Michigan, Nebraska, Columbia and Yale have eagerly taken her, before this, under their honorary wings. Miss Cather would not be surprised at anything now. For she well knows that she has accomplished, in the last decade or so, a miracle which should cause any university now extant to forget and forgive her sex. When all the rewards were going to writers of fiction who compromised with their talents and their material in order to amuse or soothe an American business culture, she, as one of her most intelligent critics has said, used her powers not in mimicking reality but in practicing fiction as one of the fine arts. She knows that she represents, to use another critical tag, "the triumph of mind over Nebraska."

She would be the first person to admit her limitations. She has admitted them, in each successive novel, by working more and more closely within them, by letting what she could not do alone. She is not a profound or subtle psychologist. Madame Colette's minute dissections of intimate personal relationships are not in

From the *New Yorker*, August 8, 1931. Reprinted by permission; Copr. © 1931, 1959 by The New Yorker Magazine, Inc.

her line. She lacks the broad canvas of Sigrid Undset. But she is a writer who can conjure up from the look of a place and the actions of people a narrative as solid as a house, written in prose as surely counterpointed as music. She produced, in *My Ántonia,* an undoubted American masterpiece, which will be read when most contemporary novels are as outdated as the publisher's blurbs on their jackets.

If you think of the author of a contemporary masterpiece as a person as solid as his own work, uncompromising, natural, nad heartily in key, Miss Cather will fit your picture. She is the antithesis of the romantic artist at odds with himself and the world— that, it may be, suppositious figure who raises himself from the pillow where lamentable habits have put him to write a few immortal words before the miasma again sets in. Her life has been free from turmoil; she is at home in her country and her society. She has not needed to expatriate herself in order to do her work, and she is as scornful of expatriate writers as she is of literary cliques and cabals. Although she now divides her time between California, where her mother lives, and a hotel in New York, she formerly lived, as much as possible, in one spot. She rooted herself in an apartment in Bank Street, in New York City, for almost ten years. Here she saw her friends, at parties and dinners always slightly tinged with formality. She refused to encourage proselytes and adorers; she picked her intimates with care. For most of the year she sat down to her desk every morning and worked at writing. Writing was her job; she accepted it as part of a natural day, as one accepts bath and breakfast. She saw few strangers and gave few interviews. She saw New York change from horizontal vistas of brownstone stoops, from gaslight and horse-cars, into a city presenting itself vertically to the eye. But Carnegie Hall remained in the same place; though Mouquin's disappeared, the Crillon and the Brevoort could be trusted to serve good food; the values of good prose persisted as always. She went each year, for rest and refreshment, to Santa Fe or Quebec. Taos and Santa Fe she has known well since 1912, long before the days of motorbuses and nationally advertised Indian Detours. Several of her books have used Southwestern material, notably *Death Comes for the*

Archbishop, which drew extensively on Southwestern legend and history. Her new novel, *Shadows on the Rock,* is about Quebec. She does not like to call it an historical novel, although its time is the seventeenth century and Count Frontenac is one of its characters.

She likes the French Canadians because they have remained practically unchanged for over two hundred years, Quebec because it is built to last, and because its buildings show the influence of French architects of France's best period. Its inhabitants like good food and simple pleasures. They are almost indestructible in their racial traits, and Miss Cather admires indestructible qualities in human character.

"Quebec never would have changed at all," she says, "if the American drunks had left it alone."

It is difficult to realize, after a glance at the Willa Cather who has shaken herself free from any influence which might hamper her work or her career, the indisputable fact that her career got off, in her first two books of prose, to a bad start. She stepped, in *The Troll Garden,* a volume of short stories, and *Alexander's Bridge,* a novel, not out onto the Nebraskan prairie but into the artist's studio and the drawing-room. This misstep, when one considers the state of American fiction at the time (the years 1905 to 1912), was only natural. Henry James, in his steady progress through tapestried and marble halls, had lugged American fiction after him. His disciple, Mrs. Wharton, save for one lapse, in 1911, when she published *Ethan Frome,* had carried on the genteel tradition. O. Henry, it is true, had reported on people in hall-bedrooms and corner saloons, with some success. His influence, however, with the young who cared for beautiful prose was negligible. Young Willa Sibert Cather wanted to write beautiful prose about temperamental, ambitious, enchanting people. She now admits that this ambition was a grave mistake. Her talents had no real scope in the drawing-rooms of New York and London.

She walked into London drawing-rooms by way of Pittsburgh. Directly after her graduation, in 1895, from the University of Nebraska, at the age of twenty, she came east, to work for two years as telegraph editor on the Pittsburgh *Leader*. A friend who knew her ambition and her desire for Eastern experience got her the job. She left the newspaper to teach English literature in the Allegheny High School in the same city. She was not much older than her pupils; she remembers them as nice, intelligent children.

In Pittsburgh a new life began for the young Nebraskan. She met, for the first time, people with money and taste, who entertained actors and musicians. Pittsburgh was one of the first stops on the road; plays arrived there fresh from the New York stage. Singers and members of the theatrical profession were more generous with their time and talents, more grateful for hospitality, in the provinces than they were likely to be in New York itself. Public entertainers in those days were not carried away by the ambition to look and act like everyone else. They never could be mistaken for other people. Miss Cather was no more afraid of hero-worship then than she is now. She wrote down her new and exotic acquaintances. She crowded everything in. The early stories are full of furniture, salon pictures, literary conversation, phrases in foreign languages, glittering clothes, sweeping opera cloaks, bouquets, and gold slippers. The Western plains appear briefly now and then, but the characters hasten to leave them as quickly as possible. Trains whistle in and out of the action; people go back, but almost immediately escape again.

After nine years of Pittsburgh Miss Cather's career took another turn, in an upward direction. *The Cosmopolitan* (then a periodical of great seriousness), *Lippincott's, Scribner's,* and finally *McClure's,* had accepted her stories. *McClure's Magazine* was far more enterprising in its editorial policies than any of the others. S. S. McClure, after his triumph in the field of newspaper syndicates, was an expert at drawing native and imported literary talent into his pages. He had published Anthony Hope, Stevenson, Kipling, and Conan Doyle. He had taken Ida M. Tarbell away from historical essays on the paving of Paris to an historical summing-up of the Standard Oil Company. Willa Sibert Cather could write as good stories as any young disciple of James. She could be trusted to know a good story when she saw it. In 1906 S. S. McClure hired her as a member of the staff of his magazine.

Miss Cather worked in New York as managing editor of *Mc-Clure's* from 1908 to 1912. She and McClure were sympathetic; they both were simple, ambitious, and straightforward. Every summer she accompanied the McClures to London, to assist in the magazine's author-seining expeditions. She went everywhere and met everyone: the older generation of authors and critics, in the persons of Edmund Gosse, Sidney Colvin, and the Meynells; and the newer generation: Chesterton, Leonard Merrick, Wells, and Galsworthy. She enjoyed everything, old and new. "I wasn't out to spy on life," she says of these days. "I was out to live it."

While she worked on *McClure's,* she published practically nothing. Samuel McClure's autobiography came out in 1912; it bears the acknowledgement: "I am indebted to the co-operation of Miss Willa Sibert Cather for the very existence of this book." *Alexander's Bridge,* that artistic stepchild, appeared the same year. "In *Alexander's Bridge* I was still more preoccupied with trying to write well than with anything else," she has since explained. "A painter or writer must learn to distinguish what is his *own* from what he admires. I never abandoned trying to compromise between the kind of matter which my experience had given me, and the kind of writing I admired, until I began my second novel, *O Pioneers!*"

Miss Cather was not a young writer, as such things go, when she wrote *O Pioneers!* She was thirty-eight. But at that age she found herself so certainly that she never again has needed to fumble about. From then on, in five succeeding books, she remembered Nebraska, where she had spent her youth. She was born in Virginia, outside Winchester, where her forebears had lived as farmers for three generations. When she was nine her father went west, and settled in south-central Nebraska, near Red Cloud. The section had previously been peopled, soon after the opening of the Union Pacific and Burlington Railways, in the late sixties, by Norwegians, Swedes, Russians, and Czechs. Much of the country was still raw prairie. Young Willa rejected a regular primary education; until the time when she entered the high school in Red Cloud, her education went on at home. She rode about and made friends with her neighbors. She learned all there was to know about the prairie, including how to kill rattlesnakes and how prairie dogs built their towns. The neighbors, although immigrants living a hard life in difficult surroundings, were of a high type, especially the Czechs and Norwegians. They were musical; their cooking, at its best, compared well with the best culinary art of Prague or Vienna. They planted trees and gardens in the bare little towns, and dreary saloons, under their influence, blossomed out into beer gardens. They were worth bringing to mind. But Miss Cather was surprised when Ferris Greenslet, of the Houghton Mifflin Company, accepted *O Pioneers!* Her first novel had opened with a description of a gentleman on his way to a tea party on Beacon Hill. Her second, in its first sentence, disclosed a Nebraska town in a high gale of wind. For Miss Cather, the wind was at last blowing in the right direction.

William Heinemann, who brought out *O Pioneers!* in England, rejected her next book, *The Song of the Lark,* on the ground that "the full-blooded method, which tells everything about everybody" was the wrong one for Miss Cather to use. She took his words to heart. She now considers the higher processes of art to be the processes of simplification. To her, the first law of writing is to be yourself and to be natural.

One can see at a glance that she herself has always been that rare accident of Nature, a perfectly natural person. She speaks, without the shadow of a doubt, in the accent she acquired as a child. Her voice is deep and resonant. Her dresses are bright in color; she likes brilliant embroidery, boldly designed materials, and exotic strings of beads. She is of medium height and of the build best described as stocky. She stands and moves solidly. She sits with an air of permanence, as though the chair were, and had always been, her home. She smokes a cigarette as though she really liked the taste of ignited tobacco and rice paper. Her eyes are fine: gray-blue and set well apart. She has a thorough smile. Her face, when she detects some affectation in another's words or actions, can lose every atom of warmth and become hostile and set. It is impossible to imagine her strong hands in a deprecatory gesture. The remarks "Oh well" and "What does it matter?" have never, in all probability, passed her lips. She admires big careers and ambitious, strong characters, especially if they are the careers and characters of women. The most fortunate and most exciting of human beings, to her mind, is a singer with a pure, big voice and unerring musical taste. She also understands men and women who are her direct opposite: delicate, capricious figures full of charm, but with no staying powers or will to endure. She knows that these last, the world being what it is, usually come to a bad end. She has nothing but contempt for people who refuse, because of indolence or indifference, to get the best they can out of life.

She does not like to work away from America, although some of *A Lost Lady* was written in Europe. In Paris she misses clear American skies, becomes absorbed in watching the changing soft colors of the Seine, and gets nothing done. She delights in the turns and sound of colloquial American speech. In literature she admires the power and breadth of the Russians even more than the delicacy and form of the French. Pushkin, Gogol, Turgenev, and Tolstoi receive her praise; she does not mention Dostoevsky and considers Chekhov too despairing and bloodless to be of the first rank. No one can convince her that sociological reasons can explain the appearance of great writers in certain places at certain times. Greatness, to her mind, is up to the individual; the culture into which he is born can be of little help and less hindrance to the complete, freely functioning artist. She would not give a penny for any literature that present-day Russia can produce. "Liberty," she says with a snap of her eyes, "sheds too much light."

She does not believe that the critical faculty, applied to literature, can really find out how the thing goes. "Anyone," she remarks, "who ever has experienced the delight of living with people and in places which are beautiful and which he loves, throughout the long months required to get them down on paper, would never waste a minute drawing up lists of rules or tracing down reasons why."

Her later novels approach more and more closely to the ideal she has set herself: human character and setting put down almost without accent, keyed to the quietest level, denuded of everything but essentials. This ideal she has herself termed "the novel *démeublé.*" *Death Comes for the Archbishop* was an example of this style, and, it may be added, her greatest financial success; it went into four times as many printings as any of her earlier books. In contemporary writing, pure style and no nonsense are her demands. She is willing to be stirred by the work of young writers, if they write in a way of which she can approve. She read *The Bridge of San Luis Rey* against her own prejudices (she thought that the wrong people had admired it), and has prayed for the fortunate continuance of Thornton Wilder's talent ever since. She likes W. R. Burnett's *Little Caesar,* because it is direct—because it sounds as if it might have been written by Little Caesar.

The ladies of Omaha commissioned Bakst, when he was in America, to paint her portrait. They made an extremely appropriate choice. For Bakst gained a subject who, in spite of her Irish-Alsatian ancestry, her American upbringing, has a strain of Tartar in her temperament. She has come through in spite of everything—unsubordinated by her material, her early sentimentality, false starts, and bad choices. Her integrity cannot be sufficiently remembered with awards, whether they be Pulitzer Prizes, medals of the American Academy, or honorary degrees. She has made herself complete mistress of her talent. Her foot is on her native heath and her name is Willa Cather.

IV

CRITICISM ON THE BARRICADES: THE SOCIAL TEMPER OF THE 1930's

A READER who confined his attention to the book columns of the newspapers and the larger circulation magazines in the thirties would probably be unable to detect any downturn in Willa Cather's reputation in that decade. The *Atlantic Monthly* and *Saturday Review* maintained exactly the same kind of receptivity and enthusiasm toward Miss Cather that they had established in the twenties. Fanny Butcher continued to write ecstatic reviews in the Chicago *Tribune*. Indeed, Miss Cather's popularity had never seemed greater, or her position in American letters more assured. *Shadows on the Rock* (1931) was a runaway best seller, the only of her novels ever to achieve that kind of immediate popularity. Nearly every mark the successful author can be awarded fell Miss Cather's way during the decade—honorary degrees from a growing list of universities, requests from publishers to include her works in textbooks, translations of her novels in all parts of the world. But for the first time a crack appeared in the critical façade. To be sure, the crack was only a minority report; but what made it ominous was that it came from a highly articulate group of young critics writing in the *Nation* and the *New Republic*, and that it mounted a full-scale attack not only on Miss Cather's new work but on the direction of her entire career.

It is quite possible that an attack of some kind, if not this then some other, was bound to come, quite apart from the special character of the thirties. Willa Cather had achieved, finally, so imposing a reputation that she had become fair game for the younger critics. In addition, her new books, *Shadows on the Rock* and *Obscure Destinies* (1932), while near the top of her apogee, were not remarkable for energy or originality when judged by the standards of *The Professor's House* or *Death Comes for the Archbishop*; while the books that came after, *Lucy Gayheart* (1935) and *Not Under Forty* (1936), are hard to defend by any standard. More to the point, these books simply did not seem important or current, as though they had been written in some other time and place. But the brunt of the attack and the form in which it came was less a reflection of Miss Cather's crimes than of the special breed of criticism developed in the thirties—a criticism that tried to alter the ground rules by which the game of literature was played, and came close to success.

The extreme examples are the frankly Marxist writings of Max Eastman and V. F. Calverton, or the reviews that appeared throughout the thirties in *The Modern Quarterly* or *The Partisan Review*. A sample is Calverton's introduction to *The Liberation of American Literature* (1931), in which he maintains that literature is a reflection of the culture that produces it, and that American literature and culture are shaped by the "class conflict." What Calverton calls the writer's "aesthetic" effects and evaluations are, says Calverton, of no importance. All that is important is the writer's "ideology"—that is, his "interpretation of the class conflict." Using such a standard, Calverton can—indeed, does—dismiss not only Willa Cather but Sherwood Anderson, Sinclair Lewis, and every other writer of significance from the period as—in his words—simply people "who lacked courage or vision and remained petty bourgeois."

Calverton had almost no literary sensitivity and had the Marxist criticism of the thirties been wielded wholly by such people it could not possibly have had much effect. But dozens of critics of superior equipment and acute sensibility who must have found most of Calverton's judgments gross oversimplifications nonetheless accepted the premises from which the judgments issued, including most of the young critics writing for the *Nation* and the *New Republic*—Edmund Wilson, Malcolm Cowley, F. O. Matthiessen, Robert Cantwell, Granville Hicks, Newton Arvin, the young Mary McCarthy. Marxist criticism, or some version of it, quickly became the American avant-garde criticism, and was to the young critics of the thirties much what aestheticism was to the twenties and Coming-of-Age criticism was to the decade between 1910 and 1920. People who ten years earlier would have been talking about "point of view" were talking about "abandonment of one's class," "bourgeois individualism," and "class solidarity," at times with strange results when their subject happened to be Willa Cather. Harlan Hatcher, for instance, writing in 1935 in the approved fashion, notes that while Lewis, Anderson, Dreiser, and Floyd Dell were "struggling desperately in the pit," Willa Cather had the good fortune "to be able to ride her own pony among the alien settlers of Nebraska," and from this favored class position produced books "which could be read in schools and women's clubs where Theodore Dreiser and Anderson would have caused a panic."

It would be a mistake to suggest that Marxist criticism, even when it was at its height about 1935 or 1936, was ever the predominant American criticism, or that it ever extended much beyond a fairly narrow intellectual fringe. But its power was enough to force a polarization, such as has been often characteristic of European criticism but seldom of American, that registered up and down the whole range of journalistic criticism in the thirties. The pole on the left was roughly defined by the sort of literary criticism appearing in the *New Masses, Science and Society,* the *Partisan Review,* and *Mainstream;* the pole on the right by the kind appearing in the *Catholic World, America,* and *Commonweal.* Much of what the right had to say was produced in reaction to the left. Partly this reaction was uninformed and irrelevant. Faulkner, for instance, was lumped with the left as a degenerate, profane, and godless exponent of violence. But even though there was little genuine dialogue between left and right and no real attention paid by either extreme to the other, essential elements in the right-wing reaction were relevant and corrective: its concern, for instance, with tradition and permanent values at a time when these were ignored or under attack from the left; and its rejection of the narrow choice Marxists were trying to foist off on the American writer—a rejection in which the right was joined by humanists, liberals, academics, and others.

Willa Cather and Thornton Wilder, who appeared as bastions of strength against the encroaching materialism of the Marxists, were the two literary darlings of the right, and the comment about them in the Catholic press was as intemperate as the opposite sort written by Calverton. Michael Williams, for example, commenting on Willa Cather's *Obscure Destinies*, could say: "If there is a bookcase in any literate household in which *Obscure Destinies* does not stand (but well-worn, often taken down for use) then such a household is to be pitied, and should be immediately rescued from its poverty." He could write, that is, as though he were commenting on a venerable classic—on Shakespeare, say—rather than on a collection of short stories issued only a few weeks before.

The essays that follow are characteristic in different ways of the left-wing response of the thirties, and are close in certain ways. But Hicks's estimate, the earlier of the two, is also the more polemical and doctrinaire statement; Trilling's the more detached, scholarly, and reflective. The right is not represented, partly because it is impossible to find interesting criticism from the rightist viewpoint, but mainly because the chapter is not intended to represent the whole spectrum of opinion of the thirties. Instead, it is intended to represent what, from the perspective of today, seems most characteristic, distinctive, and permanent from the decade. For better or worse, the attack of the left rather than the defense of the right was what made the deeper mark—and, indeed, the most frequently heard critical stereotypes about Willa Cather originated in the leftist comment of the thirties.

GRANVILLE HICKS

"The Case against Willa Cather"

In her first representative book, *O Pioneers!*, published in 1913, Miss Cather clearly indicated the subsequent development of her career. After experiments, some fortunate and some not, in the short story, and after the failure of *Alexander's Bridge*, her one book that betrays the influence of Henry James, she found her distinctive field of literary activity and her characteristic tone. *O Pioneers!* contains all the elements that, in varying proportions, were to enter into her later novels.

We observe first of all that the very basis of *O Pioneers!* is a mystical conception of the frontier. At the turning point of Alexandra's career, when, after an examination of the river farms, she decides to remain on the high land, she looks at the Divide with love and yearning: "It seemed beautiful to her, rich and strong and glorious. Her eyes drank in the breadth of it, until her tears blinded her. Then the Genius of the Divide, the great, free spirit which breathes across it, must have bent lower than it ever bent to a human will before." This exultation sustains Alexandra throughout the book, and at the end she says, "The land belongs to the future. . . . We come and go, but the land is always here. And the people who love it and understand it are the people who own it—for a little while." Miss Cather's final comment is, "Fortunate country, that is one day to receive hearts like Alexandra's into its bosom, to give them out again in the yellow wheat, in the rustling corn, in the shining eyes of youth!"

But, though Alexandra speaks of the future, her mind is fixed

Reprinted from the *English Journal*, November, 1933, with the permission of the National Council of Teachers of English and Granville Hicks.

on the past, on the days of the Bergson family's struggle, before ease had corrupted her brothers. Miss Cather, too, is concerned with that past era, and she looks back at it with nostalgia. "Optima dies . . . prima fugit" might as well be the motto of *O Pioneers!* as of *My Ántonia*. Alexandra retains to the end the spiritual qualities of the pioneer, but the novel depicts the general disappearance of those virtues after the coming of prosperity. The coarsening of Lou and Oscar Bergson and the confusions of Frank Shabata and Emil are the fruits of change. Carl Linstrum, who has lived in cities and learned to hate them, looks with apprehension at the new developments. He tells Alexandra,

This is all very splendid in its way, but there was something about this country when it was a wild old beast that has haunted me all these years. Now, when I come back to all this milk and honey, I feel like the old German song, "Wo bist du, wo bist du, mein geliebtest Land?"

Even in little things *O Pioneers!* is prophetic. We find, for example, in her depiction of Amédée's funeral service, the same fondness for the colorful ceremonies of the Catholic church that dictated so many passages in *Death Comes for the Archbishop* and *Shadows on the Rock*. We find, also, in her scorn for the agrarian radicalism of Lou Bergson and Frank Shabata, the political conservatism that is implicit in all her works. And we find the episodic method, the reliance on unity of tone rather than firmness of structure, that is so marked in the later novels.

The two successors of *O Pioneers!*—*The Song of the Lark* and *My Ántonia*—closely resemble it, especially in the qualities we have noted. Both depend upon a mystical conception of the frontier, and both look back longingly to the heroism of earlier days. The more successful portions of *The Song of the Lark* are those portraying Thea's girlhood in Colorado and her visit to the cliff-dwellings. Both of these sections are developed at greater length than the part they play in Thea's life warrants, as if Miss Cather could not resist the temptation to expand upon her favorite theme. *My Ántonia* is exclusively concerned with the frontier, and the heroine retains the pioneer virtues in poverty and hardship, even as Alexandra and Thea do in success. All three women are triumphant products of the pioneering era; in them the mystical essence of a heroic age, now unfortunately passing, is embodied.

But if these three novels were merely mystical and nostalgic we should have less to say about them. After all, Miss Cather saw at first hand the Nebraska of the eighties and nineties, and her accounts of the life there are not without authenticity. However much she emphasizes the heroism and piety of the pioneers, she does not neglect the hardships and sacrifices. And heroism and piety did play their part in the conquest of the frontier. Miss Cather's proportions may be false; she may ignore motives, conditions, and forces that are altogether relevant; but there is nevertheless a basis in reality for the picture she gives.

That is why *O Pioneers!* and *My Ántonia* have their importance in American literature. Although the story of *My Ántonia* is told by Jim Burden, with his concern for "the precious, the incommunicable past," the book does create credible pioneers in the Burdens and the Shimerdas and does give convincing details of their life. In the latter part of the book there is a passage in which several daughters of immigrants tell of their homes in the first years in Nebraska, and we realize that Miss Cather can appreciate the bleakness and cruelty of this land for the travelers from across the sea. She can understand their eagerness to escape to the towns, and she knows, too, the monotony and narrowness of the prairie city.

Against this background Miss Cather presents the unforgettable picture of Ántonia, more human than Alexandra because of her weaknesses, more likeable because of her defeats. Though the reader never doubts that Ántonia is exceptional, though he realizes how much bitterness and tragedy the frontier brought to many of its daughters, he accepts Jim Burden's account of her:

She was a battered woman now, not a lovely girl; but she still had that something which fires the imagination, could still stop one's breath for a moment by a look or gesture that somehow revealed the meaning in common things. She had only to stand in the orchard, to put her hand on a little crab tree and look up at the apples, to make you feel the goodness of planting and tending and harvesting at last. All the strong things of her heart came out in her body, that had been so tireless in serving generous emotions. It was no wonder that her sons stood tall and straight. She was a rich mine of life, like the founders of early races.

From the first, it is clear, the one theme that seemed to Miss Cather worth writing about was heroic idealism, the joyous strug- gle against nature sustained by a confidence in the ultimate ben- eficence of that nature against which it fought. In her own child- hood she had actually seen such heroic idealism in the lives of Nebraskan pioneers, and in writing of those lives she achieved not only personal satisfaction but also fundamental truth. One may feel that she deals with the unusual rather than the repre- sentative, and that what she omits is more important than what she includes. One may be conscious that the haze of regretful retrospection distorts innumerable details. But one cannot deny that here is a beautiful and, as far as it goes, faithful re-creation of certain elements in the pioneering experience.

But after *My Ántonia* was written there came a crisis in Miss Cather's career as an artist. She obviously could not go on, paint- ing again and again the Nebraska she had once known. The West was changing, as she had been forced to admit in *O Pioneers!* and the others. Could she learn to depict the new West as she had depicted the old? The story of this new West could scarcely take the form of a simple, poetic idyll. Heroism and romance, if they existed, had changed their appearance. Characters could no longer be isolated from the social movements that were shap- ing the destiny of the nation and of the world. She would have to recognize that the life she loved was disappearing. Could she become the chronicler of the life that was taking its place?

At first she tried. The earlier chapters of *One of Ours* describe a sensitive Nebraskan boy in the years before the war. Claude Wheeler, who as a youth flinches before the coarseness and ma- terialism of his father, suffers almost as much from the narrow religiosity of his wife. The joy and beauty that are so prominent in the lives of Alexandra and Antonia have vanished from Claude's Nebraska. Though he seems capable of a heroic idealism, his life is miserable and futile. Then the war comes, and he enlists, goes forth to battle in heroic mood, and dies a hero's death. Thus Miss Cather, thanks to a romantic and naïve conception of the war, was able to approximate her favorite theme. But the second part bears no relation to the issues raised in the account of Claude's unhappiness in Nebraska. For Miss Cather, as for Claude, the war provides an escape from apparently insoluble problems.

Insoluble indeed, Miss Cather found these problems, and as she looked at the life about her, her despair grew. Once she had created symbols of triumph in Alexandra, Thea, and Ántonia, but now she concerned herself with symbols of defeat. Of all the books between *My Ántonia* and *Death Comes for the Archbishop*, *A Lost Lady* is the most moving. Why Marian Forrester is lost Miss Cather never explains, contenting herself with a delicate and pathetic record of that descent. Captain Forrester has in him the stuff of the pioneers, but his wife, though one feels in her capacities for heroism, is the product of changed times, and she abandons her standards, betrays her friends, and encourages mediocrity and grossness. She is the symbol of the corruption that had overtaken the age.

But *A Lost Lady* is merely a character study, and Miss Cather felt the need for a more comprehensive record of the phenomena of decay. St. Peter in *The Professor's House* is alienated from his wife and family; he has finished the work that has been absorbing him; he realizes that he must learn to live "without delight, without joy, without passionate griefs." That, Miss Cather seemed to feel at the moment, was what we all must learn. Heroism and beauty and joy had gone. For St. Peter these qualities had been summed up in Tom Outland, dead when the story opens, and perhaps fortunately dead: "St. Peter sometimes wondered what would have happened to him, once the trap of worldly success had been sprung on him." But Tom lives in St. Peter's memory, and his story occupies much of the book. Tom is the pioneer, vital, determined, joyful, sensitive to beauty. In telling his story Miss Cather escapes from her gloom and writes with the vigor and tenderness of her earlier work. But in the end the animation of the Outland narrative only serves to accentuate her melancholy, and she is left, like Professor St. Peter, in a drab and meaningless world.

> The university, his new house, his old house, everything around him, seemed insupportable, as the boat on which he is imprisoned seems to a sea-sick man. Yes, it was possible that the little world, on its voyage among all the stars, might become like that: a boat on which one could travel no longer.

Her despair increased, and Miss Cather made one more study of defeat, in *My Mortal Enemy*. But obviously she could not continue with these novels of frustration and hopelessness. One may risk the guess that, while she was writing her studies of despair, she personally was not particularly unhappy. Her reputation and income were both established on a reasonably high level. As a person she could be as contented as anyone else who enjoyed comfort and security, and as indifferent to the woes of the world. But as a writer she had that world as a subject, and the contemplation of it filled her with sadness and regret. It was not a world in which her imagination could be at ease, for her imagination still demanded the heroic idealism of the frontier. She could deal with that world only by portraying, in a few tragic lives, the corruption and defeat of what she held dear. She could not understand why evil had triumphed or how good might be made to prevail. All she could express was her conviction that something of inestimable value had been lost. She could only repeat, "Wo bist du, wo bist du, mein geliebtest Land?"

Miss Cather has never once tried to see contemporary life as it is; she sees only that it lacks what the past, at least in her idealization of it, had. Thus she has been barred from the task that has occupied most of the world's great artists, the expression of what is central and fundamental in her own age. It was easy for her, therefore, to make the transition from *My Mortal Enemy* to *Death Comes for the Archbishop*. If she could not write as she chose about her own time, she could find a period that gave her what she wanted. The beauty and heroism that she had found in pioneer Nebraska and that seemed so difficult to find in modern life could certainly be attributed to life in mid-nineteenth century New Mexico. And thence she could turn, in *Shadows on the Rock,* to Quebec about 1700. Once more she could show men and women who were neither awed by the savageness of nature nor unappreciative of its beauty. Once more she could deal with "the bright incidents, slight, perhaps, but precious," that are to be found whenever "an adventurer carries his gods with him into a remote and savage country."

Death Comes for the Archbishop, which describes the life of two Catholic missionaries in the Southwest, is highly episodic, and the episodes are so chosen as to make the most of the colorfulness of the country, the heroism of the characters, and the contrast between the crudeness of the frontier and the religious and cultural refinement of the archbishop. As one reads, one seems to be looking at various scenes in a tapestry, rich in material and artful in design. At first one is charmed, but soon questions arise. One asks what unity there is in these various episodes, and one can find none except in Miss Cather's sense that here, in the meeting of old and new, is a process of rare beauty. What significance, one goes on to inquire, has this beauty for us? Does it touch our lives? Is this really the past out of which the present sprang? Did these men and women ever live? Is there anything in their lives to enable us better to understand our own? We ask these questions, and as we try to answer them we realize that we are confronted by the romantic spirit. Miss Cather, we see, has simply projected her own desires into the past: her longing for heroism, her admiration for natural beauty, her desire—intensified by pre-occupation with doubt and despair—for the security of an unquestioned faith.

What is true of *Death Comes for the Archbishop* is also true of *Shadows on the Rock.* Miss Cather has again created her ideal frontier and peopled it with figments of her imagination. The construction is even weaker, the events even more trivial, the style even more elegiac, the characters even less credible. The book has a certain sort of charm, for Miss Cather's dreams have beauty and are not without nobility, and it has brought consolation to many readers who share her unwillingness to face the harshness of our world. But for the reader who is not seeking an opiate *Shadows on the Rock* has little to offer. Compare Cécile with Alexandra and Ántonia; compare Pierre Charron with Tom Outland. What Miss Cather chiefly tries to do is to throw over her Quebec the golden haze of romance, and she succeeds so well that her characters are, to the reader's vision, obscured and distorted almost beyond recognition.

Apparently it makes little difference what Miss Cather now attempts to do. The three stories in *Obscure Destinies* are more or less reminiscent of her earlier work, but the honesty and enthusiasm have disappeared. As if she were conscious of some lack, she finds it necessary to rely on direct statements. In "Neighbour Rosicky" she underlines the harshness and rapacity of the city and exaggerates the security of the country, and she introduces Doctor Ed to point the moral of the tale: "Rosicky's life seemed to him complete and beautiful." "Old Mrs. Harris" is so lacking in unity that its point has to be explained in the closing paragraph: "When they are old, they will come closer and closer to Grandma Harris. They will think a great deal about her, and remember things they never noticed; and their lot will be more or less like hers." "Two Friends," concerned with two "successful, large-minded men who had made their way in the world when business was still a personal adventure," teaches that politics is much less important than friendship. Twenty years ago Miss Cather had no need of exposition, for her themes were implicit in her material, but now her romantic dreams involve the distortion of life, and she cannot permit the material to speak for itself.

The case against Willa Cather is, quite simply, that she made the wrong choice. The nostalgic, romantic elements so apparent in her recent work were present in her earlier novels, but they were at least partly justified by the nature of her themes, and they could be introduced without the sacrifice of honesty. But once she had to abandon the material her Nebraskan childhood had so fortunately given her, she had to make her choice. She tried, it is true, to study the life that had developed out of the life of the frontier, but she took essentially marginal examples of modern life, symbolic of her own distaste rather than representative of significant tendencies. And when time had shown how certainly that path would lead to impotence and ultimately to silence, she frankly abandoned her efforts and surrendered to the longing for the safe and romantic past.

Willa Cather is by no means the only contemporary author who has fallen into supine romanticism because of a refusal to examine life as it is. One thinks, for example, of Elizabeth Maddox Roberts, whose first novel, *The Time of Man*, was worthy of comparison with *My Antonia*. It is easy to understand why many writers turn from our industrial civilization. On the one hand, they cannot accept the cruelty and rapacity that are so integral a part of it and its inevitable destruction of institutions and ways of life they cherish. On the other hand, they are so much bound up in it that they cannot throw themselves, as the revolutionary writers have done, into the movement to destroy and rebuild it. Flight is the only alternative. But flight is and always has been destructive of the artistic virtues, which are rooted in integrity. If, to the qualities Miss Cather displayed in *O Pioneers!* and *My Antonia,* had been added the robustness of a Dreiser or the persistence of an Anderson, not only survival but growth would have been possib!e. But the sheltered life seldom nurtures such qualities. She has preferred the calm security of her dreams, and she has paid the price.

LIONEL TRILLING

"Willa Cather"

In 1922 Willa Cather wrote an essay called "The Novel Démeublé" in which she pleaded for a movement to throw the "furniture" out of the novel—to get rid, that is, of all the social fact that Balzac and other realists had felt to be so necessary for the understanding of modern character. "Are the banking system and the Stock Exchange worth being written about at all?" Miss Cather asked, and she replied that they were not. Among the things which had no "proper place in imaginative art"—because they cluttered the scene and prevented the free play of the emotions—Miss Cather spoke of the factory and the whole realm of "physical sensation." Obviously, this essay was the rationale of a method which Miss Cather had partly anticipated in her early novels and which she fully developed a decade later in *Shadows on the Rock*. And it is no less obvious that this technical method is not merely a literary manner but the expression of a point of view toward which Miss Cather had always been moving—with results that, to many of her readers, can only indicate the subtle failure of her admirable talent.

If we say that Miss Cather has gone down to defeat before the actualities of American life, we put her in such interesting company that the indictment is no very terrible one. For a history of American literature must be, in Whitman's phrase, a series of "vivas for those who have failed." In our literature there are perhaps fewer completely satisfying books and certainly fewer

From *After the Genteel Tradition* (New York, 1937). The essay originally appeared in the *New Republic*. Copyright 1937, © 1965 by Lionel Trilling. Reprinted by permission of The Viking Press, Inc.

integrated careers than there are interesting canons of work and significant life stories. Something in American life seems to prevent the perfection of success while it produces a fascinating kind of search or struggle, usually unavailing, which we may observe again and again in the collected works and in the biographies of our writers.

In this recurrent but heroic defeat, the life of the American writer parallels the life of the American pioneer. The historian of frontier literature, Professor Hazard, has pointed out that Cooper's very first presentation of Deerslayer, the type of all pioneers, shows him a nearly broken old man threatened with jail for shooting a deer, a pitiful figure overwhelmed by the tides of commerce and speculation. In short, to a keen observer, the pioneer's defeat was apparent even in 1823. The subsequent decades that opened fresh frontiers did not change the outcome of the struggle. Ahead of the pioneer there are always the fields of new promise, with him are the years of heartbreaking effort, behind him are the men who profit by his toil and his hope. Miss Cather's whole body of work is the attempt to accommodate and assimilate her perception of the pioneer's failure. Reared on a Nebraska farm, she saw the personal and cultural defeat at first hand. Her forebears had marched westward to the new horizons; her own work is a march back toward the spiritual East—toward all that is the antithesis of the pioneer's individualism and innovation, toward authority and permanence, toward Rome itself.

The pioneer, as seen by a sophisticated intelligence like Miss Cather's, stands in double jeopardy: he faces both the danger of failure and the danger of success. "A pioneer . . . should be able to enjoy the idea of things more than the things themselves," Miss Cather says; disaster comes when an idea becomes an actuality. From *O Pioneers!* to *The Professor's House*, Miss Cather's novels portray the results of the pioneer's defeat, both in the thwarted pettiness to which he is condemned by his material failures and in the callous insensitivity produced by his material success. "The world is little, people are little, human life is little," says Thea Kronborg's derelict music teacher in *The Song of the*

Lark. "There is only one big thing—desire." When there is no longer the opportunity for effective desire, the pioneer is doomed. But already in Miss Cather's Nebraska youth the opportunities for effective desire had largely been removed: the frontier had been closed.

A Lost Lady, Miss Cather's most explicit treatment of the passing of the old order, is the central work of her career. Far from being the delicate minor book it is often called, it is probably her most muscular story, for it derives power from the grandeur of its theme. Miss Cather shares the American belief in the tonic moral quality of the pioneer's life; with the passing of the frontier she conceives that a great source of fortitude has been lost. Depending on a very exact manipulation of symbols, the point of *A Lost Lady* (reminiscent of Henry James's *The Sacred Fount*) is that the delicacy and charm of Marian Forrester spring not from herself, but from the moral strength of her pioneer husband. Heavy, slow, not intelligent, Forrester is one of those men who, in his own words, "dreamed the railroads across the mountains." He shares the knightly virtues which Miss Cather unquestioningly ascribes to the early settlers; "impractical to the point of magnificence," he is one of those who could "conquer but not hold." He is defeated by the men of the new money interests who "never risked anything"—and the perdition of the lost lady proceeds in the degree that she withdraws from her husband in favor of one of the sordid new men, until she finds her final degradation in the arms of an upstart vulgarian.

But though the best of the pioneer ideal is defeated by alien forces, the ideal itself, Miss Cather sees, is really an insufficient one. In her first considerable novel, *O Pioneers!*, she already wrote in an elegiac mood and with the sense that the old ideal was not enough. Alexandra Bergson, with her warm simplicity, her resourcefulness and shrewd courage, is the essence of the pioneering virtues, but she is distinguished above her neighbors because she feels that, if she is to work at all, she must believe that the world is wider than her cornfields. Her pride is not that she has triumphed over the soil, but that she has made her youngest brother, "a personality apart from the soil." The pioneer, having reached his goal at the horizons of the earth, must look to the horizons of the spirit.

The disappearance of the old frontier left Miss Cather with a heritage of the virtues in which she had been bred, but with the necessity of finding a new object for them. Looking for the new frontier, she found it in the mind. From the world of failure which she portrayed so savagely in "A Wagner Matinée" and "The Sculptor's Funeral," and from the world of fat prosperity of *One of Ours*, she could flee to the world of art; for in art one may desire illimitably. And if, conceivably, one may fail—Miss Cather's artists never do—it is still only as an artist that one may be the eternal pioneer, concerned always with "the idea of things." Thea Kronborg, of the breed of Alexandra Bergson, turns all the old energy, bogged down in mediocrity, toward music. Miss Cather rhapsodizes for her: "O eagle of eagles! Endeavor, achievement, desire, glorious striving of human art."

But art is not the only, or a sufficient, salvation from the débâcle of pioneer culture. For some vestige of the old striving after new worlds which cannot be gratified seems to spread a poison through the American soul, making it thin and unsubstantial, unable to find peace and solidity. A foreigner says to Claude Wheeler of *One of Ours*, "You Americans are always looking for something outside yourselves to warm you up, and it is no way to do. In old countries, where not very much can happen to us, we know that, and we learn to make the most of things." And with the artists, Miss Cather puts those gentle spirits who have learned to make the most of things—Neighbor Rosicky, Augusta and, pre-eminently, My Ántonia. Momentarily betrayed by the later developments of the frontier, Ántonia at last fulfills herself in child-bearing and a busy household, expressing her "relish for life, not overdelicate but invigorating."

Indeed, "making the most of things" becomes even more important to Miss Cather than the eternal striving of art. For, she implies, in our civilization even the best ideals are bound to corruption. *The Professor's House* is the novel in which she brings the failure of the pioneer spirit into the wider field of American life. Lame as it is, it epitomizes as well as any novel of our time the disgust with life which so many sensitive Americans feel, which makes them dream of their preadolescent integration and innocent community with nature, speculate on the "release from effort" and the "eternal solitude" of death, and eventually reconcile themselves to a life "without delight." Three stories of betrayal are interwoven in this novel: the success of Professor St. Peter's history of the Spanish explorers, which tears him away from the frontier of his uncomfortable and ugly old study to set him up in an elegant but stifling new home; the sale to a foreign collector of the dead Tom Outland's Indian relics, which had made his spiritual heritage; and the commercialization of Outland's scientific discovery with its subsequent corruption of the Professor's charming family. With all of life contaminated by the rotting of admirable desires, only Augusta, the unquesting and unquestioning German Catholic seamstress, stands secure and sound.

Not the pioneering philosophy alone, but the whole poetic romanticism of the nineteenth century had been suffused with the belief that the struggle rather than the prize was admirable, that a man's reach should exceed his grasp, or what's a heaven for? Having seen the insufficiency of this philosophy Miss Cather must find another in which the goal shall be more than the search. She finds it, expectably enough, in religion. The Catholicism to which she turns is a Catholicism of culture, not of doctrine. The ideal of unremitting search, it may be said, is essentially a Protestant notion; Catholic thought tends to repudiate the ineffable and to seek the sharply defined. The quest for Moby Dick, that dangerous beast, is Protestant; the Catholic tradition selects what it can make immediate and tangible in symbol, and Miss Cather turns to the way of life that "makes the most of things," to the old settled cultures. She attaches a mystical significance to the ritual of the ordered life, to the niceties of cookery, to the supernal virtues of *things* themselves—sherry, or lettuce, or "these coppers, big and little, these brooms and clouts and brushes," which are the tools for making life itself. And with a religious ideal one may safely be a pioneer. The two priests of *Death Comes for the Archbishop* are pioneers; they happen to be successful in their enterprise, but they could not have been frustrated, Miss Cather implies, because the worth of their goal is indisputable.

From the first of her novels the Church had occupied a special and gracious place in Willa Cather's mind. She now thinks with increasing eloquence of its permanence and certainty and of "the universal human yearning for something permanent, enduring, without shadow of change." The Rock becomes her often repeated symbol: "the rock, when one comes to think of it, was the utmost expression of human need." For the Church seems to offer the possibility of satisfying that appealing definition of human happiness which Miss Cather had made as far back as *My Ántonia*—"to be dissolved in something complete and great . . . to become a part of something entire, whether it is sun and air, goodness and knowledge."

It is toward that dissolvement that Miss Cather is always striving. She achieves it with the "sun and air"—and perhaps few modern writers have been so successful with landscape. She can find it in goodness and in society—but only if they have the feudal constriction of the old Quebec of *Shadows on the Rock*. Nothing in modern life, no possibility, no hope, offers it to her. She conceives, as she says in the prefatory note to her volume of essays, *Not Under Forty*, that the world "broke in two in 1922 or thereabouts," and she numbers herself among the "backward," unaware that even so self-conscious and defiant a rejection of her own time must make her talent increasingly irrelevant and tangential—for any time.

"The early pioneer was an individualist and a seeker after the undiscovered," says F. J. Turner, "but he did not understand the richness and complexity of life as a whole." Though Miss Cather in all her work has recognized this lack of understanding of complexity and wholeness, and has attempted to transcend it, she ends, ironically enough, in a fancier but no less restricted provincialism than the one she sought to escape. For the "spirituality" of Miss Cather's latest books consists chiefly of an irritated exclusion of those elements of modern life with which she will not cope. The particular affirmation of the verities which Miss Cather makes requires that the "furniture" be thrown out, that the social and political facts be disregarded; the spiritual life cannot support the intrusion of all the facts the mind can supply. The unspeakable Joseph Joubert, the extreme type of the academic verity-seeker, says in one of his *pensées*: " 'I'm hungry, I'm cold, help me!' Here is material for a good deed but not for a good work of art." Miss Cather, too, is irked by the intrusion of "physical sensations" in the novel. And one remembers Joubert's hatred of energy—he believed that it hindered the good life and scorned Balzac for his superabundant endowment of it—and one sees what is so irksome in Miss Cather's conception of ordered living: it is her implied praise of devitalization. She can recognize the energy of assiduous duty but not the energy of mind and emotion. Her order is not the channeling of insurgent human forces but their absence.

We use the word "escape" too lightly, no doubt; when we think how each generation must create its own past for the purposes of its own present, we must realize that the return to a past way of thought or of life may be the relevant criticism of the present. The only question, then, is the ends such criticism serves. Henry Adams's turn to the twelfth century was the attempt to answer the complex questions of the *Education* and to discover a better direction of energy; Eugene O'Neill's movement toward Catholic theology, crude as it may seem, as the profound interest of an energetic response to confusion. But Miss Cather's turn to the ideals of a vanished time is the weary response to weariness, to that devitalization of spirit which she so brilliantly describes in the story of Professor St. Peter. It is a weariness which comes not merely from defeat but from an exacerbated sense of personal isolation and from the narrowing of all life to the individual's sensitivities, with the resulting loss of the objectivity that can draw strength from seeking the causes of things. But it is exactly Miss Cather's point that the Lucretian *rerum natura* means little; an admirer of Virgil, she is content with the *lacrimae rerum*, the tears for things.

Miss Cather's later books are pervaded by the air of a brooding ancient wisdom, but if we examine her mystical concern with pots and pans, it does not seem much more than an oblique defense of gentility or very far from the gaudy domesticity of bourgeois accumulation glorified in the *Woman's Home Companion*. And with it goes a culture-snobbery and even a caste-snobbery. The Willa Cather of the older days shared the old racial democracy of the West. It is strange to find the Willa Cather of the present talking about "the adopted American," the young man of German, Jewish or Scandinavian descent who can never appreciate Sarah Orne Jewett and for whom American English can never be more than a means of communicating ideas: "It is surface speech: he clicks the words out as a bank clerk clicks out silver when you ask for change. For him the language has no emotional roots." This is indeed the gentility of Katherine Fullerton Gerould, and in large part the result, one suspects, of what Parrington calls "the inferiority complex of the frontier mind before the old and established."

Yet the place to look for the whole implications of a writer's philosophy is in the esthetic of his work. *Lucy Gayheart* shows to the full the effect of Miss Cather's point of view. It has always been a personal failure of her talent that prevented her from involving her people in truly dramatic relations with each other. (Her women, for example, always stand in the mother or daughter relation to men; they are never truly lovers.) But at least once upon a time her people were involved in a dramatic relation with themselves or with their environments, whereas now *Lucy Gayheart* has not even this involvement. Environment does not exist, fate springs from nothing save chance; the characters are unattached to anything save their dreams. The novel has been *démeublé* indeed; but life without its furniture is strangely bare.

V

THE SEARCH FOR
HISTORICAL PERSPECTIVE

F. O. MATTHIESSEN'S *American Renaissance* (1941) was by no means the first treatment of the classical phase of American literature, nor was it the first good treatment; but it was the first good treatment of its kind. When Matthiessen tried to explain what kind it was, he did so mainly by negatives: it was not, he said, the kind Parrington had done in the twenties, nor that Granville Hicks and Newton Arvin had written in the thirties—it was not, that is, a study of the intellectual backgrounds of literature, and the impingement of social and economic forces on the writer. Instead, says Matthiessen, "I have concentrated entirely on the foreground, on the writing itself." This "kind" was to prove the most successful formula for the writing of American literary history in the forties, and a model pointing the direction literary history has followed since.

The Marxist writings of the thirties had been historical and moral criticisms, and the people who wrote American literary history in the forties—for instance, Irving Howe, Alfred Kazin, Maxwell Geismar, F. O. Matthiessen, Malcolm Cowley—either were or in all likelihood would have been, had they been older, strongly attracted to the left-wing criticism of the thirties. In other words, literary history as written in the forties was a continuation of the moral and historical critical methods of the

Marxist criticism of the thirties. But at the same time the cool history of the forties was a reaction against the hot partisanship of the thirties, a way of achieving the lost virtues of objectivity and detachment. It was a criticism trying hard to get its balance, and to mediate between polar extremes.

It was also trying to achieve balance in another and perhaps more important way: to stand upright between the kind of criticism that pushes values and the kind that assumes them. University-connected criticism in the thirties and forties—the various movements associated with Cleanth Brooks, Tate, Crane, Ransom, and others—was engaged in minute part-whole analysis, applying the "laboratory" methods of the New Criticism to pieces of literature whose value was unquestioned. It made a proud point of ignoring social, historical, and moral issues as extraneous, concentrating entirely on "the work of literature itself." There was a painful divorce between this sort of "pure" criticism and the kind written by newspaper and magazine critics, who were engaged in the much messier job of arguing values and shaping popular taste. Matthiessen, with his concentration on the "foreground," was in part trying to bridge the gap between historical criticism and "pure" criticism, as were other literary historians of the forties—Alfred Kazin, for instance, who in his preface to *On Native Ground* (1942) wrote: "I have never been able to understand why the study of literature in relation to society should be divorced from a full devotion to what literature is in itself."

Willa Cather had become a candidate for historical treatment in the forties for at least three reasons. First, enough time had elapsed so that her earliest work—the stories and poems produced between 1900 and 1905—belonged to an obviously different historical era, as to some extent did her mature work of the World War I era and the twenties. Second, she completed the record in the forties. Her last novel, *Sapphira and the Slave Girl*, was published in 1940, and, although she started another ambitious novel, she died seven years later without having finished it. Third, the generation of writers to which Willa Cather belonged —Theodore Dreiser, Sherwood Anderson, Mencken—was just beginning to define itself clearly as a generation, and to become invested with enough nostalgic patina to make it of interest to the literary historian. The definition and patina were partly manufactured by such books as Maxwell Geismar's *The Last of the Provincials* (1947), a study of the American novel between 1915 and 1925, in which Geismar suggests that Cather, Anderson, Lewis, Mencken, and Fitzgerald terminated a unique era. But quite apart from such books there was an interest in catching the most recent wave of American literature as it was in the process of slipping from the present into the past—an interest that expressed itself most spectacularly in the rash of biographies that started to appear around 1950: Irving Howe's *Sherwood Anderson* (1950), Matthiessen's *Theodore Dreiser* (1950), J. N. Berryman's *Stephen Crane* (1950), Kemler's *The Irreverent Mr. Mencken* (1950), Mizener's *The Far Side of Paradise* (1951), and others.

The historical critics asked a number of different kinds of questions. What was Willa Cather's place in American literature? What was her relation to other writers of her generation? How was she influenced by those who came before? What was the direction of her work, and the periods into which it fell? How was it connected with the social and political life of the time? What were the principal values—social, political, religious—that it affirmed? What were its stylistic features? These were hardly new questions, of course. Thomas Beer had posed and answered most of them with subtlety and wit in his essay "Willa Cather" in 1925. But what was new was the detached tone of the investigation, and the framework into which it was set.

The reviews and estimates of the thirties, reduced to the simplest possible terms, fell into two opposing camps: those which praised Willa Cather for her traditionalism; and those which condemned her for "retreating" before the realities of American life—for going, in Trilling's words, from "West" to "East." These two alternative ways of looking at Willa Cather, at last stripped of partisan polemics and clothed in decent academic rhetoric, were borrowed by the forties from the thirties, and provided the main framework for the discussion.

ALFRED KAZIN

Willa Cather

Like the younger writers, both Willa Cather and Ellen Glasgow had a brilliant sense of style and an instinct for craftsmanship. But their feeling for style demanded none of the formal declarations and laborious experiments that Hemingway and Dos Passos brought to theirs. Like so many women in modern American writing from Emily Dickinson to Katherine Anne Porter, they had a certain dignity of craft from the first, a felicity all their own. In a period so marked by devotional estheticism in writing, and one when it was easy to slip into the ornamental fancywork of men like Cabell and Hergesheimer, Willa Cather and Ellen Glasgow stood out as examples of serious craftsmanship.

Yet their art had no gestures no tricks, and—this is less true of Ellen Glasgow—no glitter. They were almost too serenely good; it was always so easy to put them into their placid niches. Yet if they seemed to be off on their own, it was largely because the experience that became the substance of their books now seemed distant and the hold of the past on them so magnetic. Willa Cather soon became a conscious traditionalist, as Ellen Glasgow satirized traditionalism; but what isolated them both was the fact that they brought the resources of the modern novel in America—and frequently not a little of the bitterness of the postwar spirit—to the persistent exploration and evocation of the past. Unlike so many of their postwar contemporaries, they used modernism as a tool; they did not make it their substance.

Sharing in the self-consciousness and freedom of the new literature, their minds persistently ranged below and beyond it. Yet
unlike writers like Irving Babbitt and Paul Elmer More, who
went directly against the current of the new literature, they were
wholly a part of it. Indeed, they testified by their very presence,
as writers so diverse as F. Scott Fitzgerald and Anderson,
Mencken and Van Wyck Brooks, Hemingway and Cabell, had already testified, to the variety and freedom of the new American
literature.

Willa Cather and Nebraska grew up together. Born in Virginia, she was taken at eight to a country moving in the first great
floodtide of Western migration in the eighties. Within a single
decade half a million people—Yankee settlers, sod-house pioneers out of the Lincoln country, Danes, Norwegians, Germans,
Bohemians, Poles—pulled up stakes or emigrated from the farms
of northern and eastern Europe to settle on the plains of a region
that had been "a state before there were people in it." Nebraska
was the first of the great settlements beyond the Mississippi after
the Civil War, and the pace of its settlement and the polyglot
character of its people were such that they seemed to mark a
whole new society in flower. The successive stages of economic
and social development were leaped quickly, but not too quickly;
as late as 1885 the state was mostly raw prairie, and for the children of the first pioneers history began with the railroad age
roaring in from the East. Nebraska was a bristling new society,
proud of its progress and of values and a morality consciously
its own. The prairie aristocracy that was to play as triumphant
and even didactic a role in Willa Cather's novels as the colonial
aristocracy had played in Edith Wharton's may have been com-
posed out of the welter of emigration; but it was a founding class,
and Willa Cather never forgot it.

Her enduring values were the values of this society, but they
were not merely pioneer and agrarian ones. There was a touch
of Europe in Nebraska everywhere during her girlhood, and
much of her literary culture was to be drawn from it. The early
population numbered so many Europeans among it that as a

young girl she would spend Sundays listening to sermons in French, Norwegian, and Danish. There was a Prague in Nebraska as well as in Bohemia. Europe had given many brilliant and restless young men to the West. Amiel wrote letters to a nephew who died among the Nebraska farmers; Knut Hamsun worked on a farm just across the state line in South Dakota; a cousin of Camille Saint-Saëns lived nearby in Kansas. One could walk along the streets of a country seat like Wilber and not hear a word of English all day long. It was in this world, with its accumulation of many cultures, a world full of memories of Grieg and Liszt, of neighbors who taught her Latin and two grandmothers at home with whom she read the English classics, that Willa Cather learned to appreciate Henry James and at the same time to see in the pioneer society of the West a culture and distinction of its own. Her first two years there, she wrote later, were the most important to her as a writer.

All through her youth the West was moving perpetually onward, but it seemed anything but rootless to her; it suggested a distinctive permanence in the midst of change, a prairie culture that imparted to her education a tender vividness. Unconsciously, perhaps, the immigrants came to symbolize a tradition, and that tradition anchored her and gave her an almost religious belief in its sanctity. Growing up in a period of violent disruption and social change, she was thus brought up at the same time to a homely traditionalism. Later she was to elegize it, as all contemporary America was to elegize the tradition of pioneer energy and hardihood; but only because it gave her mind an abiding image of order and—what so few have associated with the pioneer tradition—of humanism. Her love for the West grew from a simple affection for her own kind into a reverence for the qualities they represented; from a patriotism of things and place-names into a patriotism of ideas. What she loved in the pioneer tradition was human qualities rather than institutions—the qualities of Ántonia Shimerda and Thea Kronborg, Alexandra Bergson and Godfrey St. Peter—but as those qualities seemed to disappear from the national life she began to think of them as something more than personal traits; they became the principles which she was to oppose to contemporary dissolution.

Willa Cather's traditionalism was thus anything but the arbitrary or patronizing opposition to contemporary ways which Irving Babbitt personified. It was a candid and philosophical nostalgia, a conviction and a standard possible only to a writer whose remembrance of the world of her childhood and the people in it was so overwhelming that everything after it seemed drab and more than a little cheap. Her distinction was not merely one of cultivation and sensibility; it was a kind of spiritual clarity possible only to those who suffer their loneliness as an act of the imagination and the will. It was as if the pervasive and incommunicable sense of loss felt by a whole modern American generation had suddenly become a theme rather than a passing emotion, a dissociation which one had to suffer as well as report. The others were lost in the new materialism, satirized or bewailed it; she seceded, as only a very rare integrity could secede with dignity. Later, as it seemed, she became merely sentimental, and her direct criticism of contemporary types and manners was often petulant and intolerant. But the very intensity of her nostalgia had from the first led her beyond nostalgia; it had given her the conviction that the values of the world she had lost were the primary values, and everything else merely their degradation.

It was this conflict, one that went beyond classes and could be represented only as a struggle between grandeur and meanness, the two poles of her world, that became the great theme of her novels. She did not celebrate the pioneer as such; she sought his image in all creative spirits[1]—explorers and artists, lovers and saints, who seemed to live by a purity of aspiration that represented everything that had gone out of life or had to fight a losing battle for survival in it. "O Eagle of Eagles!" she apostro-

---

[1] "Nothing is far and nothing is dear, if one desires. The world is little, human life is little. There is only one big thing—desire. And before it, when it is big, all is little."—Old Wunsch to Thea Kronborg in *The Song of the Lark*.

"Desire is creation."—Godfrey St. Peter in *The Professor's House*.

phized in *The Song of the Lark.* "Endeavor, desire, glorious striving of human art!" The world of her first important novels—
O Pioneers!, The Song of the Lark, My Ántonia—was unique in its serenity. Its secret was the individual discovery, the joy of fulfilling oneself in the satisfaction of an appointed destiny. The material Alexandra Bergson and Thea Kronborg worked with was like the naked prairies Jim Burden saw in *My Ántonia* on the night ride to his grandparents' farm. "There was nothing but land: not a country at all, but the material out of which countries are made." It was always the same material and always the same creative greatness impressed upon it. Ántonia was a peasant and Thea a singer, but both felt the same need of a great and positive achievement; Alexandra was a farmer, but her feeling for the land was like Thea's feeling for music. The tenacious ownership of the land, the endless search of its possibilities, became the very poetry of her character.

Yet even as Willa Cather's pale first novel, *Alexander's Bridge*, had been a legend of creative desire and its frustration, so in these novels the ideal of greatness had been subtly transformed into a lesson of endurance. Even in *My Ántonia*, the earliest and purest of her elegies, the significance of achievement had become only a rigid determination to see one's life through. The exultation was there, but it was already a little sad. Her heroines were all pioneers, pioneers on the land and pioneers of the spirit, but something small, cantankerous, and bitter had stolen in. The pioneer quality had thinned, as the pioneer zest had vanished. Ántonia might go on, as Thea might flee to the adobe deserts and cliff cities of the Southwest for refuge, but the new race of pioneers consisted of thousands of farm women suffering alone in their kitchens, living in a strange world amidst familiar scenes, wearing their lives out with endless chores and fears.

On starlight nights I used to pace up and down those long, cold streets, scowling at the little, sleeping porches on either side, with their storm-windows and covered back porches. They were flimsy shelters, most of them poorly built of light wood, with spindle porch-posts horribly mutilated by the turning-lathe. Yet for all their frailness, how much jealously and envy and unhappiness some of them managed to contain! The life that went on in them seemed to me made up of evasions and negations; shifts to save cooking, to save washing and cleaning, devices to propitiate the tongue of gossip.

By 1920, the stories in *Youth and the Bright Medusa* hinted at a growing petulance, and in stories like "A Wagner Matinée" and "The Sculptor's Funeral" there was nothing to indicate that Willa Cather thought any better of small-town life than Sinclair Lewis. Yet by their very bitterness, so much more graphic than the dreary tonelessness of *Miss Lulu Bett*, these stories reveal how sharp her disillusionment had been, and when she developed the theme of small-town boorishness in *One of Ours* into the proverbial story of the sensitive young man, she could only repeat herself lamely. She was writing about an enemy—the oppressively narrow village world—which seemed only one of the many enemies of the creative spirit, but she did not have Zona Gale's inverted sentimentality, or anything like the spirit of Lewis's folksy and fundamentally affectionate satire. *One of Ours* was a temporary position for an artist whose need of an austere ideal was so compelling. Claude Wheeler was only the Midwest *révolté*; her authentic heroes were something more than sensitive young men who "could not see the use of working for money when money brought nothing one wanted. Mrs. Ehrlich said it brought security. Sometimes he thought that this security was what was the matter with everybody: that only perfect safety was required to kill all the best qualities in people and develop the mean ones." The farmer's wife in "A Wagner Matinée" had left something deeper when, after her few moments of exultation at the concert, she turned and cried: " 'I don't want to go, Clark. I don't want to go!' Outside the concert hall lay the black pond with the cattle-tracked bluffs; the tall, unpainted house with weather-curled boards, naked as a tower; the crook-backed ash seedlings where the dish-cloths hung to dry; the gaunt moulting turkeys picking up refuse about the kitchen door."

The climax in Willa Cather's career came with two short novels she published between 1923 and 1925, *A Lost Lady* and *The*

Professor's House. They were parables of the decline and fall of her own great tradition; and they were both so serenely and artfully written that they suggested that she could at last commemorate it quietly and even a little ironically. The primary values had gone, if not the bitterness she felt at their going; but where she had once written with a naïvely surging affection or irritation, she now possessed a cultivated poise that could express regret without rancor or loss without anguish. She had, in a sense, finally resigned herself to the physical and moral destruction of her ideal in the modern world, but only because she was soon to turn her back on that world entirely in novels like *Death Comes for the Archbishop* and *Shadows on the Rock.* In the person of a Captain Forrester dreaming railroads across the prairies, of a Godfrey St. Peter welding his whole spirit into a magnificent history of the Spanish explorers in America, she recaptured the enduring qualities she loved in terms of the world she had at last been forced to accept. These were the last of her pioneers, the last of her great failures; and the story she was now to tell was how they, like all their line, would go down in defeat before commerce and family ties and human pettiness.

Only once in *A Lost Lady* did her submerged bitterness break through, in her portrait of Ivy Peters, the perfect bourgeois:

Now all this vast territory they had won was to be at the mercy of men like Ivy Peters, who had never dared anything, never risked anything. They would drink up the mirage, dispel the morning freshness, root out the great brooding spirit of freedom, the generous, easy life of the great landholders. The space, the colour, the princely carelessness of the pioneer they would destroy and cut up into profitable bits, as the match factory splinters the primeval forest. All the way from Missouri to the mountains this generation of shrewd young men, trained to petty economies by hard times, would do exactly what Ivy Peters had done.

The theme was corruption, as it was to be the theme of *The Professor's House.* It was as explicit as Marian Forrester's dependence on her husband's frontier strength and integrity, as brutal as Ivy Peters's acquisition of Marian Forrester herself. And at the very moment that Willa Cather recognized that corruption, gave its name and source, she resigned herself to it. It had been her distinction from the first to lament what others had never missed; she now became frankly the elegist of the defeated, the Amiel of the novel. The conflict between grandeur and meanness, ardor and greed, was more than ever before the great interest of her mind; where she had once propounded that conflict, she now saw nothing but failure in it and submitted her art almost rejoicingly to the subtle exploration of failure. In any other novelist this would have made for sickliness and preciosity; now that she was no longer afraid of failure as a spiritual fact, her work gained a new strength and a keener radiance.

The significance of this new phase in Willa Cather's work is best seen in *The Professor's House,* which has been the most persistently underrated of her novels. Actually it is one of those imperfect and ambitious works whose very imperfections illuminate the quality of an imagination. The story of Godfrey St. Peter is at once the barest and the most elaborately symbolic version of the story of heroic failure she told over and over again, the keenest in insight and the most hauntingly suggestive. The violence with which she broke the book in half to tell the long and discursive narrative of Tom Outland's boyhood in the Southwest was a technical mistake that has damned the book, but the work as a whole is the most brilliant statement of her endeavor as an artist. For St. Peter is the archetype of all her characters and the embodiment of her own beliefs. He is not merely the scholar as artist, the son of pioneer parents who has carried the pioneer passion into the world of art and thought; he is what Willa Cather herself has always been or hoped to be—a pioneer in mind, a Catholic by instinct, French by inclination, a spiritual aristocrat with democratic manners.

The tragedy of St. Peter, though it seems nothing more than a domestic tragedy, is thus the most signal and illuminating of all Willa Cather's tragedies. The enemy she saw in Ivy Peters— the new trading, grasping class—has here stolen into St. Peter's home; it is reflected in the vulgar ambition of his wife and eldest daughter, the lucrative commercial use his son-in-law has made of the invention Tom Outland had developed in scholarly research, the genteel but acquisitive people around him. St. Peter's own passion, so subtle a pioneer passion, had been for the life of the mind. In the long and exhaustive research for his great history, in the writing of it in the attic of his old house, he had known something of the physical exultation that had gone into the explorations he described. As a young man in France, studying for his doctorate, he had looked up from a skiff in the Mediterranean and seen the design of his lifework reflected in the ranges of the Sierra Nevada, "unfolded in the air above him." Now, after twenty years, that history was finished; the money he had won for it had gone into the making of a new and pretentious house. The great creative phase of his life was over. To hold onto the last symbol of his endeavor, St. Peter determined to retain his old house against the shocked protests of his family. It was a pathetic symbol, but he needed some last refuge in a world wearing him out by slow attrition.

In this light the long middle section of the novel, describing Tom Outland's boyhood in the desert, is not a curious interlude in the novel; it becomes the parable of St. Peter's own longing for that remote world of the Southwest which he had described so triumphantly in his book. Willa Cather, too, was moving toward the South, as all her books do: always toward the more primitive in nature and the more traditional in belief. Tom Outland's desert life was thus the ultimate symbol of a forgotten freedom and harmony that could be realized only by a frank and even romantic submission to the past, to the Catholic order and doctrine, and the deserts of California and New Mexico in which the two priests of *Death Comes for the Archbishop* lived with such quiet and radiant perfection. Her characters no longer had to submit to failure; they lived in a charming and almost antediluvian world of their own. They had withdrawn, as Willa Cather now withdrew; and if her world became increasingly recollective and abstract, it was because she had fought a losing battle that no one of her spirit could hope to win. It was a long way from the Catholic Bohemian farmers of Nebraska to the eighteenth-century Catholicism of the Southwest, but she had made her choice, and she accepted it with an almost haughty serenity. As early as 1922, in "The Novel Démeublé," her essay on fiction, she had defined her rejection of modern industrial culture explicitly, and had asked for a pure novel that would throw the "social furniture" out of fiction. Even a social novelist like Balzac, she had insisted, wrote about subjects unworthy of him; for the modern social novelists she had only a very gracious and superior contempt. "Are the banking system and the Stock Exchange worth being written about at all?" she asked. She thought not, and itemized the "social furniture" that had to be thrown out of the novel, among them the factory and a whole realm of "physical sensations." It was now but a step from the colonial New Mexico of *Death Comes for the Archbishop* to old Quebec in *Shadows on the Rock* and the lavender and old lace of *Lucy Gayheart*. Her secession was complete.

The significance of Willa Cather's exquisitely futile values was often slurred over or sentimentalized; the felicity of her art was never ignored. Her importance to the older generation—a generation that was now to make room for Hemingway—was a simple and moving one: she was its consummate artist. To critics sated with the folksy satire or bitterness of the village revolt, she suggested a preoccupation with the larger motives; to critics weary of the meretriciousness of Cabell and Hergesheimer, she personified a poised integrity; to critics impatient with the unkempt naturalism of Dreiser and Anderson, she offered purity of style. As an indigenous and finished craftsman, she seemed her own way so complete that she restored confidence to the novel in America. There was no need to apologize for her or to "place" her; she had made a place for herself, carved out a subtle and interesting world of her own. If that world became increasingly elegiac and soft, it was riches in a little room.

MAXWELL GEISMAR

"Willa Cather:
Lady in the Wilderness"

A POINT OF ETHICS

In approaching our first feminine writer among the dozen or so contemporary American novelists who deserve a full literary consideration, it is essential, of course, not to consider her as a "feminine" writer.

Willa Sibert Cather made this clear herself in those early reflections on the discipline and austerity which mark the career of Thea Kronborg in *The Song of the Lark*. There are also her reflections on the character of Flaubert, who almost becomes the later Cather's model of personal behavior as well as of aesthetic excellence: the meticulous and disdainful French artist, that is, in whose case, as we are told, it was a point of ethics "to encourage no familiarity at any time." In *Shadows on the Rock*, you may remember Father Hector's little sermon to the apothecary Auclair:

Listen, my friend. No man can give himself heart and soul to one thing while in the back of his mind he cherishes a desire, a secret hope for something very different. You as a student, must know that even in worldly affairs nothing worth while is accomplished except by that last sacrifice, the giving of oneself altogether and finally.

Reprinted from *The Last of the Provincials* (Boston, 1947), by permission of the Houghton Mifflin Company.

In these brief, lucent lines you may get a sense of the lifelong dedication, the complete moral consecration which is at the base of Willa Cather's work: that final giving, as Henry James also pointed out in a memorable but more abstruse manner, which is at the root of all serious work.

The outlines of her life are simple enough. Born in Virginia, on a farm near Winchester, December 7, 1876, she came from "an established Virginia family" of English, Irish, and Alsatian extraction. At eight or nine she was taken to Nebraska and spent the years of her growth among the Bohemians, Scandinavians, Germans, and French-Canadians of a pioneer environment. Yet there may be traces of her original background in, say, that Jim Burden of *My Antonia*, who is always comparing immigrant vitality with native refinement, but who still can never quite cross a social line he sees so clearly and detests so strongly. These earliest Virginia origins of Willa Cather, obscure and almost hidden as they are, are to form an important element in her work.

Meanwhile, she spent her days on the Nebraska plains—her open western prairie scene, with its ridges and draws and blowing sea of red grass, its badgers, 'possums, cranes, earth-owls, and rattlesnakes. She learned reading and writing at home, studied Latin with a neighbor, read the English classics in the evenings. In 1891 she graduated from the state university, and took up journalism and teaching in Pittsburgh. This is also the period of her "especial delight in the work of Henry James," while her impressions of Pittsburgh—"that smoke-palled city," as she tells us in one of her earliest short stories, "enamoured of figures and grimy toil"—are not quite so pleasant.

The virtuoso publisher, S. S. McClure, whose later autobiography, edited by Willa Cather, contains an illuminating account of a frontier childhood, noticed Miss Cather's early stories and invited her to join the staff of his magazine; two years later she was made managing editor. Her relations with that nest of young radicals, muckrakers, and embryonic political reformers who developed *McClure's Magazine* remain somewhat intangible, however—she spent a great deal of her time in travel to Europe, the southwestern states, and "the New York world of art, literature, and music." In 1912 she published her first novel, and, a year later, *O Pioneers!* marked the start of the series of frontier tales which established her reputation as one of the most gifted novelists of her period.

Yet there are very ambiguous elements in these luminous chronicles of "the little beginnings of human society in the West." We shall notice the curious foreshortening of Cather's historical view, not only in terms of the contemporary scene, but in terms of this frontier period which she has chosen for herself and made her own. We shall trace the increasing sense of disenchantment in her work, and the final sense of complete spiritual defeat and withdrawal which is recorded in *The Professor's House*—that familiar Catheresque wound, "healed and hardened and hopeless," which begins to throb all over again. And certainly the religious pilgrimage of her middle period: this voyage of a spiritual malaise which pushes its way back from the epoch of the pioneers and the empire-builders to the New Mexico of the eighteen-fifties and to the French Quebec of the early seventeen-hundreds, and even there, with the passing of the "old order," yearns for a still earlier time, a still more absolute cosmos of authority and faith, since on this rock, too, there are shadows— certainly this is one of the most curious of all those curious spiritual pilgrimages in the late nineteen-twenties.

As a matter of fact, Willa Cather's is one of the most complex, if not difficult and contradictory, minds in our letters. If we must admire the conscience, it won't always be easy to follow the logic of this artist. (We shall notice that this sophisticated lady is also an advocate of the primitive impulses, or, at least, of those more direct, unprincipled, and ruthless "feminine" impulses which mark her most memorable heroines.) And it is, after all, as the work of a talented and tormented woman that her literary world takes on its particular glow and interest. Among the whole group of our feminine novelists, Willa Cather is in some ways the most interesting of them all: less restricted than Edith Wharton, more intense than Ellen Glasgow. And among the circle of novelists under consideration here, she is probably the writer who comes closest to having the sense of a human necessity whose origins are wild and whose destination is tragic.

Is it merely a coincidence, too, that Cather's belated return to the western towns of *Lucy Gayheart* should be coupled with her final declaration of belief in the enchantment *and* suffering of life?—the final acceptance of both the pleasure and pain of ordinary human experience, and the inextricable unity of these two poles of our existence: that old-fashioned "optimism" of the Middle Generation, which she, along with Sherwood Anderson, and, for all her curious delicacies and restraints, most purely exemplifies.

For this is actually a deeper and tougher sense of life than Henry Mencken or Sinclair Lewis could honestly claim to have, and one which, with Scott Fitzgerald and a new generation of cosmopolitan and primarily urban novelists, almost disappeared for a generation from the American literary scene itself. . . . Between Miss Cather's early western scene and her late return, however, lies another story, and a less fortunate one: to a large degree the story of an evasion of a social environment, of a broken creative framework, and a dissipation of the writer's true energies—a very familiar story in the national letters.

But even the limitations of Willa Cather's work are made more poignant by her long and sustained attempt to deal with them. And as early as her first novel you will realize how sure and sensitive her values are in the human area at least.

THE WILD LAND

When she looked back at her first novel, *Alexander's Bridge*, published in 1912, Miss Cather was not favorably impressed by it.

The book was "external and young," she says in her 1922 preface and in rather formal auctorial tones. It marked the thrill of novelty and the glitter of the passing show, as opposed to a writer's true "life-line." She quotes a remark of Sarah Orne Jewett, her early mentor: "Of course, one day you will write about your own country. In the meantime, get all you can. One must know the world *so well* before one can know the parish."

Yet, if there is little of the parish in *Alexander's Bridge*, there is also little of the provincial. It is a remarkably interesting first novel as a matter of fact, and not merely in terms of a prose style that is already supple and fluent, but in terms of the subject matter itself. The scene is set in Boston and in London; the story deals with a successful American architect, happily married, proud of his wife, and fond of their life together, who is nevertheless drawn back into the emotional vortex of a youthful love affair.

The point is that Cather's architect (he is actually a bridge-designer) is one of her most interesting men—one might say he is almost the only interesting man during the whole first period of her work—during the period of the Pioneer Matriarchy. And her first hero also gives us our first real indication of her own view of experience. For what Bartley Alexander has missed, in the midst of his success and fame, is simply his own former sense of energy and delight: "the impetuousness, the intense excitement, the increasing expectancy of youth." What the love affair actually means to him is a return, in the "dead calm of middle life," of his own identity. "There was only one thing that had an absolute value for each individual, and it was just that original impulse, that internal heat, that feeling of one's self in one's own breast." But there is the equal realization that the full consciousness of self, as it reaches its point of tension, touches the orbit of death.

And just as Alexander's "affair" with the English actress, Hilda Burgoyne, revives his awareness of the absolute value of life, so it begins to destroy all his formal patterns of living. The increasing recklessness of Alexander's behavior, the sense of his own guilt and folly, the knowledge that the only real emotions he has are those which are destroying him, and, at the same time, the "sullen painful delight" with which he accepts his impending ruin: these undertones of irony and suffering, which accompany and parallel the notes of an almost lyrical exaltation in the novel, are an unusual achievement for a young writer in the early teens. In the whole group of her pioneer novels, Willa Cather will do nothing better than some of her passages in *Alexander's Bridge*; and what is a little curious, too, is that the older novelist, looking back upon a pattern of feeling which is so intense, intimate, and lived, should dismiss it as superficial or remote.

Of course, the English theatrical set through which the early Cather moves here, and the opera cloaks, the calling cards, the "wonderful little dinners" of ducklings, mushrooms, and truffles which she dwells upon, *are* a little remote from the Nebraska plains; in a way this is an odd vista to be unfolded by the future historian of the frontier, one that is closer to Edith Wharton, even, than to Sarah Orne Jewett. On the London streets, Cather's lovers, in their moment of delight, in their assurance that life is the most indestructible thing in the world, are compared with the gloomy city and with the office workers who have come out to drink the "muddy lees" of the day. Beyond Charles Street, in Boston, there is apparently not much, too, except a series of labor strikes—"a general industrial unrest" in the American scene which prevents Alexander from completing his new bridge on schedule. It is this Moorlock Bridge, the "longest cantilever in the world," which collapses at the end of the novel and, by taking Bartley Alexander's life and his reputation with it, fulfills his convictions of ruin. Yet it is interesting that almost Alexander's last reflections should deal with the industrial masses, with "all these dirty people" who surround him in the train, these "poor unconscious companions of his journey . . . who had come to stand to him for the ugliness he had brought into the world." And it is actually a gang of half-crazed iron-workers who send him to his death, while Alexander, a strong swimmer, tries to beat them off in the swirling waters beneath the doomed cantilever.

In this light the framework of Cather's first western tale, *O Pioneers!* in 1913, becomes more obvious, and even a little stylized. Practically at the start of the novel, one notices the drunken traveling man who tries to flirt with Cather's woman of the plains: that foolish little clothing drummer, who has been knocking about "in little drab towns and crawling across the wintry country in dirty smoking cars," and who, when he chances upon a fine human creature, suddenly wishes himself more of a man. Running through the novel, and forming a sort of counterpoint, there are those references to "the new prosperity" which will come when the wild land has been subjugated by the early generations of pioneers; the new standards in behavior, which will appear with bathtubs and with pianos. "At home, in the old country," says Crazy Ivar, "there were many like me, who had been touched by God, or who had seen things in the graveyard at night and were different afterward. . . . We thought nothing of it, and let them alone. But here, if a man is different in his feet or in his head, they put him in the asylum."

There are harsher references, too, about the agrarian disturbances which appeared in the eighteen-nineties upon a western horizon that had seemed so illimitable. Politics is the natural field, according to Cather, for such persons as Lou Bergson, who "has not got a fox's face for nothing"; while the Populist reform movement that centered around Bryan is viewed as a local engagement between the anarchists and J. P. Morgan. In a more notable passage, Carl Linstrum, returning to the prairies from Chicago and New York, expresses the real point of the novel:

"Here you are an individual, you have a background of your own, you would be missed. But off there in the cities there are thousands of rolling stones like me. We are all alike; we have no ties, we know nobody, we own nothing. When one of us dies, the scarcely know where to bury him. Our landlady and the delicatessen man are our mourners, and we leave nothing behind us but a frock-coat and a fiddle, or an easel or a typewriter, or whatever tool we got our living by. All we have ever managed to do is to pay our rent, the exorbitant rent that one has to pay for a few square feet of space near the heart of things. We have no house, no place, no people of our own. We live in the streets, in the parks, in the theatres. We sit in restaurants and concert halls and look about at the hundreds of our own kind and shudder."

And this helps to explain the kind of affection with which *O Pioneers!* delineates the background of the first settlers on the windy Nebraska tableland—of those earlier immigrants who owned the land for a little while because they loved it.

For the descriptions of the wild land in *O Pioneers!* and of the half-wild frontier eccentrics like Crazy Ivar who have again become part of the land; and of those first small colonies of Russians, Swedes, Czechs, French, or Bohemians who then set out rigorously, persistently, inch by inch, to tame the land, almost as though they themselves represented an opposing natural force and displayed something of Nature's own relentless will as against the infinite extent of her willfulness—all this is certainly well done here. From that first glimpse of Alexandra Bergson's wagon by night, "a moving point of light . . . going into the dark country," to Amédée's twenty French cousins, this is surely the chronicle of "the little beginnings of human society" on the endless western plains. And in the daily patterns of pioneer activity—the colorful weddings, dances, and costume parties, the all-night gatherings to the tune of a *dragharmonika* or a fiddle, the games, choral societies, and family readings that accompanied the axe, the plow and the Bible—Miss Cather very early suggested the resources of that frontier life which was to seem so harsh and sterile to a subsequent generation of western rebels and expatriates.[1]

Such portraits as those of "Old Mrs. Lee," or Frank Shabata, for example, are among the first of those vignettes which will add a peculiarly native grave to Willa Cather's frontier tales. The sometimes elaborate, almost Jamesian cadences of her earlier prose ("and however one took him, however much one admired him, one had to admit that he simply wouldn't square") have been refined down to a homelier western idiom. "He knew the end too well to wish to begin again," Cather says of John

[1] In a sense one can understand how a Henry Mencken, as a rising Baltimore luminary, an ex-newspaper man with a yen for cosmopolitan culture, and a wit, set the tone for the later movement, while such a writer as the young Scott Fitzgerald, at once innocent and obsessed, was a natural victim of the debunkers. More curious is the fact that a Sinclair Lewis, coming out of the prairie towns and dealing, in his earlier novels, with almost the same frontier matrix as Willa Cather, should have had so little regard for it. But possibly the decade between Cather's youth and Lewis's, the decade, roughly, of the eighteen-nineties, actually marked a sort of dividing line between the immigrant settlers and the native realtors.

Bergson, dying alone in the wilderness. "He knew where it all went to, what it all became." And the unmistakable accents of suffering—

Spring, summer, autumn, winter, spring; always the same patient fields, the patient little trees, the patient lives; always the same yearning, the same pulling at the chain—until the instinct to live had torn itself and bled and weakened for the last time, until the chain secured a dead woman, who might cautiously be released. . . . How terrible it was to love people when you could not really share their lives!

—the accents of intense suffering, as well as the Catheresque sense of the sweetness and splendor of life, are now linked to the forces of pioneer aspiration and pioneer fate, to the seasons, and almost to Nature itself.

Yet it is interesting that this familiar pattern of feeling, this emotional dualism of the inevitable pain and the implicit ec-stasy of life which was the dominating pattern of *Alexander's Bridge,* is relegated to the story of Marie Shabata in *O Pioneers!*: to a secondary place in the novel, while the heroine, Alexandra Bergson, now wears the mask of the stoic—that "impervious calm of the fatalist" which, as Cather notes, is always disconcert-ing to people "who cannot feel that the heart lives at all unless it is still at the mercy of storms; unless its strings can scream at the touch of pain." One notices the increasing references to Ca-tholicism and to that little French Church in the wilderness, "pow-erful and triumphant there on its eminence," with its music and pageantry and hallowed rituals of suffering, with the gold cross flaming on its steeple, and offering that kind of rapture in which one can love forever "without faltering and without sin." As a matter of fact, Alexandra Bergson, as the central figure of *O Pioneers!*, as the symbolical pioneer woman, and as Cather's superior individual, is almost *too* stoical, remote, and unfalter-ing. "What a hopeless position you are in, Alexandra," says the devoted but ineffectual Carl Linstrum. "It is your fate to be al-ways surrounded by little men." In a way, for a woman of feel-ing, this must be a dull position: at least it begins to seem so in the case of Cather's next and more renowned pioneer heroine.

In many respects, *My Ántonia* marks a gain in Cather's craft. Probably the accounts of the frontier land are even more graceful here; that childhood visit of Ántonia and Jim Burden to "dog town" is a perfect little episode; while the story of Ántonia's Bohemian family, the Shimerdas, almost summarizes the story of all those "strange uprooted people" who were among the first citizens of our western plains.[2] But it is around Black Hawk, Nebraska, that *My Ántonia* centers, as Cather carries forward the chronicle of the frontier settlers to the framework of early western town life and the merchants and farmers, the commercial travelers, the eccentrics, and outcasts of what was almost a society of outcasts. Such portraits as Wick Cutter, the dissolute moneylender, or Lena Lingard, the Swedish farm girl; or scenes like those Saturday night operas in Black Hawk or the evenings at the Vannis's dancing pavilion; or frontier legends like that of Blind d'Arnault, the traveling Negro pianist who plays as though "all the agreeable sensations possible to creatures of flesh and blood were heaped up in those black and white keys": these are among the most attractive passages in Miss Cather's early novels. She is shrewd too about "the curious social situation" which arose in Black Hawk—that is, the class distinctions which developed between the merchants' daughters and the "hired girls"— between native refinement and immigrant vitality—and the consequent effect of a whole new ethos of respectability upon the middle-class children. To dance "Home, Sweet Home" with Lena Lingard, she says, was like coming in with the tide, while the bodies of the town girls never moved inside their clothes,

---

[2] Parenthetically, it may be interesting to compare the death of Mr. Shimerda in *My Ántonia* with the death of Addie Bundren in William Faulkner's *As I Lay Dying,* or with Ernest Hemingway's tale of a mountain death, "An Alpine Idyll." The literary elements in these three accounts are almost identical. But while Cather includes both an idiot son and a frozen corpse in the ordinary context of frontier life, the later writers isolate one or another of these elements in a context of human degradation—in the milieu of Faulkner's "poor-whites" and of the young Hemingway's "peasants."

and their muscles seemed to ask but one thing—not to be disturbed.

The Black Hawk boys looked forward to marrying Black Hawk girls and living in a brand-new little house with best chairs that must not be sat upon, and hand-painted china that must not be used. But sometimes a young fellow would look up from his ledger, or out through the grating of his father's bank, and let his eyes follow Lena Lingard, as she passed the window with her slow, undulating walk, or Tiny Soderball, tripping by in her short skirt and striped stockings. . . . The country girls were considered a menace to the social order. Their beauty shone out too boldly against a conventional background. But anxious mothers need have felt no alarm. They mistook the mettle of their sons. The respect for respectability was stronger than any desire in Black Hawk youth.

And this guarded mode of existence, Cather's Jim Burden also thinks, was almost like living under a tyranny, where every individual taste, every natural appetite, was bridled by caution. These people tried to live like the mice in their own kitchens; "to make no noise, to leave no trace, to slip over the surface of things in the dark."

Yet the middle sections of *My Ántonia*, the sections on the hired girls and on Lena Lingard herself, represent a sort of climax in the novel's action. Cather's narrator is captivated alike by the physical charms of Lena Lingard and the moral stature of Ántonia Shimerda. (And there is that interesting split again between the ostensible heroine, Ántonia, the epitome of the frontier spirit, and Lena, who represents merely the frontier flesh, but who almost runs away with the show.) However, Jim Burden, the descendant of a Virginia family, can never actually make the break, and can never cross that social line which he sees so clearly and despises so heartily. Indeed, as he draws away from the western scene in later life, becomes legal counsel for a big railway, has a wife who plays patroness to the new poets and painters, and himself frequents London or Vienna, Jim Burden's memory of Ántonia becomes more precious. "She lent herself to immemorial human attitudes which we recognize by instinct as universal and true. . . . She was a rich mine of life, like the founders of the early races." Very much like Scott Fitzgerald's western observer in *The Great Gatsby*, Willa Cather's narrator, when he decides to revisit the scene of his youth, has the sense of coming back home to himself. "Whatever we had missed, we possessed together the precious, the incommunicable past." [3]

All the same, that closing scene of the novel in which we actually *see* Ántonia has some curious undertones. "You really are a part of me," Jim Burden tells her. "I'd have liked to have you for a sweetheart, or a wife, or my mother, or my sister—anything that a woman can be to a man." "Ain't it wonderful," Ántonia answers, "how much people can mean to each other?" Is it merely in the shadow of Burden's continental sophistication that Ántonia now seems so much cruder in sensibility and expression, as well as rather battered in appearance—as though she had reverted in some degree to the line of her peasant ancestors while Jim Burden has moved closer to his own more or less aristocratic forebears? The difference between them has never been quite so apparent as it is just when Jim Burden believes that the same road of "Destiny" which has separated him from Ántonia has now brought them together again. . . . Meanwhile, in 1915, three years before *My Ántonia*, Willa Cather had published a novel in which the pattern of her pioneer tales is defined even more clearly.

In terms of its content, as well as in its actual size, *The Song of the Lark* is also, of course, the "big" book of Cather's first

[3] The similarity of theme and tone between the closing sections of *My Ántonia* and *The Great Gatsby* has probably not been sufficiently noticed by historians of literary craft: a similarity which extends through phrases and rhythms of the writing to the almost identical "dying-fall" of Fitzgerald's last sentence in *Gatsby*: "So we beat on, boats against the current, borne back ceaselessly into the past." It seems likely, that is, that Fitzgerald drew upon Willa Cather's work for his own development of the theme, although, since both writers also use the structural device of the "sensitive observer," there is the common influence of Henry James or the school of James.

period, and it deserves the wide popular recognition it brought to her work as a whole. (It is no mean feat, incidentally, to choose an opera singer for one's heroine, as she does in the case of Thea Kronborg, and to establish an artist's love for music as the central passion of a novel.) Moreover, when Cather moves southwest to the mining town of Moonstone, Colorado, when her familiar Swedish and German immigrants meet the more volatile Mexicans who, like Spanish Johnny, have learned "to dive below insults or soar above them," the early sections of *The Song of the Lark* take on a warmer and richer color, like the sky above the southwestern desert, or like those linden trees of Mrs. Kohler's which have a honey-colored bloom in summer, with a fragrance "that surpasses all trees and flowers and drives young people wild with joy." Professor Wunsch, the drunken musician to whom the young Thea recalls "standards, ambitions, a society long forgot"; Ray Kennedy, the railroad worker who gives his life to the cause of Thea's career; and Thea herself, the gifted, generous child whose close associates were Mexicans and sinners, are all part of this admirable early drama in the dunes. There is the climax of the drama, too: the scene in which Thea, alienated from her home and family by her own "desires, ambitions, revulsions," and finding refuge among the Mexicans, realizes for the first time what such a people can give to an artist—feels "as if all these warm-blooded people debouched into her": that scene in which Cather somehow manages to put the ecstasy and anguish of a whole race of aliens into the description of a soprano voice which leaps and plays about those "dusky male voices" at night on the desert. "*Die Thea,*" whispers Mrs. Kohler, listening to the music across the gulch. "*Ach wunderschön!*" And so it is.

In passing, it is interesting to notice the descendants of the New Hampshire farmers whom Miss Cather also portrays in *The Song of the Lark* as hard workers and close traders—"with good minds, mean natures, and flinty eyes." Are these merchants among the citizens who have contributed to the "general scramble of American life" which Cather's heroine meets in Chicago? For the account of Thea's later musical career in the metropolis is interesting: in these pages, and often very eloquently, Cather stresses her own belief in an individual integrity and personal fulfillment as well as in the technical achievement of the artist. Here are the Catheresque glimpses of those bright moments in life "which are few, after all, and so very easy to miss," or of those good things "which are never complete in this world," while in the parallel relationships of Harsanyi, who tells the truth to Thea in order to make her free, and of Fred Ottenburg, who deceives her in order to keep her free, we realize again the spaciousness of Cather's view of human relationships.[4]

Yet it is difficult to ignore the increasing accents of auctorial bitterness, almost of contempt, which mark the story of Cather's heroine's increasing fame as a singer. Is it a Chicago musical society itself, in the days when "the lumbermen's daughters and the brewer's wives contended in song," that seems such "a common, common world" to Thea? Or is it the industrial city as a whole—the rich, fat, noisy city, whose chief concern is with its digestion, as Cather says, whose money and office are "the consolations of impotence," and the majority of whose citizens, like the Poles of Packingtown, live chiefly in the saloons, where one can buy for a few hours "the illusion of comfort, hope, love —whatever one most longs for"? Certainly the accounts of "the cosmopolitan brewing world of St. Louis," or of "the plunging Kansas City set," form some of the most acute sections in *The Song of the Lark,* and Cather treats these native manifestations of a *haute bourgeoisie* with a light touch that, from Dreiser to Tom Wolfe, is particularly rare in our social novelists. And yet one notices that the Jessie Darcy who is the operatic darling of the Chicago Northwestern Railroad, or that rather fascinating Miss Beers who is a racy product of "a long packing-house purse," or, to some degree, Fred Ottenburg himself, when he uses the

---

[4] Notice the passage in which Ottenburg asks himself whether, between men and women, all ways were not more or less crooked. "He believed those which are called straight were the most dangerous of all. . . . In their unquestioned regularity lurked every sort of human cruelty and meanness, and every kind of humiliation and suffering. He would rather have any woman he cared for wounded than crushed. He would deceive her . . . to keep her free."

tongues of Bayreuth to entrance an interstate meeting of the *Turnverein,* are all more or less dismissed here as being merely "Stupid Faces."

Equally so are the native political reformers, those "few dull young men who haven't the ability to play the old game the old way," whom Doctor Archie dismisses with some scorn when his mining interests have become so large that his political influence is considerable. And Thea Kronborg herself, having completed her escape from "a smug, domestic, self-satisfied provincial world of utter ignorance," as Cather adds in her later preface to *The Song of the Lark,* and having established her place as an artist in "an idle, gaping world which is determined that no artist shall ever do his best," is not without a similar element of arrogance, or of a rather complacent provincial ignorance of her own. The material conveniences, the trappings of luxury with which Cather's heroine is surrounded at the end: the fur coat which she leaves for her maid to pick up, the instructions she transmits to her assistant, Mr. Landry, to have tea at five, the cab which is always waiting at her door, the intimate little dnners, or the delicate underclothing which, to her annoyance, has been misplaced by some worthless hotel "nigger"—is all this a sort of compensation for the travail of an artist in a society of so many material conveniences? And is a mere glimpse of the great Sieglinde, and Thea's gracious bow, quite sufficient to bring happiness to her old friend, Spanish Johnny? Still, that closing section of *The Song of the Lark,* in which Cather's fashionable primadonna chats of London and Dresden with her two rich and devoted masculine admirers, *is* a curious resolution to the tale of an immigrant girl from Colorado. And it is in terms of this scene of wealth and cultivation which Cather dwells upon both at the start of her first novel and at the close of this one, which forms such an elegant framework for her pictures of a more primitive life, that we must consider the work of her first period.

There is no doubt that Cather's pioneer portraits are foreshortened in perspective to a certain degree, a little reduced in size, and also, after one has escaped from the spell of the craft itself, curiously static in their final effect, almost like a tableau of Grant

Wood's. Both *O Pioneers!* and *My Antonia* are georgics of the frontier, or idylls of western fortitude, and it seems just as clear that Cather went back to the past, to her childhood memories of the Nebraska plains, to achieve this effect. As early as her first novel we noticed her distaste for the murky cities, the white-collar office workers, and the industrial masses of her time; while the collapse of the defective cantilever which symbolizes the ruin of her engineer-hero in *Alexander's Bridge* is certainly meant to be projected outward into the larger context of an engineering society. In the first of her frontier tales we noticed an almost equally sharp aversion to those modern "politicians" who appeared on the western horizon so shortly after the first glow of the pioneer effort had faded—those agrarian "agitators" who seem to be identified in her mind with the unnecessary economic disturbances as well as the increasing standardization of thought and personality in the later stages of her western society. It is against this whole emerging pattern of both rural and urban life in America that Cather has actually set her earlier western individualists, her pioneer makers and ancestors, as an example of a better, a freer, a more heroic and worthy time.

In some part this accounts for both the eloquence of Cather's frontier tales and the final effect they produce of being isolated and almost static episodes, as I say—of being separated *out* of a larger and more complex historical situation. If this is a return to the childhood world of the artist, it is also a sort of childlike return. Moreover, as the chronicle of the pioneers is carried forward through the early western towns of *My Antonia* to the metropolitan centers of *The Song of the Lark*, there is the same note of isolation and hostility in the later defense of the artist in a purely materialistic society. . . . And yet there are other elements and more curious undertones here. Does the central emotional pattern of Cather's work—that particularly Catheresque sense of an intense splendor in life and of its inevitable loss, of a brief ecstasy and of a long and bitter resignation to suffering—stem back to her first novel, which contains, in fact, not only the fullest statement of this theme, but the most complete human relationship of the first period of her writing? After *Alexander's*

Bridge the lyrical note is increasingly subordinated to the stoical, while the line of her superior matriarchs is established, and Thea Kronborg again expresses their central conviction of "standing up under things," of "meeting catastrophe without any fussiness," of "dealing with fate bare-handed."

That, too, is admirable, of course, but is it also the fate of Cather's dominant and increasingly inaccessible women to be "always surrounded by little men," as in the case of Alexandra Bergson, to be worshiped from afar and to marry for convenience, as in the case of Ántonia Shimerda, and to sacrifice marriage, love, and, finally, friendship in the interests of an artist's career, as in the case of Thea Kronborg? Isn't it something of a catastrophe to avoid all deeper human involvements, as her women really seem to be doing here, though it may be in the interests of the most admirable or illustrious cause? Nor will that life of fame and luxury which Cather returns to and which she conveys so well quite answer this question either, as Thea herself admits when she reflects that the unexpected favors of fortune, no matter how dazzling, do not mean very much in comparison with those things "which in some way met our original want."

As a matter of fact, one *could* view Willa Cather's representation of her pioneer and artistic heroines as a turning-away, not only from a distasteful contemporary society, but also from a sensitive and crucial area of emotional experience: that is, from all the more or less involved consequences of what we call ordinary human relationships. In any case, the work of her second period will record the stress of an increasingly acute spiritual conflict, if not that of an actual psychic wound. For there, indeed, her figures will learn to live without delight, as she says, and will fall out of "all domestic and social relations." . . .

THE TRAGIC NECESSITY

The three tales in *Obscure Destinies* are an exposition of those ties with the earth and the farm animals and growing things "which are never made at all unless they are made early." If they center around an idyllic agrarian existence, however, they also present glimpses of a sort of industrial inferno.

"To be a landless man was to be a wage-earner, a slave all your life; to have nothing, to be nothing," Neighbour Rosicky thinks, while in the country what you had was, after all, your own:

You didn't have to choose between bosses and strikers and go wrong either way. You didn't have to do with dishonest and cruel people. . . . In the country, if you had a mean neighbour, you could keep off his land and make him keep off yours. But in the city, all the foulness and misery and brutality of your neighbours was part of your life. The worst things he had come upon in his journey through the world were human,—depraved and poisonous specimens of man. To this day he could recall certain terrible faces in the London streets. There were mean people everywhere, to be sure, even in their own country town here. But they weren't tempered, hardened, sharpened like the treacherous people in cities who live by grinding or cheating or poisoning their fellow-men.

And you cannot miss the bitterness of this indictment; the whole mixture of contempt and frustration which has been absent from Cather's work during the long sabbatical from her own society.

It may be worth mentioning that Cather's "Old Mrs. Harris" is no longer living among the southern gentry of her youth, "where there were plenty of landless people glad to render service to the more fortunate," but in a snappy little western democracy "where every man was as good as his neighbour and out to prove it." In turn, the Mr. Dillon and the Mr. Trueman who represent success and power in a little wooden town in a shallow Kansas River valley at a time when "business was still a personal adventure," who, indeed, inhabit a Main Street that Sinclair Lewis never knew, long before the period of pushing and boasting, of "efficiency and advertising and progressive methods," are contrasted with the little "hopper men" of the new economic order. Are these "Two Friends" rather quaint figures to serve as Cather's spokesmen for the depression years—to appear at almost the exact time when business had become a sort of national calamity? All the same, she has managed to suggest the end of an epoch in the break-up of the old friendship during the political disturbances of the eighteen-nineties. In these final reflections of the story on an old "scar," an old uneasiness—"the feeling of something broken that could so easily have been mended; of something delightful that was senselessly wasted, of a truth that was accidentally distorted"—you may catch the haunting refrain of an entire line of American writing which, from Howells to Hemingway, has been confronted with the latest developments of American life.

On a worldly level, the essays and sketches which are collected in *Not Under Forty*, in 1936, throw further light on a special literary temperament. This is Cather's only volume of non-fiction, and even the title which our author has selected for her first major public appearance indicates a deliberate and sylized retreat to the past, and to the recusant stand of "age":

This book will have little interest for people under forty years of age. The world broke in two in 1922 or thereabouts, and the persons and prejudices recalled in these sketches slid back into yesterday's seven thousand years. . . . It is for the backward and by one of their number, that these sketches were written.

In much the same vein the essay on "148 Charles Street" deals with the salon of Mrs. James Fields, where the young Willa Cather first met Sarah Orne Jewett and a whole circle of cultivated personages who assembled under the shadow of the distinguished Boston publisher and were held together by the firm social tutelage of the publisher's widow. Is this harmonious drawing room—"an atmosphere in which one seemed absolutely safe from everything ugly"—a little remote from the true creative sources of the New England tradition it represents: from Thoreau's hut, or the booms and jibs of Melville's whalers? Is it really essential for Cather to tell us that "nobody can cherish the flower of social intercourse, can give it sun and sustenance and a tempered clime," without also being able very completely to dispose of anything that threatens it—"not only the slug, but even the cold draught that ruffles its petals"? Now, indeed, the Lady in the Wilderness is almost completely the Lady. And yet that cultivated Boston home of Mrs. Fields's had, at least for the older novelist who looks back upon it, another and deeper meaning. It was not only a place where the past lay in wait for one; it was a place where the past lived on, "where it was protected and cherished, had sanctuary from the noisy push of the present"—where the ugliness of the world, and "all possibility of wrenches and jars and wounding contacts" seemed securely shut out.

These wrenches, jars, and wounding contacts are familiar to us. Are they *all* encompassed by that garage which now stands at 148 Charles Street, which has "altogether taken the place of things formerly cherished on that spot," and which, as Cather adds, seems to represent the only real development in our national culture since that earlier flowering of learning, of talent, and of the finer amenities of life? In any case, what is interesting to notice is the change in the volume's tone after the crack-up of this earlier and in a sense rather derivative and second-class drawing room society. Thus, by comparison with the Salvini or Modjeska of Mrs. Fields's group, the appeal of Dickens or Scott is primarily for "the great multitudes of humanity" who have no feeling for the form of any art, who, indeed, do not want quality but quantity, change, a succession of new things "that are quickly threadbare and can be lightly thrown away." [5] The younger generation is interested only in contemporary writers, "the newer the better," while the neglect of Sarah Orne Jewett, as we are told in one of Cather's more impassioned periods, implies a growing contempt not only for the English language but for the entire tradition of Anglo-Saxon culture.

"Imagine a young man or woman, born in New York City, educated at a New York university, violently inoculated with

---

[5] In terms of Cather's evaluation of her own European literary models in *Not Under Forty*, Turgeniev is listed as her favorite among the "great group of Russian writers," while Doestoevski isn't mentioned. Just so, Balzac is subordinated to Flaubert in the French group, while Zola is completely ignored. And if Dickens and Scott represent the nineteenth-century English writers, as above, D. H. Lawrence himself is viewed as an example of the distinction "between emotion and mere sensory reactions." But the real distinction here seems almost to be that between literary perfection and literary force, or depth, and similarly most of Cather's objections to contemporary realism or naturalism have a concealed bias, and are almost directed at the *existence* of the naturalistic novel.

Freud, hurried into journalism, knowing no more about New England country people (or country folk anywhere) than he has caught from motor trips or observed from summer hotels: what is there for him in *The Country of the Pointed Firs?*" And furthermore:

This hypothetical young man is perhaps of foreign descent: German, Jewish, Scandinavian. To him English is merely a means of making himself understood, of communicating his ideas. He may write and speak American English correctly, but only as an American may learn to speak French correctly. It is a surface speech: he clicks the words out as a bank clerk clicks out silver when you ask for change. . . . Moreover, the temper of the people which lies behind the language is incomprehensible to him. He can see what these Yankees *have not* (hence an epidemic of "suppressed desire" plays and novels), but what they *have*, their actual preferences and their fixed scale of values, are absolutely dark to him. When he tries to put himself in the Yankee's place he attempts an impossible substitution.

Nor is the "adopted American" alone in being cut off from the old moral harmonies, Cather adds; there is also the new American whom George Santayana described as "the untrained, pushing cosmopolitan orphan." It is amusing that to make her point Cather should draw upon the phrase of the Spanish-born philosopher, the uneasy child of mixed cultures who was himself, during the American twenties and thirties, an illustrious example of the gifted and retroverted cosmopolitan orphan. And where else but in some such source as this could you find an appropriate phrase during the entire period when so many "hypothetical" young men of foreign descent, "aliens" and adopted Americans, sons and grandsons of immigrants, such as the "German" Dreiser or the "Portuguese" Dos Passos or the "Swedish" Sandburg or the "Irish" Fitzgerald, to name only a few, were making their major contributions to the national letters? Or when, for instance, the cosmopolitan Thomas Mann, to whom Cather pays such a glowing tribute in a neighboring essay of *Not Under Forty*, was drawing upon the great Viennese Jew, Freud, for the core of his own writing; not to mention in this connection any other Bohemian,

French, or Scandinavian artisans or farmers who, in her own earlier life, had given her an initial sense of the traditions, standards, and craftsmanship, as well as of the music, dancing, and gaiety of life in those primitive little "American" settlements on the untamed plains of Nebraska.

But very clearly here, in the uncertain tone of this artist who usually appears so serene, in these more importunate accents of malice and prejudice which recall at once the Continental jargon of Mencken and the cold academic purity of Stuart Sherman's view of our native scene in that strange ethnological debate that raged over the "New Literature" of the post-war period, we may see the symptoms of a running feminine distemper as it were, which has not yet been soothed by Cather's attempt to achieve a spiritual harmony. You may notice, incidentally, that interesting reference to the rhythms of a new American language that is clicked out "as a bank clerk clicks out silver when you ask for change"—a reference which stands by itself in the midst of all this veiled racial nonsense. Just so, the peroration to perhaps the most famous of these essays, "The Novel Démeublé"—

How wonderful it would be if we could throw all the furniture out of the window; and along with it all the meaningless reiterations concerning physical sensations, all the tiresome old patterns, and leave the room as bare as the stage of a Greek theatre, or as that house into which the glory of Pentecost descended!

—betrays a certain uneasy consciousness of the real truth about Cather's own novels of religious sensations and ecclesiastical trappings. And her later remarks about the artist who spends his life in pursuing "the things which haunt him," in having his mind "teased" by them, are coupled, in the closing essay of *Not Under Forty*, with those extraordinary reflections on the everyday existence of an ordinary "happy" family, each member of which, as she says, is "clinging passionately to his individual soul, is in terror of losing it in the general family flavour":

As in most families, the mere struggle to have anything of one's own, to be one's self at all, creates an element of strain which keeps everybody almost at the breaking-point. . . . One realizes that even in harmonious families there is this double life: the group life, which is the one we can observe in our neighbour's household, and, underneath, another—secret and passionate and intense—which is the real life that stamps the faces and gives character to the voices of our friends. Always in his mind each member of these social units is escaping, running away, trying to break the net which circumstances and his own affections have woven about him. One realizes that human relationships are the tragic necessity of human life; that they can never be wholly satisfactory, that every ego is half the time greedily seeking them, and half the time pulling away from them.

For what one realizes here is the singular nature of Cather's picture of "reality"—those final overtones of fear or dread which linger on in our minds after this description of normal "everyday" experience. The disparate nature of our group lives and our personal lives is surely one of the most ironical facts of our existence. Still, is our private life quite so secret, passionate, and intense—*always* marked by this element of strain and tension at the breaking point? Those human relationships which are in fact the tragic necessity of human life, which are never wholly satisfactory, while their continuous imperfections form, indeed, the real dynamics of ordinary affairs—can they never be even partly satisfactory? Moreover, while the ostensible play of this passage is on the attraction, the actual need, of ego for ego, the final stress is on the mutual repulsion of these tormented selves, on an almost frantic clinging to one's own identity, a pulling away from, an actual *breaking* of that net which, indeed, circumstances and our own affections usually weave about us—a stress on fear, on flight, on escape. And this is a passage which comes close, if not to the realities of experience, at least to Cather's view of them; while to a large degree it defines the real psychological milieu of one of her last and most illuminating novels. *Lucy Gayheart*, published in 1935, does mark a return in both theme and tone to the pattern of her earlier writing. But it is very far from the "lavender and old lace" which has been generally used to describe it.

As a matter of fact, Cather almost deliberately points up both the typical and the incongruous elements in the story. Lucy herself is pretty, eager, "delighted with everything," as her surname suggests; the whole picture of the town of Haverford, on the Platte River in Colorado, at the turn of the century, is idyllic, innocent, quaint. Similarly, our first impression of Clement Sebastian, the middle-aged singer whom Lucy meets in Chicago, is not entirely exhilarating. Sebastian is a famous baritone, but he is also plump, his torso is "unquestionably oval," and he is married. Moreover, with his valet Giuseppe and his assistant, Mr. Mockford, his morning coats and smoking jackets, his complete aversion to anything that might "tarnish his personal elegance," he is an exaggerated and artificial symbol of that cosmopolitan elegance which has figured so largely in Cather's work. On its superficial levels *Lucy Gayheart is* a standard and almost stereotyped story in our literature: the love affair of the young provincial girl who seeks an artistic career and the sophisticated city-man who represents all the glamour of artistic success. We see this very clearly, and then, as it were, gradually stop seeing it altogether.

For what Cather has managed to create in the reader of her story is hardly so much that "willing suspension of disbelief" which the literary critic delights in, but a sort of inevitable and unwitting acceptance of the artist's intention—an intention that is hardly limited to a picture of love's delights. The Chicago musical world of *Lucy Gayheart* is attractive, to be sure. The descriptions of Chicago, its buildings, streets, crowds, and climate, probably rank among Cather's best recreations of the first mystery and enchantment of the large city for the provincial aspirant: the city of flowers and music, as it first seems to Lucy, in which it was hard to believe that there was anything in the world she could not have—which gave one the freedom "to spend one's youth as one pleased, to have one's secret, to choose one's own master and serve him in one's own way."

For here, in this late heroine of hers, are those "feudal" responses which are the real secret of Cather's women: those deeper and more authoritarian patterns of feminine affection, and that whole underlying view of the love relationship as a deliberate return to the primitive experiences of the individual—as a *willed* bondage between master and servant, or between parent and child. But the lyrical opening of the central romance in *Lucy Gayheart* is soon qualified by the unpleasant revelations of love: by Lucy's "discovery" that passion, dark and terrifying, can drown like black water. Indeed, her first feeling for Sebastian "had already destroyed a great deal of her," as Cather says:

Some people's lives are affected by what happens to their person or their property; but for others fate is what happens to their feelings and their thoughts—that and nothing more.

Moreover, with Lucy's realization that Sebastian also has been broken by his feelings, that he has in fact resolved that "nobody would ever share his life again," and has to a large extent resorted to the refuge of Catholicism; and with Sebastian's sudden death, we reach the real center of the novel.

Now, for such a scrupulous artist as Cather, it *is* curious that the pattern of this love story should be so familiar, not merely in terms of its main elements but as to matters of detail. The repetition, for example, of the scenes in the Chicago Art Museum, where a "rather second-rate French painting" suggested the title for *The Song of the Lark*; the return to a musical environment which has been such a central preoccupation of Cather herself, and which here again helps to maintain Lucy Gayheart's belief in "an invisible, inviolable world," very much as the religious hymns did for the Marie Shabata of *O Pioneers!*; the sense of personal defeat in the midst of worldly success which marks both the Bartley Alexander of her first novel and the Clement Sebastian of this one, not to mention that final death by drowning, which occurs to her hero in both *Alexander's Bridge* and *Lucy Gayheart*—these are certainly among the elements of a central love story which vibrates and echoes in all of her early works; which has been submerged during the whole period of her own religious refuge, and which here at last has been given its final and fullest expression: its *actuality,* perhaps even down to that odd final touch, that author's warning, used for the first time in the whole span of her work. "The characters and situations in this work are wholly fictional and imaginary."

In any case, just as *Lucy Gayheart* contains the most complete love relationship in the range of Cather's work, with the possible exception of *Alexander's Bridge,* it is also among her most convincing works. The sense of immediacy that we have in regard to both the scene and the emotions of the central story is a remarkable achievement for an artist who is approaching her sixties. (You may note, incidentally, that the Chicago scene of the novel is by no means the harsh urban society of *Obscure Destinies* and the later Cather.) And here, as Lucy returns to Haverford on the Platte and struggles to patch up her life after the death of Sebastian, and listens to the advice of such country characters as Cather's "Mrs. Ramsay"—

"Nothing really matters but living. Get all you can out of it. I'm an old woman, and I know. Accomplishments are the ornaments of life, they come second. Sometimes people disappoint us, and sometimes we disappoint ourselves; but the thing is, to go right on living."

—and makes her own decision at last to go back to Chicago, to her work and to life itself—"Let it come! Let it all come back to her again! Let it betray her and mock her and break her heart, she must have it!"—we get that sense of a final catharsis, of a human rebirth, which, as we have seen, Cather has constantly struggled for but has actually failed to achieve in the formal "humanity" of her religious works. For one may also lose one's soul by gaining it, so to speak, under false pretenses; and it is only here that she has achieved a true as against a ceremonial "resurrection" of the spirit—a celebration of life in the midst of death, rather than a glorification of life without end.

Yet, on the plane of critical speculation, you might say that the true inner pattern of Cather's early work is that of a kind of traumatic wound; that the whole burden of her middle period is the attempt to reach a spiritual equilibrium through a formal mode of religious conversion—and that it was only *after* this conversion, and within the framework of its security, that the original emotions of the writer could approach something like a full aesthetic expression. . . . You may notice that in the later sections of *Lucy Gayheart* Cather does at least reach down into the mystery and drama, or even the mingled splendor and terror, of that *ordinary* human life, that common everyday existence of humanity which, lying directly between her need for worldly glamour and her sense of religious guilt, has constantly eluded her grasp. The description of the domestic relationships in the Gayheart family, of Haverford society in general, and of such townspeople as Harry Gordon or Mrs. Ramsay are among the best examples of Cather's realism, just as that brief passage of hers—

In little towns lives roll along so close to one another; loves and hates beat about, their wings almost touching. On the sidewalks, along which everybody comes and goes, you must, if you walk abroad at all, at some time pass within a few inches of the man who cheated and betrayed you, or the woman you desire more than anything else in the world. Her skirt brushes against you. You say good-morning and go on. It is a close shave. Out in the world the escapes are not so narrow.

—almost summarizes the whole nature of small-town life in America. Here Cather expresses that "mysteriousness of the general" which is at the center of Sherwood Anderson's study of our earlier form of communal organization, and our older and deeper mid-American roots.

It may be worth mentioning that her next novel, *Sapphira and the Slave Girl*, in 1940, marks a return to her own earliest and hitherto almost obscure origins: to the more or less "aristocratic," semi-feudal, pre-Civil-War Virginia society from which she traces her own family ancestry. Certainly she has the material of a rich novel in her picture of a typical Virginia plantation, whose master, Henry Colbert, an upright Dutch dissenter, stands out, against that whole generous, careless, easy, slave-owning, horse-racing Tidewater group to which his wife, Sapphira, belongs. And the central story of the novel—Colbert's increasing affection for the slave girl Nancy, and Sapphira's cold-blooded attempt to ruin the Negress through having her seduced by Colbert's younger brother—deals with a very sensitive area of Negro-white relationships in the South.

In its central framework *Sapphira and the Slave Girl* is probably Cather's most ambitious book, the first of her novels to attempt to come to grips with a difficult and complex social environment. It is interesting to notice how close she comes to the psychological implications of this environment; that is, to the underlying sexual corruption which was attendant upon the institution of slavery; the debasement of the deepest human drives which was implicit in the buying and selling of human flesh, as well as of human souls, and which in a way did less fundamental harm to those who were the "material" of the merchandising than to the merchants themselves. For the white male could hardly be expected to attribute a human status to a relationship that, in an adjacent area, could be viewed in such completely different terms, and was, indeed, for economic reasons, deliberately relegated to a subhuman status, while the "innocence" of the Southern Lady was achieved, in turn, by deliberately excluding from her view everything she knew to be true and saw at every moment around her. At least Sapphira, who has married Nancy's mother to a "capon man" for her own domestic convenience, and who sets "the worst rake in the country" upon the track of the young Negress, while she laughs at the "old jokes" of the Negro slaves who mock at their own sexual inclinations, can hardly be viewed as an incarnation of pure white southern womanhood. And in the "legend" of Jezebel, the fierce African tribeswoman, who is captured, examined, and sold almost purely for her value as a sexual animal, Cather defines the real background, and the basic moral issues, of *Sapphira and the Slave Girl* in less than a dozen pages. However—there is a curious hiatus in the working-out of her southern story.

It is surely legitimate for the novelist to represent the different points of view in her central situation. But maybe Cather's attempt to give a balanced picture of the Negro-white relationships in her novel is a little *too* successful. Henry Colbert's daughter, Mrs. Blake, has gone over to the Quakers and Abolishers. Yet

Colbert's own conclusion that, although he has a legal right to manumit any of his wife's Negroes, it would be an outrage to Sapphira's feelings and an injustice to the slaves themselves, while, after all, are we not all in bonds?—is a model of private sensibility in the midst of a historical crisis. Those "good" southern plantation owners of Cather's who never "sell off their slaves to strangers" may sound, again, rather like the Hemingwayish hunter of the *Green Hills of Africa* who never shoots a kudu he has met before, while there is, in fact, altogether too much stress here on the scriptural appearance, the filial loyalty, and the "childlike trust" of the faithful Negro slaves themselves. For such a subtle novelist as Cather, it seems odd that the slave girl Nancy, the original inspiration and the chief victim of the story, should turn out to be so timid, superstitious, and hysterical. Her despair at being pursued by Sapphira's agent is not entirely alluring ("I'm goin' to throw myself into the millpawnd, I am!"), just as, at the moment of the novel's climax, when she is being rescued and sent off to the North as a free woman, she turns completely irresponsible and dozes off. Still more curious, it is Sapphira herself, the cold, proud, aristocratic mistress of the house, who emerges, at least in her more benevolent moments, as the real heroine of the novel. "There are different ways of being good to folks," Henry Colbert says to his dying and repentant wife. "Sometimes keeping people in their place is being good to them."

You may notice other ambiguous elements in Cather's southern story. There is that "foolish, dreamy nigger-side" of Nancy's nature; or that "soft darky laugh" which makes her, apparently, more attractive. And the Virginia mountaineers—the hill people who are midway between the plantation owners and the Negroes in the story's social scale—are viewed in a curiously ambivalent light: both as sturdy individualists, like Cather's old-fashioned Mandy Ringer, and as an ignorant and vicious mob, like the young Keyser boys of the story. . . . But isn't the main trouble with *Sapphira and the Slave Girl* the fact that nothing really happens in the end?—that a novel which has the material for half a dozen tragedies, and which is set against the fury, the intrigue, and the rhetoric of probably the most crucial period of our history, should turn out to be so pale and remote? And that the novelist herself, who has constantly reiterated her belief that all that is necessary for a drama is four walls and one passion, should manage to achieve, out of all these conflicting personalities and beliefs, only an unlikely "happy ending"? Just as clearly here as in the acrid social commentary of *Not Under Forty* we may see the evidence of a final division in Cather's values which hasn't been altogether bridged by the synthesis of extremes at the conclusion of her religious pilgrimage. Only in this case the conflict in her thinking is most sharply revealed in just that muting and softening, that "balancing-off," and that final literary stalemate which marks her attempt to deal with the basic historical issues of *Sapphira and the Slave Girl.*

For the whole range of Cather's values, standards, tastes, and prejudices, her tone, is that of an inherent aristocrat in an equalitarian order, of an agrarian writer in an industrial order, of a defender of the spiritual graces in the midst of an increasingly materialistic culture. Miss Cather is quite aware of her predicament. Her work is filled with its intimations. What other meaning is there, indeed, to the series of farewells—to the Pioneers, to the Empire Builders, to the Washington Square society of the early nineteen-hundreds—which constitutes the whole burden of her earlier writing? Yet playing all around the edges of this primary western scene, skipping from the immigrant settlers to the last of the railroad builders, delighted, in the salons of Boston and New York, with the areas of sensibility produced by, and all the cultivated by-products of, the great American fortunes, she has nowhere reached the real center of her material. Selecting and enhancing the most subtle effects of wealth, she has, rather like Samuel Dodsworth's wife, either looked down upon or ignored the whole process of creating wealth. Writing so discreetly about the age when business was a personal adventure, she has neglected to mention the most typical forms of the adventure. And Cather's narrow and almost deliberately naïve view of the past, of history, and therefore of human nature itself, has also affected the whole texture of her work.

As a matter of fact, is it the *instinctive* taste of "the great multitudes of humanity" which has created that succession of new things "quickly threadbare and lightly thrown away" that she describes in *Not Under Forty*? Or can this be attributed in some measure also to the economic pattern—if not to the economic necessity—of an industrial set-up whose mechanisms of production have so far outrun its methods of distribution? In terms of an older agrarian order, or at least for its more privileged members, the banking system and the stock exchange may have no proper place in imaginative art, as Cather again declares. But have they no place at all in the imaginative art of a predominantly financial republic—particularly, when, during the years of her own artistic maturity, the banking system and the stock exchange were in fact determining the lives, the habits, and even the mythology of the great multitudes of people who perched, rather uneasily, on the crest of the boom market or wallowed in its trough? Miss Cather's belated return to the soil in those agrarian idylls of *Obscure Destinies* might have seemed a little ironical to the migrant Okies of John Steinbeck's *The Grapes of Wrath,* or to those later immigrants who, unlike Neighbour Rosicky, had not been so fortunate as to remove themselves from the stricken urban centers of the depression years.

Miss Cather's stress on the moral elements of character is important, to be sure. Her emphasis, as a craftsman, on whatever is felt upon the page without being specifically named there—on the "inexplicable presence of the thing not named, of the overtone divined by the ear but not heard by it"—is admirable. But perhaps her view of both that older American world which, as she says, broke in two in the early nineteen-twenties, and that whole new American world of the corporations and the cartels, and of the untrained pushing orphans of finance capitalism is a little *too* intangible. We have noticed those uneasy glimpses of the "bosses and strikers" with whom you go wrong either way, or of those "adopted" Americans who are probably not so different from the admirable immigrants of her youth, but who almost come to be blamed, in Cather's later years, for whatever has happened to American life. In these later tones of hostility and malice, of isolation, and reversion to the past, as well as in the reluctance to treat a historical situation whose implications appear throughout her work but whose true nature is never faced, indeed, we may almost see the symptoms of a sort of cultural wound. For the general relationship of the cultural and the temperamental factors in a writer's work is usually clear enough. It is the more precise relationship, the weight, the balance, the interaction of these forces that is difficult to judge.

Was it the intense emotional crisis at the center of Cather's literary work which forced her to retreat so completely from the real issues of her own time? Or was it her initial aversion to the whole context of an industrial and financial society which, as early as 1912, in her first parable of Alexander the bridge-builder, forced her back into such a narrow and intense psychological sphere? . . . In a way, too, as I said in opening, the limitations of her work are made more poignant by her long and sustained attempt to transcend them, as well as by those wonderful areas of sensitivity which we have noticed, and by her actual achievement. If only she hadn't needed to go so far afield for her spiritual sanctuary, when a less remote and less ornate mode of salvation might have done! If only the common people of her tales had been allowed to experience a little more of that exquisite torment of life which she portrays so well—or if, in turn, both the promise and the gallantry of life in America had not disappeared quite so completely with the arc light and the hansom! . . . Then, indeed, which one of our novelists would have served as a better chronicler of that last softly lighted, discreetly sparkling evening scene of the great American fortunes at the turn of the century?

GEORGE SCHLOSS

"A Writer's Art"

Admired, even honored while alive, Miss Cather is still neglected. In many of the more important studies of current literature she is hardly mentioned. Put off on the one hand by the literary jingoists who by incorrectly coupling her with a Sandburg or a Benet use her as a weapon against the expatriates—spiritual or otherwise—or on the other by the heirs of the genteel tradition (cf. Stephen Tennant's harmless introduction to this book) [1] who have adopted her but against whom she herself rebelled, most serious critics and writers have never bothered to read her —at least seriously. Yet by both precept and example she points a hopeful way for the modern writer.

The landscape of the American artist has often been painted as a battlefield, a place where Paleface meets Redskin, the one armed with an imported consciousness, intellect and aesthetic, the other with nothing more than the primitive experience of the frontier or concrete jungle. The overall contribution of Miss Cather's work is, I think, a partial transcendence of these opposing forces into something that looks like, if not a victory, at least a peace.

In the truncated essay here on Katherine Mansfield, [2] Miss

Reprinted from *The Hudson Review*, Vol. III, No. 1 (Spring, 1950). Copyright 1950 by The Hudson Review, Inc.

[1] The "harmless introduction" is Stephen Tennant's introduction to *On Writing,* a posthumous collection of Miss Cather's critical writings published by Knopf—ED.

[2] The essay on Katherine Mansfield is from *Not Under Forty,* reprinted in *On Writing*—ED.

Cather sighs over the bad luck that deprived the overwrought New Zealander from ever putting into practice a phrase one of her characters uses in an early story: "Easy does it." "Easy does it" is an attitude Willa Cather raised almost to a method and it is not the least important of the lessons she has to teach.

Her life followed the classical pattern of growth and fulfill-ment. Beginning brightly, she paused for a time, then continued through a period of trial and error until, mature, she was ready to bring her work to fruition. During this space of ten or fifteen years she achieved not one but five or six fine books, of which three—*My Ántonia, A Lost Lady* and *Death Comes for the Arch-bishop*—certainly stand out. At the end, although she diffused some of her force and seemed really to be exhausted, she was still in command of her material, and this alone is a rare enough qual-ity to distinguish her in our literary history.

Serene in her own confidence, neither brittle nor folksy, she avoided the two traps that often waylay the American: the tenu-ousness of an excessive alienation or the bluntness of regional chauvinism. To her, art was a "rather personal thing after all, too . . . human to be very great" or very important "except to those who have an ear for it or an eye for it." She could point out to her more ponderous colleagues too, the condition under which it best flourishes: "a condition free," she says in her pertinent letter on "Escapism," "not so much from restriction, as from adul-teration; considerations and purposes which have nothing to do with spontaneous invention."

Her tools sharpened by the European culture she not only did not fear but loved, she turned them towards what she knew best, first to a world of artists and businessmen, then, more success-fully, to her pioneer West, and she created, as far as is possible, a conscious rational art. The distance between Sherwood Ander-son's Ohioans and Miss Cather's Nebraskans is only a thousand miles, but the distance between the development of their makers is infinite. The one, the best of his kind, produced spasmodically and ended up pathetically tongue-tied and lost; the other, *no less critical of the American scene,* and in the end surely much less sentimental, knew exactly where she was going and went there.

Yet she came at a bad time. Younger than Sarah Orne Jewett, James and Henry Adams, she was still more than a literary generation away from Ftizgerald, Hemingway and Faulkner. Her only *real* contemporaries in prose fiction were Stephen Crane, who died young and whom, in one of these prefaces, she indicates she admired, Edith Wharton and Ellen Glasgow. The decline of the old New England intellectual values and the frontier social values as they yielded to the new monopolied vulgarity and its own later postwar counter-revolt isolated her, accounted for her elegiac bias; yet this isolation may have been fortunate. It forced her to go her own way and permitted her to become both a bridge between the best and a counter-irritant against the worst aspects of both periods. Perched between two eras she could see the true and the false in each; though unhappily, in the press of the "new writing" her own best work, produced between 1918–1931, was passed over by the "revolutionaries" whom it might have benefited most.

Evading academicism of every kind—the hothouse variety from which she emerged, the muckraking realism of her youth, and the harsh, abstract urbanity which surrounded her later life —she was able to keep her balance. Because she preserved what was worthwhile in the past, she could welcome the essentially new. An admirer of Proust, Mann, Stravinsky, and the modern painters especially, she could detect the obscurantism of many of their camp followers and the coarseness of the growing, tough, wise-guy journalism she so much deplored, deplored yet understood:

"I should say the greatest obstacles that writers today have to get over are the dazzling journalistic successes of twenty years ago. . . . The whole aim of that school . . . was novelty—never a very important thing in art. They gave us altogether poor standards—taught us to multiply our ideas instead of to condense them," and art, she writes in her essay on fiction, "should simplify. That indeed, is very nearly the whole of the higher artistic process; finding what conventions of form and what detail one can do without and yet preserve—the spirit of the whole—so that all that one has suppressed . . . is there to the reader's consciousness as much as if it were in type on the page. . . . Whatever is felt upon the page without being specifically named there . . . that is created."

This theme, rendered in her fiction, is dominant in her criticism and is a good antidote to the textbook competence of the creative writing courses which, getting hold of a half-truth, subtly lose sight of the larger issue: art—design—as something more than competence. She is willing to lose her life to find that mysterious "gift of sympathy" that comes from an indefinable process of "persistence, survival, recurrence in the writer's mind," emerging from "shapes and scenes that have teased the mind for years."

Still, she commends competence as far as it goes, and rebukes a facile romantic attitude towards personal expression:

The novelist must learn to write and then he must unlearn it; just as the modern painter learns to draw, and then learns when utterly to disregard his accomplishment, when to subordinate it to a higher and truer effect. In this direction only . . . can the novel develop into anything more varied and perfect than all the many novels that have gone before.

This is the archetypal approach of the conservationist, the values of whom we of the liberal persuasion, both in art and in politics, are learning to recognize and appreciate. As we can see, if only in three of the letters published here tracing the evolution of *Death Comes for the Archbishop, Shadows on the Rock* and perhaps the imperfect *The Professor's House,* by holding to the traditional as a base she enlarged rather than restricted her area of mobility, and was constantly and quietly experimenting.

Like many American writers she was never completely at home in the conventional dramatic novel. She had to find her own form —a form that could attain the force of her elegiac mood, could express at once her love for nature and for the native past. After a few failures and partial successes where the content splashed over the sides, she devised a panoramic narrative strong enough to hold both her subject and her emotion. Compared to so much of our mechanistic well-made fiction even her failures are refreshing, conditioned as they are not by mere lack of technique, but by a searching effort to create something new. Discussing a writer's development she notes what must have been a reflection of her own struggle, that "the courage to go on without compromise does not come to a writer all at once," and adds wisely, "nor does the ability."

Unlike many women of talent she never got lost in the jade rooms of sensibility. Her prose, primitive yet articulate, neither circumlocutory nor infantile, is always clear, and even at its most musical never evaporates into just sound. It is charged with that echoing vibration she sought as one of the definitions of a literary art. To say, as has often been said, that she was limited—which she was and knew she was—is to say nothing. Given her gift, she realized her potential. She did the best she could possibly have done and most of the time, I suspect, tried to do a great deal more. It may have been this that led her into a too frequent use of the archaic in language and thought, but since she is seldom tedious, I, for one, am willing to forgive her almost anything. She has the rare ability, certainly in her fiction, but even in her critical writing, to create that electric *scenic* quality which in her scathing appraisal of Defoe's *Roxana* (what must be one of the most uncomplimentary prefaces ever written; she not only damns an author she is inviting you to read, but a whole materialist culture as well) she finds lacking, a quality that can vitally record in the memory an experience of any kind, whether of life or of literature.

Humorous, even reasonably tolerant, she is one of our few writers who can be reread with increasing excitement and pleasure, and her rank, however modest, is assured in that catholic hierarchy she so much respected: Tolstoy, Turgenev, the French prose masters of the nineteenth century, and the Americans, Hawthorne, Twain, Jewett and James.

More versatile than most of her contemporaries, more well rounded, there are points where the best of her achievement is comparable only to, say, the best of the painter Marsden Hartley's. Her relation to Flaubert resembles Hartley's to Cézanne. Neither *Death Comes for the Archbishop* nor the Katahdin series could be quite the same without *Salammbo* or the studies of Mont St. Victoire. In richness of color, imaginative intent and not least, sheer persistence, both Americans approximate each other—right down to their occasional gaucheries. Both went to the center of Western culture and came back, renewed, to their own peripheries. Ironically, it was through this recognition and acceptance of their provincialism that they rejoined the main body and enlarged it.

Becoming somewhat of a popular writer as she grew older, Miss Cather, by her example of integrity, patience, and sanity in face of the chaotic, indicated, in this and her other work, how she found her way. As a consequence she points out some of the means with which others, if they wish, can find theirs.

HENRY STEELE COMMAGER

Willa Cather

To Willa Cather the past was significant for its moral qualities, and only gradually did romanticism triumph over morality. Throughout her long literary life she was engaged in an elaborate remembrance of things past—the past of the pioneers who had built the West, of the immigrants who had carried with them into the New World their sense of beauty and art, of those earlier spiritual pathfinders, the Franciscans and Jesuits, who had served their fellow-men and their God so selflessly. And all her novels and stories—those of the Arcadian Virginia of her childhood, of the golden Nebraska of her youth, of the New York she had known as a young journalist, of the shimmering Southwest that belonged to the past even in the present, and the Quebec that seemed to have only a past—were animated by a single great theme as they were graced by a single felicitous style. The theme was that of the supremacy of moral and spiritual over material values, the ever recurrent but inexhaustible theme of gaining the whole world and losing one's soul.

Willa Cather was a traditionalist and a conformer; the tradition that she so triumphantly maintained was peculiarly American, the standards to which she so instinctively conformed those that had sufficed her mentors, Sarah Orne Jewett and Henry James and, in an earlier day, Hawthorne. Her roots were deep in the American and the Christian past; she had inherited the best of Virginia—not the Tidewater, but that Valley where

Reprinted from "The Traditionalists," Ch. VIII of *The American Mind: An Interpretation of American Thought and Character Since the 1880's* (New Haven, 1950) by permission of the Yale University Press.

Ellen Glasgow finally found her vein of iron; she had known the Middle Border in the days of its primitive beauty and all her life drew strength from it; she had lived and worked in eastern cities and abroad and could re-create the artistic world of New York with flawless deftness, but she never came to terms with that world. "It's a queer thing about the flat country," she once wrote, "it takes hold of you, or it leaves you perfectly cold. A great many people find it dull and monotonous; they like a church steeple, an old mill, a waterfall, country all touched up and furnished, like a German Christmas card. I go everywhere—I admire all kinds of country. I tried to live in France. But when I strike the open plains, something happens. I'm home. I breathe differently."

Miss Cather rejected the "overfurnished" novel as she rejected the overfurnished countryside—rejected alike the furniture of sociology, of psychology, and of physiology, for "a novel crowded with physical sensations is no less a catalogue than one crowded with furniture." She thought the traditional themes of love and despair, truth and beauty, the struggle with the soil and the struggle for artistic honesty, far from exhausted; indeed she held, with Henry James and Ellen Glasgow, that these were the only themes capable of inspiring great art. "Ideals," she wrote, "were not archaic things, beautiful and impotent; they were the real sources of power among men," and unlike so many of her contemporaries —Hemingway, for example—she was not embarrassed by this vocabulary. Sarah Orne Jewett had admonished her, when she was scarcely more than a girl, that "you must write to the human heart, the great consciousness that all humanity goes to make up. Otherwise what might be strength . . . is only crudeness, and what might be insight is only observation, sentiment falls to sentimentality—you can write about life but never write life itself." From *Alexander's Bridge* to *The Old Beauty* she wrote life itself, wrote it so passionately that the characters she created seem to us more authentic than the characters of history.

The best of Miss Cather's novels all deal with the frontier, in one sense or another, but the frontier is never the object but rather the setting, and her stories are never, as with Bret Harte or Hamlin Garland, frontier stories. For just as Turner, when he placed himself on the vantage point of the frontier, was able to see the significance of the whole of American history, so Willa Cather, when she looked out upon life from the prairie or mesa or from one of those Rocks which figure so largely in her books, was able to see, from those vantage points, the real meaning of life in America. It was because the frontier simplified, clarified, and dramatized universal moral problems that she returned to it again and again for inspiration, and rarely in vain.

What was it about the pioneer West that inspired Miss Cather's elegiac mood, commanded her affection and respect, and, by contrast, made the busy world of the East seem so brash and pushing? It was, first of all, the land itself, and Miss Cather indulged in that pathetic fallacy which ascribed to the land not only spaciousness and beauty but endurance and serenity and strength. "It fortified her," she wrote of Alexandra Bergson, "to reflect upon the great operations of nature, and when she thought of the law that lay behind them she felt a sense of personal security." She subscribed to that romantic tradition, so strong in American literature and art, that saw nature splendid in all its manifestations and man virtuous only when he accommodated himself to nature—the tradition that stretched, politically, from Jefferson to Bryan, that found literary expression in so many writers from Cooper to Rølvaag, that was reflected in the work of naturalists like Burroughs and Muir and in landscape painters from the Hudson River school to Winslow Homer and Grant Wood. Thus when Thea Kronborg heard the "New World Symphony" she recalled

The sandhills, the grasshoppers and locusts, all the things that wakened and chirped in the early morning; the reaching and reaching of the high plains, the immeasurable yearning of all flat lands. There was home in it, too; first memories, first mornings long ago; the amazement of a new soul in a new world, that had dreamed something despairing, something glorious, in the dark before it was born.

And thus, in a somewhat different vein, of the Rock of Acoma:

the rock, when one came to think of it, was the utmost expression of human need; even mere feeling yearned for it; it was the highest comparison of loyalty in love and friendship. . . . The Acomas, who must share the universal human yearning for something permanent, enduring, without shadow of change, had their idea in substance.

Nature, however, was usually something that seemed to belong to the past; modern man had ignored it or exploited it, and therein lay its weakness. But those pioneers who had first gone out to the high plains, Miss Cather asserted, had been concerned with more than material conquest or exploitation: it was a romantic assertion, to be sure, and not wholly supported by the facts, but it was a mark of Miss Cather's triumph that she made nature and history conform to her art. The pioneers had a special relationship to the soil and drew from the soil strength and courage; they came not merely to make money but to live, and they built not merely an economy but a civilization, and there was integrity and dignity and piety in their work and their lives.

When an adventurer carries his gods with him into a remote and savage country [she wrote in *Shadows on the Rock*—and the words apply as well to the Nebraska pioneers], the colony he founds will, from the beginning, have grace, traditions, riches of the mind and spirit. Its history will shine with bright incidents, slight perhaps, but precious, as in life itself, where the great matters are often as worthless as astronomical distances, and the trifle dear as the heart's blood.

But after the pioneer and the builder, after the Ántonias and the Alexandras, the Captain Forresters and the Tom Outlands, came the exploiters and the spoilers. Thus Niel Herbert, who loved the Lost Lady,

had seen the end of an era, the sunset of the pioneer. He had come upon it when already its glory was nearly spent. So in the buffalo days a traveler used to come upon the embers of a hunter's fire on the prairie, after the hunter was up and gone. . . . This was the very end of the road-making West; the men who had put plains and mountains under the iron harness were old; some were poor; and even the successful ones were hunting for rest and a brief reprieve, death. It was already gone, that age; nothing could ever bring it back.

Nothing could ever bring it back, but Miss Cather found a sort of mournful consolation in recalling its heroic virtues.

This moral is implicit in all the early novels—notably in *O Pioneers!* and *My Ántonia*. With *A Lost Lady* and *The Professor's House*—both dating from the early twenties—it becomes explicit. "The whole world broke in two in 1922 or thereabouts," Miss Cather later wrote, and it was perhaps a consciousness of the passing of that old world that gave such poignancy to her recollection of the past. *A Lost Lady* is almost an allegory. The lovely Marian Forrester draws her strength, even her beauty and her charm, from that husband who represented all the old integrities. "It was as Captain Forrester's wife that she most interested Niel," says Miss Cather,

and it was in her relation to her husband that he most admired her. Given her other charming attributes, her comprehension of a man like the railroad-builder, her loyalty to him, stamped her more than anything else. That, he felt, was quality. . . . His admiration for Mrs. Forrester went back to that, just as, he felt, she herself went back to it.

When the Captain fails and then dies, Mrs. Forrester is indeed lost; her beauty remains and something of her charm, but they are tarnished, as the Old West was tarnished, because put to shabby use. That the gross and greedy Ivy Peters should supplant Captain Forrester is symbolic of the triumph of the speculator over the builder:

The Old West had been settled by dreamers, great-hearted adventurers who were unpractical to the point of magnificence; a courteous brotherhood, strong in attack but weak in defense, who could conquer but could not hold. Now all the vast territory they had won was to be at the mercy of men like Ivy Peters, who had never dared anything, never risked anything. They would drink up the mirage, dispel the morning freshness, root out the great brooding spirit of freedom, the generous, easy life of the great land-holders. The space, the colour, the princely carelessness of the pioneer they would destroy and cut up into profitable bits, as the match factory splinters the primeval forest. All the way from the Missouri to the mountains this generation of shrewd young men, trained to petty economies by hard times, would do exactly what Ivy Peters had done when he drained the Forrester marsh.

The passing of this pioneer generation meant, to Miss Cather, the passing of all the old virtues, and she was incapable of believing that there could be different virtues in a civilization whose standards were those of the countinghouse, whose habits were predatory, and whose rewards were social and ostentatious rather than spiritual and private. "We must face the fact," she said in a tribute to Nebraska penned just as she finished *A Lost Lady,*

that the splendid story of the pioneers is finished, and that no new story worthy to take its place has yet begun. . . . The generation now in the drivers' seat hates to make anything, wants to live and die in an automobile, scudding past those acres where the old men used to follow the corn-rows up and down. They want to buy everything ready-made: clothes, food, education, music, pleasure. Will the third generation—the full-blooded joyous ones just coming over the hill—be fooled? Will it believe that to live easily is to live happily?

Miss Cather's next novel—in many ways her most interesting —answered this rhetorical question with a clear negative. If *A Lost Lady* was an allegory, *The Professor's House* was a morality play, its characters authentic enough but symbols, each of them, of virtues and vices. It presented the contrast between spiritual integrity and worldly success even more dramatically than had *A Lost Lady.* For here, as if to underline the moral, were two complementary themes: Professor St. Peter's devotion to scholarship, threatened by the social ambitions of his family, and Tom Outland's passion for his miraculous mesa, thwarted by commercialism. The professor's house is a symbol of all the artistic and moral values he cherishes, the shabby house with the attic room which he shared with Augusta's "form," where he had written the eight volumes of his Spanish Adventurers, where he had known the happiest hours of his life, just as the new house he had built for his ambitious wife and spoiled daughters is a symbol of the pretentiousness of the new day. As for Tom Outland —the elusive Tom who had come out of nowhere and slipped away as quietly—the symbol is the mesa where he had discovered the remains of an extinct civilization, the mesa so remote, so private, so far above mere exploitation, a work of art, a projection, almost, of his own spirit. But the professor's house was doomed to abandonment; Tom Outland was killed, leaving a formula which made others rich, and greedy hands put the lovely pots and jars and tools he had found to commercial use. In the end, St. Peter found solace only in a crumbling diary which recalled for him the one stirring experience of his life.

The Professor's House was an acknowledgment of defeat, and after that Miss Cather seemed to give up even the pretense of finding something worth while in contemporary life. "The United States," she wrote, "had got ahead wonderfully, but somehow ahead on the wrong road." She turned back, instead, to Spanish New Mexico, to French Quebec, to ante-bellum Virginia. It was entirely natural that her search for the permanent should have led her, as it led Henry Adams, to the Catholic church, with "its safe, lovingly arranged and ordered universe, not too vast, though nobly spacious."

"It takes a great deal of history to produce a little literature," Henry James had written, and the sense of history was strong in Willa Cather, stronger by far than in most of those "historical" novelists whose recreation of the past was so calculated and so artificial. Better than any of her literary contemporaries, she represented the force of tradition in twentieth-century America— the tradition of the artist, the tradition of the pioneer, the tradition, eventually, of the universal church.

MORTON D. ZABEL

"Willa Cather:
The Tone of Time"

In 1927, at fifty-four, Willa Cather, after three decades of steady and patient labor in her craft, stood at the height of her career, with fifteen years of her best work behind her and her most popular book, *Death Comes for the Archbishop,* claiming an unstinted admiration. When she died twenty years later,[1] she had already come to appear as the survivor of a distant generation, remote from the talents and problems of the past two anxious decades. This estrangement was no surprise to her. It was of her own choice and election. In 1936, in prefacing her collection of essays then called *Not Under Forty,* she admitted that her writing could have "little interest for people under forty years of age." "The world broke in two in 1922 or thereabouts," she said, and it was to "the backward, and by one of their number," that she addressed her later books. She had, in fact, so addressed her work ever since she first found her real bearings in authorship with *O Pioneers!* in 1913. Backwardness was with her not only a

From *Craft and Character in Modern Fiction* (New York, 1957), copyright 1940, 1947 by Morton Dauwen Zabel. Reprinted by permission of The Viking Press, Inc. The essay is based on two pieces that appeared in the *Nation,* the first in 1940 and the second in 1947.

[1] On April 24, 1947. The date of Willa Cather's birth, long recorded as 1876, was discovered by E. K. Brown and Leon Edel in their biography of her (1953) to have been December 7, 1873. Her book of essays, *Not Under Forty,* was retitled *Literary Encounters* when she included it in her collected edition in 1937.

matter of her material and temperament. It was the condition of her existence as an artist.

She was one of the last in a long line of commemorators and elegists of American innocence and romantic heroism that virtually dates from the beginnings of a conscious native artistry in American literature. Her books, once she found her natural voice and métier, and once she had put aside her Eastern subjects and earlier themes of rebellious protest, had become elegies, and Irving, Cooper, Hawthorne, Mark Twain, and Sarah Orne Jewett figure in their ancestry. When, on rare occasions, she praised her fellow-craftsmen, from Miss Jewett to Katherine Mansfield, Thornton Wilder, or Thomas Mann (who "belongs immensely to the forward-goers. . . . But he also goes back a long way, and his backwardness is more gratifying to the backward"), it was usually because they also turned to the past and rooted their values there.[2]

She was quite aware of the false and bogus uses to which the historic sentiment had been put in American fiction. Its products surrounded her in the early 1900s when she was feeling her way toward her career: "machine-made historical novels," "dreary dialect stories," "very dull and heavy as clay"—books by John Fox, Jr., James Lane Allen, Mary Johnston, and their successful competitors, the memory of which today she likened to "taking a stroll through a World's Fair grounds some years after the show

[2] This sympathy in Willa Cather was confirmed in the last years of her life in a project she did not live to complete: "to place the setting of a story straight across the world, quite far into the past—leaving America entirely—in the setting of medieval Avignon." She was "no longer at any pains to conceal her disillusion and aversion to most of the life about her." An account of this project has recently been given by George N. Kates in "Willa Cather's Unfinished Avignon Story," in *Five Stories* by Willa Cather (New York: Vintage Books, 1956). Mr. Kates says further of this story, whose title was to be *Hard Punishments*: "Willa Cather reached first for the stars over the pure air of Nebraska, and then, when their light became obscured, would accept nothing less beautiful in their place simply because it was American." Also: "Like many people of plain origins, her first great need had been to be reassured, to still the youthful panic of seeming to possess only an inferior brand of everything that her more fortunate brothers and sisters took as naturally theirs. This was a prime need; but she had conquered it in her own way, which was the way of genius."

is over." She knew Miss Jewett shone like a star in that lustreless company; that Henry James's "was surely the keenest mind any American had ever devoted to the art of fiction"; that Stephen Crane "had done something real." She also had to learn the secret of their distinction the hard way: she came out of the West at-tracted by the prairie girl's mirage of the East—its cities, salons, opera houses, studios, Beacon Hill sanctities, the fever and ex-citement of New York, the lure of Atlantic liners, with the shrines of Europe beyond. Her early stories, many never collected in her books, are full of this worshipful glamour, and she was past thirty-five when she tried to make something of it in her first novel, which combined a problem out of Edith Wharton, a setting and something of a manner out of Henry James, and an outsider's clumsiness in handling them, with inevitable results in self-con-scious stiffness and crudity of tone.

Only then did she remember the advice Sarah Orne Jewett had once given her: "The thing that teases the mind over and over for years, and at last gets itself put down on paper—whether little or great, it belongs to Literature." "Otherwise," as Miss Jewett had also said, "what might be strength in a writer is only crudeness, and what might be insight is only observation; senti-ment falls to sentimentality—you can write about life, but never life itself." Willa Cather put Beacon Hill and Bohemia behind her. She returned to Nebraska, to a prairie town trying hard not to be blown away in the blast of a winter wind. She found the local habitation of her talent, and her serious career in art be-gan.

From that point she began her journey into lost time, going back beyond Nebraska, Colorado, and Kansas to colonial New Mexico, to eighteenth-century Quebec, and finally to the pre-Civil War Virginia of her family, every step taking her deeper into the values and securities she set most store by. She had, to help her, her rediscovered devotion to the scenes of her early youth, the Western fields and skies she called "the grand passion of my life," her brilliant gift for rendering landscape and weather in the closest approximation to the poetic art of Turgenev and Gogol our fiction has seen, her retentive sympathy with the life of farms, small towns, prairie settlements, immigrant colonies, and Southwestern outposts and missions. In all the tales of regional America that have been produced in the past forty years nothing has exceeded her skill in evoking the place-spirit of rural America in her finest books—*My Antonia, A Lost Lady, The Professor's House,* and *Death Comes for the Archbishop.*

The pathos of distance by which she induced her special poetry into these scenes was, of course, stimulated by her feeling that the inspiring landscape of the prairies, deserts, and mountains, no less than the gracious charms of colonial Virginia or old New York, had been obliterated by a vulgar and cheapening modernity. The garage that now stands on Charles Street in Boston on the site of the house where Mrs. James T. Fields had once held court to "Learning and Talent" was symptomatic for Willa Cather of a general and humiliating degradation. So the old wagon roads of the West, "roads of Destiny" that "used to run like a wild thing across the open prairie," had been resurveyed and obliterated to make highways for tourist and motor traffic. The railways once "dreamed across the mountains" by a race of Titans, highways in the heroic conquest of the West, were streamlined for commuters between New York and California. Wooden houses and piazza'd mansions, once landmarks of pioneer fortitude and hospitality, came down and suburban Tudor or sham Château went up in their place. The frontier universities that had once fostered a scholarship of vision and historical passion yielded to academic power plants thick with politics and careerism. She despised such a world, whose literature itself she saw as mere statistics and "sensory stimuli," and apparently she preferred to be despised by it.

The interesting thing about Miss Cather's career is that it started in protest against and flight from the very world she ended by idealizing and mourning. It recapitulates a characteristic American pattern of rebellion and return, censure and surrender. The prairie and small town, the Western hinterland and the neighborly community, as she presented them in her best early stories—"A Wagner Matinee," "Paul's Case," "The Sculptor's Funeral," "A Death in the Desert"—were objects of a moral reproach and castigation as severe as anything she later directed against the vulgarizing influences of the modern world. She was, indeed, a pioneer in the twentieth-century "revolt from the village," and she spared no scorn in describing the provincial spirit. It had created the life of a "dunghill," of petty existences, of "little people" and a small humanity, of stingy hates and warping avarice that made generous spirits shrivel and ardent natures die. The savagery of her indictment was perhaps the strongest passion she ever summoned in any of her works. Her frontier in those days was not the West; it was the East and the world of art, with desire the goad of her heroes and heroines and the running theme of her stories, as much as it was of Dreiser's.

It was in young artists—the dreaming, headstrong, fractious, or unstable young, fated to defeat or bad ends by the materialism and ugliness of their surroundings—that she first envisaged the heroic ideal. Paul, Katharine Gaylord, Harvey Merrick, and Don Hedger are the defeated or dishonored "cases" that foreshadow the triumphant lives of Alexandra Bergson, Thea Kronborg, Ántonia Shimerda, Archbishop Machebeuf, and Nancy Till, and that lend their note of desire or vision to the middle terms of Miss Cather's argument—the inspired spirits who do not succeed but who, by some force of character or apartness of nature, lend significance to the faceless anonymity around them. These characters—the "lost lady" Marian Forrester, Myra Henshawe, Tom Outland, Professor St. Peter, even the slighter Lucy Gayheart in a later novel—are the most persuasive of Miss Cather's creations, her nearest claims to skill in a field where she was admittedly and obviously incompetent—complex and credible psychology. But somehow she could never bring her opposites into full play in a novel. They remained irreconcilably differentiated, dramatically hostile, morally and socially incapable of true complexity.

The full-bodied and heavily documented novel was never congenial to Miss Cather; she rightly understood her art to be one of elimination and selection, which eventually meant that it was an art of simplification and didactic idealization. *The Song of the Lark* and *One of Ours* drag with detail. *My Ántonia* and *A*

Lost Lady are her finest successes because there her selection defines, suggests, and evokes without falsely idealizing. When she seized a theme of genuine social and moral potentiality in *The Professor's House* or *My Mortal Enemy,* she pared away its substance until she produced what must always be, to her admirers, disappointingly frugal and bodiless sketches of two of the most interesting subjects in the America of her time. And when she decided to model *Death Comes for the Archbishop* on the pallid two-dimensional murals of Puvis de Chavannes, she prepared the way for the disembodied idealization, making for inertness and passivity, that overtook her in *Shadows on the Rock,* weakest of her books and portent of the thinness of her final volumes.

What overtook her plots and characters is the same thing that overtook her version of American life and history. She could not bring her early criticism into effective combination with her later nostalgic sentiment. She represents a case analogous to that of Van Wyck Brooks, who started by vigorously but disproportionately castigating American literature, and has ended in a sentimentalization equally unbalanced and simplistic. So Miss Cather, having never mastered the problem of desire in its full social and moral conditioning, passed from her tales of ambitious artists and defeated dreamers, worsted by provincial mediocrity or careerism, to versions of American idealism and its defeat that never come to satisfactory grips with the conditions of society and personal morality. As her lovers, her artists, her pioneers, and her visionary Titans become disembodied of complex emotion or thought, so her America itself became disembodied of its principles of growth, conflict, and historical maturity. There obviously worked in her nature that "poetic romanticism" to which Lionel Trilling has referred her case: what Parrington called "the inferiority complex of the frontier mind before the old and established"; the pioneer's fear of failure but greater fear of the success which comes "when an idea becomes an actuality"; the doctrine of American individualism to which F. J. Turner credited the pioneer's failure to "understand the richness and complexity of life as a whole." So to Willa Cather's early veneration for the distant goals and shining trophies of desire, ambition, and art, there succeeded a veneration for lost or distant sanctities which gradually spelled her diminution as a dramatic and poetic craftsman. The village, the prairie, the West, the New Mexican missions thus became in time abstractions as unworkable, in any critical or moral sense, as her simplified understanding of Mann's Joseph cycle. Art itself, in her versions of Flaubert, Gogol, Mann, or Katherine Mansfield, took on a remote ideality and aesthetic pathos that do much to explain her distaste for Dostoevsky or Chekhov. And the Church, to which she finally appealed as a human and historical constant, became in her unimplicated and inexperienced view of it the most abstract of all her conceptions, a cultural symbol, not a human or historical actuality, and the least real of any of the standards she invoked in her judgments and criticism of the modern world.

She defended her art in an essay, "The Novel Démeublé," in 1922, which belongs among the theorizings by artists which constituted for Henry James an "accident" which is "happiest, I think, when it is soonest over." At best, it shows Miss Cather's temerity in venturing into "the dim wilderness of theory"; at its worst it must be taken as one of those ventures which justify themselves only because they tell what a restricted view of art some writers must impose on themselves in order to get their own kind of work done. In 1922 it had some value as a warning against the excesses of realism and documentation in fiction, as a preference for feeling and insight over "observation" and "description." But when it went on to assert that Balzac's material—not merely Paris and its houses but "the game of pleasure, the game of business, the game of finance"—is "unworthy of an artist," that the banking system and Stock Exchange are scarcely "worth being written about at all," and that "the higher processes of art are all processes of simplification," it set Miss Cather down as an aesthetic fundamentalist whose achievement was bound, by the nature of her beliefs, to be sharply curtailed and inhibited. She stood by the essay; she reprinted it unmodified in her later editions. And there it shows, *post factum,* how little a principle of deliberate simplification can serve its believer if he is also an artist. Willa Cather set up a standard directly opposed to Zola's program of naturalism—and similarly deluding and disabling in its literalness and crudity. For both sensibility and naturalism arrive at the same impasse when they deny art its right to richness of thought and complexity. What such principles limit is not merely craftsmanship; it is subject-matter itself. Miss Cather saw as little as Zola did that to inhibit craftsmanship or content is to inhibit or starve the sensibility and insight that nourish them, and to arrive at the sterility of high-mindedness and the infirmity of an ideal. It is artists who have denied their art and theory no possible risk, challenge, or complexity who have arrived at the surer lease on creative life; it is to James and Conrad, to Yeats, Eliot, and Valéry, that we turn, in their theory no less than in their practice, for the more responsible clues to endurance and authority in modern literature.

Yet it was by such means of simplification, discipline, curtailment, that Willa Cather made her achievement possible and wrote the books of her best years—books which, if essentially minor in substance, are wholly her own, and if elegiac in their version of American history, revive a past that was once, whatever its innocence, a reality, and that required, in its own delusions as much as in the versions of it she created, the correction and resistance of a later realism. The boy who told the story of *My Ántonia*, finding himself transported from Virginia to the prairies of Nebraska, said: "I had the feeling that the world was left behind, that we had got over the edge of it, and were outside man's jurisdiction. I have never before looked up at the sky when there was not a familiar mountain ridge against it." For thirty years Willa Cather found her clue to the heroic values of life in that Western world of open plains and pioneer struggle, lying, with its raw earth, untested possibilities, and summons to heroic endeavor, beyond the familiar jurisdiction of codes and laws. But when, in her last novel, *Sapphira and the Slave Girl* in 1940, she at last turned back, for the first time in her literary career, from Nebraska to the Virginia of her birth and earliest memories, to a country of older laws and severer customs—to Back Creek Valley west of the Blue Ridge and to the house of Henry Colbert, the miller, and his wire Sapphira, a Dodderidge of Loudon County—she brought the air of the more primitive Western world into it, the insistence on primary or primitive emotion.

The story offered the familiar features of her Western books —there is the retreat to the past, now 1856, when human dignity and honor were not yet outlawed by the confused motives and vulgar comforts of modern times; there is the idealizing pathos of distance and lost beauty; there is an epilogue that brings the story twenty-five years nearer—but only to 1881—when time has dissolved old conflicts, relaxed old tensions, and healed old wounds by its touch of grace and humility. There is a stoic husband, asking no questions of an unkind destiny. There is an imperious wife who finds herself exiled in the rough country over the Blue Ridge as earlier heroines like Marian Forrester and Myra Henshawe were exiled in the rough country of the West, self-confounded by her pride and fear of truth, defeating herself rather than allow victory or happiness to others. There is also a young girl, the Negro slave Nancy, on whom Sapphira vents her defeat and jealousy, another embodiment of the spirit of youth and natural grace which had already appeared in Alexandra, Thea, Ántonia, Tom Outland, and Lucy Gayheart—the pure in heart whom no evil can defeat wholly and on whom Miss Cather fixed for her faith in character in an age of warring egotisms and debasing ambition.

Willa Cather thus risked not only a repetition of characters and effects in which her expertness had already passed from mastery to formulation. She duplicated her matter and her pathos so narrowly as to make unavoidable the sensation that what was once a sincere and valid theme had been subjected to a further attenuation of sentimental argument and special pleading. This effect was emphasized by the insistent plainness and simplicity of manner to which she adhered—that conscious simplicity, fiction most decidedly and stubbornly *démeublé*, which at times (in *My Ántonia* and *A Lost Lady* particularly) she raised to a point of conviction and lyric poignance that must remain her one indisputable achievement as an artist, but which on other occasions (*One of Ours, Shadows on the Rock*) she permitted to lapse either into a kind of didactic dullness of sobriety or into a sentimentality that begs the whole question of creating and substantiating character by means of words, sensation, and observed detail.

Her devotion to the past and its perished beauty was sincere but inevitably limited by a didactic principle and threatened by the inflexibility of an idealistic convention. Only when her sentiment was toughened by personal or atmospheric realism did she bring off her pathos successfully, and only when her idealism was grounded in a hard sense of physical and regional fact was she able to avoid banality and abstraction. To reread the whole of her work is to realize how deliberately she accepted her risks and limitations in order to win her prizes. It is to see that the subtlety and scope of her themes—*The Professor's House* remains the most significant case—could readily fail to find the structure and substance that might have given them life or redeemed them from the tenuity of a sketch. It is to realize that her novels reduce to a single motive and pattern whose sincerity is undeniable but rudimentary and which eventually becomes threadbare. But it is also to admit, finally, that in her best work Willa Cather brought to a kind of climax and genuine epic vision the work of the American women who preceded her—Rose Terry Cooke, Sarah Jewett, Mrs. Freeman—and that she sublimated to its elements a conception of pioneer life and native energy which in other hands has generally lapsed into vulgar romanticism and the more blatant kinds of American eloquence.

It was her honesty and persistence in rendering this quality that made possible her real contribution to contemporary, and to American, writing. She defined, like Dreiser, Scott Fitzgerald, and a few other of her contemporaries between 1910 and 1930, a sense of proportion in American experience. She knew what it meant to be raised in the hinterland of privation and harsh necessities; knew what it meant to look for escape to Chicago and the world beyond; knew how much has to be fought in one's youth and origins, what the privileges of the richer world mean when they are approached from the outposts of life, what has to be broken away from and what has to be returned to for later nourishment, and how little the world appears when its romantic distances and remote promise are curtailed to the dimensions of the individual destiny. This sense of tragic limitation forms the saving leaven of realism and moral necessity in Dreiser's novels; Scott Fitzgerald gave superb expression to the experience in the last eight pages of *The Great Gatsby* and in *Tender Is the Night*; Katherine Anne Porter has given another and classic version of it in her work. Willa Cather unquestionably had something to do with preserving for such artists that proportion and perspective in American experience.

The space of seventy years is too short in human history, even in modern history, to permit anyone to claim that he saw the world break in two during it. The measure of the human fate is not to be calculated so conveniently, even in a century of disturbance like the twentieth, and least of all in the moral perspective to which the artist or serious moralist must address himself. To do so is to impose a personal sentiment on something too large to contain it. It was to such sentiment, with its attendant didacticism and inflexibility, that Willa Cather came to submit. But it must also be granted that she lived through a cleavage and a crisis in something more than American life; that she saw "the end of an era, the sunset of the pioneer"; that it "was already gone, that age; nothing could ever bring it back"; and she defined the pathos, if not the challenge and moral imperative, its passing imposed on every survivor and writer concerned with it. She did not succeed in surmounting the confines of her special transition and the resentment it induced in her, and she did not write the kind of books that assure the future or the energy of a literature. That opportunity she consciously rejected. Talents who came after her have written books that surpass hers in conflict and comprehension, as in difficulty and courage—*The Enormous Room, The Sun Also Rises, Tender Is the Night, None Shall Look Back, All The King's Men, A Curtain of Green* and *Delta Wedding, Flowering Judas* and *Pale Horse, Pale Rider, The Sound and the Fury* and *Light in August*. Yet she did something in a time of distraction and cultural inflation to make the way clear for them, as much by the end she defined for one tradition as by the example of tenacity and personal scruple she set for herself. No one who read her books between 1915 and 1930 can forget their poetry of evocation and retrospective beauty—no sensitive reader can miss it today—particularly if he shared, as most Americans have shared, whether intimately or by inheritance, any part of the experience that went into their making. And Willa Cather also did something the aspirant to permanent quality rarely achieves: she wrote a few books—*My Antonia* and *A Lost Lady* chief among them—that are not only American elegies but American classics, and that can still tell us, in a time of sanctified journalism and irresponsible sophistication, how much of a lifetime it costs to make that rare and expensive article.

VI

THEMATIC AND MYTHIC
CRITICISM: RECENT VIEWS

THE pieces of criticism included in this chapter have at least
one point in common: they have all been published very recently.
Apart from that, it is hard to generalize about them, although
two or three more tentative and more interesting generalizations
can probably be ventured.

One is that some of the essays included here and most of the
recent articles on Willa Cather not included here seem to aim
modestly at the minor. For example, a few years ago *American
Literature* published an article, a good one, about Willa Cather's
uncollected stories. Later another critic wrote a long study of
Willa Cather's 1903 poems. Without much question, the uncollected stories and the 1903 poems are among the least readable
works Willa Cather published. Another group of recent studies,
while dealing with undeniably major works, have dealt with undeniably minor topics, for instance music in *My Antonia*,
with the derivation of certain names, with sources of certain
allusions in the stories, rather than with anything that could possibly be considered a pivotal critical issue.

The reason for this tendency is fairly obvious. It follows from
the enormous proliferation of literary studies of all kinds, and
the need or desire on the part of late-arriving critics to discover
some area which is relatively uninhabited. But compared to

most of the literary figures scholars have been exploring for the past fifteen or twenty years—Melville, James, Faulkner— Willa Cather is a very small critical backwater. The process euphemistically referred to as "specialization" has had little need to be carried far in her case. There is no Willa Cather "industry," and there are still significant questions to be scouted; but perhaps because the minor, specialized, and delimited has become something of a fashion or habit for article writers there is a noticeable trend, even in Willa Cather criticism, to look for nooks, corners, and dusty places.

A second and in some ways opposite characteristic of the newest criticism is its interest in broad thematic questions. Mostly these have to do with Willa Cather's depiction of, or arguments for, certain values and ideas: for instance, the value of the urban versus the bucolic life, the past versus the present, the East versus the West, American civilization versus European, an ordered versus a frontier society—contrasts which have to do in some way with ideal civilizations. It has been recognized generally for at least thirty or forty years that civilizational ideals play a crucial role in Willa Cather, much as in Henry James; but the novelty of the recent criticism is that it has not subordinated its thematic investigation to evaluation. Critics in the twenties and thirties were occupied with assessing Willa Cather's talent, gauging its strength, weakness, scope, and limits. They wanted to determine which novels were good. Those of the thirties and forties were occupied with assessing the drift of her development, and evaluating her place in American literature. They wanted to compare her with other writers of her time. By and large the concern with her "themes" and "ideas" was incidental in these earlier essays, and merely a way of getting at some other issue. But recent criticism, which has engaged in a detailed investigation of themes, has done so independently. John H. Randall's *The Landscape and the Looking Glass* (1960) is a good example.

Almost inevitably, the thematic approach works in close harmony with, and depends on, a symbolic approach. Willa Cather is seldom so inartistic as to announce that "the country is preferable to the city." Instead, nearly all of her abstract propositions remain, as Joseph Wood Krutch rather chemically put it, in "suspension," without being allowed to "crystallize." The suspension is for the most part a complex and often poetic structure of symbols, working on the levels of character, incident and image. Consequently the critic who wants to crystallize Miss Cather's ideas must go through some process of converting her structures into symbols, often doing violence to her writing in the process but sometimes arriving at insights. The original insights into Willa Cather have been reached recently by such a pairing of theme and symbol, especially using "clusters" of images taken from different parts of her work—a black plow outlined against the sun, an image of red grass, of yellow wheat—as in the fashionable Shakespeare criticism of the past decade.

The most noteworthy brand of the thematic-symbolic criticism comes in what is now often called "mythic" or "archetypal" criticism. It is impossible and probably silly to try to date the beginning of this kind of criticism; but it is possible to say that about fiften years ago a number of pieces of writing, including Richard Chase's *The Quest for Myth* (1949), Henry Nash Smith's *Virgin Land: The American West as Symbol and Myth* (1950), and an unexpectedly seminal article in *The Kenyon Review* by Northrop Frye, "The Archetypes of Literature" (1951), all proved influential in bringing about a certain direction in criticism. These writers were trained differently and were trying to do different things—Chase, a literary critic, to connect literature and myth; Smith, a historian, to connect American history and American literature; and Frye, a critical theorist, to draw up an ambitious program for a new literary criticism. But they all helped to draw attention to the power of myth as a key to literature, or to the power of the mythic elements in literature as keys to an understanding of the processes of history.

The "mythic" and "archetypal" criticism has spread rapidly. About five years ago Philip Young, a Hemingway critic who is himself a proponent and practitioner of mythic criticism, rather assertively declared before a national gathering of professors of English that the New Criticism was dead and mythic criticism had taken its place. He may have underestimated the importance of the New Criticism and exaggerated the importance of the mythic, but without much question mythic criticism is the only recognizable "school" of criticism today with a program, young disciples, a vocabulary and the power, like Marxist criticism of the thirties, to provoke quarrels.

The head of the movement and the inventor of the term "archetypal criticism" is Northrop Frye, who is interested in developing criticism into a "science" which, like astronomy or sociology, would grandly transcend mere differences of language and locality. But there are local branches, including an American branch, which has developed out of American Studies, and which finds its chief organ of expression in *The American Quarterly*. The originator of the key terms and concepts of the purely American mythic criticism is Henry Nash Smith, who explains in *Virgin Land* that the image of a "vast and constantly growing agricultural society in the interior of the continent became one of the dominant symbols of nineteenth-century American society —a collective representation, a poetic idea that defined the promise of American life," and which he is able to trace in detail as a controlling idea from Cooper's Leatherstocking tales to Frederick Jackson Turner's "The Significance of the Frontier in American History"—all of them expressions of what Smith calls the "Garden of the World myth." The notion has been a persuasive one and seems to have given rise to dozens of similar and competitive studies "fusing symbol and myth"—most notably R. W. B. Lewis' *The American Adam* (1955) (although Mr. Lewis explains that he did not see Smith's study until his own was near completion). Lewis' book in turn has been influential, and the sheer volume of materials generated from it and Smith's has been of such a magnitude as to suggest almost the creation of a new branch of studies.

It is significant that both the major critical books about Willa Cather which have appeared in the sixties, John Randall's *The Landscape and the Looking Glass* and Edward and Lillian Bloom's *Willa Cather's Gift of Sympathy* (1962), have been in the mythic tradition. John Randall acknowledges his debt to Smith and to Leo Marx, a student of Smith and author of *The Machine in the Garden* (1965); and he draws rather heavily on Smith's notion that the "garden of the world" was the controlling American myth. Randall's book has chapter headings and subheadings with such titles as "The Establishment of the Garden" and "The Fruition of the Soil: the Garden of the World." Perhaps the most important influence on Randall, however, was Smith's persistent dialectical opposition of "civilized" versus "frontier" values, which Randall takes over and applies to Willa Cather both as a matter of method and as his central issue. The Blooms are also concerned with the confrontation of the values of the frontier and of civilization in Willa Cather. "Fundamentally, we have concluded that she was interested in three major themes," they wrote in their introduction. These were "the spirit of the frontier in both modern and ancient times; the threat to that spirit in the encroachments of materialism and selfish acquisitiveness; and the nature of the artist." But the Blooms arrived at their conclusion differently, over a period of many years. As early as 1949, before the publication of *Virgin Land,* they had published an article in *American Literature,* "Willa Cather's Novels of the Frontier: A Study in Thematic Symbolism," the first of the "thematic-symbolic" treatments of Willa Cather, and they followed this with another study, "Willa Cather's Novels of the Frontier: the Symbolic Function of 'Machine-Made Materialism,' " in 1950. Their book is largely a refinement and extension of these early articles.

A number of the following pieces, including those by Howard Mumford Jones and Bernice Slote, are varieties of mythic criticism; but they were not chosen to represent that approach. They were chosen as pieces that deal individually with interesting works or groups of works by Willa Cather. Thus we have the Blooms on *Death Comes for the Archbishop,* John Randall on *My Ántonia,* my own essay on *The Professor's House,* Howard Mumford Jones on the stories, Bernice Slote on the poetry. The choice of works was based on what seemed likely to be of most use to the reader; but the choice also reflects the tendency of modern criticism to deal with individual works, and the tendency of the modern critic to take the book as his unit rather than—as in older criticism—the *oeuvre,* the "middle period," or some such thing.

HOWARD MUMFORD JONES

Excerpt from *The Bright Medusa*

In the myth, Medusa was divinely beautiful, but when she violated the sanctity of the temple, she was punished by acquiring the beauty of terror, so much so that whoever looked upon her was turned to stone. Perseus, using his shield as a mirror, so that he looked upon only the reflection of her face, broke the spell. Let us not forget, however, that from the blood of Medusa, Pegasus was born. Only by the death of horror do we come to the horses of inspiration.

The stories which make up *Youth and the Bright Medusa*, seven in number, were written between 1903 and 1920. The best known of them is "Paul's Case," a memorable study of adolescence, illness, obsession with music, the theater, and luxury, and of moral degeneration and eventual suicide. But I shall content myself with some of the others, despite the excellence of this better known narrative. In all these stories the accent is on youth, and the bright Medusa represents the fascination of art, or at least of aesthetic experience, as this works its havoc or its charm. Again and again, tension in these tales arises from the conflict between the desire of the artist to pursue beauty and the necessity of the craftsman, if he is to live, to make some practical adjustment to the workaday world.

Excerpted from the chapters "The Artist" and "The Poet" in *The Bright Medusa* (Urbana, Ill., 1952); reprinted by permission of the University of Illinois Press. This discussion of Miss Cather's stories is part of a longer thesis: that the important books of the twenties "tend to concentrate upon the self as the measure of value,"—a "special self," the artist as autonomous poet. Professor Jones's complete analysis of course is better than any one of its parts.

An early story is called "The Sculptor's Funeral," dated 1903, a sketch not much beyond the range of a bright literary under-graduate. The theme is the conflict between beauty and reality. A sculptor named Merrick has left the little Kansas village where he was born, gone East, made a success, and died young. Now his disciple, one Steavens, is bringing the body home. Steavens says of his master—and the language is significant—that what-ever he touched revealed its holiest secret. The funeral trip is Steavens' first venture into the hinterland, here represented by a raw, ugly, ignorant community in Kansas. He is horrified by the banality of Merrick's home and by the vicious gossip among members and friends of the sculptor's family, none of whom has any comprehension of the life of the free spirit in art.

The climax comes when a drunken lawyer pours his scorn upon his fellow townsmen in a fashion anticipatory of *Main Street*, a book not to be published for seventeen years. The lawyer and the sculptor had gone to school together, each had resolved to make something of himself, but Merrick, by going away, had ful-filled his ideal, whereas the lawyer had remained and succumbed to pettiness. "I came back here to practise," he rages,

and I found you didn't in the least want me to be a great man. . . . I . . . became the damned shyster you wanted me to be. You pretend to have some sort of respect for me, and yet you'll stand up and throw mud at Harvey Merrick, whose soul you couldn't dirty and whose hands you couldn't tie. . . . Now that we've fought and lied and sweated and stolen and hated as only the disappointed strugglers in a bitter, dead little Western town know how to do, what have we got to show for it?

The last glimpse vouchsafed us of the dead sculptor's face shows him "still guarding something precious."

Obviously this is 'prentice work, which offers very little new. The drabness and cruelty of American village life had furnished a theme for Ed Howe's *Story of a Country Town* in 1883, and the escape of aesthetic youth into the city had been in part the theme of Garland's *Rose of Dutcher's Coolly* in 1895. The law-yer's speech is heavy-handed. But it is for that very reason revealing. The story is at once a passionate defense of youth and art, which keep from others "something precious," and a passionate denunciation of American domesticity and of small-town democracy. Merrick's death is immaterial; what matters is Merrick's life, dedicated to self-fulfillment. That life represented the revolt of youth in the service of art against customary culture. Merrick had never, as Scott Fitzgerald would say, become "really insincere."

This theme is more subtly treated in the latest story of the volume, one entitled, "Coming, Aphrodite!" This is mature, even though the central episode sounds a bit ridiculous in the telling; and in order to get the ridicule out of the way, let me say that it concerns a young man staring every afternoon through a knothole in his bedroom closet at a naked young woman doing exercises in the next apartment. The fact that Miss Cather raises this episode from the vulgarity of voyeurism to beauty shows how she had developed between 1903 and 1920.

The tale concerns one Hedger, a painter, living in a ramshackle apartment house in Washington Square. Into the adjoining apartment moves Edna, or Eden, Bower, already on the road to becoming a successful opera singer. She has come to New York to stay until a wealthy Chicagoan and his sister are ready to take her to Europe. Eden is vigorous, attractive, healthy, curious; and after some preliminary stages of irritation, Hedger falls in love with her, for, as he watches her naked body, it seems to his painter's eye, utterly beautiful. Their acquaintance ripens; and when she learns of his peeping, she is not offended. They go to Coney Island, where Eden once more irritates Hedger by substituting, on impulse, for a trapeze artist making a balloon ascension. Since part of the trick is that an evening gown shall fall from the shoulders of the trapeze artist, revealing a lady in tights, Hedger is again annoyed, but the annoyance leads into the love affair, which is happy and healthy and pagan.

However, Eden Bower is a musical performer on the make rather than a creator; and since she knows it takes money and backing to succeed in the concert world, she assumes the same conditions exist in the world of painting. When, therefore, she has wheedled a fashionable portrait painter into taking some notice of her lover, she is furious to discover that Hedger will have nothing to do either with the society racket or with commercialism. He rests content in his youthful integrity. They quarrel. He leaves, and when, remorseful, he returns, he discovers that Eden's wealthy patrons have carried her off to Europe, leaving him a memory, a dressing gown, and a letter.

What Miss Cather writes about Eden's childhood is pertinent to our theme:

People like Eden Bower are inexplicable. Her father sold farming machinery in Huntington, Illinois, and she had grown up with no acquaintance or experiences outside of that prairie town. Yet from her earliest childhood she had not one conviction or opinion in common with the people about her—the only people she knew. Before she was out of short dresses she had made up her mind that she was going to be an actress, that she would live far away in great cities, that she would be much admired by men and would have everything she wanted. When she was thirteen, and was already singing and reciting for church entertainments, she read in some illustrated magazine a long article about the late Tsar of Russia, then just come to the throne or about to come to it. After that, lying in the hammock on the front porch on summer evenings, or sitting through a long sermon in the family pew, she amused herself by trying to make up her mind whether she would or would not be the Tsar's mistress when she played in his capital. Now Edna had met this fascinating word only in the novels of Ouida—her hard-worked little mother kept a long row of them in the upstairs storeroom, behind the linen closet. In Huntington women who bore that relation to men were called by a very different name, and their lot was not an enviable one; of all the shabby and poor, they were the shabbiest. But then, Edna had never lived in Huntington, not even before she began to find books like "Sapho" and "Mademoiselle de Maupin" secretly sold in paper covers through Illinois. It was as if she had come into Huntington, into the Bower family, on one of the trains that puffed over the marshes behind their back fence all day long, and was waiting for another train to take her out.

You will note that in this passage the birth of an artist is inexplicable—that is, it is placed outside the ordinary chain of cause and effect.

In "The Sculptor's Funeral" Miss Cather's purpose was principally to indict. The village heretic there is merely a mouthpiece for the author, the dead sculptor is a stereotype, and his friend Steavens, through whose eyes the conflict between art and reality is revealed, is but the shadow of a shade. In "Coming, Aphrodite!" however, two human beings are fully studied in their strength and their weakness. Miss Cather does not manage the story, nor does she insist upon a moral. If, from Hedger's point of view, Eden betrays the high responsibility of the artist who must never compromise his vision, to Eden, Hedger is an obstinate, impatient, impractical young man with small sense of humor and no willingness to have fun. She cannot understand why he does not appreciate her lowering her own pride in order to wheedle a successful painter into looking at Hedger's work.

But though Miss Cather is apparently impartial, when we analyze what she tells us of Eden's childhood, we discover a deft indictment of American domesticity. Family life, village life are again represented as hostile to the artist. We read that Eden is inexplicable as a product of Huntington—as if the artist were somehow a miraculous creation. We learn that she and the community had not a single conviction or opinion in common. Her dream was, as soon as she could, to flee to the metropolis, to develop her personality, to be admired, and to escape vulgarity, especially the crass polarity of female types in the village—whores or wives. Her father sells farm machinery, her mother is hard-worked and hides naughty novels behind the linen closet. We learn nothing else about Eden's girlhood except that somehow or other she must have submitted to the discipline of music lessons, that she was bored on Sundays, and that, on long summer evenings, dreaming in the hammock, she thought a great deal was going to happen to her. The story concerns one of the earlier stages in her making things happen; and if Eden's adolescent notions of luxury are naïve, we must remember that her information was limited.

Yet, for all her seeming impartiality, Miss Cather makes one deadly comment when she writes that Eden "did not guess her neighbor [Hedger] would have more tempestuous adventures sitting in his dark studio than she would find in all the capitals of Europe, or in all the latitude of conduct that she was prepared to permit herself." If Miss Cather recognizes the validity of the revolt of youth in the name of art, she also insists upon an essential difference between the ethos of the artist—in this case, Hedger—and the ethos of the mere practitioner, or follower—in this case, Eden Bower. If life is to be lived experimentally, it makes a great deal of difference by whom the experiment is conducted. Unlike Fitzgerald, Miss Cather, in addition to dramatizing the revolt of youth in the name of art, evaluated as well the rebel personality.

Other stories in the collection concern the central conflict between the arts and the economic order; as, for example, the right of relatives to exploit a singer. But for richer treatment of the ambivalent lure of art one turns to her novels. The earliest, *Alexander's Bridge,* appeared in 1912. Bartley Alexander, a successful builder of bridges, comfortably married to a Boston wife and apparently happy, rediscovers on a solitary business trip to London that Hilda Burgoyne, the lost love of his youth, has become a mature and fascinating actress. Despite every effort of his moral will, he succumbs to the timeless promise, the immortal memory of youth and art. The climax comes with the simultaneous collapse of a bridge, built too near the safety margin, and of Alexander, who dies in the river, a victim of a similar error in the human equation. Hilda lives, on the whole enriched as an artist by suffering because she represents the autonomy of art. The story is in ten chapters and an epilogue; precisely at the end of the fifth chapter we find this tribute to universal Pan:

But Alexander was not thinking about his work. After the fourth night out [on the steamer taking him back to London], when his will suddenly softened under his hands, he had been continually hammering away at himself. More and more often, when he first awakened in the morning or when he stepped into a warm place after being chilled on the deck, he felt a sudden painful delight at being nearer another shore. Sometimes, when he was most despondent, when he thought himself worn out with this struggle, in a flash he was free of it and leaped into an overwhelming consciousness of himself. On the instant he felt that marvellous return of the impetuousness, the intense excitement, the increasing expectancy of youth.

In view of the pagan mysticism of this passage one almost expects Bartley to have sight of Proteus rising from the sea. He is the victim of the Dionysiac fascination, the Bacchic appeal, the illusion of youth, which create in him a new and overwhelming feeling of self, sensed in a series of mystical insights superior to his normal self and eventually controlling it.

Alexander's Bridge dwells upon the destructive powers of the bright Medusa, but in *The Song of the Lark* three years later Miss Cather reversed the legend and wrote a profound and subtle study of the growth into selfhood of a great artist, tracing the life of Thea Kronborg from her childhood in Moonstone, Colorado, to golden triumph as a Wagnerian singer at the Metropolitan. The title comes from Millet's painting, "The Song of the Lark," in the Chicago Art Institute, not from Thea's voice, and the picture is chiefly significant in the novel as a symbol of wordless communication between the peasant girl and the unseen singer in the sky. In a preface dated 1932 Miss Cather was unnecessarily apologetic about what she calls the descending curve of the story—that is, she argued that the life of the successful artist is less interesting than the life of a talented young girl making her way. Perhaps so. What I think more important is that she also points out she had reversed *The Picture of Dorian Gray* by Oscar Wilde. As Thea is more and more released into artistic fulfillment, her life as artist becomes more self-absorbed and her life as person grows less interesting. Only as artist is the happy, free, and real.

Certain basic elements in the story require analysis. One notes the assumption that there exists a secret community of persons capable of discovering and accepting instinctive values— a mystery cult of art, a fraternity of the initiate. Let us borrow a phrase from Schumann's famous piano piece and call this the *Davidsbündler*—the League of David against the Philistines.

Training does not bring one initiation, only temperament can do that. Thus Thea's vocal teacher does not "belong," whereas the Mexicans in Moonstone enjoy membership—visiting them, she found "there was no constraint of any kind . . . but a kind of natural harmony." As Wunsch, Thea's first teacher, tells her: "Some things cannot be taught. If you do not know in the beginning, you do not know in the end." Although Thea cannot communicate her deepest thoughts to the devoted pianist, Harsanyi, he understands her because he too was born a member of the *Davidsbündler*. He realizes that "one must take where and when one can the mysterious mental irritant that rouses one's imagination. . . . It is not to be had by order." The *Davidsbündler* is a race apart—Thea's birthright in it is symbolized by her acquiring a room of her own in the crowded household—and forms a natural league against the Philistines. As Thea tells her devoted admirer, Doctor Archie:

If you love the good thing you must hate the cheap thing just as hard. I tell you there is such a thing as creative hate! A contempt that drives you through fire, makes you risk everything and lose everything, makes you a long sight better than you ever knew you could be.

The section of the book in which Thea breaks with her family is entitled "Stupid Faces," and it is against the stupid faces of the world that the artist must rebel.

A second component is passion—not necessarily the passion of love, but will, strength, an unquenchable vitality that creates the self. That Thea possesses passion in this sense comes to her in successive revelations. When Wunsch first implies that she is destined for something better than Moonstone, she is shaken by a passion of excitement, she feels a kind of "warm sureness." She develops the will to effort, she overcomes difficulties without verbal comprehension of them, she lifts, as it were, weights greater than herself. After her first experience of symphonic music, a great rush of power floods her being, making her hands cold with excitement, and it seems to her a hostile world would like to rob her of this vitality, but, she meditates, "As long as she lived that ecstasy was going to be hers. She would live for it, work for it, die for it." At the end of the novel Harsanyi's comment is: "Her secret? It is every artist's secret . . . passion. That is all. It is an open secret, and perfectly safe. Like heroism, it is inimitable in cheap materials." And at the moment of her triumph as Sieglinde: "Not for nothing has she kept it so severely, kept it filled with such energy and fire. All that deep-rooted vitality flowered in her voice, in her very finger-tips. She felt like a tree bursting into bloom."

But the vitality is expendable, the tree must have its roots and sap. Nourishment of the artist's self depends upon an intermingling of the senses and the soul. This neither conventional ethics nor Philistine psychology can ever comprehend. The sensuous renewal comes to Thea at intervals, but never more importantly than in Part IV, entitled "The Ancient People," when she goes out to an Arizona canyon near an abandoned cliff-dwelling. Note how, in the introductory paragraph, Miss Cather sets the stage for this part of the story, insisting upon selfhood, incommunicability, and the healing power of an ancient, chthonic way of life:

The San Francisco Mountain lies in northern Arizona, above Flagstaff, and its blue slopes and snowy summit entice the eye for a hundred miles across the desert. About its base lie the pine forests of the Navajos, where the great red-trunked trees live out their peaceful centuries in that sparkling air. The piñons and scrub begin only where the forest ends, where the country breaks into open, stony clearings, and the surface of the earth cracks into deep canyons. The great pines stand at a considerable distance from each other. Each tree grows alone, murmurs alone, thinks alone. They do not obtrude upon each other. The Navajos are not much in the habit of giving or of asking help. Their language is not a communicative one, and they never attempt an interchange of personality in speech. Over their forests there is the same inexorable reserve. Each tree has its exalted power to bear.

Into this silence Thea Kronborg comes from her struggle in the city, and there she learns the last secret of selfhood and of art. She had got back to the earliest sources of gladness that she could remember—the sun, the brilliant sand, the sky, the night.

Slowly music comes to her as sensuous form rather than something to be struggled with. Her power of thought ceases to be intellection or communication, it is converted "into a power of sustained sensation. She could become a mere receptacle for heat . . . or . . . color . . . or a continuous repetition of sound." In this fallow mood her love affair with Fred Ottenberg, who is married, though Thea does not know it at the time, is merely part of the world of sense and soul, so that what might have broken a Philistine is for her an increment. The last secret is this:

The stream and the broken pottery: what was any art but an effort to make a sheath, a mould in which to imprison for a moment the shining, elusive element which is life itself—life hurrying past us and running away, too strong to stop, too sweet to lose? The Indian women had held it in their jars. In the sculpture she had seen in the Art Institute, it had been caught in a flash of arrested motion. In singing one made a vessel of one's throat and nostrils and held it on one's breath, caught the stream in a scale of natural intervals.

Much earlier in the story Thea had had a foreshadowing of this experience, when, as she lay in her hard-won little room, "life rushed in upon her through that window—or so it seemed," but, comments Miss Cather,

In reality, life rushes from within, not from without. There is no work of art so big or so beautiful that it was not once all contained in some youthful body like this one which lay on the floor in the moonlight, pulsing with ardor and anticipation.

so, in her fulfilling time, in the ancient canyons of Arizona, youth and art to Thea Kronborg become timeless and one thing, for the paradoxical reason that youth is translated out of time into form and energy.

Finally, the completed act of art is a completed act of truth. Neither Thea nor her creator can tell us the way by which she comes to truth, all they can tell us is that she finds it and unshakably knows she has found it. The story of her musical education—that is, of the development of the artist into maturity—is a chronicle of the inadequacy of words to communicate meaning. Wunsch finds in her "something unconscious and unawakened," but he cannot touch her with speech. She is unable to talk to Harsanyi, largely because of this doctrine of the secret—something to be guarded against the Philistines. Miss Cather writes of her:

Hitherto she had felt but one obligation toward [her genius]—secrecy; to protect it even from herself. She had always believed that by doing all that was required of her by her family, her teachers, her pupils, she kept that part of herself from being caught up in the meshes of common things. . . . It was as if she had an appointment to meet the rest of herself sometime, somewhere.

Once, singing for Harsanyi, she sings wrong, he tries to correct her, he gets nowhere, and then suddenly light dawns, and Harsanyi meditates:

He had often noticed that she could not think a thing out in passages. Until she saw it as a whole, she wandered like a blind man surrounded by torments. After she once had her "revelation," after she had got the idea that to her—not always to him—explained everything, then she went forward rapidly. But she was not always easy to help.

Yet at the very end of the novel Miss Cather's comment is:

Artistic growth is, more than anything else, a refining of the sense of truthfulness. The stupid believe that to be truthful is easy; only the artist, the great artist knows how difficult it is.

Whether this organicism, this nonrational approach (one scarcely knows whether to call it suprarational or subrational) be sound or socially right—it has embarrassing relations to the doctrine of thinking with one's blood—there is an eternal contradiction between artistic truth arrived at by instinct and revelation, and the truth of a world in which analysis and computation—the slide rule, the butcher's scale, the bank balance, the chemist's analysis—are paramount.

If Miss Cather's subtle study of the development of youth into art antedates and diminishes *This Side of Paradise,* it is a commonplace of literary history that *The Song of the Lark* in turn had its predecessors—Robert Herrick's *The Common Lot* (1904), a study of an architect; Theodore Dreiser's *Sister Carrie* (1900), in which a huge and vital tide carries Carrie Meeber to success on the stage; or the three novels of Arlo Bates, *The Pagans* (1884), *The Philistines* (1889), and *The Puritans* (1898), which, dated in many respects, yet have the root of the matter in them. Of about 125 fictional titles by Henry James something over a fifth have to do with the development of the artist—painter, actress, writer—with the nature of artistic truth, and with the irrelevance of secular measurements of the divine fire. Typical is *The Tragic Muse* (1890), in which, by contrary motion, Nicholas Dormer gives up matrimony and politics for painting, and Miriam Rooth gives up domesticity for acting and matrimony. Two passages illustrate James's adumbration of the theme. Of political speaking Dormer roundly says, "It has nothing to do with the truth, or the search for it; nothing to do with intelligence, or candor, or honor." In contrast, the fascination of art, embodied in Miriam Rooth, is thus set forth:

But the great thing, to his mind and, these first days, the irresistible seduction of the theatre, was that she was a rare incarnation of beauty. Beauty was the principle of everything she did and of the way, unerringly, she did it—the exquisite harmony of line and motion and attitude and tone, what was most general and most characteristic in her performance. Accidents and instincts played together to this end and constituted something which was independent of her talent or her merit, in a given case, and which in its influence . . . was far superior to any merit and to any talent. It was a supreme infallible felicity, a source of importance, a stamp of absolute value. To see it in operation, to sit within its radius and feel it shift and revolve and change and never fail, was a corrective to the depression, the humiliation, the bewilderment of life.

This is persuasively, this is beautifully said, but if, like jesting Pilate, we ask what is truth and unlike him, stay for answer, no clear explanation is forthcoming. The assertion that superior truth is expressed by the artist raises the same difficulties that appear when a great religious leader asserts that he expresses superior truth. In *The Varieties of Religious Experience* William James examined the various modes by which the religious person comes to the belief that he has or has had a special vision of truth, but so far as I am aware, no one has made a similar study of varieties of religious experience, so to say, expressed as art. Our studies of aesthetic principles are, perhaps rightly, metaphysical and formal; but when the artist abandons any formal system of values and of truth—say, for example, Platonic philosophy or Christian belief—he faces very great difficulties. And these difficulties are not the sort arising out of the old Art-for-Art's-sake movement, inasmuch as the modern artist does not, like these earlier men, give up the ethical problem as irrelevant, but on the contrary assumes that the ethical problem is solved in the work of art itself. If one burns with a hard, gem-like flame, if one lives so that he can say to this or that passing moment, "Tarry awhile, thou art so fair," individual experience is, indeed, the center of the statement, but no assumption is made about human dignity, whereas the tacit assumption of Miss Cather and, for that matter, of Scott Fitzgerald, is that human dignity is enhanced in being the creator of a work of art—an assumption which becomes more and more perilous, the more one meditates upon it and upon the biographies of artists, particularly those of artists in modern times. It is a theory which requires a greater degree of support than solipsism can offer, and yet no very clear sustaining hypothesis seems to be at hand. It is sometimes said the artist may be sustained by something called myth, and it is sometimes said he is sustained by something called culture or society.

Let us glance at some attempts to remake myth in the name of art, and at certain aspects of the artist's relation to culture, particularly to republican culture. I prefer this term as having certain theoretic values not found in a phrase like "the democratic way of life," an awkward concept to keep clear of mere propaganda. But first, for art and myth.

In the phrase "Youth and the Bright Medusa" we agree to embody the enigmatic lure which the life of art often holds for youth, and which it held most evidently and most disastrously for youth in the nineteen-twenties. The pathetic career of Scott Fitzgerald, partially foreshadowed in *This Side of Paradise*, dramatizes a legend, and at the end of that decade—that is, in 1929—*Look Homeward, Angel* announced another heaven-storming genius that burned itself out too quickly in the name of art. In a general sense, since the death of Thomas Wolfe, the youth movement has virtually disappeared, but it has not utterly vanished. Contemporary writing has produced other sacrifices to the bright Medusa which it might be embarrassing to discuss. And our problem is a two-fold one: first, to ascertain whether this youth movement is what legend makes it out to be—a product of postwar disillusion in the twenties—or whether its sources and significance are not deeper and more important than, let us say, the light of Miss Millay's candle which, burning at both ends, shed on friend and foe its lovely and ephemeral light. This inquiry in turn leads into the second question: what support can be given the implied doctrine of a superior truth in art, supposed to justify the sacrifice of youth?

I have assumed that special light is shed on the nature of an artist's development (especially on the nature of development of art into truth) in the fiction of Willa Cather; and if I seem to slight the claims of Henry James in this regard, it is not because his fiction fails to interest itself in art and in artists. True, he says little about music, but his narratives do concern the sculptor, the painter, the actress, and the writer. But there is a radical difference between the approach of Henry James to this problem and the approach of Willa Cather. For James the problem is one of culture; for Miss Cather it is a problem of energy. The one pays homage to Apollo, the other to Dionysius, and though both agree that the artist is possessed of a secret and superior truth, for James the problem is Platonic, whereas Miss Cather narrates the unfolding of her singer in terms of Orphic initiation. Culture, it is James's hope, will eventually lead into that study of perfection which is art; but in Miss Cather's world the initiates already recognize each other by signs too subtle for the multitude. Art for the one is wisdom; for the other it is radiance.

LEON EDEL

"Willa Cather:
The Paradox of Success"

It is a great pleasure to commemorate the name and the work
of Willa Cather in this city and in this Library under the aus-
pices of the Gertrude Clarke Whittall Poetry and Literature
Fund. I do not have to remark upon the appropriateness of the
place. Concerning Willa Cather and this city, however, a few
words might be said. She was of two minds about the capital. I
suppose many Americans are. About the city as symbol of American life she had many eloquent things to say: its stateliness, its
power, its art, could hardly be lost upon her. But there were
certain misgivings which I suppose the most patriotic Washing-
tonian is likely to experience at one time or another. The sense
of a capital's largeness, its labyrinthine character, its impersonality—these were matters upon which she seems to have brooded
with an intensity that is reflected in *The Professor's House,* in
Tom Outland's account of his stay in Washington. It is one of
the most moving sections in the novel: Tom's feeling that he
spent all his days in the capital in outer offices, in which persons
like himself, imbued with some ideal, wait and wait, and find
themselves the object of a sharp indifference; the overwhelming
helplessness sometimes of the individual before what we speak
of as the *machinery* of government. All this oppressed Willa
Cather's young hero.

Reprinted from *Willa Cather: The Paradox of Success* (Washington, 1960)
by permission of the Library of Congress and Leon Edel.

Willa Cather mistrusted machinery, whether of the farm or of the Government. Some of you may have read one of her lesser novels, *One of Ours*—considered good enough in the 1920's, however, to have been given the Pulitzer prize—and you may recall her account, often humorous, of the second generation on the Nebraska farmlands, purchasing all kinds of machinery to do the work of the pioneers; and how, after a while, the machines piled up in cellar and yard, a rusty wilderness of gadgets and implements. If we look at Miss Cather from our angle of vision, from the electronic age, we might say that she doubtless made too much of a virtue out of the farmer's sweat of his brow; but the deeper meaning of her protest must not be allowed to escape us. It has been reiterated by William Faulkner in one of his rare letters to the press, in which he expressed a fear that fliers who fly by instruments alone are abdicating their human role. This is what Willa Cather was trying to say. She expressed it on one occasion in a newspaper interview when she said: "Restlessness such as ours, success such as ours, do not make for beauty. Other things must come first: good cookery, cottages that are homes, not playthings; gardens, repose. These are first-rate things, and out of first-rate stuff art is made. It is possible that machinery has finished us as far as this is concerned. Nobody stays at home any more; nobody makes anything beautiful any more."

One expects such utterances from old persons, set in their ways, and quite content to do things as they did them in their youth. But Miss Cather gave this interview in her prime. To understand her refusal to move with her era—and her refusal was adamant —we must recognize that Willa Cather was not a child of the twentieth century. She had been a child of the frontier; and long after the frontiers were gone she yearned—with an ache that had all the poetry of youth and adolescence in it—for the old, the cherished things she had known. This she expressed in one form and another in twelve novels; it is the best aspect of her talent and the one that gives her a claim upon us on this occasion. It also reflects the limitations of her talent. Our task will be to try to understand this, in order that we may the better define that essence in her work which has had—and still has—so strong an appeal to her public.

I must confess to a certain constraint in speaking to you of Willa Cather now, on the periphery of the 1960's—constraint because we have moved so far away from her world. It is gone, gone as if it had never existed, save for the fact that it does exist in some of the best pages of her writing. To use an exaggerated image, I would say that to talk of Miss Cather's world is a little like trying to extol the Stone Age to a Renaissance man. We must remind ourselves, as we survey the big-finned automobiles, conquering more space than any human being is entitled to on the highway, that Miss Cather belonged to the age when there were still horses hitched to hitching posts in the Western towns; when one walked a good deal more and wrote letters instead of telegraphing or telephoning; when life in the small remote community and on the farm was more isolated and lonely than it is today—and offered more time for reading and reflection; and it was a life that was hard indeed by our cushioned standards, hard with the work of the hands, and not of the same hands running machines. This was before the broad and smiling countenance of our country was offered the sonorities of the jet in the sky, or the cacophony of the dishwashing machine in the kitchen, or the vibrations of Hi-Fi and television within the walls of our dwellings. It is indeed of an ancient world that I must speak tonight if I am to do justice to Miss Cather—and to Miss Cather's problem of reconciling herself to a time in which life altered so radically that even those of us who have bridged some part of this period still rub our eyes in amazement. We wonder, sometimes, whether we have awakened from the realities of our childhood into the fantastic world of science fiction. I am just old enough, and was just young enough, to have lived in a semi-frontier town and to have seen the old farmcarts hitched to hitching-posts and the horses knee-deep in mud; and I watched the last of the peasants, immigrants from the old world, being transformed from Europeans into North Americans. I sometimes wonder, when I fly in a plane, or read about our spacemen, whether I am the same person who used to walk to school in terrible blizzards without benefit of the school bus and knew the joys of the horsedrawn sleigh on frosty winter nights.

The questions Willa Cather raised about the changes in her time are extremely important in this second half of our century, for they relate to the whole problem of art in an age of science, to the role of the artist when he is faced by a self-assured technology, supremely aware of the comforts it brings to man. C. P. Snow, the English novelist, has written much about this. He was a scientist before he recognized that art could express for him something that lies beyond the boundaries of science; and he has sought, with high seriousness and great imagination, to establish a bridge over the gulf that exists between the specialists of science, who converse in their own particular language, and the creative artists who deal in words, and who use them to express the quick impulses, the ready feelings by which men discover their kinship with one another. In his Rede lecture, delivered at Cambridge earlier this year, Sir Charles was forthright about this chasm, and quite right, I think, in suggesting that there is a great deal of ignorance on both sides. Those of us who are concerned with imaginative literature must recognize that this *is* the age of science, and that we live in a time of great scientific wonder and adventure. But we know what Willa Cather would say if C. P. Snow pointed out to her that man's new discoveries necessitate new ways of seeing the world. She would say, as she made the Indian say in *Death Comes for the Archbishop*: "Men travel faster now, but I do not know if they go to better things."

Sir Charles Snow is certain that men are going on to better things, thanks to technology; and he feels that the answer to the alienation of the two cultures, those of the scientists and the nonscientists, lies in educating the world to understand that technology is an irreversible process: for machines, at their best, and in spite of new problems which they have created, have made life better and often much less arduous. There can be no turning back from the bulldozer and the dishwashing machine even though these create, I'm afraid, more noise than man or animal was intended to hear. There can be no turning back from social progress save through violence and war; as Sir Charles remarked, man is no longer resigned to wait for periods longer than a person's lifetime. But if this is the optimistic side of the Machine Age, I am reminded of the words I heard Alberto Moravia address to a congress of writers last July. He spoke, in a sense, like Miss Cather, not of the achievements of technology, but of the relationship of the human being to them. Novelists, after all, write about men, not machines. Signor Moravia was justifiably querulous about humans who are asked to do something, or feed something, into the maw of a machine on some eternal and irreversible assembly line. He wanted to know what could be done to keep such men from becoming a part of the mechanical continuum into which they are drawn, and the effect it has upon their lives. It was understandable that Moravia, with his quick sense of human values, should point to the heart of the problem, as Willa Cather had done before him. The novelist wants to know, when he is confronted with a machine, whether it will confer new benefits or new slaveries upon man. The discussion is not new; it has been going on since the dawn of the Industrial Revolution, ever since those primitive days when the machine-breakers hoped to wipe out sudden unemployment by destruction of the metal Frankensteins. Their lives had been disrupted overnight; they protested in the only way they knew at that time. The novelist protests out of a concern with man's spirit, and out of his quick insight into the new feudalism: that of a science which now bids man to obey and be mastered and offers him, instead of the old iniquities, the narcotics of cushion comfort. The ambiguity of this was not lost upon Willa Cather. She was caught, in the end, in a revolt against the very achievements she had praised, the very successes—that of the pioneers of our land—of which she made herself the fictional historian. But this only partly expresses what I meant when I proposed to speak to you tonight of the "paradox" of success in the literary career of Willa Cather.

The story of Willa Cather's literary career is an American success story of the most charming kind. She spent her childhood in Virginia, member of a then-increasing and ultimately large Southern family. She was taken, before adolescence, to Nebraska, in that movement westward of the American population in which the Southerners encountered westward-drifting New Englanders on the common ground of the prairie—there to encounter new pioneers from Europe. This episode in Miss Cather's life, her uprooting from old familiar things at an early age, has been well told both in E. K. Brown's critical biography (which I completed after his death) and in the memoir written by Edith Lewis, who knew Miss Cather during the greater part of her writing years. Willa was nine when she was transferred from a South still filled, in the early decades after the Civil War, with a sense of an old aristocratic way of life, to the life of the prairie, with its new dynamism, that of creating everything from scratch. To have lived in a stately rambling house in Virginia and then to discover the sod houses of the settlers on the Divide, was revelation enough for a pre-adolescent girl. Willa Cather's experience was common to most of the members of her migratory generation in Nebraska: they had been uprooted out of older places, many out of centuries of civilization in the Old World. The difference between her and her contemporaries is that she was an observer from the start: an observer in the little town of Red Cloud, Nebraska, who came to know the countryside intimately. She played with the children of the pioneers; they lived their lives on the prairie; and Willa was to write about the lives they lived. Somewhere she quotes the words of Virgil: *Primus ego in patriam mecum . . . deducam Musas.* She was indeed the first to woo the muse in her wild land. The early and late settlers were essentially non-literary: they could hardly have been otherwise. They were concerned with doing, on the plane of struggle and conquest. To take hold of the land, to tame it, to build on it, to make it yield life; the goals were simple, and they were among the most difficult of all of man's goals. Schools, culture, wise words, all this had to come in good time. The Bible had wisdom enough for them as they did their rude tasks; and those who came from other lands brought their memories of song and dance and tale out of the old cultures with which to relax after their toil.

Willa Cather at first does not seem to have dreamed of being a writer. She would be a scientist, or a doctor; there was a phase during which she sought for truth by dissection, like Turgenev's young men and their frogs; and looked at the stars and had a vision of new worlds. In this period of her girlhood the only hint of her later aesthetic idealism might have been found in her addiction to reading. What we discover in Miss Cather's personal life, which the literary biographer must explore if he is to understand the later public life of the writer, is that in Nebraska, amid the pioneers, she was caught up in the very heart of the "American dream": opportunity, equality, competition for achievement, above all the idea of "success." One *had* to succeed. One could not be a failure. And if one's individuality and courage were not appreciated in the home town, then success was the way to conquest. The sculptor who left the Nebraska town to become famous, and whose funeral we attend in one of Willa Cather's early stories, is eulogized in these words: "There was only one boy ever raised on this borderland between ruffianism and civilization who didn't come to grief, and you hated Harvey Merrick more for winning out than you hated all the other boys who got under the wheels."

She was determined to "win out," and from her first days in Lincoln when she went to the city to prepare for college, she addressed herself to this end. Her early essays won the admiration of her teachers and they published them in the local paper as examples of a literary gift on the frontier. Willa obtained thereby a precocious local fame. The story of her striving years is a record of a persistent and highly determined young woman possessed of an assertive ideal of achievement: the dawn could not come soon enough for Willa Cather during those years when she rose at five and built a fire in her coal stove with coal she had herself carried up a flight of stairs, and sat down in her small room in snow-piled Lincoln to study her Greek and her Latin. Happy day indeed when our youth rose as early as this—and to study the old languages! Miss Cather, we might add, passed first in a class of fifty-three. Throughout her works we come upon such phrases as "the passionate struggle of a tenacious will," and the "loyalty of young hearts to some exalted ideal and the passion with which they strive." The passion was in the striving. Ultimately she was to say that "success is never so interesting as struggle—not even to the successful."

We will have to come back to this statement, made years later, when she herself had tasted the fruits of success and yet found the world to be out-of-joint, and longed nostalgically for the older time when there were still frontiers to conquer. Her own frontiers had been conquered by the process of doing things for herself, knowing what she wanted to do, and taking every step of life as a challenge: what we speak of as "rugged individualism." From Lincoln, after she graduated, she went to Pittsburgh, and, after a decade of journalism and teaching, published her first volumes—her verses and a book of her tales. After that there came the further temptation of a high position on a national magazine, *McClure's,* and to this she gave several of her best years. Only then did she find her true path and, turning her back on journalism and administration forever, she settled down to be a novelist. But ten or fifteen years were to elapse before her work would become widely read and receive the recognition every novelist desires. Willa Cather was almost fifty by the time she reached the end of her strivings and became famous. No wonder that she looked back and murmured the third *Georgic* of Virgil: *optima dies . . . prima fugit,* "the best days are the first to flee."

It has become fashionable among certain of our critics to talk of literature as if it were a created object, an ingenious contrivance, a vase, a mechanical butterfly—and to insist upon the impersonality of art. Literary art, it seems to me, is the most personal creation of man: it is the use of words to express feeling and experience in story and poem, in metaphor and simile. Far from ignoring the life of an artist, as these critics would have us do, we must encounter that life in the artist's work. We can hardly avoid it, for the work is a kind of supreme biography of the artist: it is by his work that the artist asserts himself, and writes his name, his voice, his style—his and no one else's—into the memory of men. These may be truisms but we have listened to so much talk about the function of criticism that I find myself pressed to reassert them on an occasion such as this one, in the interest of the things I want to say.

What I want particularly to say is that if we examine the work of any novelist in the sequence in which it was written we can always discover an inner core of narrative, and an inner pattern— due caution being taken, as it must, to read the pattern *out of* and not *into* the work. I speak inevitably of the writer of genius, and not of the hack, the artist who creates out of personal necessity, not out of the expediencies of journalism. Creative writers do their work out of profound inner dictates, they write in compliance to an imperious self-demand for expression. With all the world to choose from, they almost invariably select subjects closest to their hearts, even though the story they write may seem on the surface remote and unrelated. This can be stated as a literary axiom; and the subject selected more often than not reveals some emotion the writer had to express, some particular state of feeling, some view of life which demanded articulation. In this sense it might be said that writers—and writers of fiction in particular—are engaged in creating parables about themselves.

Thus, if we listen carefully to Tolstoy as he tells us the story of Anna Karenina, we discover that he is not merely writing a novel about his overt subject: the consequences of blind passion. His novel is a novel about two persons, both in a state of despair, and we are shown the different solutions each finds to his dilemma. I speak of Anna and of Levin. And if we turn to Tolstoy's life, we have very little difficulty in discovering that the despair projected into this work was his own: indeed there were days when he thought of taking Anna's solution, and others in which he reasoned himself into the states of mind of Levin. So, if we try to listen to what Willa Cather is really saying in her sequence of novels, we can discover a pattern ineluctably woven through her work; and an analysis in sequence enables us to discover the meaning of the particular parables Miss Cather was impelled to write.

Let us take her short stories first of all, since they reflect her earliest moods. These deal largely with artists and what they must do in a world that tends to be hostile to art and in which artistic success can be obtained only by bitter toil and often at a forbidding price. These stories represent largely the phase of Willa Cather's revolt against Nebraska and her strong conviction that the prairies would have confined her talent. They express the artist's need to overcome the tyranny of family and the pressures of environment, the need to move out into a receptive world in order to conquer. Professor Howard Mumford Jones, some years ago, used Miss Cather's image of Youth and the Bright Medusa (the title of her best-known collection of tales) as the subject for a vivid series of lectures on artists, poets, and radicals. The tension in Miss Cather's tales, he observed, arises from the "conflict between the desire of the artist to pursue beauty and the necessity of the craftsman, if he is to live, to make some practical adjustment to the workaday world." The Bright Medusa, she who could lure but who also turned those lured into stone, represents, said Professor Jones, "the fascination of art, or at least of aesthetic experience, as this works its havoc or its charm." And in a happy contrast between Miss Cather's tales of artists and the stories on the same subject written by Henry James, Professor Jones remarked that for James the problem was one of culture, whereas for Miss Cather the problem was one of energy. This strikes me as profoundly true. On rereading the stories recently, I was inclined to add that this fascination for art, and the art world, on the part of Miss Cather's heroes and heroines, was a fascination essentially with success; the energy represented is not aesthetic, it is that of conquest; of overcoming nature and competition and standing firm and free among the Philistines and resisting their inevitable demands that talent become as mediocre as themselves.

Miss Cather's central theme is that of people who pull themselves up by their bootstraps. What is interesting for us in a novel such as *The Song of the Lark* is that once the would-be opera star, Thea, arrives at her goal, the story has nowhere to go. The love affair Miss Cather created in the novel is artificial; it has had little meaning beside the main impulse, which was Thea's, to be a great singer and a great star. And when the characters meet sometime afterwards, I think in Denver, on a crisp starry night, all they can do is to be very smug about all that they have accomplished. They discover, perhaps, what Henry James meant when he remarked that success was like having a good dinner. All that you can say is that you have had it.

The inner voice of the early novels of Willa Cather suggests this fascination with, and need to describe, various forms of success—but also certain forms of failure. The drive to power in these books is overriding, with the result that the novels contain no complicated plots, no complexity of human relationships, no love affairs that we can take seriously. Her heroines, those women with feminized masculine names, Alexandra, Ántonia—and the name Alexandra itself reminds us of one of history's greatest conquerors —have tenacious wills and an extraordinary capacity for struggle. Miss Cather's first four novels seem to say that a great engineer may build his bridges, but bridges sometimes collapse; that the pioneer must do what he is ordained to do as Alexandra is ordained to conquer the land and finish the task her pioneer father had but half completed—and in the process impose her will on her brothers; and that the children of the pioneers who remained within the tradition of struggle had hard lives, but in the end achieved a rugged kind of happiness. Already in *O Pioneers!*, and in the finest of the prairie novels, *My Ántonia*, the younger rebel in Willa Cather is making her peace with the Nebraska she had fled and is discovering a deep love for the place and the people she had known.

When a writer turns to things as they were, and conveys them with an ache as powerful and poignant as Willa Cather's, we can wonder whether this may not express a profound uneasiness with things as they are. There is always a certain ache, inevitably, for old days and bygone experiences which we cherished; the question is the degree to which that ache prevails in the midst of the here and the now. Miss Cather's novels, those she wrote in her second phase, leave no doubt that for her the here and the now was deeply depressing. This is what the inner voice says in the four novels Miss Cather wrote during the early 1920's. In *One of Ours*, to which I have already alluded, the hero makes an unhappy marriage and escapes from it and the prairie by going overseas during the First World War; he escapes also from the new machines and the new men who are betraying the promise of the pioneers. Death in battle comes to him as a happy release. The title of the next volume expresses a further stage in this mood of despair, decay, death. *A Lost Lady* expresses the nostalgia for a lost aristocratic order on the frontier. This short novel, which achieved extraordinary popularity during the 1920's, paints with vividness and economy a heroine who cannot yield the old for the new, but who in her love of pleasure is prepared to accept shallow compromises. The story conveys to us a kind of lonely ache for the swagger of the railroad pioneers and the early tycoons. *The Professor's House*, which followed, tells us much more. If the lost lady is lost indeed, the professor has everything to live for: he is a prize-winning historian, his work is recognized, he is about to become a grandfather. There is a forward movement in the life around him, but also within it a decline in old high values; and his reaction to this decline is to decline himself into apathy and bitter premature old age. Indeed, he all but commits suicide. *My Mortal Enemy,* the last novel in this group, ends in the death of the heroine, and in it Willa Cather seems to offer herself a kind of ambiguous resignation and the possible solace of religion. But the novel is of a piece with its immediate predecessors and the view of life in it is dark and ominous.

What, then, emerges from these eight novels, representing two stages in Willa Cather's artistic progress? If we seek their essence —and I am not concerned for the moment with their beauty as narrative and their lyrical quality—we discover in them two subjects: conquest and death. The triumph and achievement of the pioneer yields to disillusion, and disillusion harbors in it a wish for extinction. A whole world has been lost and seems irretrievable save in memory. It was Miss Cather who spoke of "the precious, the incommunicable past." The present, we take it, had ceased to be precious to her. "Some memories," she said, "are realities, and are better than anything that can ever happen to one again." There is a deep pessimism in this statement. Let me digress for just a moment to underline that I am not suggesting that Willa Cather should have been other than she was; nor am I of the opinion that writers should be optimists. The critic and the literary biographer are concerned only with things as they are, or as they have been; a critic is presumptuous indeed when he tells a writer how he should have written his work; a biographer is worse than presumptuous if he tells his subject how he should have lived his life. The task in each case is one of trying to perceive, to understand, to place in context, to evaluate—but not to sit in judgment. For Miss Cather, the American past was heroic, and it had been her privilege to witness one phase of it. The present seemed drab. Her picture of soldiers returning from the First World War and finding life an anticlimax after the excitement and danger of the field of battle is consonant with her feelings about the conquest of the frontier. The past was splendid; the present was dull and she seems to have arrested her experience of the old splendor at its moment of triumph; nothing that came after could equal it. The process of growing older, the calm of quieter years, the dropping away of early intensities for later insights, could offer little satisfaction. The only thing that had possessed fundamental meaning for Willa Cather were her striving years. And this brings me to what I have spoken of as the "paradox of success" in the work and in the life of Willa Cather.

There is, in *A Lost Lady*, a highly significant passage. Miss Cather, speaking in the voice of the omniscient author, expresses contempt for the new generation which succeeded the pioneers on the frontier, the young men who were diluting the achievements of their parents and destroying the values of the earlier world. (The new men are Bayliss Wheeler of *One of Ours*, Wick Cutter of *My Antonia*, Ivy Peters of *A Lost Lady*, and the smooth-talking Louie Marsellus of *The Professor's House*.) This type of man would, Willa Cather wrote, "drink up the mirage, dispel the morning freshness, root out the great brooding spirit of freedom, the generous, easy life of the great landholders. The space, the colour, the princely carelessness of the pioneer, they would destroy and cut up into profitable bits, as the match factory splinters the primeval forest. All the way from the Missouri to the mountains this generation of shrewd young men, trained to petty economies by hard times, would do exactly what Ivy Peters had done when he drained the Forrester marsh."

We can respect the feeling in this passage, but we must recognize the curious fallacies it contains. It is written on the assumption that a shimmering mirage can last, that early morning freshness can continue throughout the day, that "princely carelessness" can be possible to all generations. It is precisely the "princely carelessness" of the first-comers, to whom the riches of nature seemed endless, that brought on the duststorms of later years, and created a need, doubtless unprincely and parsimonious, to start conservation of our resources lest our entire heritage be swept away. But with an emotion such as Miss Cather's one cannot be logical: and the beauty of her statement is its high romanticism and the firmness with which she clung to the fine old things. To such a person, who cannot tolerate change, it is useless to say that change is simply one of the hard facts of life. Moreover, it is difficult to say this, since change is not always for the better, and certainly some of the sterling pioneer qualities did decline. Miss Cather remained unreconciled. The drama of the frontier had been too vivid; it came to seem miraculous. She could not believe, she did not like to believe, that the curtain had come down. She became involved in one of those anomalies of human existence in which, when the struggle ceases, there seems to go with it all reason for pursuing anything new. The land was tamed and productive; it was being re-worked and re-parceled by a new generation. And like her pioneers Willa Cather had conquered too. She had made herself powerful as a writer; her books were read; she had financial ease. She, too, had been a pioneer and now she had her success. She could live and work for her art, but apparently this was not enough, as it might have been in other circumstances and to other artists. If it had been, she would have been capable, in the large way of the great novelists, of being forever immersed in the world around her; she would have found it constantly interesting and curious and filled with abiding truths of human character and an ever-continuing battle between good and evil. Balzac died with dozens of novels unwritten. Dostoyevsky dropped his pen only when his physical strength failed him. Henry James' notebooks are crammed with tales he never had time to write, and he wrote ceaselessly. Miss Cather, coming of a different race of novelists and driven by a single vision, does not seem to have possessed such resources. As she looked back at her heroine in *The Song of the Lark* many years after the book was written, she remarked: "The life of a successful artist in the full tide of achievement is not so interesting as the life of a talented young girl 'fighting her way' as we say. Success is never so interesting as struggle—not even to the successful, not even to the most mercenary form of ambition." And when we open this particular novel which tells of the singer's career, step-by-step, a prairie girl's rise to the operatic stage, we find that as epigraph Willa Cather placed the following words from Lenau's *Don Juan* on her title page: "It was a wondrous lovely storm that drove me."

It was a wondrous lovely storm that drove Willa Cather, and what she cared for above all was the storm. With success achieved, she was like her professor in *The Professor's House*. She felt depressed. She didn't know what to do with success; or rather, she seems to have experienced a despair altogether out of proportion to the actual circumstances of her achievement. She blamed it on the changed times: on the bothersome little men who seemed to clog a foreground formerly filled with giants; on machines; on new and less simple values; on complexities which had not existed in the early flush of the American dawn. She had, in her personal triumph, outdistanced competition—had surpassed her classmates, her father, her brothers—and yet she could not give herself up to the enjoyment of the fruits of her success. This was the paradox, and it is more common in American life than one might think. I do not propose here to generalize on it, save to remark that I suppose it is a part of our endless consuming energy and our need to go on endlessly doing, endlessly creating the bigger and sometimes the better, without pausing to grasp fully what we have. It must be a part of our belief, like Willa Cather's, that the dew of morning will not go away, even after the sun is already high on the horizon, if only we can maintain a life of consuming action. Success, by the very testimony of the tales she wrote, created for Willa Cather a deep despair and even a wish for death, as with the pioneer farmer in her story "Neighbour Rosicky," who wanted to go on pitching hay, after the doctor told him he had a bad heart and reminded him that he had strong sons to pitch the hay for him. When the frontiers have been conquered, the alternatives would seem to be simple: one accepts this fact and goes on to new problems or one mourns for their disappearance as if they could have existed forever.

I suspect that the more Miss Cather succeeded in her career, the more despair she experienced without quite understanding why. We get evidence of this not only in the turn she gave to her tales, but in the ways in which, for instance, she chose to put together her essays. The essays in themselves were a series of reminiscences about old and valued things: her days in the Charles Street house of Mrs. Fields in Boston, where all the Brahmins used to visit and where Dickens and Thackeray had once stayed; her friendship with Sarah Orne Jewett; her meeting with Flaubert's niece. To these essays, in their book form, she gave the provocative title, *Not Under Forty*. She herself was past fifty then, and the preface which she wrote was a belligerent explanation of the title. The essays, she said, were for those who were not under forty, because anyone younger could not understand or appreciate what they meant. And in this preface she said that "the world broke in two in 1922 or thereabouts," choosing the year in which she stood on the threshold of her fiftieth birthday. We need not go here into the other circumstances which may have contributed to this belligerency. I have dealt with them in a long chapter in my book on literary biography. I am concerned tonight principally with the aspect of success in Miss Cather's career.

Many are the consequences of success. Some persons understandably thrive on it and even revel in it. Others seem to do their utmost to turn it into failure. And some are even killed by it. We have read of persons so driven by their pursuit of their life goals that they collapse utterly when these goals are reached. Overnight their lives acquire an emptiness that can be overwhelming. There had been such a tremendous expenditure of energy in the struggle that there is still too much left to accept a halt. Much more might be said about this wondrous lovely storm which drives such persons. But alas, storms blow themselves out and calm follows. Youth does not last. The best days are doubtless the first to flee, and for Miss Cather the rest seemed to be defeat. Yet her career did not end here as well it might have. She saved herself from defeat in two ways: one was by the instinct to write about her feelings and thereby ease herself of inner burden. The other resided in the intensity with which she clung to her embeddedness in her personal past. Out of that intensity she had already created the powerful nostalgia which illuminates *My Ántonia*. And now she found another way of defeating this static element within herself. It was a happy and resourceful solution. But it had an uncomfortable circumstance in it. It made her more successful than ever.

To understand the burden of my theme tonight, it is necessary once more to underline the process of my reasoning. In seeking the inner voice of Willa Cather's novels, I started with the axiom that the individuality of a novel resides particularly in its being a reflection of the novelist himself. It is a truism to say that a poem is the poet's, and the novel, no less than the poem, is the novelist's. "Poetry," said Thoreau, "is a piece of very private history, which unostentatiously lets us into the secret of a man's life." No one but Willa Cather has written anything quite like her novels for the simple reason that they are tissued out of *her* memories, memories of experience as well as of reading, stories lived and stories told, the materials of her life gathered and re-experienced in words. We can say this of any novelist whose writings lay claim to a personality and to a style. And in saying this, I reject the old belief that a story just "flies" into a novelist's mind, that creation is a fortuitous circumstance, a happy inspiration. It is nothing of the kind. Inspiration there may be, but the flight of the story is, if anything, outward from within; it comes from the mind and the heart and the whole consciousness of the artist. I predicate a series of choices open to the artist. Of all the frontier stories available to Willa Cather, why, we can ask, did she particularly cling to this one rather than that; why did a night of talk with a blue-eyed girl at some party in the 1890's, a girl whose name was Gayhardt, end in a novel almost half a century later titled *Lucy Gayheart*; why had it long been dreamed of as a story to be called "Blue Eyes on the Platte?" Some buried intensity of experience, some deep core of meaning had existed for Miss Cather in the blue eyes and the bright talk of the Gayhardt girl, and in the fullness of time this became the novel we can read. But this novel contained in it other materials also tissued out of old experience; it was again the story of an active young woman setting out on a career; she is again a musician; she has a love affair with an older man; and of importance also in the story is Lucy's relationship with her father; and significant too is Lucy's early death. The novel dissolves itself in the break of a bright promise; and Lucy's death is as arbitrary as death can be. The novelist had the choice of giving the heroine life and adventure, but she chose a skating accident as a way of ending her novel.

I have used this novel as I might any other of Miss Cather's, to show that a work of fiction, like a poem, is a reflection of a state of feeling in the writer. As I say, Willa Cather might have chosen some other girl in Nebraska, when she came to write this novel; another Alexandra or Ántonia or Thea, but she chose Lucy instead, and she might have given her victory and success as she does her earlier heroines, but she *chose* to give her an early death. These were choices made by the writer for reasons she could doubtless have explained rationally, and for deeper reasons of which she was unaware and about which we speculate now by examining the choices made in her other works, and noting similarities and dissimilarities. Since the novels all issued out of the single consciousness, we are likely to discover more similarities than dissimilarities in the fundamental treatment of the material, in the predicaments pictured, the solutions reached.

If we had had the opportunity to ask Miss Cather why, when she reached the impasse of near-death with the professor in *The Professor's House* and the death of Myra in *My Mortal Enemy*, she then turned to a distant past and wrote *Death Comes for the Archbishop*, she might have answered that she had for long been interested in the work of the early French missionaries in the

American Southwest; that she had read such-and-such books about them; that she had conceived the idea of writing a novel about them. What I would like to submit to you is that the inner story of *Death Comes for the Archbishop* is something quite other than the overt material shows: it illustrates the marvelous way in which the creative consciousness operates in an artist as determined as Willa Cather, as tenacious in keeping her personal world intact and allowing neither time nor world upheaval to alter it. Indeed we might observe that Miss Cather instinctively found a solution, a triumphant solution, in terms of her personal as well as her artistic needs. Up to this time she had lived over her Nebraska past and the past of her Southwest in her novels, as well as her memories of Pittsburgh and her life in New York. Then her world broke in two, as she said, and she wrote out her despair in *A Lost Lady, The Professor's House,* and *My Mortal Enemy.* Where her theme had been power and conquest, it had become frustration and death. And now she wrote a novel of an older pioneering time which had required the same courage as that of her Nebraska pioneers, and even greater hardihood. If the Western frontiers of her own time had disappeared, Miss Cather's inner voice seemed to say to her, there were still older frontiers available—those which existed before her time and which she could relive in the history books, in anecdote, in memories other than her own, and then retell them. Stated in other terms, Miss Cather's greatest fictional success, her chronicle of two missionaries in the Southwest carrying out their great religious and civilizing tasks, was a discovery that she could still—and indeed better than ever—do what she had always done. But see how insistent inner claims can be! The word Death is the first word in the title, even though the novel is once again a novel of conquest, conquest alike of a new land and of the souls of men. Indeed, for all the insistence of the title, the book is in reality not about death; it is about Archbishop Latour's courage and steadfastness, his gentleness and his worldly wisdom. His death at the end is simply the death that comes to all men—but in giving it significance, Miss Cather may have betrayed her deepest awareness that she was herself engaged in this novel in an act of exhuming the dead past.

Miss Cather had embodied all her major themes in the *Arch-bishop*. Yet she dealt with them on a different footing; they could touch her less in a personal way, being remote in time. She could write this book without the anxieties betrayed in the novels which preceded it. Her friend Miss Lewis testifies to this when she tells us that the writing of the *Archbishop* gave Miss Cather such an intense joy that she promptly tried to recapture it by writing another historical fiction. She went, for the material of *Shadows on the Rock*, into an even more remote time—seventeenth-century Quebec. Miss Lewis writes: "I think Willa Cather never got so much happiness from the writing of any book as from the *Archbishop*; and although *Shadows on the Rock* is of course altogether different in conception, in treatment and in artistic purpose, it may have been in part a reluctance to leave the world of Catholic feeling and tradition in which she had lived so happily for so long that led her to embark on this new novel." There is doubtless a fund of truth in this; but a curious critic might still ask why Miss Cather experienced a pleasure so intense, even allowing for the intellectual and emotional interest she (herself an Episcopalian) found in the history of Catholicism in America. I would be inclined to the view that Miss Cather experienced great joy in writing the *Archbishop* because for the moment she had laid aside all the frustrations which had engendered the despair reflected in the books of her middle period. *Death Comes for the Archbishop* could be written in a kind of easy freedom, a joy of identifying herself with the old things, the great wide American out-of-doors of her childhood which touched all that was deepest in Willa Cather and in which she could roam while remaining firmly embedded in her own past.

Shadows on the Rock sold even more copies than the *Archbishop* and was an even greater material success. But it was not as good a book. For in it old problems began to intrude again: and, as E. K. Brown has shown, in writing about the apothecary in Quebec and his twelve-year-old daughter, Miss Cather was returning to her own early adolescence and reliving some of the memories of her father, who had recently died. She had found in the pages of history what her own time could no longer furnish her and she could do again what she had done before. These two books were the sum of her escape from her fundamental dilemma; and their overwhelming success revived a sense of frustration again. Then illness and late middle age closed in upon her. Two more novels were written, both retrospective, but Miss Cather's best work was done. Unlike some other writers, she could create only from what had happened to her, or what had happened in a history to which she was personally attuned.

One more word about *Shadows on the Rock*: in choosing the rock of Quebec for her story, and that part of society on this continent which has undergone the least change since the old time, Miss Cather was once again testifying to her own reluctance to accept change. She spoke of the rock, indeed, as "the utmost expression of human need." A strange statement, for rocks are hard and singularly unfertile; they symbolize stratification and rigidity. Miss Cather's formulation suggests that for her the symbol of the rock means none of these things. Rather, it symbolized for her something that expressed durability, steadfastness, something to which one could cling. Well, this *is* the use it had for her, and we must recognize that Willa Cather needed something to hold on to; her life had assumed, given its particular circumstances, an inescapable bitterness. A last story upon which she was working and which she ordered destroyed (but the content of which Miss Lewis has revealed to us) would have taken her even farther into the past, the past of the Avignon of the Popes.

You will say to me that I have given you a strange account of Willa Cather; that I came here to commemorate her and that instead I have drawn boundaries about her and shown how, for her, life seemed to become static and despairing once she achieved her goals. My account is not strange, however, for it is in some such searching light that we in the second half of our century must place the writers of the first half. Moreover, I have taken Miss Cather at her own word. She wrote of Sarah Orne Jewett, who deeply influenced her, and to whom she was devoted: "To note an artist's limitations is but to define his talent." This cuts through to a valuable critical truth and it is indeed by seeing Miss Cather's limitations that we can see her whole. I have told you what her struggles were, with what deep and bitter problems she had to contend, problems of life and of the inner spirit. In doing so I am proclaiming the triumph, not the defeat, of her talent. It is the triumph of any artist to be able, in the teeth of difficulties, to achieve artistic utterance. I have said that Miss Cather's life and work constitute a success story of the most characteristic kind. Her books, her best books, are, in their simple and direct appeal, success stories, uncomplicated by subtleties of analysis or complexities of plot. She is a writer of people in action; and their action is characteristically American. She was one of those whose energies in a pioneering world were boundless; Tennyson's words, wafted over the seas during the Victorian century, to strive, to seek, to find—and he added also *but not to yield*— meant much to the pioneers who were striving and seeking and finding and seldom yielding. And Willa Cather had experienced her early life with such extraordinary intensity that she refused ever to let it go. It is this life, when it flows into her novels, that gives them their warm glow and reveals what Justice Holmes called her "gift of the transfiguring touch." Those novels of hers which are suffused with all the ache and nostalgia of youth, those elegiac pages which speak for the joy and sorrow of things gone by—these are the lyrical pages of her novels which touched the heart of her generation and will probably touch those who read her in the future. It is something for a writer— a writer with Miss Cather's distinct limitations—to have so warmly encountered her own time and to have done so with dignity and devotion to her art and with an unfaltering belief in her world that amounted to dogma, an unshakable faith in the old true things. If this belief made life hard for her in a civilization as addicted to shaking up the old things as our own, it was also often a solace to her and to many of her readers.

Willa Cather clung to her rock no matter what tide swept in and swept by. She would certainly have been happier, I think, if she could have been a little more yielding. That which is new is not always a destruction of the old; it can also be a phenomenon of re-birth, of things rising from the ashes of older things to new life and new achievement. Nevertheless, I admire the consistency, the stubbornness, the pride, and the hard and rugged individualism with which Willa Cather lived and wrought. That which diminished her work also proved its strength; the very collapse of her world gave her that radiance of spirit by which Archbishop Latour and Father Vaillant traveled on in the strange land, remote from familiar things, and carried their faith with them. As I say, to have wrought this with distinction and feeling is achievement enough in our time, and indeed in any time.

JOHN H. RANDALL, III

Interpretation of My Ántonia

THEMES OF MY ÁNTONIA

My Ántonia is the most famous of Willa Cather's prairie novels and is generally considered to be her best. It contains the fullest celebration ever to come from her pen of country life as opposed to the life of the cities, for the book is one long paean of praise to the joys of rural living and shows her a passionate advocate of the virtues of a settled agricultural existence. In *My Ántonia* the rural-urban conflict hardly seems to exist. The characters pass from farm to town or city and back again without feeling any incompatibility between value systems; instead they manage to extract the maximum of joy from each. But it is always the country to which they return; Ántonia permanently after a brief sojourn in Black Hawk (Red Cloud) and Denver, and the narrator Jim Burden periodically whenever he can get away from his job in a large Eastern city. Native born or immigrant, all the good characters in the book sooner or later yield to the spell of the land, and there is no doubt in the author's mind as to whether country or city is the real America.

My Ántonia thus clarifies certain values which *O Pioneers!* had left up in the air. It is as if Willa Cather had finally made up her mind that her true allegiance was to the soil. The earlier book had shown that life on the farm yielded satisfactions which were deep but narrow; certain things essential to civilized existence just were not to be found there. In the later work all that any-one could ever hope for is pictured as being found on a farm. Án-

Reprinted from *The Landscape and the Looking Glass* (Boston, 1960) by permission of the Houghton Mifflin Company.

tonia has managed to make her husband happy for twenty-six years in one of the loneliest regions in the world, even though he was a city man and occasionally had spells of homesickness for the theaters and lighted cafés of the Old World.

But more important than this, the two books show different stages in the development of civilization. In *O Pioneers!* the greatest interest centers on the actual taming of the earth, the breaking of the virgin soil; only incidentally is it concerned with the attempt to found a family. The love of Emil and Marie is snuffed out and so cannot take root, and the proposed marriage of Carl and Alexandra is postponed until after the book's ending. In *My Ántonia,* on the other hand, there is much less emphasis on pioneering. What interested Willa Cather here is the quality of life on the plains, and for once in her career she focuses squarely on and affirms human relations. Much of the book deals with the attempts of the internal narrator and his heroine to come to grips with their emotional involvement with people. This finally results in Ántonia's establishing a domestic household as a going concern and the narrator's failing to do so. Ántonia's great achievement and the chief subject of the book is the founding of a family.

ÁNTONIA AND JIM: THE CONTRASTING LIFE CYCLES

My Ántonia has an interesting and rather peculiar introduction or prologue. In it Willa Cather pretends to have met Jim Burden, the fictitious narrator of the tale, on a train and has them agree that each one of them shall set down on paper his impressions of Ántonia, a mutual friend of their childhood. After months go by they meet again to find that Jim is the only one who has written anything; the rest of the book purports to be his manuscript. Thereafter Willa Cather herself drops out of the story as a separate character. The book that follows really consists of the parallel stories of Ántonia and Jim. The narrator points this out to us while explaining what he has written. "I simply wrote down what of herself and myself and other people Ántonia's name recalls to me. I suppose it hasn't any form. It hasn't any title either." Then he clinches the fact that this is to be the story of a relationship rather than of an individual by changing the wording on the front of the manuscript from "Ántonia" to "My Ántonia."

My Ántonia is usually called a novel with a single protagonist —the heroine—and the narrator has been considered relatively unimportant. I would like to suggest a different interpretation, because the role played by Jim Burden seems to me far too important to be merely that of a first-person onlooker who is relating someone else's story. He enters into the action too much, for one thing. In the early part of the book the Burden family is continually trudging over to their neighbors the Shimerdas to see if they can help them out. Later on there is a long section in which Jim attends the University of Nebraska and flirts with Lena Lingard; here Ántonia scarcely even appears. Even in the parts of the book where Ántonia and Jim appear together, Jim's reactions to events are at least as important as hers. If Willa Cather wanted her heroine to hold the undisputed center of the stage, she should have focused less attention on her narrator. As it is, the center of interest shifts back and forth between Jim and Ántonia, and the result is best understood as the story of parallel lives.

In her later novels Willa Cather often has a double protagonist such as this, one of whom resembles herself and the other someone who is not herself but whom she admires. One of these usually stands for the contemplative life, the other for the life of action. The use of a double protagonist has certain advantages: it allows one character to be an actor and the other a spectator; one can be youth which performs and accomplishes unthinkingly, the other middle age which can interpret the significance of action in others but itself has lost the capacity to act. In *My Ántonia* this double protagonist consists of Jim Burden and Ántonia, who, true to the best traditions of the romantic movement, stand for head and heart, respectively. It is as if Ántonia actually lives life, while Jim merely records it, or at best lives vicariously through her. When he is with her, Jim is a complete personality and reaches his highest development as a human being, but his personal life falls apart when he leaves her, however successful he may be in his professional role. Later in the book when he returns to visit Nebraska after a twenty years' absence, he finds out just how far Ántonia has forged ahead of him during that time. He is generous enough to rejoice in her good fortune, but it merely underlines his own lack of progress, and even regression, during that same interval. The more she tells him about her successful present, the more his mind wanders back to thoughts of their childhood together. Together he and the friend of his youth make a complete personality, but it is Janus-faced, one of them looking forward and the other back. Ántonia has the whole future for her domain; Jim Burden has only the past.

The principle on which this parallel story is constructed is that of development by contrasts. For in spite of early childhood experiences shared together, the lives of the two protagonists are radically unlike. Ántonia comes to Nebraska as an immigrant and in addition to other hardships of the plains has to face a language barrier; Jim Burden comes from Virginia and faces no such problem. Ántonia comes from a family wracked by internal dissensions, and her father is so unhappy that he commits suicide, largely because her mother is not a homemaker; Jim's family is a well-knit group in which order and happiness are maintained by a pair of extremely competent homemakers, his grandparents. The Shimerdas suffer from poverty for a great many years; the Burdens never have to meet this particular difficulty. As a result Jim can leave home and receive a university education, while Ántonia cannot even afford to take time off from the farm to attend grade school and learn English properly. Finally Jim leaves Nebraska for good to make his home in a large Eastern city where he enters into an unhappy and childless marriage; Ántonia stays on in Black Hawk and after a single unsuccessful effort succeeds not only in marrying but in founding a dynasty, having eleven children by the time Jim comes back to visit her twenty years later.

Although the two lives run parallel and are given almost equally extensive treatment, no doubt is left in the reader's mind that Ántonia is the one who has achieved the real success. Willa Cather loads the story in Ántonia's favor, not only by emphasizing Jim's obvious admiration for her, but by making all the significant action take place in Nebraska; Jim Burden's marriage and Eastern career are mentioned merely in passing. Accordingly, the early years on the plains are heavily stressed. This is not surprising, since the two main characters see relatively little of each other after childhood. But it does contribute mightily to the mood of nostalgia which is so strong an ingredient in Jim Burden's personality and which swells toward the end of the book into a hymn of praise for the past which Willa Cather aptly sums up in a line quoted from Vergil: *"Optima dies . . . prima fugit"* (*Georgics*, III, 66–67).

HUMAN RELATIONS: THE FAMILY AS RITUAL

If we consider *My Ántonia* as the story of two parallel but contrasting lives the book reveals a threefold thematic division. The first part deals with two opposed family groups, the Shimerdas and the Burdens, and their struggles with their environment. The second, beginning with the Burdens' removal to Black Hawk, deals mostly with the contrasting modes of life in country and town. This forms the major part of the book. The third, which describes Jim's return to Black Hawk after an absence of twenty years, shows Ántonia's final success in achieving her great goal in life, a family of her own. This last section fails to carry out the parallel structure of the previous parts except in briefest outline. The introduction tells us that in the intervening period Jim Burden has contracted an unfortunate and childless marriage which differentiates him from the fecund and happily married Ántonia. This would have given Willa Cather a splendid opportunity to develop the theme of the rootless city marriage versus the more stable country union, a theme which appeared later in *A Lost Lady* and *My Mortal Enemy*. But evidently Willa Cather did not care to develop the theme at this point, for she barely alludes to Jim's marriage in this final section of the book. This gives the concluding section a one-sided quality; the story here is almost entirely Ántonia's, and Jim merely stands to one side and worships her. One cannot help feeling that the ending would have been better if Jim Burden had been more dramatically implicated in it, as he had been in the previous sections. But, of course, given the nostalgic tone of the book, he couldn't have been.

As in *O Pioneers!* the first part of *My Ántonia* deals with the period of breaking the sod. Here again the precariousness of civilization on the plains is made to stand for the precariousness of life. But Willa Cather now uses different means to express this: the toughness of reality is now symbolized, not by the unwillingness of the land to be tamed, but among other things by the rigors of a continental climate. The extremes of hot and cold to be found in the Middle West stand for the best and worst life has to offer; heat is correlated with vitality and the great enemy of life is the cold. During a description of a December evening in which the Burden family is snowbound, Jim says:

I was convinced that man's strongest antagonist is the cold. I admired the cheerful zest with which grandmother went about keeping us warm and comfortable and well-fed. . . . Our lives centered around warmth and food and the return of the men at nightfall.

Here warmth obviously stands for something more than physical warmth and well-being; it represents the satisfaction of congenial family relations as well.

In other places warmth takes on a somewhat different meaning. In the introductory conversation on the train between Jim Burden and herself Willa Cather says:

We were talking about what it is like to spend one's childhood in little towns like these, buried in wheat and corn, under stimulating extremes of climate; burning summers when the world lies green and billowy beneath a brilliant sky, when one is fairly stifled in vegetation, in the color and smell of strong weeds and heavy harvests; blustery winters with little snow, when the whole country is stripped bare and gray as sheet-iron.

This suggests the sequence of birth and death as outlined in the vegetation myth, that age-old interpretation of the cycle of the seasons. On the side of warmth we have life, color, fecundity, and organic material; on the side of coldness we have death, lack of color, sterility, and sheet metal, which is something mechanical with no life in it. But more is to come. An elaboration of the statement that man's worst enemy is the cold carries us further:

Winter comes down savagely over a little town on the prairie. The wind that sweeps in from the open country strips away all the leafy screens that hide one yard from another in summer, and the houses seem to draw closer together. The roofs, that looked so far away across the green tree-tops, now stare you in the face, and they are much uglier than when their angles were softened by vines and shrubs.

In the morning, when I was fighting my way to school against the wind, I couldn't see anything but the road in front of me, but in the late afternoon, when I was coming home, the town looked bleak and desolate to me. The pale, cold light of the winter sunset did not beautify—it was like the light of truth itself. When the smoky clouds hung low in the west and the red sun went down behind them, leaving a pink flush on the snowy roofs and the blue drifts, then the wind sprang up afresh, with a kind of bitter song, as if it said: "This is reality, whether you like it or not. All those frivolities of summer, the light and shadow, the living mark of green that trembled over everything, they were lies, and this is what was underneath. This is the truth." It was as if we were being punished for loving the loveliness of summer.

We now begin to get an idea why the cold is man's greatest enemy. It represents the light of truth, and this as Willa Cather conceives it is always unpleasant, something to be hidden. Cold fact, she feels, is mankind's greatest enemy—the fact of his mortality, his frailty, his vulnerability before the forces of nature and before himself. These insights, which other people have erected into a tragic vision, she regarded as something to be put aside. Nor was this the limit of her fear of life—that fear which later led her into so much evasion. She felt that beauty, warmth, light, and loveliness—all the things she herself loved— were somehow lies. She also felt that they were evil, and that she would be punished for loving them.

The hostility of the climate turns out to threaten something that is vitally important to Willa Cather—the family unit. It will soon be time to see just what she meant by this all-important group. We have seen how in the Burden establishment Jim's grandmother kept the family going in spite of the cold. The family there is a center of warmth and affection, against not only the coldness of nature but also the coldness of life. This affection, however, is not of the dangerous explosive spontaneous kind which we have seen Willa Cather shying away from in *O Pioneers!* In a word, it is not sexual. Instead, as we shall see, it is affection such as the members of a large closely knit family feel for each other. The ways of feeling are clearly laid down, they are socially acceptable, and they have none of the dangerous destructive aspects of passion—or of the creative ones either.

To understand Willa Cather's portrayal of the family unit it is necessary to know the kind of family in which she herself grew up. She was the eldest child of seven, the daughter of a strong-willed aggressive mother and a charming but ineffectual father. The family came from Virginia but moved to the Nebraska frontier in the years following the Civil War. Willa Cather's father was the last of his family to move to Nebraska, leaving ten years after his brother and six years after his father had gone there. When he went, it was to live in the house of his father. Previous to this remove, he and his wife lived in the house of his mother-in-law, Willa's grandmother, whom they took along to Nebraska with them. Thus when Willa Cather first came to the frontier she lived in a family consisting of several brothers and sisters, a father and mother, a grandfather, and two grandmothers. In other words, her family was a multi-generation affair, quite large and closely knit.

The importance of this becomes clear when we examine her portrayal of the family unit in her fiction. Time after time the family is represented as being the source of all civilized values; it is the only social unit which she conceives of with any degree of intensity. She was able successfully to portray human relations in a family of the kind she had known in a way in which she was not able to portray, for instance, passionate love between a man and a woman. The interesting thing about her conception of the family is that it constitutes a Platonic hierarchy. Each member is assigned his own individual role, his status being defined by his duties toward the family considered as a corporate group. There is a regular ladder of rank starting with the children and proceeding up through the parents to the grandparents, who in *My Antonia* are regarded as the ultimate repositories of wisdom.

In *My Antonia* such a family is presented in the Burdens, the family of the narrator. Jim is an orphan who goes west at the age of ten to grow up with his grandfather and grandmother, but the place of parents is at least partly filled by other adults of his parents' generation who live with the family. In particular their place is taken by the cowboy Otto Fuchs and the hired hand Jake Marpole, who has come to Nebraska with Jim all the way from Virginia. So, even in the Burden family, Willa Cather's three-generation pattern is maintained. It is hard not to feel that the omission of the parents in *My Antonia* is significant in view of Willa Cather's general pattern of rejecting her immediate environment. They are dead, but their place is taken up by the goodhearted but essentially simple-minded Otto and Jake, whom Willa Cather can like but at the same time looks down on. Thus, while some of her attitudes have changed since her world-of-art period, others have persisted. However she may have changed about the Middle West, it seems likely that she still feels rebellious toward her parents.

When a Willa Cather character of this period thinks of home, however, he thinks not only of his relatives but also of the homestead. In a very real sense the universe of the prairie novels is a local, small-scale affair, embodying the family on the family farm presided over by local deities. That is why Jim Burden is so impressed when he goes to the university by his Latin professor's exposition of the beginning of the third book of Vergil's *Georgics*: *"Primus ego in patriam mecum . . . deducan Musas"*; "for I shall be the first, if I live, to bring the Muses into my country."

Cleric had explained to us what "patria" here meant, not a nation or even a province, but the little rural neighborhood on the Mincio where the poet was born. This was not a boast, but a hope, at once bold and devoutly humble, that he might bring the Muse (but lately come to Italy from her cloudy Grecian mountains), not to the capital, the *palatia Romana,* but to his own little "country"; to his father's fields, "sloping down to the river and to the old beech trees with broken tops."

Later on Jim wonders "whether that particular rocky strip of New England coast about which he had so often told me was Cleric's *patria*" because the concept of the family on the family land is so important to him. For the youthful Jim *patria* has meant his father's farm under the Blue Ridge of Virginia which he has to leave in his tenth year because of the death of his parents. This sudden uprooting and change of scene is devastating. When he is shipped out west to be reared by his grandfather it is as if he had moved to an entirely different universe where he is completely unknown. He feels he has outrun his lares and penates, and even the guardian spirits of his dead parents seem left behind. So homeless does he feel that he is not even sure that in this remote country God can hear his prayers:

There was nothing but land; not a country at all, but the materials out of which countries are made. . . . I had never before looked up at the sky when there was not a familiar mountain ridge against it. But this was the complete dome of heaven, all there was of it. I did not believe that my dead father and mother were watching me from up there; they would still be looking for me at the sheep-fold down by the creek, or along the white road that led to the mountain pastures. I had left even their spirits behind me. The wagon jolted on, carrying me I knew not whither. I don't think I was homesick. If we never arrived anywhere, it did not matter. Between that earth and that sky I felt erased, blotted out. I did not say my prayers that night: here, I felt, what would be would be.

If Jim had continued in this vein, he would have yielded to despair. Being young, however, he goes to sleep in the wagon and wakes to bright sunlight in a room in his grandparents' house. He awakens to find his grandmother looking down on him: "a tall woman with wrinkled brown skin and black hair. . . ."

"Had a good sleep, Jimmy?" she asked briskly. Then in a very different tone she said, as if to herself, "My, how you do look like your father!" I remembered that my father had been her little boy; she must often have come to wake him like this when he overslept.

The family is back in the picture once more; Jim has a grandmother who is very much alive and a dead father who yet lives vividly in her memory of him. A few household details provide a reassuring contrast to the last night's experience of the wildness and strangeness of the new land, and serve as a reminder that even in this remote country civilized domestic life is possible. Jim's grandmother is able to allay his fears by using a well-recognized formula for the expressing of emotion within the family framework. The home has become a kind of sanctuary; for Willa Cather the one thing that alleviates the terrible insecurity of emigration is the emotional protection furnished by the accepted modes of thought and feeling found within the family unit.

THE BURDENS AND THE SHIMERDAS: ORDER VS. CHAOS

From the beginning the Shimerda family is contrasted with the Burdens. They are pictured as being much less able to cope with the soil than their American neighbors. To be sure, they are at a tremendous disadvantage because they do not know English at first, and therefore have to depend on a fellow countryman of theirs named Krajiek, who is thoroughly dishonest. He has sold them his home, which is merely a cavelike dugout in the side of a hill, and has overcharged them for it. (The Burdens, by way of contrast, live in the only wooden house west of Black Hawk, itself a sign of civilization.) He exploits them in every way he knows how, but although they realize it they do not know how to get rid of him, for he is the only one they can turn to until the Burdens start giving them neighborly advice. Krajiek is the first evil thing they come across in the wild new land. He represents an early and somewhat abbreviated Willa Cather portrait of man's cruelty to men. In the old country the Shimerdas would never have gotten into a position where he could have taken advantage of them, but in the new West he is able to make the very conditions of life serve his own wily ends:

During those first months the Shimerdas never went to town. Krajiek encouraged them in the belief that in Black Hawk they would somehow be mysteriously separated from their money. They hated Krajiek, but they clung to him because he was the only human being with whom they could talk or from whom they could get information. He slept with the old man and the two boys in the dugout barn, along with the oxen. They kept him in their hole and fed him for the same reason that the prairie dogs and the brown owls house the rattlesnakes—because they did not know how to get rid of him.

But quite aside from the possession of such a dangling parasite, the Shimerdas are not equipped for life in the wilderness. They are improvident, for one thing, and are always giving away articles which please their friends. This characteristic, an important trait of all Willa Cather heroines, is better suited to an economy of abundance than to an economy of scarcity such as that found on the frontier. More important, they seem to lack know-how, the knowledge of how to make the most out of their scanty resources. It doesn't occur to Mrs. Shimerda to start a henhouse going in the fall so that her family will be able to have fresh eggs and poultry during the winter. For a while they are reduced to a diet of prairie-dog meat until the Burden family undertakes to revictual them with enough food to last them through the winter.

Mostly it is Mrs. Shimerda's fault that the family does so poorly. In *O Pioneers!* Willa Cather had indicated the important role she felt that women played in maintaining the usages of traditional civilization in an alien land. Of Mrs. Bergson, Alexandra's mother, she says:

For eleven years she had worthily striven to maintain some semblance of household order amid conditions that made order very difficult. Habit was very strong with Mrs. Bergson, and her unremitting efforts to repeat the routine of her old life among new surroundings had done a great deal to keep the family from disintegrating morally and getting careless in its ways. . . . Alexandra often said that if her mother were cast upon a desert island, she would thank God for her deliverance, make a garden, and find something to preserve.

Mrs. Shimerda has no such talent. She is not a homemaker; her house is a chaos, and she does nothing to bolster the morale of her gentle, mild-mannered husband, who is pining away with homesickness for his native Bohemia. It is quite understandable that Mr. Shimerda feels happiest when he is visiting with the Burdens, where everything is well regulated in a civilized manner. Willa Cather gives more than a hint that the despair which finally drives him to suicide is due at least in part to his wife's poor housekeeping:

I suppose, in the crowded clutter of their cave, the old man had come to believe that peace and order had vanished from the earth, or existed only in the old world he had left so far behind.

In marked contrast to this disorder is the well-ordered home run by the Burden family. The civilized quality of the life here is felt rather than described, although vivid little details go to build up an impression of it: the statement that the family lives in a wooden house rather than a sod hut, the fact that even in the basement the earthen walls are plastered and whitewashed; the description of the heavy copper-tipped rattlesnake cane which Grandmother used for killing rattlers she found in the garden, itself a token of the emphatic superimposition of civilization upon the country's wildness. The key words Willa Cather uses in describing the Burdens' existence are order, tranquillity, and regularity. No wonder Mr. Shimerda, with his "fixy" ways, feels when he is with them that he is among civilized people.

The head of the whole family group is the grandfather, a wonderful fountain of common sense. A good idea of what he was like is seen in his attitude toward the Indian ring:

Beyond the pond, on the slope that climbed to the cornfield, there was, faintly marked in the grass, a great circle where the Indians used to ride. Jake and Otto were sure that when they galloped round that ring Indians tortured pioneers, bound to a stake in the center; but grandfather thought they ran races or trained horses there.

Grandfather has a realistic mind, in contrast to the romantic attitude of the cowboy Otto and the fieldhand Jake, who are child men, strong in body and in loyalty, but untutored in the ways of the world. When trouble develops between the two families over a badly used piece of farming equipment the Shimerdas had borrowed and as a consequence Jake knocks Ambrosch Shimerda down, it is Grandfather who suggests that Jake go to the town justice of the peace, tell him the story and pay the fine for the assault, thus forestalling any action that the vindictive and litigious Mrs. Shimerda might take. And it is Grandfather who finally resolves the ensuing feud between the two families by hiring Ambrosch to help harvest his wheat crop and asking Ántonia to help with the feeding of the crews in the kitchen. When the danger of religious antagonism between Catholic and Protestant seems imminent, Grandfather Burden averts it by saying, "The prayers of all good people are good," and when the Shimerdas are unable to get a priest to conduct a service over Mr. Shimerda's grave because he was a suicide, Grandfather himself undertakes to say a prayer. Grandfather's opinion on any matter is always the final court of appeal because he is such a repository of sanity and common sense.

If Grandfather is the person to whom all religious and ethical problems are referred, Grandmother is the source of all judgments on aesthetic matters. She knows instinctively what is the right thing for a woman to do. She worries about the heavy farm work that Ambrosch makes Ántonia do after their father's death. "Heavy field work'll spoil that girl. She'll lose all her nice ways and get rough ones," she says, and she is right, since for a while Ántonia's hard life does make her lose all charm. Thus the Platonic hierarchy of assigned roles and qualities in the family is carried through as regards Grandfather and Grandmother Burden.

The most interesting results of the contrast between the Burden and Shimerda families are the quiet judgments that Willa Cather implicitly makes on what a family should be. The Shimerda family is not a unit. It breaks down into little groups which work at cross-purposes to one another. The grasping Mrs. Shimerda and her surly and arrogant son Ambrosch form one of these groups; Ántonia and her father form another. Old Mr. Shimerda is the most civilized person in the family and exemplifies the Old World traits that Willa Cather would most like to see carried over the seas. But unfortunately he is not strong, and we have already seen in the case of John Bergson, of *O Pioneers!*, that imagination and aesthetic sensitivity without strength are powerless to survive in a rough-and-ready new land. His wife, who might have been a prop and support to him if she had been a homemaker like Mrs. Bergson, only undermines her husband's morale. Her disorderly housekeeping, rather than emphasizing the continuity between life in Bohemia and life on the western plains, points up the disparity between the two. Her disorderly ways help contribute to her husband's despair by making his present life the exact opposite of everything he wanted his life to be, and in the end, driven beyond his endurance by misery, he commits suicide.

The Burden family, on the other hand, is a little commonwealth presided over by Grandmother and Grandfather. The latter's commands are obeyed unquestioningly since his authority comes to him straight from God—he is represented as being intensely religious—and he always uses that authority for the good of the family as a whole, not for any particular unit in it, as well as for the good of the pioneer community of which it forms a part. Grandmother Burden plays a more subdued but no less important role as maintainer of domestic routine; she succeeds in all the practical matters in which Mrs. Shimerda fails. Jake and Otto are the faithful family retainers, the men children, strong of back though weak of mind, whose devotion to Jim's grandparents is almost feudal. Their particular province is dealing with children; they teach Jim how to ride a pony, keep him entertained with stories of the Wild West, build a sleigh for him, cut down and bring in a tree for him at Christmas and decorate it with Christmas ornaments. To a certain extent the traditional roles of parents' and grandparents' generations are reversed, since the parent surrogates Otto and Jake play with Jim all the time and it is Grandfather and Grandmother Burden who are the disciplinarians.

There is an ironic twist at the end of *My Antonia* that heightens the contrast between the two families and tells a good deal about the novel's values. The Shimerdas are an anarchic disintegrating family group which seems bent on its own destruction, and yet it produces Ántonia, who emerges at the end of the novel as the family founder *par excellence.* All these traits she learned from the Burdens, and rightly so for they form a model family. But in spite of all its good qualities, it is the Burden family which dies out. The improvident family turns out to be the one that produces the most successful homemaker and the model family produces no one capable of carrying on its traditions. But the spirit of Grandmother and Grandfather Burden has been passed on to Ántonia. That is one reason why Jim admires her so much.

The reason for this interchange of roles between the two families has to do with one of Willa Cather's deepest feelings about the value of a family living on the family land. For after Jim Burden has been living in Nebraska for three years, his grandparents become too old for heavy farm work and decide to move into town. This produces a change of the profoundest significance in the nature of the Burden family. It makes Otto and Jake want to leave the Burdens' employ for one thing. Both men are such dyed-in-the-wool children of the wide-open spaces that they would be lost in town. Willa Cather says of them:

Jake and Otto served us to the last. They moved us into town, put down the carpets in our new house, made shelves and cupboards for grandmother's kitchen, and seemed loath to leave us. But at last they went, without warning. Those two fellows had been faithful to us through sun and storm, had given us things that cannot be bought in any market in the world. With me they had been like older brothers; had restrained their speech and manners out of care for me, and given me so much good comradeship. Now they got on the west-bound train one morning, in their Sunday clothes, with their oilcloth valises—and I never saw them again. Months afterward we got a card from Otto, saying that Jake had been down with mountain fever, but now they were both working in the Yankee Girl Mine, and were doing well. I wrote to them at that address, but my letter was returned to me, "unclaimed." After that we never heard from them.

The departure of Jake and Otto combined with the removal to Black Hawk makes the Burdens a rootless town family which no longer consists of several generations. When this happens they lose their country roots and can no longer absorb all the special virtues which Willa Cather saw as emanating from a life lived close to the land. The agrarian myth has it that the virtuous yeoman is virtuous no longer once he migrates to the city, even if the city turns out to be only a small town like Black Hawk. That is why the Burden family dwindles to nothing; Jim ends up a landless, childless failure, in marked contradistinction to Ántonia, who stays on the land.

DEATH IN WINTER AND THE HARDNESS OF LIFE

One of the strong points of *My Ántonia* as compared with Willa Cather's other novels is that in it she comes closer than she usually does to facing the problem of evil and suffering in life. This frankness in recognizing the reality of problems which are ultimately insoluble gives the book an emotional depth which one looks for in vain in much of her work. If by evil we mean anything impairing the happiness or welfare of a person or depriving him of good, there is a good deal of evil in *My Ántonia*. Briefly, the varieties Willa Cather describes can be summed up under three headings: natural or external nonhuman evil, man-made evil inflicted by other people, and evil which is self-inflicted.

Natural evil is the simplest of the three and in a sense is no problem at all. One meets it on the frontier or elsewhere by pitting oneself against the forces of nature, and one either succeeds or fails. Sometimes one proves oneself a man by overcoming natural forces, as does the youthful Jim when he kills the great rattlesnake which attacks him in prairie-dog town. Sometimes it is the forces of nature which triumph over man.

Man-made evil inflicted by other persons is more complicated and cannot be summed up so easily. I have described how the Bohemian Krajiek exploited his fellow countrymen the Shimerdas. Another example is Wick Cutter, the Black Hawk money lender, whom Willa Cather treats as a comic character in spite of the ferocious reputation she gives him. He fastens like a bloodsucker upon the poverty-stricken farmers of the neighborhood, and Grandfather Burden has had to rescue more than one poor

devil from his clutches. He has an interestingly unhappy relation
with his wife which can be summed up by her remark to him
when, in exhibiting some of her chinaware to a caller, he accidentally drops a piece: "Mr. Cutter, you have broken all the
commandments—spare the finger-bowls!" As they grow older
they quarrel continually over the disposal of his estate should
she survive him; he is afraid that it will all go to her "people,"
whom he hates. He finally solves the problem melodramatically
by murdering her and then shooting himself an hour later, after
firing a shot out the window to insure the presence of witnesses
to testify to the fact that he had survived his wife and that therefore any will she might have made would be invalid. Willa
Cather's comic treatment of Wick Cutter tends to preclude any
real consideration of the moral implications of his acts, since he
is turned into a character in a grand farce. As a comic figure of
evil he lacks reality and seems to have no relation to the world as
we know it; evidently Willa Cather does not intend to have him
taken too seriously.

A more telling example of man-made evil inflicted by others
can be found in Ántonia's pregnancy. She falls in love with a
railroad conductor named Larry Donovan, a "train-crew aristocrat" who fancies himself a ladies' man; he lures her to Denver
with promises of marriage and then deserts her, leaving her with
a child on the way. Unlike the love passages in *O Pioneers!* this is
not presented directly to the reader. Instead of being narrated
by Jim Burden, it is told to him by another person, the Widow
Steavens, since the episode has occurred after Jim has left the
University of Nebraska for Harvard. The Widow Steavens is a
pioneer, an older woman of the same generation and stature as
Jim's grandparents, and so her comments on the tale carry a moral
authority which they would not if they had issued from the lips
of a younger person. In her mouth the story of Ántonia's seduction
assumes overtones that are almost tragic: the bad prosper, the
good come to misfortune through their very virtues, and no one
knows why:

"Jimmy, I sat right down on that bank beside her and made lament.
I cried like a young thing. I couldn't help it. I was just about heart-

broke. . . . My Ántonia, that had so much good in her, had come home disgraced. And that Lena Lingard, that was always a bad one, say what you will, had turned out so well, and was coming home here every summer in her silks and her satins, and doing so much for her mother. I give credit where credit is due, but you know well enough, Jim Burden, there is a great difference in the principles of those two girls. And here it was the good one that had come to grief!"

For all her heartbrokenness the Widow Steavens does not turn against Ántonia as Jim does; with the ferocity of youth he cannot forgive her for becoming an object of pity. The Widow Steavens, on the other hand, is able to accept the fact that there is a tragic incomprehensibility in the fates meted out to human beings; she can admit that Ántonia has made a mistake and still believe in her. This makes her superior to Jim, whose immediate reaction to Ántonia is one of rejection as soon as the image he has of her is broken. Jim is a typical Willa Cather character in this; he makes a hard-and-fast rule about people and things and prefers to see the world in terms of black and white.

But Ántonia does not remain an object of pity for long. Like Hester Prynne, she gains from suffering a new kind of strength, and finally is accepted even by the community:

"Folks respected her industry and tried to treat her as if nothing had happened. They talked, to be sure; but not like they would if she'd put on airs. She was so crushed and quiet that nobody seemed to want to humble her."

Her bitter experience has given her more self-knowledge than Marie Shabata ever had a chance to learn; she now knows the dangers as well as the delights of unbridled spontaneity and of absolute commitment to the objects of one's affection. As she tells Jim when he comes back to visit her twenty years after, "The trouble with me was, Jim, I never could believe harm of anybody I loved."

One would expect the birth of Ántonia's illegitimate child to form the climax of the book, but no. The whole episode is only thirty pages long and is related to Jim Burden by a third person, the Widow Steavens. In other words, the reader is not once removed from the action but twice removed from it. This in itself is the most significant thing about the whole event. It shows a trait highly characteristic of Willa Cather's fiction—that in it she did not really want to present directly any sort of serious human conflict. The really emotional situations, the scenes in which it was necessary to face up to the hard facts about human nature and passions, she avoided if she could. Of *My Antonia* she said:

> There was material in that book for a lurid melodrama. But I decided that in writing it, I would dwell very lightly on those things that a novelist would ordinarily emphasize, and make up my story of the little, every-day happenings and occurrences that form the greatest part of everyone's life and happiness.

If this was her attitude one may ask why she bothered including the story of the birth of the baby at all. For she was not bound to follow in every detail the life of the person upon which the character of Ántonia was based. The fact that she chose both to include the episode and to treat it in the precise way that she did indicates that she was bent on devaluing some of the devastating conflicts that occur in life, particularly those relating to sex. And if this is so she is being dishonest and evasive, and her representation of the human scene suffers from distortion in consequence.

From what has gone before it seems clear that Willa Cather tended to make light of the difficulties raised by man-made evil inflicted by other persons. It is natural for her to do so, since this sort of evil runs directly counter to her belief in the overriding power of the heroic will, and to admit its potency to hurt us is to admit the inadequacy of that will. For this reason the real interdependence of men and women is minimized in her novels; she is more interested in making them appear independent.

But there is one other kind of man-made evil in *My Antonia*, and one to which a person who aspires to be independent is particularly prone. This is self-inflicted evil or despair, and its logical result is suicide. Two acts of despair and self-destruction are described in the book, one minor one which is mentioned as an anecdote in passing and an important one which forms a major part of the book. The important one is the suicide of Ántonia's father, Mr. Shimerda.

The minor one has to do with a tramp who arrives at Black Hawk during harvest time. He comes up to a crew running a threshing machine and remarks to Ántonia, who is one of them: "The ponds in this country is done got so low a man couldn't drown himself in one of 'em." Ántonia objects:

"I told him nobody wanted to drownd themselves, but if we didn't have rain soon we'd have to pump water for the cattle.

" 'Oh, cattle,' he says, 'you'll all take care of your cattle! Ain't you got no beer here?' "

The tramp offers to help run the threshing machine, and after cutting bands for a few minutes, jumps into the hopper. By the time they get the machine stopped, he is cut to pieces. The incident itself is not so important as the way Willa Cather treats it. This is what she supplies by way of comment:

"Now wasn't that strange, Miss Frances?" Tony asked thoughtfully. "What would anybody want to kill themselves in summer for? In thrashing time, too! It's nice everywhere then."

"So it is, Ántonia," said Mrs. Harling heartily. "Maybe I'll go home and help you thresh next summer. Isn't that taffy nearly ready to eat? I've been smelling it for a long while."

The discussion then shifts to another field. Here in a nutshell is one of Willa Cather's most glaring weaknesses: when her mind is presented with something unpleasant, it shies away from it. The problem of evil is posed, but not commented on. Instead she is evasive and changes the subject.

The best example in the book of self-inflicted evil resulting from despair is the suicide of Mr. Shimerda. Willa Cather treats this differently from the death of the tramp; for once she faces the problem of evil squarely and gives a satisfactory artistic presentation of it. For there is no flinching from the reality of death in the description of Mr. Shimerda's suicide and its consequences. When he can stand things no longer, he washes with hot water, dresses up in clean clothes, and goes out to the barn where he puts the barrel of a gun in his mouth and pulls the trigger. What happens to the people around him after that, the Shimerdas and the Burden family and the community at large, Willa Cather describes at length and deals with not in terms of what death means to the individual but of what it means to the people who survive him.

The reason Mr. Shimerda kills himself is that he cannot stand life on the Divide. Like John Bergson in *O Pioneers!* he is a prime example of a man who has imagination enough to be a pioneer, but not the strength. Except his death, every single important event in his life had been determined for him by others. He need not have married Mrs. Shimerda in the first place—as Ántonia tells Jim, he could have paid her some money instead. He had not wanted to come to America at all, but was browbeaten into coming by his ambitious wife. As her daughter puts it, "All the time she say: 'America big country; much money, much land for my boys, much husband for my girls.'" When he is exposed to the chaos and squalor of the Shimerda farm it apparently never occurs to him to pick up and leave—to go back to an Eastern city, or even to Europe. He is not a man of action, and any other kind of man is lost on the frontier. Unable to use force against the external world, he finally raises his hand against himself.

This causes consternation among his family, since aside from the abdication of responsibility involved he is a Catholic and suicide is not allowed to him. But through her narrator Jim Burden Willa Cather makes clear that she is sympathetic with Mr. Shimerda's act:

"As I understand it," Jake concluded, "it will be a matter of years to pray his soul out of Purgatory, and right now he's in torment."

"I don't believe it," I said stoutly. "I almost know it isn't true." . . . Nevertheless, after I went to bed, this idea of punishment and Purgatory came back to me crushingly. I remembered the account of Dives in torment, and shuddered. But Mr. Shimerda had not been rich and selfish; he had only been so unhappy that he could not live any longer.

The details of the suicide itself are handled very briefly, in the space of a couple of pages. The rest of the episode describes the effect of Mr. Shimerda's death on his family, his friends, and the pioneer community. Willa Cather does not dwell on the emotional reactions of the Shimerda family except to say that the oldest son Ambrosch was "deeply, even slavishly, devout," sitting with a rosary in his hands and praying all morning while the Burdens make arrangements for his father's burial. Significantly enough Ántonia's responses are hardly mentioned. What Willa Cather does describe is the emotional impact of the calamity on the Burden family. The Burdens rise to the occasion to fill their friends' needs. It is they who do most of the work in preparation for Mr. Shimerda's burial, and it is their emotional reactions which Willa Cather seems to find most interesting. Grandfather is the usual fountain of good sense, the grandmother, in the maternal role once again, gives food and comfort to the younger Shimerdas, who now have nobody to look after them. But it is Otto Fuchs, the Austrian cowboy, upon whom the burden of meeting the crisis devolves. It is he who relates the circumstances of Mr. Shimerda's death to Grandmother Burden and young Jim. He volunteers to make the long ride through the snow into Black Hawk in order to fetch the priest and coroner. And it is he who volunteers to make a coffin, and by his cheerful matter-of-fact awareness and acceptance of death helps the people around him to realize that in spite of disaster life can and does go on:

"The last time I made one of these, Mrs. Burden," he continued as he sorted and tried his chisels, "was for a fellow in the Black Tiger mine up above Silverton, Colorado. . . . It's a handy thing to know, when you knock about like I've done."

"We'd be hard put to it now, if you didn't know, Otto," grandmother said.

"Yes, 'm," Fuchs admitted with honest pride. "So few folks know how to make a good tight box that'll turn water. I sometimes wonder if there'll be anybody about to do it for me. However, I'm not at all particular that way."

The pleasure he gets from handling his carpenter's tools shows that, far from being squeamish or afraid of death, he readily accepts it. He is able actively to enjoy the job at hand, since he realizes its constructive and even religious nature; his intellectual simplicity does not prevent him from recognizing death as one of the great facts of existence:

All afternoon, wherever one went in the house, one could hear the panting wheeze of the saw or the pleasant purring of the plane. They were cheerful noises, seeming to promise new things for living people: it was a pity that the freshly planed pine boards were to be put underground so soon. The lumber was hard to work because it was full of frost, and the boards gave off a sweet smell of pine woods, as the heap of yellow shavings grew higher and higher. I wondered why Fuchs had not stuck to cabinet work, he settled down to it with such ease and content. He handled the tools as if he liked the feel of them; and when he planed, his hands went back and forth over the boards in an eager, beneficent way as if he were blessing them. He broke out now and then into German hymns, as if this occupation brought back old times to him.

Another effect of Mr. Shimerda's suicide is that it makes the pioneers much more talkative than they usually are. It releases speech in the people who hear about it, and thus unites the living into a closer-knit group than they had formed before. Since their talk is mostly about the deaths of others they have known of or heard about, it serves to tighten the organic bonds of the little frontier community in much the same way as a funeral service is supposed to do:

One pleasant thing about this time was that everybody talked more than usual. I had never heard the postmaster say anything but "Only the papers, to-day," or "I've got a sackful of mail for ye," until this afternoon. Grandmother always talked, dear woman; to herself or to the Lord, if there was no one else to listen; but grandfather was naturally taciturn, and Jake and Otto were often so tired after supper that I used to feel as if I were surrounded by a wall of silence. Now everyone seemed eager to talk. That afternoon Fuchs told me story after story; about the Black Tiger mine, and about violent deaths and casual buryings, and the queer fancies of dying men. You never really knew a man, he said, until you saw him die. Most men were game, and went without a grudge.

The rallying together of the community's forces enables the people better to face up to the unpleasant reality of the hardness of life. To express that hardness Willa Cather refers to the already mentioned rigors of the continental climate in a submerged metaphor based on her statement that "man's greatest enemy is the cold." The submerged metaphor is that of frozen blood. It is hard in both the literal and figurative senses; the very stuff of life itself has been reduced to immobility by nature's indifference:

The dead man was frozen through, "just as stiff as a dressed turkey you hang out to freeze," Jake said. The horses and oxen would not go into the barn until he was frozen so hard that there was no longer any smell of blood. They were stabled there now, with the dead man, because there was no other place to keep them.

Mr. Shimerda lay dead in the barn four days, and on the fifth day they buried him. All day Friday Jelinek was off with Ambrosch digging the grave, chopping out the frozen earth with old axes. On Saturday we breakfasted before daylight and got into the wagon with the coffin. Jake and Jelinek went ahead on horseback to cut the body loose from the pool of blood in which it was frozen fast to the ground.

The fact that the pioneers are willing to chop Mr. Shimerda's body loose from the pool of frozen blood shows that they are facing unflinchingly the toughness of reality, the hardness of life. It is no accident that the body is frozen, or that the death occurs in the midst of winter. According to the old vegetation myth winter is the death of the year, because all crops have died down in the fall, and are not to be reborn until spring. The meaning of the myth is that death is not final; one year's crop dies, but next year's crop takes its place; in human terms, the individual dies but the community lives on. This is just what happens in *My Antonia*; the chapter following the one describing the burial of Mr. Shimerda, and dealing with the further fortunes of his family, begins with a description of the coming spring.

COUNTRY VS. TOWN:
THE SUPERIORITY OF THE COUNTRYSIDE

The middle portion of the book, which is largely the story of Jim's school and college days, deals with a problem which we have seen was left unsolved at the end of *O Pioneers!* and which is unresolved in Willa Cather's work as a whole. It is the problem of the relative advantages between country and town. Although the book ends with a glorification of the life of the country, it turns out to be a qualified glorification. Ántonia may become an earth-goddess, but she gets many of her good qualities from her father, who was a town dweller. Thus Willa Cather's idea of the good country life really turns out to be that of one in which urban and rural traits which she considers desirable are combined.

My Ántonia's middle section opens with the removal of the Burdens from farm to town. Just as in the book's first part the edge is taken off the strangeness of Jim's arrival in the West by a description of the cozy life led by Jim's grandparents, so the town is rendered more friendly to him by the description of another family whom he admires, the Harlings. These nextdoor neighbors are as much paragons of town life as the Burdens were of life in the country. The father and eldest daughter are in business—a calling which the later Willa Cather comes to detest; yet she has nothing but approval for them. The father is quite authoritarian: when he is at home no one is allowed to make any noise, and he insists on having all his wife's attention to the exclusion even of his children. He is much more authoritarian than the bearded patriarch who was his country counterpart, for Mr. Harling is not shown as having a saving sense of humor; but, far from resenting this, Jim seems to find it interesting and rather grand. There is no doubt that Willa Cather enjoyed the portrayal of authoritarian personalities. The oldest daughter, Frances Harling, is her father's business associate and takes care of his transactions for him while he is away on trips. Jim admires her, too, and finds her quite as satisfactory a human being as if she were a man.

Into this ménage Willa Cather introduces Ántonia, who, tiring of the rough life she knows on the farm, comes into town to "go into service," thus hoping to earn money for the folks back home and at the same time see a little more of life than had hitherto come her way. Through the agency of the Burden family she goes to work for the Harlings. She immediately becomes popular with her employers, and they carry on the process of education which had been begun by her father but which would never have gotten very far if it had been left in the tender hands of the grabby Mrs. Shimerda and the sullen Ambrosch. Jim, too, finds himself drawn to the brightly lighted Harling home, from which seem to emanate all the most desirable things in civilization:

Frances taught us to dance that winter, and she said, from the first lesson, that Ántonia would make the best dancer among us. On Saturday nights, Mrs. Harling used to play the old operas for us,—"Martha," "Norma," "Rigoletto,"—telling us the story while she played. Every Saturday night was like a party. The parlor, the back parlor, and the dining room were warm and brightly lighted, with comfortable chairs and sofas, and gay pictures on the walls. One always felt at ease there. Ántonia brought her sewing and sat with us—she was already beginning to make pretty clothes for herself. After the long winter evenings on the prairie, with Ambrosch's sullen silences and her mother's complaints, the Harling home seemed, as she said, "like Heaven" to her.

Part of the reason Mrs. Harling is able to educate Ántonia is that, town-bred or not, she is essentially the same kind of person that Ántonia is. Both have a deep instinctive response to life:

There was a basic harmony between Ántonia and her mistress. They had strong, independent natures, both of them. They knew what they liked; and were not always trying to imitate other people. They loved children and animals and music, and rough play and digging in the earth. They liked to prepare rich, hearty food and to see people eat it; to make up soft white beds and to see youngsters asleep in them. They ridiculed conceited people and were quick to help unfortunate ones. Deep down in each of them there was a kind of hearty joviality, a relish of life, not over-delicate, but very invigorating. I never tried to define it, but I was distinctly conscious of it. I could not imagine Ántonia's living for a week in any other home in Black Hawk than in the Harlings'.

In spite of her great fondness for her employers, Ántonia finally leaves them. One night a young man who has escorted Ántonia home from a dance tries to kiss her, and when she protests—because he is going to be married the following Monday—he uses strong-arm tactics and she slaps him. The autocratic Mr. Harling has heard all this and puts his foot down: she will have to stay away from Saturday night dances or else find a new place. Ántonia utterly refuses: nothing is going to make her give up her good times, and so she and the Harlings part.

Ántonia's revolt against the Harlings is only one extension of the rebellion she had already begun against her own family. It is a rebellion in favor of the good things of life; years of drudgery on a remote farm with only an unpleasant mother and brother for company had begotten in her a fierce desire to enjoy life's sweets. To us the rebellion seems mild, since it consists chiefly of having a good time and going out with young men to dances, although it culminates in her being "fooled" by Larry Donovan's promise of marriage and having a baby by him after he had abandoned her. The significance of her rebellion is that it shows Ántonia's asserting her independence from her family as well as from the Harlings. This is a vitally important step for Willa Cather's early heroines, since they seem to feel that without completely rejecting parental authority they cannot be individuals in their own right.

My Ántonia is unique in Willa Cather's early writing in that in it she for once represents a happy marriage and a family at its best; that is, she is able to feel more attraction for the family than revulsion against it. Later on, Ántonia, this nonconformist and rebel against the family, lives to marry and found a family of her own; having experienced many sides of life, she now knows a good deal of what life is about, and is all the better a mother for it. To achieve this effect, Willa Cather has manipulated the plot so that Ambrosch and Mrs. Shimerda are as unattractive as possible; thus a revolt from them is a revolt toward life itself. Ántonia must rebel against a bad family before she can set up a good family. Thus she is able both to be a rugged individualist and later on to enjoy the advantages of group membership too.

If the youthful Ántonia is spirited enough to be rebellious, the same cannot be said of the town girls. One of the most explicit contrasts between town and country which Willa Cather makes in the book is that between the farm-bred females and the girls of Black Hawk. Other girls besides Ántonia get tired of the country and go into service in Black Hawk in order to make the most of town life. When Jim Burden is growing toward manhood he becomes their great admirer. Here is what he has to say about them:

> There was a curious social situation in Black Hawk. All the young men felt the attraction of the fine, well-set-up country girls who had come to town to earn a living, and, in nearly every case, to help the father struggle out of debt, or to make it possible for the younger children of the family to go to school.
>
> Those girls had grown up in the first bitter-hard times, and had got little schooling themselves. But the younger brothers and sisters, for whom they made such sacrifices and who have had "advantages," never seem to me, when I meet them now, half as interesting or as well educated. The older girls, who helped to break up the wild sod, learned so much from life, from poverty, from their mothers and grandmothers; they had all, like Ántonia, been early awakened and made observant by coming at a tender age from an old country to a new. [It is a matter of interest to note that Willa Cather herself came from Virginia to Nebraska at the tender age of nine.] I can remember a score of these country girls who were in service in Black Hawk during the few years I lived there, and I can remember something unusual about each one of them. Physically they were almost a race apart, and out-of-door work had given them a vigor which, when they got over their first shyness about coming to town, developed into a positive carriage and freedom of movement, and made them conspicuous among Black Hawk women.
>
> Unlike the town girls, they had had the hard jolt of coming from one civilization into another of an entirely different kind; they were not able to take for granted habits and customs which were after all only peculiar to one time and place, but were less likely to be conformist and more likely in a given situation to

think things out for themselves. This is Jim Burden's analysis of the "strong, independent natures" which he admires so much.

For the town girls he has nothing but a qualified contempt. "Girls who had to walk more than half a mile to school were pitied," he says:

There was not a tennis court in the town; physical exercise was thought rather inelegant for the daughters of well-to-do families. Some of the High School girls were jolly and pretty, but they stayed indoors in winter because of the cold, and in summer because of the heat. When one danced with them their bodies never moved inside their clothes; their muscles seemed to ask but one thing—not to be disturbed. I remember those girls merely as faces in the schoolroom, gay and rosy, or listless and dull, cut off below the shoulders, like cherubs, by the ink-smeared tops of the high desks that were surely put there to make us round-shouldered and hollow chested.

Such is Jim Burden's attack on the genteel tradition whose ideal of feminine refinement is an anemic passivity which regards any form of physical activity as vulgar. The contrast between the hired girls and their mistresses is the opposition between country and town life, between vitality and listlessness. The townspeople, blissfully unaware of their own shortcomings, looked down on the prairie-bred girls because they earned their living, because they were "foreigners," and (so Willa Cather hints) because they were so attractive. As Jim Burden tells us:

The country girls were considered a menace to the social order. Their beauty shone out too boldly against a conventional background. But anxious mothers need have no alarm. They mistook the mettle of their sons. The respect for respectability was stronger than any desire in Black Hawk.

And he goes on to tell the story of Sylvester Lovett, the half-hearted swain who becomes so infatuated with Lena Lingard that he is unable to make his bankbooks balance, but who manages to cure himself by running away with a widow six years older than himself, "who owned a half-section." Jim Burden is perfectly furious with him when this cure takes: he had "hoped that Sylvester would marry Lena, and thus give all the country girls a better position in the town." In this incident we have Willa Cather's commentary on the social history of Black Hawk: All the young men of good families were afraid to marry the immigrant girls. If they hadn't been the old New England stock might have been rejuvenated by mating with a more vital breed—vital because it was able to profit from being transplanted into new surroundings—and might not have gone on to produce a generation of Wick Cutters.

This failure of town and country to mingle spells the death the town. In her next novel, *One of Ours*, Willa Cather gives her view of what happened to communities like Black Hawk when the descendants of the original settlers lost whatever vitality their progenitors possessed. They became completely immersed in a conventional commercial existence in which they learn a great deal about how to make money but nothing at all about how to spend it wisely. Willa Cather here shows striking similarities to Sherwood Anderson, Sinclair Lewis, and others who figured in the post-World War I revolt from the village. This attitude is present in *My Ántonia* also:

> On starlight nights I used to pace up and down those long, cold streets, scowling at the little, sleeping houses on either side, with their storm-windows and covered back porches. They were flimsy shelters, most of them poorly built of light wood, with spindle porch-posts horribly mutilated by the turning-lathe. Yet for all their frailness, how much jealousy and envy and unhappiness some of them seemed to contain! The life that went on in them seemed to me made up of evasions and negations; shifts to save cooking, to save washing and cleaning, devices to propitiate the tongue of gossip. This guarded mode of existence was like living under a tyranny. People's speech, their voices, their very glances, became furtive and repressed. Every individual taste, every natural appetite was bridled by caution. The people asleep in their houses, I thought, tried to live like the mice in their own kitchens; to make no noise, to leave no trace, to slip over the surface of things in the dark.

This last simile is a good example of the "do I dare to eat a peach" attitude; the townspeople feel that they are intruders in a universe in which they have no business to be. Usually, however, the narrator's impatience with Black Hawk is treated in a lighter vein. As the adolescent Jim Burden tramps the streets looking for things to do, he finds that most of the people around him are as bored as he is. There is for example this fine description of small-town ennui:

One could hang about the drug-store, and listen to the old men who sat there every evening, talking politics and telling new stories. One could go to the cigar factory and chat with the old German who raised canaries for sale, and look at his stuffed birds. But whatever you began with him, the talk went back to taxidermy. There was the depot, of course; I often went down to see the night train come in, and afterward sat awhile with the disconsolate telegrapher who was always hoping to be transferred to Omaha or Denver, "where there was some life." He was sure to bring out his pictures of actresses and dancers. He got them with cigarette coupons, and nearly smoked himself to death to possess these desired forms and faces. For a change one could talk to the station agent; but he was another malcontent; spent all his spare time writing letters to officials requesting a transfer. He wanted to get back to Wyoming where he could go trout-fishing on Sundays.

From the stifling confinement of small-town life Jim turns with relief to the open air. The gay country girls come to signify for him the joyful expansiveness of country life as opposed to the contraction of the circle of living which oppresses him so much in town. The highest point of the book's middle section occurs when he goes with Ántonia and the hired girls on a picnic. They spend an idyllic day by the shores of the river, and in a long passage meant to celebrate the joys of country living the girls point out their fathers' farms to him, talk about them, and boast of the things they are going to get for their families. Then comes the passage which is meant to be the climax:

"Jim," Ántonia said dreamily, "I want you to tell the girls about how the Spanish first came here, like you and Charley Harling used to talk about. I've tried to tell them, but I leave out so much."

They sat under a little oak, Tony resting against the trunk and the other girls leaning against her and each other, and listened to the little

I was able to tell them about Coronado and his search for the Seven Golden Cities. At school we were taught that he had given up his quest and turned back somewhere in Kansas. But Charley Harling and I had a strong belief that he had been along this very river. A farmer in the county north of ours, when he was breaking sod, had turned up a metal stirrup of fine workmanship, and a sword with a Spanish inscription on the blade. He lent these relics to Mr. Harling, who brought them home with him. Charley and I scoured them, and they were on exhibition in the Harling office all summer. Father Kelly, the priest, had found the name of the Spanish maker on the sword, and an abbreviation that stood for the city of Cordova.

"And that I saw with my own eyes," Ántonia put in triumphantly. "So Jim and Charley were right, and the teachers were wrong!"

The girls began to wonder among themselves. Why had the Spaniards come so far? What must this country have been like, then? Why had Coronado never gone back to Spain, to his riches and his castles and his king? I couldn't tell them. I only knew the school books said he "died in the wilderness, of a broken heart."

"More than him has done that," said Ántonia sadly, and the girls murmured assent.

We sat looking off across the country, watching the sun go down. The curly grass about us was on fire now. The bark of the oaks turned red as copper. There was a shimmer of gold on the brown river. Out in the stream the sandbars glittered like glass, and the light trembled in the willow thickets as if little flames were leaping among them. The breeze sank to stillness. In the ravine a ringdove mourned plaintively, and somewhere off in the bushes an owl hooted. The girls sat listless, leaning against each other. The long fingers of the sun touched their foreheads.

Presently we saw a curious thing: There were no clouds, and the sun was going down in a limpid, gold-washed sky. Just as the lower edge of the red disc rested on the high fields against the horizon, a great black figure suddenly appeared on the face of the sun. We sprang to our feet, straining our eyes toward it. In a moment we realized what it was. On some upland farm, a plough had been left standing in the field. The sun was sinking just behind it. Magnified across the distance by the horizontal light, it stood out against the sun, was exactly contained within the circle of the disc; the handles, the tongue, the share —black against the molten red. There it was, heroic in size, a picture writing on the sun.

Even while we whispered about it, our vision disappeared; the ball dropped and dropped until the red tip went beneath the earth. The fields below us were forgotten, the sky was growing pale, and that forgotten plough had sunk back to its own littleness somewhere on the prairie.

Coronado stands for the spirit of adventure and romance, and the kind of life young people dream about. The pedantic mind, which is the enemy of Coronado and all his kind, denied that that Spanish *conquistador* had ever set foot between the Republican River and the river Platte; Nebraska, it holds, is too mundane ever to have been part of the realms of romance. But the young people's own experience gives this the lie; they are sure Coronado has been along this very river, and sure enough, a Spanish sword is plowed up, with an inscription and an abbreviation of Cordova on the blade. So the spirit of romance has been to this dry, flat country; but the spirit of romance is not enough. It can see things, but it cannot persevere. Coronado never did find what he was looking for, but died in the wilderness of a broken heart. But if the spirit of romance had been to this country, so has the spirit of civilization. This is symbolized by the plough against the sun. The agricultural implement is made the symbol of a whole way of life; as it stands with its tongue and shares contained within the circle of the sun it becomes representative of everything Willa Cather has been glorifying. Willa Cather prepares for this symbol, as she does for others, by the use of light as a transfiguring agent. The world as seen under ordinary light, the common light of day, looks as ordinary and commonplace as the pedantic mind can conceive of it as being, but when illuminated by some special kind of light, such as sunset, it becomes transfigured and the real glory that lies latent in everyday things is brought out. In this manner a perfectly ordinary, homely farming tool is made the symbol of a settled agricultural civilization, which is thereby given a kind of cosmic approval.

Coronado and the plough against the sun are two opposites which, taken together, are meant to embrace the whole of life; neither one is sufficient alone, but together they suffice. Coronado had his heart broken by the plains country, but the plough conquered it. In her choice of the plough as a symbol, Willa Cather shows that the people she is most interested in are not the nomadic pioneers but the tillers of the soil who come after them; her symbol stands in marked contrast to the hunting dog and musket grouped around the dying Leatherstocking at the end of Cooper's novel, *The Prairie.*

Jim Burden now fully realizes the superiority of country life to life in a small town, but so far he has little acquaintance with the world outside the rural areas: his vision is still bounded by the horizon of his neighbors' cornfields. Desperately wanting to get into the great world outside, he looks forward to going off to Lincoln to attend the university. Once there, he finds out what an important part the countryside has played in the history of civilization itself. He falls under the influence of Gaston Cleric, a brilliant young scholar newly made head of the Latin department. Cleric introduces him to the great artistic tradition of the Western world, the tradition of ornate dignity and the grand style stemming ultimately from Vergil. It is from him that Jim learns that the word "patria" has a purely local meaning, and that Vergil had loved the little rural neighborhood as much as he himself loved his grandparents' farm. He begins to get some faint glimmering of the way in which human existence is the same in all times and at all places, but he does not yet know how to correlate art and life:

Although I admired scholarship so much in Cleric, I was not deceived about myself; I knew that I should never be a scholar. I never could lose myself for long among impersonal things. Mental excitement was apt to send me with a rush back to my own naked land and the figures scattered upon it. While I was in the very act of yearning toward the new forms that Cleric brought up before me, my mind plunged away from me, and I suddenly found myself thinking of the places and people of my own infinitesimal past. They stood out, strengthened and simplified now, like the image of the plough against the sun. They were all I had for an answer to the new appeal. I begrudged the room that Jake and Otto and Russian Peter took up in my memory, which I wanted to crowd with other things. But whenever my consciousness was quickened, all those early friends were quickened within it, and in some strange way they accompanied me through all my new experiences. They were so much alive in me that I scarcely stopped to wonder whether they were alive anywhere else, or how.

Like many another young person going off to college, Jim Burden considers the things he knows about to be supremely unimportant, and the things he doesn't know about to be of crucial importance. He underrates his own past and is irate when the people in it keep bobbing up in his consciousness. What do Otto Fuchs and Russian Peter have to do with Vergil? It is too early for him to know that his little world is part of the great world; he hasn't yet seen that his life is not unique but that he is part of humanity. He still doesn't understand his background, but he is beginning to realize that it is important.

In his second year at Lincoln, Jim has an experience which helps to clarify for him the relation between life and art. Lena Lingard, one of the country girls he admires so much, comes to Lincoln and they strike up a friendship. On the evening of her first visit he is already in the mood to see new relations between things:

One March evening in my Sophomore year I was sitting alone in my room after supper. . . . On the edge of the prairie, where the sun had gone down, the sky was turquoise blue, like a lake, with gold light throbbing in it. Higher up, in the utter clarity of the western slope, the evening star hung like a lamp suspended by silver chains—like the lamp engraved upon the title page of old Latin texts, which is always appearing in new heavens, and awakening new desires in men.

By the very act of thinking of such a comparison, he is beginning to see how his life fits in with the classic past.

I propped my book open and stared listlessly at the page of the *Georgics* where tomorrow's lesson began. It opened with the melancholy reflection that, in the lives of mortals, the best days are the first to flee. "Optima dies . . . prima fugit."

Then Lena Lingard knocks at the door, and for a time Jim is dragged back very pleasantly into the present. He has had recurrent dreams about Lena, and now the dreams seem about to translate themselves into reality. He and she have some kind of love experience together, but Willa Cather gingerly avoids telling us of what it consists. After Lena leaves, he realizes for the first time that the things he has experienced are the kind of things people write about, that literature is a reflection of the experience of real people, and that life and art coincide:

> When I turned back to my room the place seemed much pleasanter than before. Lena had left something warm and friendly in the lamplight. How I loved to hear her laugh again! . . . When I closed my eyes I could hear them all laughing—the Danish laundry girls and the three Bohemian Marys. Lena had brought them all back to me. It came over me, as it had never done before, the relation between girls like those and the poetry of Vergil. If there were no girls like them in the world, there would be no poetry. I understood that clearly, for the first time.

Jim Burden has a great insight as he stands in his room after Lena has gone. In seeing the relation between girls like her and Vergil's *Georgics* he has made a discovery important enough to rank as a creative act: he has succeeded in bringing Nebraska in line with the great tradition. And the great tradition—as Willa Cather sees it, at least—is a rural tradition; one need only think of the importance which the Vergil of the *Georgics* and the Horace of the *Odes* gave to the countryside. No longer does Jim have to feel like a young man from the provinces who comes up to the metropolis and is looked down upon, nor does he have to accept the inferiority of America to Europe; he has seen the unity of all life and all art everywhere; he has seen the ultimate unity of human experience.

THE FRUITION OF THE SOIL: THE GARDEN OF THE WORLD

If one of the main themes of *My Antonia* is the superiority of the countryside and the excellence of rural life, the chief image that Willa Cather uses to express that excellence is one we have already come across in discussing *O Pioneers!*: that of the garden of the world. It is in fact the basic metaphor of the whole book: everything in the novel leads up to the final section in which Ántonia has become the mistress of a large and fertile farm.

The garden image is present in the minds of both Willa Cather and some of her characters. Not the least of Grandfather Burden's insights is his ability to understand the larger meaning of the enterprise in which he and his neighbors are engaged. To the hundreds of thousands of toiling individuals who settled the West it must have seemed that each of them was seeking solely to improve his own lot, but according to the thinking of the time they were actually fulfilling a much larger destiny. The settlement of America was considered to be a part of a divine plan. When the great basin of the Mississippi Valley was completely populated, it was to become not only an earthly paradise for the inhabitants, who would thus live in a latter-day Garden of Eden, but also the whole earth's granary; by means of its immense fertility it would feed the people of Europe and Asia as well. Willa Cather had hinted at this in *O Pioneers!*; in *My Ántonia* she makes it quite explicit:

July came on with the breathless, brilliant heat which makes the plains of Kansas and Nebraska the best corn country in the world. It seemed as if we could hear the corn growing in the night; under the stars one caught a faint crackling in the dewy, heavy-odored cornfields where the feathered stalks stood so juicy and green. If all the great plain from the Missouri to the Rocky Mountains had been under glass, and the heat regulated by a thermometer, it could not have been better for the yellow tassels that were ripening and fertilizing each other day by day. The cornfields were far apart in those times, with miles of wild grazing land between. It took a clear, meditative eye like my grandfather's to foresee that they would enlarge and multiply until they would be, not the Shimerdas' cornfields, or Mr. Bushy's but the world's cornfields; that their yield would be one of the great economic facts, like the wheat crop of Russia, which underlie all the activities of men, in peace or war.

This is one way in which Willa Cather adjusts Nebraska to the macrocosm and gives local happenings a cosmic importance.

But it is not merely the garden that Willa Cather is celebrating in *My Antonia;* it is a garden with people living in it, and the people form one of those tightly knit Willa Cather families. The ultimate achievement of Willa Cather's heroine in *My Antonia* is the setting up of a family. The whole drive of her nature is toward this; we could have guessed it from the description of the basic likeness between Ántonia and her town employer, Mrs. Harling:

They loved children and animals and music, and rough play and digging in the earth. They liked to prepare rich, hearty food and to see people eat it; to make up soft white beds and to see youngsters asleep in them.

Ántonia makes two attempts at marriage and the founding of a family: the first is unsuccessful but the second succeeds. The unsuccessful attempt with Larry Donovan has already been discussed. Ántonia's second attempt comes to a better fruition. Jim Burden does not witness the events leading up to it, since after graduation from college he has moved east permanently, but he does hear that another Bohemian has married her, that they are poor, and that they have a large family. He does not come back to visit his home town for nearly twenty years, and when he does he is afraid to visit Ántonia. "In the course of twenty crowded years one parts with many illusions," he says. "I did not wish to lose the early ones. Some memories are realities, and are better than anything that can ever happen to one again." In such brief passages as this he lets the reader know that he has become disappointed in life, that he has been beaten in the things that really count. But his dread turns out to be needless, for Ántonia when he sees her is not a disappointment to him; she has become old and battered, but her vitality is undiminished. She is surrounded by a large happy brood of eleven children, all of whom either come tumbling around him in curiosity to see the man their mother has talked so much about, or else are attractively shy. Ántonia's fecundity is a sign of vitality and success, and the nicest compliment she can pay to some friends of their youth, the three Bohemian Marys, is that they are now married and have large families of their own. The lack of offspring, on the other hand, she regards as a sign of failure. Significantly enough, when she hears that Jim Burden has no children she becomes embarrassed, and tries to shift the conversation to a more neutral subject.

The relation between the various members of this large and happy family are of intense interest to Jim, who feels that he himself has failed at human relations. He observes that there is a kind of physical harmony between them, and that they are not afraid to touch each other. They take great pride in each other, and particularly in their wonderful mother. He describes the attitude of husband and wife toward each other as being "easy friendliness touched with humor." Father Cuzak in particular seems to express his affection for his family by finding them highly amusing: "He thought they were nice, and he thought they were funny, evidently." It is clear that love is the tie that binds them all together, and that they are very happy in one another's affection. And yet there is some slight suggestion of tension between Cuzak, the city-bred man, and Ántonia, the country girl. In the struggle between the sexes envisaged by Willa Cather, Ántonia seems to have gotten the upper hand:

I could see the little chap, sitting here every evening by the windmill, nursing his pipe and listening to the silence; the wheeze of the pump, the grunting of the pigs, an occasional squeaking when the hens were disturbed by a rat. It did rather seem to me that Cuzak had been made the instrument of Ántonia's special mission. This was a fine life, certainly, but it wasn't the kind of life he had wanted to live. I wondered whether the life that was right for one was ever right for two!

This last comment brings into question the entire feasibility of a city-country union. Willa Cather seems to have doubts as to whether the two modes of life can ever be rendered compatible. In addition, it also recalls her distrust of marriage in general. The marriage of the Cuzaks is as idyllic a union as she was ever to portray in any of her novels, and yet even here there is the suggestion not only of female dominance but of marriage as being inevitably frustrating.

The human fertility of the Cuzak homestead is matched by the fertility of the soil. The years of backbreaking labor spent tending the crops has at last yielded a rich fruit. Ántonia is especially proud of her orchard, which has been planted in the painstaking way that orchards are in Willa Cather's novels: every tree had to be watered by hand after a hard day's labor in the fields. The result is a yearly apple crop that far surpasses that of any of their neighbors. At the center of all this fertility is a symbol of civilization. Years before, Ántonia had told Jim she was homesick for the garden behind her father's house in Bohemia which had had a table and green benches in it where they could entertain their friends and talk about such things as music and woods and God and when they were young. This garden image seems to stand in her mind for exactly the right relation between human beings and the nature in which they are placed, a nature modified and well stocked with benches so that civilized people need not get their clothes dirty when they discuss philosophical problems and wish to sit down. Now Ántonia leads Jim to the center of her orchard, and there he finds a grape arbor with seats along the sides and a warped plank table. She has reproduced in the middle of her ideal farm her own idea of the civilized garden. Jim's detailed description of it enhances its importance:

We sat down and watched them. Ántonia leaned her elbows on the table. There was the deepest peace in the orchard. It was surrounded by a triple enclosure; the wire fence, then the hedge of thorny locusts, then the mulberry hedge which kept out the hot winds of summer and held fast to the protecting snows of winter. The hedges were so tall that we could see nothing but the blue sky above them, neither the barn roof nor the windmill. The afternoon sun poured down on us through the drying grape leaves. The orchard seemed full of sun, like a cup, and we could smell the ripe apples on the trees. The crabs hung on the branches as thick as beads on a string, purple-red, with a thin silvery glaze over them. Some hens and ducks had crept through the hedge and were pecking at the fallen apples. The drakes were handsome fellows, with pinkish gray bodies, their heads and necks covered with iridescent green feathers which grew close and full, changing to blue like a peacock's neck. Antonia said they always reminded her of soldiers—some uniform she had seen in the old country, when she was a child.

This passage contains a cluster of images, all of which contribute to the agricultural image used also in *O Pioneers!*, that of the garden of the world. Several ideas are at work here. First, there is the idea that at the center of all this fertliity of farm and family is a place of quietness, a place which contains the deepest peace which human beings can know. The still center is protected from the outside world by a triple barrier which excludes not only strangers (the wire fence) but also extremes of heat and cold, with their connotation of everything else which man finds unpleasant. But aside from shutting out, it also shuts in; it confines the inhabitants of the garden so they cannot tell what is going on in the outside world; they can't even see their farm or windmill, the symbols of the way in which they earn their living. Thus the garden becomes another of those images of sanctuary and retreat which we have seen as giving so important a clue to Willa Cather's attitude toward life. The orchard resembles a cornucopia; it is full like a cup, and the fragrance of its fruit hangs over it. The concept of plenitude finds further development in the idea of roundness, when the crab apples on the trees are compared with beads on a string. Finally Ántonia's comparison between the iridescent shimmeringness on the necks of her ducks and the uniforms of soldiers she had seen as a child in Bohemia suggest that the aesthetic response to life has been carried from Europe to America, but instead of being aroused by an artificial and destructive product of civilization, it is now tamed and rendered beneficent by being brought closer to nature, and is simulated by such a harmless and thoroughly natural creature as a barnyard fowl.

In the middle of this earthly paradise stands its Eve, the now victorious Ántonia. She has triumphed over adversity and over nature; she has wrestled with life and imposed an order on it, her order, just as she has imposed order on the wilderness of Nebraska by converting part of it into a fruitful farm with a garden at its center. In her double role as founder of a prosperous farm and progenitor of a thriving family she becomes the very symbol of fertility, and reminds us of Demeter or Ceres of old, the ancients' goddess of agriculture. Willa Cather herself points up the comparison, and it is of value to her to do this, for she makes an earth-goddess of Ántonia; the mortal who struggles with the adverse powers of nature and conquers them becomes the type of all successful human endeavor and passes over into the realm of myth. That Willa Cather quite deliberately makes an earth-goddess of Ántonia is seen in the following passage:

She lent herself to immemorial human attitudes which we recognize by instinct as universal and true. I had not been mistaken. She was a battered woman now, not a lovely girl; but she still had that something which fires the imagination, could still stop one's breath for a moment by a look or gesture that somehow revealed the meaning in common things. She had only to stand in the orchard, to put her hand on a little crab tree and look up at the apples, to make you feel the goodness of planting and tending and harvesting at last. All the strong things of her heart came out of her body, that had been so tireless in serving generous emotions.

It was no wonder that her sons stood tall and straight. She was a rich mine of life, like the founders of early races.

And what becomes of the other protagonist in the story, Jim Burden? When he revisits his past by returning to Black Hawk, it gives him no clue to his identity or to the meaning of life such as he has found in the Cuzak farm. He is not able to build on his past as Ántonia is on hers:

My day in Black Hawk was disappointing. Most of my old friends were dead or had moved away. Strange children, who meant nothing to me, were playing in the Harlings' big yard when I passed; the mountain ash had been cut down, and only a sprouting stump was left of the tall Lombardy poplar that used to guard the gate. I hurried on.

The town no longer means anything to him, although the country still does. It has changed too much; the children and the trees are gone. The town families he had known had had no roots, since the community in which they lived had given them none, and so they had passed on to other places. But there are parts of the country that haven't changed at all. Jim takes a long walk out of town and stumbles upon an old road, the first road built from Black Hawk to the north, in fact the very same road over which Ántonia and he had traveled on the first night of their arrival in the Midwest. The road becomes a symbol of the unchanging quality of the countryside, and carries him back to the region of childhood memories:

I had only to close my eyes to hear the rumbling of the wagons in the dark, and to be again overcome by that obliterating strangeness. The feelings of that night were so near that I could reach out and touch them with my hand. I had the sense of coming home to myself, and of having found out what a little circle man's experience is.

The wheel has come full circle, and the same road which had first brought him to Black Hawk now carries him away from an unsatisfying present and into a nostalgically remembered past. Nothing could illustrate better than this final contrast between the Cuzak farm and Black Hawk the difference between country and town, Ántonia and Jim, the yea-saying and nay-saying attitudes toward life. Both had been set down in the Middle West without any previous training which would help them, both had once literally traveled down the same road, but their circumstances and temperaments were different. Ántonia now prefers the country because it gives her a greater chance to fulfill herself; Jim because it has changed less than the city and because it is linked with the past, to which he turns because it is all he has:

For Ántonia and for me, this had been the road of Destiny; had taken us to those early accidents of fortune which predetermined for us all that we can ever be. Now I understood that the same road was to bring us together again. Whatever we had missed, we possessed together the precious, the incommunicable past.

Perhaps the best way of summing up the meaning of *My Ántonia* is to recapitulate the story of each of the three sections in terms of the dominant imagery. The first part, concerning the struggle of the Burdens and the Shimerdas with the wild land, is described in terms of animal imagery; as in *O Pioneers!* the central symbol is the unbroken colt. This represents inchoate material waiting to have form imposed upon it, vitality ready to be harnessed by order. Ántonia too is waiting to have form imposed upon her; by her father, by the Burden family, and by the Harlings, form being in this context the stamp of civilization itself. The imposition of form on wild nature is a difficult thing, as those who do not have the strength to achieve it find out; Mr. Shimerda fails at the task and kills himself, while even Ántonia barely survives. But she does survive.

In the book's second part the dominant image is the plough. Both Ántonia and the land are now ready to be creative and fertile; to produce children and crops. This section contains the struggle between town and country traditions, with Ántonia absorbing both: she first learns from and then emancipates herself from the Harlings. Unlike her father, she is able to triumph over adversity—in her case, an unfortunate love affair.

In the third section of the book the dominant image is the earth-goddess in the garden of the world. This section shows the final fruition of both woman and land, which comes about because Ántonia is able to combine the vitality of nature with the order of civilization, both in her own life and in the life of the land. In this section Jim Burden meets adversity and is inspired by Ántonia.

The importance to her career of Willa Cather's two prairie novels can hardly be overestimated. In them she gives the fullest expression she ever gave to one of her major themes, the meaning of the European experience in America. The exact significance of America differs in the two prairie novels. In *O Pioneers!* America functions as pure raw material; it is the land where the creative will best can operate. *My Ántonia* does not contradict this, but the emphasis has shifted; America is now the land in which "Europe" can reach its finest flower. For Willa Cather as for many other nineteenth-century people Europe and America stood for pairs of opposites: Europe was tangibly the past, America tangibly the present; Europe stood for order, America for chaos. The two are connected, since the present is always visibly chaotic and needs to have order imposed upon it by applying the lessons learned in the past. The most important antithesis of all, however, was that America stood for nature whereas Europe represented civilization. The difference between the two novels is that in *O Pioneers!*, even while Alexandra is struggling to conquer it, it is the wildness of nature which is being celebrated, the untamed vitality of the frontier, whereas in *My Ántonia* the vitality and the discipline of civilization are combined to form a new synthesis, which provides the basis for a settled agricultural society like that eulogized by Horace and Vergil.

I have shown that at a certain point in her career Willa Cather gradually ceased looking to the world of art for subject matter and began seeking it in the world of nature. But this did not mean that she gave up her belief in the world of art as a source of value. Because she did not her former cultural ideal came into conflict with her present one, for the world of urban sophistication has little in common with the world of simple homely virtues associated with the countryside. This conflict between cultural ideals was by no means peculiar to Willa Cather but was part of a much more general conflict present in the minds of nineteenth-century Americans concerning their ideas about themselves; it revolved around the question of whether they owed their allegiance to the concept of primitivism or the concept of civilization and the stages of society. According to primitivism, since nature is seen as the source of all value, the closer a man lives to nature the better off he is, physically, mentally, and morally. According to the concept of the stages of society, all men progressed through certain stages of development proceeding from the most primitive to the most civilized, starting with the nomadic and proceeding upward through the pastoral and agricultural until finally they reached the industrial and commercial stages. These last two— the agricultural and industrial-commercial—correspond to the rural and urban stages, which I have discussed under the headings of country and town. In the nineteenth century the two turn up over and over again as contrasting ideals as to how life should be lived, the best literary expression of this being in the novels of James Fenimore Cooper. As we have seen, Willa Cather herself vacillated between the two, as indeed Americans traditionally have done. In *O Pioneers!*, she merely states the case for both sides, without making any choice between the two. But in *My Antonia* she resolves the conflict in the direction of a highly civilized and sophisticated rural civilization, and this remains her ideal for the rest of her career, although in her later books (starting with her very next novel) she believes it to be an ideal impossible of achievement.

But this highly civilized and sophisticated rural way of living which she celebrates is actually a little too good to be true. It is doubtful whether anybody could achieve that particular combination of urban-bred sensibility and rural rootedness and strength which she envisaged. When this is seen as combined with a hierarchal three-generation family unit in which the roles are assigned and the whole is sustained by ritual, ironically enough the place where it is most likely to be found is not in the country at all but in the city. Such a pattern is common among orthodox Jewish families who (like the Cuzaks) are not too far removed from their immigrant ancestors. But this is hardly where Willa Cather looked for her heroines.

The concepts of primitivism and civilization have an all-pervasive influence on Willa Cather's fiction. They affect, for instance, her presentation of her heroines. In *O Pioneers!* she emphasizes the heroine as a solitary individual; in *My Antonia* she emphasizes the heroine as part of a group, first as a member of a family and then as its head. Similarly the differing treatment of the prairie in the two books like-wise shows the influence of the two concepts. In *O Pioneers!* the land being eulogized is the entire Great Divide; Willa Cather tells us. "Alexandra's house is the big out-of-doors." In *My Antonia* the center of attention has been narrowed down to the family living on the family farm; in other words, the homestead. This shows Willa Cather dealing in literary terms with a vitally important historical reality. The entire trans-Mississippi region was settled in the post–Civil War period by farmers called homesteaders; in fact, the Homestead Act of 1862 was conceptually based on just such a family unit as the Cuzaks.

O Pioneers! forms a sharp contrast to *My Ántonia* in structure as well as subject matter. In structure the earlier book has a superimposed form while the form of the latter is largely organic and arises from the cycle of the seasons. The organizing principle of *O Pioneers!* is the theme of the creative will directed, first toward the world of nature, then toward the world of man; the organizing principle of *My Ántonia,* as we shall see later, is the vegetation myth. Of the two *O Pioneers!* has the tighter structure, popular opinion to the contrary. In *My Ántonia* the part tends to be greater than the whole: one remembers fine but isolated passages such as Jim Burden's killing of the rattlesnake or the description of the plough against the sun.

To study the spirit behind the form of an artistic work is a fascinating albeit highly speculative occupation. In the case of the two prairie novels some light is shed on structure by what we know of Willa Cather's biography and temperament. What she was trying to do in *O Pioneers!* was evidently to show that the power of love, although it can succeed with the land, must fail when it comes to people. But this is highly idiosyncratic, and reflects her own inner fears rather than any universal human truth. What she was trying to do in *My Ántonia* was somewhat different. Leaving the vegetation myth aside for a moment, a part of the book's form is still superimposed. Willa Cather has constructed the novel as a series of snapshots or vignettes, each of them commemorating some important event. Since we know that she tended to omit struggle and conflict from both books, as well as the direct presentation of evil, it seems that her vignettes are meant to present only life's happy and successful moments, and such as showed the triumph of the will. If this is true, she was willfully failing to see life steadily and see it whole, or to give an artistically convincing representation of the entire human scene as she knew it.

In spite of its flaws, *O Pioneers!* on the whole is a successful portrait of an important American historical era. In the larger sense, it can be regarded as a kind of allegory on Western man and his entire history. It shows him—as he has historically been—as much more successful in dealing with his physical environment than with his fellow man: Alexandra's saga follows a success-failure pattern as she moves away from relatively simple problems and toward the more complex. I find it necessary to make separate judgments on the two parts of the book. In the main I believe Willa Cather is aesthetically and historically right when she takes the wild frontier as a symbol of the challenge offered to heroic souls by the precariousness of human existence, and sees the westward expansion in nineteenth-century America as a working out of the romantic aspiration toward a better life. But I believe she is dangerously idiosyncratic in seeing spontaneous relations between the sexes as being as uniformly dangerous and unrewarding as she makes them out to be. This view reflects her own particular upbringing and temperament—particularly the latter—and it severely limits her art. Nevertheless, in spite of its limitations, *O Pioneers!* is a convincing novel; in it Willa Cather comes as close as she ever does to a frank and square confrontation of the conflicts inherent in human life. But this is all she does; she faces them but is unable to resolve or transcend them. And even in *O Pioneers!* she turns her face away from the conflict before the book is over.

My Ántonia, in some ways more successful than *O Pioneers!*, in other ways is less successful; it is more affirmative but less honest. If in the first book Willa Cather gives a frank portrayal of her gloomy and one-sided view of human relations, in the second she is willing to falsify the material she has at hand in order to make the final triumph of the heroine appear almost effortless. *O Pioneers!* is the more original in form, with its brilliant linking of plots to project the success-failure motif; *My Ántonia* is more conventional in theme, if not in content, since it comes at the end of a long tradition of literary works written in praise of husbandry. It is an agrarian idyl, and its real subject is man's right relation to nature. The right relation turns out to be, not that defined by primitivism, but that of the agrarian tradition, a version of the concept of civilization which held that the stages of society culminate in the settled agricultural level, and that any further development in the direction of the city is a step downward.

In the largest sense the structure of *My Ántonia* is based on the vegetation myth. The core of this age-old mystery, as we have said, is the taking of the cycle of the seasons as the pattern for all recurrent rhythmical processes in nature, including human death and birth. It regards birth as rebirth and holds that, although death is inevitable, every person is "born again" through his children; the individual dies but the community lives on. *My Ántonia* is about this mystery of death and birth. Mr. Shimerda dies in the dead of winter, and when Ántonia is reborn as the head of a group of her own she is described in terms of the sensuous summer imagery of the garden of the world. In a sense when Mr. Shimerda dies, a good part of his daughter dies too; all her more civilized attributes wither away. She gives up her fine manners and becomes coarse and crude like her brother Ambrosch. She is reborn to civilization when she goes to town to live and relearns nice ways of doing things from the Harlings. Finally, after learning all she has to learn, she is ready to take her place in society by starting a family of her own and is reborn once again into the human community.

If we compare the two prairie novels in terms of their use of vegetation myth, we find that *O Pioneers!* deals with the death of nature and *My Ántonia* with its rebirth. *O Pioneers!* presents fertility of the soil and sterility in human beings; *My Ántonia* shows fertility of both the soil and human beings. Thus, in a profound sense *My Ántonia* is the most affirmative book Willa Cather ever wrote. Perhaps that is why it was her favorite.

But we have seen that as an author Willa Cather could not face certain facts of human experience—as, in *My Ántonia*, the problem of apparently motiveless evil involved in Larry Donovan's seduction and abandonment of Ántonia. It is also true that in her work as a whole she could not accept the emotional profundity of the vegetation myth as for the most part she did in this novel. In brief, she could accept fertility in crops more easily than in human beings, the reason being her fear of physical passion and the dependence upon others which it entails. This is evident even in *My*

Ántonia, which of all her novels most celebrates fecundity. As far as the reader is concerned, Ántonia's family is produced ready-made. Never once is a pregnancy or birth directly presented in Willa Cather's novels; what we do see is the corn growing. This implies that she only half understood the vegetation myth; she understood the cycle of the seasons but did not understand its application to the life of human beings and to their recurrent crises of birth, love, and death. She substituted in its stead, as we shall see in her later novels, an almost Platonic belief in essences, and the desire to freeze the world in the grip of form once the ideal is achieved.

EDWARD A. and LILLIAN D. BLOOM

"On the Composition of a Novel"

Even when Miss Cather attempted in her criticism to eluci-
date certain technical mannerisms or to trace creative lines which
she had followed, she seemed to fall back in spite of herself upon
a language of subjective response. For all the eloquence of her
explanations, they frequently elude clear definition. This hazi-
ness—if such it may be called—was unavoidable, for she was reflecting rather than asserting, and her subject matter was of such
private intensity that it simply did not lend itself to a critical rationale. Miss Cather, it seems to us, invited the sympathy of her
readers to both her fiction and her critical explanations. She took
for granted a measure of kindred feeling, assuming that in the
absence of a perhaps intuitive understanding of her aims no definition or objective enlargement could instill the emotions which
she portrayed and hoped to share. This is by no means a suggestion that she was indifferent to her audience, but she was well
aware that neither she nor any other author could hope to reach all
readers. The fact, however, that she has attained such wide circulation is rather convincing evidence that she succeeded in communicating and sharing her feelings without resort to an essentially objective rhetoric. Terms such as "desire," "yearning," and
"spirit" may seem elusive when attempts are made to compress
them into terse definitions. They are abundantly clear in narra-

From *Willa Cather's Gift of Sympathy* (Carbondale, Ill., 1962), copyright
© 1962, by Southern Illinois University Press. Reprinted by permission of
the Southern Illinois University Press. An earlier version of "On the Composition of a Novel" appeared under the title "The Genesis of *Death Comes for
the Archbishop*" in *American Literature* in 1955.

tive context, however, generally eliciting the response of feeling when incisive statement is inadequate.

For these reasons Willa Cather's critical attitudes must frequently be "felt," or reasoned with some difficulty, even when she sets them down in the shape of pronouncements. As an example, she once described the texture of *Shadows on the Rock* as "mainly anocoluthon," but she did not bother to connect this term specifically to her novel. She knew what she meant, and she assumed that anyone interested enough would establish the relationship for himself.

Classically, the purpose of anacoluthon was to evoke an emotional or moral effect through a temporary suspension of completeness—that is, like a series of minor suspenses—within the individual actions of the principal framework. Once identified, the term has great bearing on the working out of *Shadows*. The seeming disjunction implied by the term she attained by initiating episodes and then disclosing their resolutions in subsequent appropriate phases of the novel. It is an example of Miss Cather's critical density, her tendency to put undefined or meagerly defined theories into esthetic practice. Anacoluthon as a critical term had particular meaning for her. She suggested it as the basis of the form she used, but was not concerned with pursuing it as a critical academic matter. And it is not of any great consequence to the general reader for whom *Shadows* is primarily a warm, imaginative experience. The critic whose reading of the novel is somewhat more formal, however, seizes gladly upon the bare hint and finds his task of explication facilitated and enriched.

Occasional hints of this nature are helpful to a deeper understanding of Miss Cather's aims and accomplishments, particularly since her major novels represent unobtrusive experiments with concept and form. *The Professor's House*, as we have already seen, was cast in the approximation of the musical sonata, and other novels were worked out according to subtle patterns that might slip by unheeded without some casual word from the author. Sometimes, however, the experimentation is compounded of elements which Miss Cather has not noted directly. The wells of unconscious memory, perhaps, autobiographical incidents, former acquaintances, travel, even diligent research in libraries —all may play their part in a novel, absorbed silently and artistically into a created masterpiece. Then it becomes valuable to turn to a confidante or a chapter of biography or a historian in an effort to work out answers that may broaden one's reading. A novel such as *Death Comes for the Archbishop* is an unusually engrossing subject for detailed study, providing a synthesis of Willa Cather's attitudes—toward the frontier and the past—her moral sensitivity, and above all—at least for the purpose of this chapter—her manner of composition. To follow the delicate trail of the *Archbishop* from its unconscious beginnings to its auspicious appearance is to become aware of the summing up of a distinguished talent, mind, and moral agent.

For Willa Cather as for Henri Bergson, whom she admired, literary creation—that is, the choice of subject matter and the technique enforced by it—was an "intuitive" rather than an "intellectual" process. When she stated in an introduction to *Alexander's Bridge* that the novelist dealing with material that is deeply a part of his conscious and unconscious being has "less and less power of choice about the moulding of it," she was expressing her belief in esthetic inevitability. Great art, because it centered in the moods of the self, is an outpouring of intimate associations; and because all art as Miss Cather understood it is emotively representational, it is compulsive in its need for release. Certainly in the *Archbishop* she was engaged with familiar material, or as she would say, her "own material," which she knew and lived instinctively. Yet she was incapable of rendering personal experience or emotion literally, and she always sought new ways of communicating. That is, experimentation with form was as integral to her as was the moral substance of the themes she wished to narrate.

Of all her many novels the *Archbishop* was the most candidly and deliberately experimental. Preferring the term "narrative" to that of "novel," she shaped the *Archbishop* as a legend in the medieval tradition of Christian saints' lore, and of self-imposed necessity she eschewed all obvious dramatic treatment. Instead of the rising action and complexities which propel more conventional novels, Miss Cather drew scenes of a simplicity characteristic of her general practice and gave equal stress to each. The incidents, then, she selected with exceeding care, not for the evocation of suspense but for a cumulative effect.

It was toward this end that she integrated the details of theme, plot, characterization, and mood which make up the novel. For many years, she admitted in an essay. "On Death Comes for the Archbishop," she had been tantalized by the possibility of emulating a pictorial model in prose. Since her student days, when she had first seen the Puvis de Chavannes frescoes of the life of Saint Geneviève, she had hoped to write "something without accent, with none of the artificial elements of composition." As in the Golden Legend, where the commonplace events of saints' lives receive the same emphasis as their martyrdoms, she wished to show how all human experiences—noble and trivial—project from "one supreme spiritual experience . . . The essence of such writing," she said, "is not to hold the note, not to use an incident for all there is in it—but to touch and pass on." In adapting technical treatment to subject matter and in selecting locale and situation, she was affected by numerous determinants—her theory of literary genesis, her personal experiences and friendships, her readings. All these factors entered significantly into the composition of the *Archbishop*. And though we have neither space nor need to explore every condition which led to the publication of the novel, we propose to sample those most pertinent to its being.

Like all of Willa Cather's novels of the frontier, the *Archbishop* allegorizes the individual's withdrawal from cold reality toward sanctified purpose. Believing that time and space are irrelevant to the pioneer impulse, she merely extended her focus to create the two major historical novels, the *Archbishop* and *Shadows on the Rock*. And, of course, she had previously intimated the broadening of her interests in the idyllic interludes about the cliff dwellers in both *The Song of the Lark* and *The Professor's House*. In her historical imperative nothing is superfluous but that which is temporal or material. When she writes about prehistoric aborigines, seventeenth-century Canadians, or nineteenth-century priests, Mexicans, and Indians, she does not look for the surprising oddities of custom and event which distinguish particular eras but for the profundities of faith which unite all men of all time. Each frontier becomes a stronghold of private need, but it is a need which widely disparate men have experienced and satisfied. The broad thesis of Miss Cather's frontier philosophy is probably best served by the *Archbishop*, for here she was encouraged to speak out directly for religious principles that not only were hers by choice but that in their prevalence brought a beautiful purpose to a country ripe for their influence. When she wrote *Shadows on the Rock* she was in effect reiterating the judgments of the earlier *Archbishop* and had nothing essential to add to them. Through the course of her novels, it might be said, she was developing creative strength and collecting a store of knowledge as though in anticipation of the *Archbishop*.

She long cherished an affection for the Southwest and its mythology even before her first visit in 1912. Considerably before this date and undoubtedly long before the idea of the *Archbishop* came to her, she had become intrigued by a legend which tells of how a tribe of Indians, a thousand or more years ago, were isolated from their home on Katzímo, a vast New Mexican mesa-top, forbidding and impregnable to hostile Indians. This people, according to the legend, farmed the fertile desert at the foot of their *mesa encantada* or enchanted mesa. One summer while almost all the members of the tribe were harvesting, a fierce storm destroyed the sole passage leading to the summit of their island of rock. Hopelessly cut off, the tribe moved on to Ácoma mesa, where they established their now traditional home.

From these materials, Miss Cather created her short story "The Enchanted Bluff" (1909), an interesting forerunner of her spiritual interpretation of the Ácoma mesa in the *Archbishop*. Although vague in its outlines, this early story is yet significant in that it conveys some of the sense of yearning and seeking which gives tonality to the Ácoma incident in the *Archbishop*. When Miss Cather set down her story, the Katzímo legend was already something of a *cause célèbre*. The controversy over its authenticity, engaged in by Charles F. Lummis, Professor William Libbey, and Frederick Webb Hodge, had flared in newspapers, magazines, and scientific publications. That Miss Cather was familiar with the quarrel is evident from "The Enchanted Bluff," in which she had her characters prepare to scale Katzímo by a unique method used by Professor Libbey. At the same time she repudiated Libbey's skepticism, accepting the authenticity of the legend as it was proposed by Lummis and Hodge. Thus she took sides in an issue which at the time had no immediacy for her except that of imaginative curiosity; she had not seen Katzímo and was not destined to do so until 1926.

Almost from the beginning, then, Miss Cather was "teased" by the magic of the Southwest. While she and her brother Douglass were still children in Nebraska, they had talked of exploring the Southwest together, even as the youngsters in "The Enchanted Bluff" dreamed of a similar exploit. Then in 1912 she visited Douglass in Winslow, Arizona, where he was employed by the Santa Fe Railroad. Her first trip to this storied country became the realization of a childhood dream, and she was imbued with the satisfaction expressed by Father Joseph in the *Archbishop*: "To fulfill the dreams of one's youth; that is the best that can happen to a man." She remained several months and, according to Miss Lewis, "a whole new landscape—not only a physical landscape, but a landscape of the mind, peopled with wonderful imaginings, opened out before her." She visited Arizona again in 1914, although it was not until 1915 that she made her first lengthy sojourn in New Mexico, and she returned in 1916 once more.

Ardently attracted to the natural splendor of the territory and desirous of understanding people such as she had never known before, she did not concern herself with the possibilities of literary exploitation. Only after her love of the land had matured and become implanted with its significance did she put into words the *Archbishop*, her most profound and in some ways her most meaningful novel. Its technical conception came to her appropriately enough when she returned to New Mexico after a nine-year absence, and it was seemingly inevitable. In a single evening during that summer while she was stopping at Santa Fe, as she often said, the idea of the *Archbishop* emerged essentially as she afterward wrote it.

That Miss Cather should have been so long in the concrete formulation of the novel fits in admirably with her theory of literary genesis. In her ennobled view of the writer's function, as she once postulated in an essay on Sarah Orne Jewett, a merely good story is not enough and the process by which superlative art is achieved is very different from that which supports mere competence. Hard pressed as usual to define a concept, she concluded the main characteristics to be "persistence, survival, recurrence in the writer's mind." Only those things and events which have long tantalized the mind, "when they do at last get themselves rightly put down, make a very much higher order of writing, and a much more costly, than the most vivid and vigorous transfer of immediate impressions." Never one to settle consciously for the second best, Miss Cather had long given herself over to this kind of deliberate—taxing yet the most satisfying—process before she could write the *Archbishop*.

Significantly, she made the above observation just before her crucial trip to New Mexico in 1925. She returned from New Mexico to Jaffrey, New Hampshire, in the autumn of that year and, almost at a sitting it seemed to Miss Lewis, she wrote the introduction to the novel. All that winter in New York she continued to work on the *Archbishop* happily and with calm assurance. But as the novel progressed she realized that there were many things and places she needed to learn about, many details that she wished to verify. And so once more, in July of 1926, she went to her beloved New Mexico.

These trips to the Southwest not only made concrete for her the physical landscape, but they also introduced her to people and experiences invaluable for the genesis of the novel. For example, on her first trip to Arizona she met a friend of her brother, the Reverend Father T. Connolly, the Catholic priest in Winslow. Frequently Willa Cather accompanied him on his long drives to distant parishes, and they talked about the country and the people, and about the old Spanish and Indian legends that still survived.

Later she met Father Haltermann, a Belgian priest, who lived with his sister in the parsonage behind the church at Santa Cruz, New Mexico. This hearty, bearded clergyman, whose duties among his eighteen Indian missions had brought him close familiarity with the native traditions, endeared himself to the novelist through his animation and intellectual acuteness.

Of these priests who devotedly served in the Southwest, Miss Lewis recalls that her friend was impressed by the "tact and good sense so many of them had with their Mexican parishioners, and the cultivation of mind that gave them a long historical perspective on the life in these remote little settlements." Indeed, from Father Haltermann and his colleagues, among others, Miss Cather learned about many of the religious and secular traditions of the area, and about the simple and yet devout Catholicism of their parishioners. Observant and retentive, in this fashion she gleaned for her book details that became almost as much a part of her as if she had experienced them at first hand. From her church friends she also discovered many of the unofficial and intimate details about the construction and financing of the Cathedral of Santa Fe which appear in the *Archbishop*.

Further details of the novel owe their realistic presentation to the author's acquaintance with several Indians native to the region. Foremost among these, Tony Luhan made an immediate impression upon Miss Cather. Her companion describes him as "a splendid figure, over six feet tall, with a noble head and a dignified carriage; there was great simplicity and kindness in his voice and manner." Arrayed in his purple blanket and silver bracelets, this commanding individual accompanied Miss Cather to some of the most remote and barely accessible Mexican villages in the Cimarrón Mountains. He revealed much to her about the country that an outsider could not have discovered alone. And though he was characteristically taciturn, his infrequent conversation was wise in content and poetic in quality. Tony in all likelihood became the model for Eusabio, the Navajo Indian portrayed in the *Archbishop* as "extremely tall . . . with a face like a Roman general's of Republican times. He . . . wore a blanket of the finest wool and design. His arms, under the loose sleeves of his shirt, were covered with silver bracelets . . ." Like Tony Luhan, Eusabio, wearing an expression of "religious" seriousness, "talked little, ate little, slept anywhere, preserved a countenance open and warm, and . . . he had unfailing good manners."

Associations of this kind reconfirmed Willa Cather's faith in human simplicity and her detestation of artfulness. The fact that in her sophisticated times such fundamental piety and natural courtesy could thrive was a further testimony of the greatness of the frontier spirit. The basic truths she had sought so long came to life for her in the desert, and the certainty that they existed enabled her to inspirit her novel.

The *Archbishop*, like her other frontier novels, was an intensely personal experience, in conception and creative growth. It was not so much a piece of fiction—a mere story—as it was her vision of life and attitude toward truth. The point at which actuality and invention merged was invisible, for except in necessary mechanical details Miss Cather herself made no such arbitrary distinction. Her experiences of life were the book and the book was her life. Like a great metaphor, the novel became a subtle evaluation of her attitudes and felt emotions.

Even as she drew upon knowledge from individuals to express a philosophy and mood, she drew also from events which she experienced in the Southwest. Every year in Santa Fe, for instance, a procession honoring the Virgin commemorated De Vargas' recapture of the city for Spain in 1692. Recorded historical details of the procession were of course available to Miss Cather, but the fact that she had witnessed the procession and reacted emotionally to its spiritual implications was even more important than her readings. In the novel she directs her focus to the image of the Virgin Mother carried through the streets by the participants. She concentrates on utterly simple elements to describe the love which the Mexicans cherished for the holy figure. Although this incident is organically inseparable from the sympathetic portrayal of religious love which is the secondary thematic concern of the novel, Miss Cather pauses briefly to inject a few lines of exposition for the fuller clarification of her meaning. She has

Father Latour reflect that the poor Mexicans were expressing themselves as part of a spiritual tradition. After all, the Virgin Mother had been celebrated in great art, music, and cathedral architecture. Even "before Her years on earth, in the long twilight between the Fall and the Redemption, the pagan sculptors were always trying to achieve the image of a goddess who should yet be a woman." Concerned with the continuum of tradition, Willa Cather implies a spiritual if not a doctrinal link between heathen and Christian rites. The question she raises is not one of judgment upon idolatry, for example, but of sympathy with a universal religious need. The fulfillment of that need is basically more important than the crude manner of its fulfillment. Miss Cather no less than Latour was touched by this sign of devotion, and she translated her experience into a brilliant scene.

Other events in the *Archbishop*, such as that related in the chapter "The Lonely Road to Mora," have autobiographical bases. One of the most striking portions of the novel, the chapter describing Father Latour's introduction to Ácoma, reveals Miss Cather's typical fusion of personal experience, interpretation, and random reading. From her own visit to the mesa she stored up an impression which has been recorded by Miss Lewis: "As we passed the Mesa Encantada (the Enchanted Bluff) we stopped for a long time to look up at it. A great cloud-mesa hung over it. It looked lonely and mysterious and remote, as if it were far distant in time—thousands of years away." The same experience emerges thus in the *Archbishop*:

Ever afterward the Bishop remembered his first ride to Ácoma as his introduction to the mesa country. One thing which struck him at once was that every mesa was duplicated by a cloud mesa, like a reflection, which lay motionless above it or moved slowly up from behind it. These cloud formations seemed to be always there, however hot and blue the sky. Sometimes they were flat terraces, ledges of vapour; sometimes they were dome-shaped, or fantastic, like the tops of silvery pagodas, rising one above another, as if an oriental city lay directly behind the rock. The great tables of granite set down in an empty plain were inconceivable without their attendant clouds, which were a part of them, as the smoke is part of the censer, or the foam of the wave.

Fittingly, the sensitive priest is made to describe a phenomenon which invites not only a poetic response but a religious one as well. Only a person from a cultured background would be aware of the exotic naturalism, and only a person of strong religious inclinations would at such a time think of Catholic ritual. Willa Cather, sharing Latour's refinement and some of his inner repose, was able to elaborate this natural wonder as she did.

But if much of her knowledge of Ácoma and the nearby Mesa Encantada was informed by acute observation, it was probably derived also from historical and quasi-literary sources. For some of her factual details she was indebted to Charles F. Lummis' volumes and to Twitchell's treatment of New Mexican history.[1] From Lummis especially she derived her references to Fray Juan Ramirez, "a great missionary, who laboured on the Rock of Ácoma for twenty years or more," his mule trail, "the only path by which a burro can ascend the mesa, and which is still called 'El Camino del Padre,' " his massive church with its beams drawn from the San Mateo Mountains. There are further allusions— drawn from Lummis and Twitchell—to the military invincibility of the Ácomas, their single defeat at the hands of the Spaniards, the picture of St. Joseph and its magical rain-producing properties.

These real details, verifiable as they are in recorded sources, lend the novel a comfortable verisimilitude. Empowered, as it were, by the authority of history, Miss Cather could create a reasonable sense of the historical past. But the chronicle format was after all a mere convenience, since her purpose was larger than that of decoration and the reconstruction of past events. In short, although her specific details are vital to the narrative frame, they are far less important than the intuited significance of the Ácoma

[1] *Mesa, Cañon and Pueblo* (New York and London, 1925), pp. 264 ff.; *Some Strange Corners of Our Country* (New York, 1915), pp. 262 ff.; Ralph Emerson Twitchell, *Leading Facts of New Mexico History* (Cedar Rapids, Iowa, 1912), I, 199–200.

mesa. Her purpose, having to do with the interior essence rather than the exterior fact, is served through her paticular understanding and symbolic transference of the rock in which she synthesizes everything she means by sanctuary. Latour is again granted the imaginative intelligence that makes him her spokesman:

All this plain, the Bishop gathered, had once been the scene of a periodic man-hunt; these Indians, born in fear and dying by violence for generations, had at last taken this leap away from the earth, and on that rock had found the hope of all suffering and tormented creatures—safety. They came down to the plain to hunt and to grow their crops, but there was always a place to go back to. If a band of Navajos were on the Ácoma's trail, there was still one hope; if he could reach his rock—Sanctuary! On the winding stone stairway up the cliff, a handful of men could keep off a multitude. The rock of Ácoma had never been taken by a foe but once,—by Spaniards in armour. It was very different from a mountain fastness; more lonely, more stark and grim, more appealing to the imagination. The rock, when one came to think of it, was the utmost expression of human need; even mere feeling yearned for it; it was the highest comparison of loyalty in love and friendship. Christ Himself had used that comparison for the disciple to whom He gave the Keys of His Church. And the Hebrews of the Old Testament, always being carried captive into foreign lands,—their rock was an idea of God, the only thing their conquerors could not take from them.

In the chapter as a whole she has refined and intensified a great natural phenomenon through artistry; but she has also projected a deeply personal commitment, expressing her inner state through a peculiarly apt religious symbolism, with its mingling of the pagan and the Christian. Her analysis of the symbolic meaning of the Ácoma mesa leaves no doubt in the reader's mind. Nor is it an isolated—hence eccentric—symbol, for in slightly altered form it appears repeatedly in *The Song of the Lark, The Professor's House,* and *Shadows on the Rock.* Consistency like this is synonymous with the "persistence, survival, recurrence in the writer's mind" that she held to be the substance of lasting art.

The genesis of the *Archbishop*, finally, appears to owe much historically and philosophically to the many source works which

Miss Cather read. Michael Williams in an article for *Commonweal* rightly pointed out that in order to write her book she had read and studied a great deal. Miss Lewis, who was in a position to know, has substantiated Williams' remark with specific observations on the novelist's avid researches. Among the books she read were the Rev. J. H. Defouri's *Historical Sketch of the Catholic Church in New Mexico* (San Francisco, 1887); J. B. Salpointe's *Soldiers of the Cross* (Banning, California, 1898); the *Catholic Encyclopedia*; the works of Lummis; Bandelier's *The Gilded Man*; the Rev. Francis Palou's *Life of Ven. Padre Junipero Serra* (San Francisco, 1884); Twitchell's *Leading Facts. of New Mexico History*; and the translation by G. P. Winship (in the 14th annual report of the Bureau of American Ethnology) of Castenada's *The Coronado Expedition*.

Although Miss Cather does not openly acknowledge her use of any of these books, her indebtedness becomes readily apparent in certain details, a character sketch or two, and casual historical allusions. To one volume, however, she was overtly indebted. This was *The Life of the Right Reverend Joseph P. Machebeuf* (Pueblo, Colorado, 1908) by William Joseph Howlett, a priest who had worked with Father Machebeuf in Denver. It was from this volume that she drew most of her biographical data about Father Latour (in real life Archbishop Lamy) and Father Joseph Vaillant (Father Machebeuf). Mrs. Bennett relates that after the publication of the *Archbishop*, when the author had forgotten to mention Father Howlett's book, the priest gently reminded her of the oversight. Contritely, Miss Cather sent an open letter to *Commonweal* explaining how she came to write the novel and crediting Father Howlett as a source. At the same time she sent him an autographed copy of the *Archbishop*, apologized for her omission, and asked his blessing. As further acknowledgment, she gave autographed copies of the book to the St. Thomas Seminary in Denver, Father Machebeuf's diocese, and again admitted her debt. Later, in her essay on the novel, she stated that in the work of Father Howlett "at last I found what I wanted to know about how the country and the people of New Mexico seemed to those first missionary priests from France." There can be no question, then, of the esteem in which she held the basic printed source of the *Archbishop*.

The reading which shaped the component elements of the novel must not be confused with rigid, unimaginative paraphrase. She molded her materials rather according to artistic necessity. To achieve an aura of realism—and it must be remembered that Miss Cather's technical intention of emulating a legend allowed for no more than a peripheral reconstruction of facts—she borrowed from her reading seemingly casual historical references. To bolster her primary purpose—thematic reevocation of pioneer striving, its success and in some instances its failure—she gleaned from her reading a series of characterizations and contrasting character sketches. Her purposeful selection of characters, further, made necessary the delineation of an appropriate religious backdrop for their activities. For this end also, her reading equipped her with essential details, and it sharpened her insight. All these materials she manipulated to fuse a relatively sophisticated Catholicism with the ancient paganism of Indian rites on the one hand, and with primitive Mexican devotion to Catholicism on the other.

The least important of Willa Cather's borrowings may be found in her use of historical facts, which she characteristically subordinated to the novel's structural totality. Since reportorial accuracy was distant from her aims, she consciously developed a power of selectivity supported, as she herself admits in "The Novel Démeublé," by Mérimée's estimate of Gogol. Choosing from among the innumerable aspects of nature, the former had said, is a much more difficult literary achievement than impartial observation and literal rendering. Consequently, Miss Cather never introduces facts as such or for their own sakes. And rather than linger over them she mentions them briefly and without pedantry. Twice in the course of the *Archbishop*, for instance, she touches on the massacre of Governor Bent, which occurred in 1847. This readily verifiable event she could have encountered in any history of New Mexico.

In all likelihood, however, Miss Cather based her account on the more familiar volume by Father Howlett. He mentioned (p. 227) a generally circulated rumor that Father Martinez had an active part in the uprising by Indians and Mexicans at Taos when, on January 19, 1847, the Governor and a number of Americans and Mexicans loyal to him were slain. Martinez "at least shared with the Indians and Mexicans in hatred for the Americans, and, in their ignorance of events and conditions outside their little valley, they imagined they were but beginning a patriotic war which would result in freeing their country from the foreigner, who was supposed to be an enemy to their race and to their religion."

More forthright than most of the other chroniclers of the affair, Father Howlett was cautiously convinced of Martinez's guilt, even though a United States tribunal absolved the padre of direct complicity. Working from such unresolved hints, Miss Cather in her first mention of the massacre is but vaguely allusive, mentioning by name neither the Governor nor the supposed leader of the revolt. Early in the *Archbishop* she records dispassionately: "Only last year the Indian pueblo of San Fernandez de Taos murdered and scalped the American Governor and some dozen other whites. The reason they did not scalp their Padre, was that their Padre was one of the leaders of the rebellion and himself planned the massacre." Convinced of the priest's guilt, she merely set the stage and then temporarily abandoned it.

One hundred and thirty pages later, when she mentioned the affair a second time, she was like Father Howlett much more explicit, identifying by name the priest who engaged her attention in one of the central incidents of the novel: "It was common talk that Padre Martinez had instigated the revolt of the Taos Indians five years ago, when Bent, the American Governor, and a dozen white men were murdered and scalped. Seven of the Taos Indians had been tried before a military court and hanged for the murder, but no attempt had been made to call the plotting priest to account. Indeed, Padre Martinez had managed to profit considerably by the affair." Her first allusion broadly suggests the hazards of pioneering under the zealous but subverted state of religious belief which prevailed in New Mexico. The second allusion occurs much later, after she has introduced Father Martinez as an antagonistic character. Now, when she wishes to expose the priest's ruthless, materialistic aspirations, she makes concrete his complicity in the massacre. For her purposes, indeed, she does not allow herself even Father Howlett's charitable suspension of absolute judgment. Miss Cather, it would appear, accepted Father Howlett's suspicion, and then manipulated the evidence to conform to the shape of her novel.

Father Martinez himself acts as her spokesman in another use of historical data. Conversing with Father Latour, the renegade priest comments on the historically famous revolt of Popé in 1680, "when all the Spaniards were killed or driven out, and there was not one European left alive north of El Paso del Norte." He boasts that Popé, a San Juan Indian, operated from Taos. Once again this particular fact is common knowledge, although the fullest account of it probably available to Miss Cather appears in H. H. Bancroft's *History of New Mexico and Arizona* (San Francisco, 1889). Bancroft emphasizes, as Miss Cather does, that the revolt originated among the pueblo communities in their effort to rid themselves of foreign domination. Father Martinez's reference to the Popé rebellion is thoroughly consistent with Miss Cather's characterization of the unruly priest. By implication Popé becomes the archetype of Martinez; by indirection Father Latour is being warned that Martinez, likewise operating out of Taos, will not brook foreign interference.

The threat veiled in the reference to Popé is, indeed, all the more sinister for its obliqueness, dangerously enhancing Martinez's cool warning that future European meddling will be met with violence. He says, "You are among barbarous people, my Frenchman, between two savage races. The dark things forbidden by your Church are a part of Indian religion. You cannot introduce French fashions here." Vastly effective, this entire episode is a crucial part of the novel. The parallel between historical reality and Miss Cather's theme is so close that her embroidery is imperceptible and the conflicts stand forth with dramatic rightness.

Many of her historical facts Miss Cather selected because they convey her faith in the human longing for sanctuary. Symbolically expressive of this kind of yearning is her interpretation of the Navajos' struggles: their slaughter by white troops at the supposed impregnable Cañon de Chelly, their enforced exile to the Bosque Redondo, and their eventual return to the lands of their fathers. As she manipulates these historical incidents, they take on a mystical, religious significance. She imagines the canyon a spiritual fortress, where the Navajos "believed their old gods dwelt . . . the very heart and centre of their life." The Indians' exclusion from the fastness she sees as their tragic loss of sanctuary, without which they must perish physically as well as spiritually. The Navajos' ultimate return becomes for Miss Cather a presage that genuine faith, and this not necessarily Christian, will assert itself against base aspirations and abuse.

No authoritative work on the religion and mythology of the Navajos supports her proposition that their gods dwelt in the canyon. But what is apparent is that the struggles of the Navajos have for her a mystic significance comparable to those of the Ácomas. Her visit to the Cañon de Chelly in 1925, enhanced by romantic legends of its supposed inaccessibility, gave shape to her interpretation. The traditional Navajo nostalgia for homeland, poignantly stated in many of their commonly sung chants, complemented further her literary needs and spiritual bent.

Historical eras widely separated in time challenged rather than inhibited Miss Cather in her artistic constructions. Frequently this separation afforded her a basis for believing that man's problems are eternally reiterated, and that they are distinguished only by external details of history. For her only the inner meaning is the essential one, enabling her boldly to link events which had occurred centuries apart, in order that the early occurrence should serve as a parable for the later one. This is the kind of spiritual union which she achieves in recounting the decline of the Pecos tribe from the splendor it had enjoyed in the sixteenth century to its pathetic moribundity in the nineteenth.

Through the sensitive eyes of Father Latour, Miss Cather witnesses the contemporary atmosphere of death and decay—"empty houses ruined by weather and now scarcely more than piles of earth and stone." She chose to interpret the process of decay as beginning with Coronado and his men who "set forth . . . on their ill-fated search for the seven golden cities of Quivera, taking with them slaves and concubines from the Pecos people." As she frequently does, she recalls here ideas or events that have long engaged her. Her interest in Coronado and his search for the cities of Quivera had even found its way into *My Antonia*, where she inserted an unrelated discussion of the explorer's activities. The waste begun by the white man in the sixteenth century culminated in the ravages of the modern white man, whose civilized diseases—she wrote in the *Archbishop*—"were the real causes of the shrinkage of the tribe."

Drawing her account—particularly the description of the Pecos pueblo—from several nineteenth-century sources, she establishes a series of contrasts as a *memento mori*. She offers first the contrast between the thriving Cicuyé of the sixteenth century and the dying Pecos pueblo of the nineteenth. She then places against the strong Indians of Cicuyé the yet stronger Spaniards of Coronado who in their hungry search for gold and new worlds were destroyed, as she sees it, by the dissipation of a noble dream into the lust of materialistic desire. Through the adroitly analogical fusion of historical time, Miss Cather accentuates the perpetual conflict between spiritual serenity and greedy turbulence. In so doing she accommodates one of her favorite themes: that sophisticated civilizations are acquisitive, and that materialism is a betrayal of man's spiritual wants, leading to negation and destruction. The *Archbishop* brings together and stabilizes in its most acute rendering a theme which breaks down temporal barriers. A Spaniard in armor or a modern money-lender are equally the poorer for the dislocation of inner cause; and a Tom Outland or a Father Latour are equally the richer for the reverence of ideal values. Accidents of time and place are merely sobering reminders that in a world of seeming flux there is always one immutable point.

Characterization is of primary importance in the *Archbishop*, for Miss Cather relied strongly upon her principals to communicate the concept of the pioneer quest within the superficially simple format of the legend. Once again recorded history gave her sound, convenient models for her human portraits. But only for the outlines of events and people did she go to sources, and these outlines she enriched with her deliberate imagination. From the works of Howlett and Lummis she derived the patterns of her major characters, Latour, Joseph, Martinez, and Chavez, making each representative of a pioneer type and yet as individualized as it is possible for a type to be. All are motivated by an intangible, spiritual seeking. Fathers Latour and Joseph undergo a metamorphosis from the functional, historical treatment of Howlett's biography, where Latour (Lamy) especially is an incompletely and nebulously drawn personality. In Miss Cather's hands they are contrasted gently, even lyrically, as symbolic of the complete flowering of the pioneer type. Although Latour and Joseph are impelled by comparable spiritual motives, they are constituted differently. Father Latour, an aristocrat and philosopher, is strengthened by an introspective power of love for all individuals; in his rare moments of uncertainty he is never torn by doubts about the sanctity of his mission but rather by fears of his own capacity for love. Father Joseph complements his friend by his practicality. Lacking his superior's philosophical penetration, he drives onward by bustling activity and never-questioning acceptance of his mission and capacities. For several reasons Father Latour remains a comparatively shadowy figure throughout the novel, while Father Joseph becomes more and more realistic.

By his very nature Father Joseph is dynamic and essentially not "intellectual" as is Latour. Howlett, moreover, concentrates mainly on Joseph, and hence, it might reasonably be expected, gives Miss Cather a more tangible working model. Finally, she deliberately idealized Latour as her representation of the esthetically refined qualities of the pioneer search. As Father Joseph evaluates the life and work of the Archbishop, he reflects: "Perhaps it pleased Him to grace the beginning of a new era and a vast new diocese by a fine personality. And perhaps, after all, something would remain through the years to come; some ideal, or memory, or legend." From the mosaic of scenes through which Miss Cather achieves finally a total impression (rather, perhaps, than a portrait which connotes an exact or full reconstruction) of the man, the reader carries away the belief that for Miss Cather the memorable quality of Father Latour is the essence, and that while physical substance like Joseph's has great charm and inspiration his ultimate purpose is to carry out the beautiful designs promulgated by his Bishop.

Against these two monumental figures Miss Cather sets up Father Martinez, drawn from Howlett, and Don Manuel Chavez, from Lummis. Both characters, historically and fictionally, have a passionate desire to safeguard their pioneer frontier against the inroads of the people whom they regard as "foreigners," as despoilers of the "wild land" and the old order. But both are made to represent the pioneer of warped aims who falls short of complete realization because of the flaw which renders him incapable of love. And because both are trying to preserve the unpreservable, they must be destroyed, figuratively if not literally. As Miss Cather says of Father Martinez: "The American occupation meant the end of men like himself. He was a man of the old order . . . and his day was over." Somewhat reminiscent of Captain Forrester, at least conceptually, Martinez and Chavez are admirable dramatic foils to Latour and his positive idealism. That history could provide Miss Cather with such dynamically probable contrasts is a token of her ability to weigh human values, for discoveries such as these could come only with discrimination and with esthetic-moral sensitivity.

Without overestimating the importance of historical sources to the *Archbishop*—for, as we have repeatedly indicated, reading was no more to the author than a rough frame is to a sculptor—Father Howlett's biography gave a firm base to Miss Cather's creative scheme that a comparison between the two books will vivify. The large number of details, incidents, and psychological qualities that she borrowed only to remold may be suggested briefly in the following catalogue:

	ARCHBISHOP	HOWLETT
Latour's shipwreck at Galveston, the loss of his worldly goods (see also Salpointe, pp. 195–96, and Defouri, p. 33).	p. 18	p. 156

	ARCHBISHOP	HOWLETT
Latour's trip across Texas, his fall in a jump from a wagon (cf. Defouri, p. 33; Salpointe, pp. 195–96).	18	157
Latour's entrance into Santa Fe.	19–20	164
Latour's visit to the Bishop of Durango and its results (cf. Defouri, pp. 34–5; Salpointe, p. 196).	20, 32	178
Father Joseph as a cook.	35	95
Father Joseph's theory of "rest in action."	35	29
Father Joseph's description—his nickname.	37	50, 412–13
Father Joseph's nostalgic reference to his life at Sandusky, his "alleged" hesitance at going any farther into the wilderness.	39–41	152–53
The miracle of the bell.	42 ff.	152–53
The white mules.	52 ff.	216 ff.
Reference to Father Joseph's sister Philomène.	65	*passim*
The coming of the Sisters of Loretto.	78	187
The suspension of Father Gallegos.	118	191–92
Father Joseph's illness, his nickname of "Trompe-la-Mort."	199 ff.	77, 325
The portrait of Padre Martinez, his biography, his excommunication along with Father Luceros (cf. Defouri, p. 125).	193 ff.	227 ff.
Father Joseph's function *à fouetter les chats.*	164	227 ff.
Father Joseph and the month of May.	202 ff.	22, 25, 33–35
The religious character of the Mexicans—their childishness and their faith.	206 ff.	164
Boyhood and early training of the two priests, Joseph's father as a baker, Joseph's fear of his father and his desire to join the army.	225 ff.	20–21, 26–27

	ARCHBISHOP	HOWLETT
Father Joseph as a beggar (cf. Salpointe, p. 231).	228	300–301
Father Joseph at Rome.	230–31	128–29
Father Latour's recall of Father Joseph from Arizona.	239	256 ff.
The Colorado territory.	246 ff.	256 ff., 286
Father Joseph's wagon.	252	286
Joseph's letters to his brother and sister just before his departure to Colorado.	255–56	286
Father Joseph's accidents.	260	290–310
The begging trip of Father Joseph.	260–63	300–301
The departure of the two young priests for America.	286 ff.	43, 46

For the most part, Miss Cather admits that she follows her basic source faithfully—but not slavishly. On a few occasions, however, she uses Father Howlett's book merely as a jumping-off point; that is, on these occasions she takes merely the kernel of an idea which was suggested by Father Howlett and develops it into a fully detailed incident. For example, one of the most terrifying episodes of the novel—the character and death of Father Lucero —grew out of the following brief statement (*Archbishop*, pp. 164–74; Howlett, p. 228): "There was a Mexican priest, Mariano de Jesus Lucero, at Arroyo Hondo . . . whom Bishop Lamy was obliged to suspend for irregularities and schismatical tendencies, and who was a former pupil and great friend of Father Martinez. These two now joined their forces and continued their opposition to Bishop Lamy, until he was obliged . . . to pronounce upon them the sentence of excommunication." Similarly, one of the most delightful interludes in the book—"The Bishop Chez Lui"—is based on but a single sentence in a letter of Father Machebeuf to his sister, May 26, 1841: "But necessity, the mother of invention, has taught us a little of the science of the kitchen, and I am able to give the cook a few lessons." (*Archbishop*, pp. 35 ff.; Howlett, p. 95.)

But this kind of creative expansion is rare for Miss Cather, who usually reproduces situations more closely than in the above instances. Indeed, she will sometimes carry over in an incident not only the ideas, point for point, but much of the language as well.

Archbishop (pp. 202–3):

He smiled to remember a time long ago, when he was a young curate in Cendre . . . how he had planned a season of special devotion to the Blessed Virgin for May, and how the old priest to whom he was assistant had blasted his hopes by cold disapproval. The old man had come through the Terror, had been trained in the austerity of those days of the persecution of the clergy, and he was not untouched by Jansenism. Young Father Joseph bore his rebuke with meekness, and went sadly to his own chamber. There he took his rosary and spent the entire day in prayer. *"Not according to my desires, but if it is for thy glory, grant me this boon, O Mary, my Hope."* In the evening of that same day the old pastor sent for him, and unsolicited granted him the request he had so sternly denied in the morning. How joyfully Father Joseph had written all this to his sister Philomène, then a pupil with the nuns of the Visitation in their native Riom, begging her to make him a quantity of artificial flowers for his May altar. How richly she had responded!—and she rejoiced no less than he that his May devotions were so largely attended, especially by the young people of the parish, in whom a notable increase of piety was manifest.

Howlett (pp. 33–35):

At the approach of the month of May, Father Machebeuf wished to make preparations for May devotions. This was quite natural for him, but it was a new departure for the old pastor. It was a novelty! an innovation! The lingering consequences of Jansenism were yet visible, and new forms of devotion were not encouraged by the old pastors. Special devotions to the Blessed Virgin were of the suspected class. The aged priest may have partaken of this prejudice . . . but in any case, he was old, and it is difficult to move old men. . . .

Not discouraged, however, the young curate went to his room, and taking his rosary, he spent the rest of the day in prayer. He prayed, not that he might have his own way, but that whatever was for the glory of God might be done, and he felt confident that Mary would arrange all things for the best.

. . . [The pastor consents to the fete.] . . .

Immediately he wrote to his young sister, who was a pupil with the nuns of the Visitation in his native village of Riom, expressing his lively joy and requesting her to make up and send to him at once a supply of artificial flowers for his May altar. This she did with great pleasure, and she was delighted to learn and to record the fact that the May Devotions were numerously attended and resulted in a great increase of piety in the parish of Cendre.

Most frequently Miss Cather borrows to preserve the basic situation of an incident, and then elaborates only enough to concretize it, to make it more credible. This is exactly what she has done in her depiction of Father Joseph at Rome. The matter-of-fact account in Father Howlett's book is now enlivened not only by Father Joseph's personality and humor, but by the inclusion of the procedure followed during an audience with the Pope. This last piece of information, she obtained, as she herself admits in "On Death Comes for the Archbishop," from conversations with Father Fitzgerald in Red Cloud, Nebraska.

Archbishop (p. 230):

Joseph had stayed in Rome for three months, living on about forty cents a day and leaving nothing unseen. He several times asked Mazzucchi to secure him a private audience with the Pope. The secretary liked the missionary from Ohio; there was something abrupt and lively and naïf about him, a kind of freshness he did not often find in the priests who flocked to Rome. So he arranged an interview at which only the Holy Father and Father Vaillant and Mazzucchi were present.

The missionary came in, attended by a chamberlain who carried two great black valises full of objects to be blessed—instead of one, as was customary. After his reception, Father Joseph began to pour out such a vivid account of his missions and brother missionaries, that both the Holy Father and the secretary forgot to take account of time, and the audience lasted three times as long as such interviews were supposed to last. Gregory XVI, that aristocratic and autocratic prelate, who stood so consistently on the wrong side in European politics, and was the enemy of Free Italy, had done more than any of his predecessors to propagate the Faith in remote parts of the world. And here was a missionary after his own heart. Father Vaillant asked for blessings for himself, his fellow priests, his missions, his Bishop. He opened his big valises like pedlars' packs, full of crosses, rosaries, prayer-books, medals, breviaries on which he begged more than the usual blessing. The astonished chamberlain had come and gone several times, and Mazzucchi at last reminded the Holy Father that he had other engagements. Father Vaillant caught up his valises himself, the chamberlain not being there at the moment, and thus laden, was bowing himself backward out of the presence, when the Pope rose from his chair and lifted his hand, not in benediction but in salutation, and called out to the departing missionary, as one man to another, *"Corraggio, Americano!"*

Howlett (pp. 128–29):

The great event of his visit was his audience with His Holiness, Pope Gregory XVI, on November 17. The Holy Father was greatly interested in his account of missions, and gave him apostolic benediction for himself and his flock, and Father Machebeuf still further remembered his flock by asking the Pontiff to bless for them the supply of rosaries, crosses and medals with which he had provided himself for the purpose and occasion.

The interview made a lasting impression upon him, and the words of the Holy Father—"Courage, American!"—were never forgotten by Father Machebeuf, who often recalled them afterwards, and always with a strengthening effect.

On another occasion Miss Cather has fused two characterizations from her original source to make up a single, complete portrait, for the fully developed study of Padre Martinez which appears in the *Archbishop* is in reality based upon the combined sketches of Fathers Martinez and Gallegos in Father Howlett's book. The biographical details of Father Martinez's life which Miss Cather presents are historically accurate, but his career as libertine, carouser, Don Juan, and dissipator was suggested rather by Father Howlett's description (pp. 191–92) of Father Gallegos, another priest whom Archbishop Lamy was forced to excommunicate.

The Padre [Gallegos] was very popular with certain classes in the parish, and these were the rich, the politicians and business men, few of whom had any practical religion. With these he drank, gambled and danced, and was generally a good fellow. He was a man of more than ordinary talent, and on that account he received considerable respect and deference. His conduct, however, gave scandal to the good within the fold, and also to those without the fold, for it furnished them an occasion for reviling the church.

To round out the details of Father Latour's portrait, Miss Cather drew from the writing of still another churchman, Father Salpointe, who had come to the archdiocese of Santa Fe only nine years after Father Lamy. *Soldiers of the Cross* was the source of valuable factual information, particularly for details of the Archbishop's declining years. In that work (p. 275) Salpointe mentions the country place Lamy purchased in 1853, and to which he withdrew after his retirement in July, 1885. Shortly after taking possession of the land, he had a small house and chapel built; and when the burdens of age and administration dictated rest, he would seek it in this refuge. Those familiar with the *Archbishop* will readily identify a parallel situation in the description of the country house where the aged Latour spent many hours in tranquil meditation.

From Salpointe's book, too (p. 233), Miss Cather drew the inspiration for the extremely moving description of Father Joseph's funeral and the devotion of Father Raverdy, himself mortally ill, as he rushed from France "to make his report to Bishop Vaillant and die in the harness." The scene in the novel reaches poignant culmination when the "dying man, supported by the cab-driver and two priests," makes his way through the mourners and drops to his knees before Father Joseph's bier. And, finally, Miss Cather derived wholly from *Soldiers of the Cross* (p. 275) details about the Archbishop's death: his catching cold at his country house, his desire to return to Santa Fe, the nursing ministrations of the Sisters of Loretto, and his request for the Holy Viaticum.

For Chavez, the fourth of her important characterizations in the *Archbishop*, Miss Cather went to Lummis' *A New Mexico David* (New York, 1891, pp. 190–217); and this reading she substantiated through reference to Twitchell's history (II, 383–84). Chavez's derivative portrait contains such elements as his aristocratic lineage, his pride, his skill with the bow and arrow, his anti-Americanism, the murder of his brother by Navajos, his own near death when he was eighteen, his two-day march across the desert while he was wounded, his home in the San Mateo Mountains. All these matters were verifiable. But while she accepted factual details about Chavez, Miss Cather subjected them to an interpretation which would weave them into the fabric of her conceptual scheme. In her eyes Chavez was a pioneer diverted from his genuine purpose by unfortunately distorted values. Her sympathies, unlike those of Lummis, were for the Indians, not Chavez; and in altering superficial details to accommodate her inherent attitude, she acted in thorough consistency with her artistic purpose. Willa Cather measured the significance of Chavez's actions less by their place in history than by the broader, moral meaning which she could infer from them.

Because her major pioneer characters were men of faith, she was obliged to provide for them a locale which combined the frontier and profoundly contrasting religious attitudes. Her serious reliance upon contrast for the development of both background and characterization is, indeed, a notable aspect of her technique. Against the sophisticated scholarly introspection of Father Latour and the practical religious activity of Father Joseph, she sets forth the muted simplicity of Mexican faith and the barbaric continuity of Indian ritual. Finally, as a historic and symbolic parallel to the efforts of the two French priests, she recounts the arduous toil of Father Junípero Serra, the priest whom she identifies so closely with the Western missionary spirit as to make him a symbol of its heroism. All this information for her religious backdrop Miss Cather absorbed principally from her observation and interpretation of the area, as well as from conversations with informed persons. But as always her reading provided invaluable suggestions and partially developed ideas.

Among the religious elements which attracted her early in her involvement with Southwestern culture was the primitive artistry of Mexican religious images. She speculated in the *Archbishop* on the motivating force behind the creation of these images, concluding that for these simple people "who cannot read—or think" the image is "the physical form of Love!" Here, as in other aspects of her concern with the spiritual problem, she was drawn to instinctive goodness unalloyed by rational considerations. She sensed also that these images were expressions of an entire culture, individually created in the reflection of native poverty and struggle as well as elementary devotion. Father Latour found the wooden saints in the humble Mexican homes "much more to his taste than the factory-made plaster images in his mission churches in Ohio —more like the homely stone carvings on the front of the old parish churches in Auvergne."

Although Miss Cather makes no obvious statements about Father Latour's mild censure of the mass-produced statuettes, her implication is sufficiently clear: they are to be equated symbolically with the disappearance of the frontier under the pressures of "machine-made materialism," and they spell the attrition of individualized, emotional worship. In the New Mexico of Father Latour's day this enervating force was not yet at work. Later, however, in her own trips to the Southwest Miss Cather was to see the beginnings of this same negated idealism.

Writing "On Death Comes for the Archbishop," she deplored the fact that "conventional factory-made church furnishings from New York" were replacing the traditional if homely ornamentation and images. She feared that only after it was too late would Catholics regret the loss of these artistically and historically valuable symbols. How much better, it seemed to her, if "all these old paintings and images and carved doors that have so much feeling and individuality" were to remain in the old churches, than to be transported to some New York or Chicago gallery where their innate meaning would vanish. She felt this trend toward desensitized ugliness and uniformity reflected the loss of creative imagination which she deemed essential to the pioneer spirit.

In juxtaposition to the gentle, simple devotion of the Mexicans which she stresses (she devotes an entire chapter to the history of the Shrine of our Lady of Guadalupe, but makes only passing reference to the fanatic piety of the Penitentes), Miss Cather represents the age-old pagan rites of the Indians. She even magnifies their barbarism and antiquity by viewing them through the agency of the fastidious Father Latour. Thrown into physically close proximity to Indian ritual, he is repelled by its antediluvian nature. Seeking shelter from a snow storm, he entered the Pecos ceremonial cave and "was struck by a reluctance, an extreme distaste for the place. The air in the cave was glacial, penetrated to the very bones, and he detected at once a fetid odour, not very strong but highly disagreeable." And though nothing remarkable happened at the time, years later the cave "flashed into his mind from time to time, and always with a shudder of repugnance quite unjustified by anything he had experienced there. It had been a hospitable shelter to him in his extremity. Yet afterward he remembered the storm itself, even his exhaustion, with a tingling sense of pleasure. But the cave, which had probably saved his life, he remembered with horror." From this concretized incident with its mere echoes of ancient ritualism, Willa Cather moves to more specific details of pagan worship. In their recording she has an opportunity to display her knowledge of Pecos religious legends, such as their year-round care of an undying fire, snake worship, and the hidden shrine in a cavern of the Pecos hills.

Treating these Indian rites and legends in evocative fashion, Miss Cather is yet purposely vague about them; again and again she points out that her sources are mainly rumor and hearsay. We may take her word, then, in assuming that common talk probably brought her attention to the notion of a sacred cave known only to the descendants of the Pecos Indians. The secret of its contents and location was supposed to have been successfully withheld from any white man. Earle R. Forrest, for example, in *Missions and Pueblos of the Old Southwest* (Cleveland, 1929), records this information as being a popularly disseminated rumor.

Similarly, she may have derived her information about actual religious practices from common knowledge. But it is also possible that she learned of them from Lt. J. W. Abert's official report (*Executive Documents . . . of the Senate*—Washington, 1847—IV, 30–40). He alluded to one belief that immense serpents were kept in their temples, and another that a perpetual fire kindled by Montezuma and guarded by a member of the tribe was an object of worship. "As the severity of their vigils always caused the death of the watchers, in time this tribe became extinct [Miss Cather speaks of this perhaps fanciful interpretation in the *Archbishop*]. Again, I have been told that some six or eight of their people were left, and that they took the sacred fire and went to live with the Pueblos of Zuni." Lt. Abert expressed amazement at the interest in Pecos religious superstitions shown by "enlightened man."

Always, whether she treats the religious faith of the Mexicans or the mysterious ceremonies of the Indians, Miss Cather succeeds in creating an atmosphere of religious continuity which can be stifled only temporarily but never destroyed. She creates, in short, a sense of spiritual timelessness rooted in the unrecorded past and extending toward an unfathomable future. This emanation of pious continuity is symbolized in part by the fourteenth-century Spanish bell, the story of which Miss Cather borrowed directly from Howlett. For over a hundred years the bell hung in the Church of San Miguel at Santa Fe, and then lay for another hundred in a cellar from where it was once more resurrected, this time by Father Joseph. A thing of metal, the bell yet had been founded for an inspirational cause that made inevitable its restoration so that it could help celebrate an eternally true devotion. The same tones that had been heard centuries ago in the desert would continue to remind the devout that they were Christians. The same conviction of timelessness is given substance even more overtly in a single incident related in the *Archbishop* by Father Joseph:

Down near Tucson a Pima Indian convert once asked me to go off into the desert with him, as he had something to show me. He took me into a place so wild that a man less accustomed to these things might have mistrusted and feared for his life. We descended into a terrifying canyon of black rock, and there in the depths of a cave, he showed me a golden chalice, vestments and cruets, all the paraphernalia for celebrating Mass. His ancestors had hidden these sacred objects there when the mission was sacked by Apaches, he did not know how many generations ago. The secret had been handed down in his family, and I was the first priest who had ever come to restore to God his own. To me, that is the situation in a parable. The Faith in that wild frontier, is like a buried treasure; they guard it, but they do not know how to use it to their soul's salvation. A word, a prayer, a service, is all that is needed to set free those souls in bondage. I confess I am covetous of that mission. I desire to be the man who restores these lost children to God. It will be the greatest happiness of my life.

Although Miss Cather brought to the episode a sanctified interpretation that is her own the physical occurrence is by no means her invention; the history of the Southwest contains numerous comparable incidents. The Catholic clergy in the uncertain days of their missionary toil frequently were compelled to bury their sacred treasure in anticipation of Indian raids, and subsequent discoveries such as the novelist recounts were fairly common. She may have heard of a find like this during one of her many visits to New Mexico; and certainly she read of similar incidents, particularly in the work of Salpointe (p. 227) and in the diaries of two Army officers who visited the area in 1853 (Smithsonian Inst., 1855 *Annual Report*, pp. 296–316). Out of legend and record, she distilled the materials which make up the present scene.

Miss Cather saves for the conclusion of the *Archbishop* the story of miracles experienced by Father Junípero, augurs of piety which she employs as climactically as her legend-like construction of the novel will permit. From Palou's biography (pp. 12–13, 21–22) she selects three wonders which befell the missionary priest: the miraculous fording of the river, the "manna" in the desert, and the visitation of the Holy Family in the guise of poor Mexicans. But she develops only the last supernatural occurrence —at once the most inspirational and the most dramatic of the three—into a full-blown incident or scene. At its conclusion she meditates upon what it signifies to her:

There is always something charming in the idea of greatness returning to simplicity—the queen making hay among the country girls— but how much more endearing was the belief that They, after so many centuries of history and glory, should return to play Their first parts, in the persons of a humble Mexican family, the lowliest of the lowly, the poorest of the poor,—in a wilderness at the end of the world, where the angels could scarcely find Them!

Through Willa Cather's presentation of the miracles she makes her complex intention most apparent. Here she concretizes the religious simplicity of her frontier locale. Here, also, she recreates Father Junípero as a figure heroically parallel to Father Latour, and in so doing she reiterates her faith in the Archbishop not only as a remarkable individual but as the representative of a hardy, sanctified breed.

And finally, she points to the ameliorations of those hardships which beset the religious missionary. This last goal she states positively by reminding her readers that "no man could know what triumphs of faith had happened there, where one white man [the early missionary] met torture and death alone among so many infidels, or what visions and revelations God may have granted to soften that brutal end." The naïveté of humble acceptance becomes an instrument of transcendent reality. Stated artlessly as an ultimate truth to which there can be no alernative, the divinity represented by miraculous intervention invites no argument from rational skeptics. The token of supernal will is there to be believed—the loss is his who somehow fails to respond.

For her deeply felt imaginative purposes, then, Willa Cather has made rich application of literary borrowing and personal experiences and observations. Surprisingly, despite manipulation of data, she never distorts information or makes serious departures from historical authenticity. She alters facts only twice, to increase dramatic impact in certain scenes, and in each instance she anticipates the reader's knowledge and probable objections. She has Father Joseph die before Father Latour, a circumstance which is not historically accurate, as she herself points out in "On *Death Comes for the Archbishop*." Moreover, she consciously alters the date of the abandonment of the Pecos pueblo. When dealing with rumor or common supposition, she is in most cases careful to point that out. Yet it should be abundantly evident by now that her concern is not with facts as such but, rather, with facts as they convey ethical meaning through their symbolic or metaphorical nature. Surely Coleridge's belief that "veracity does not consist in saying, but in the intention of communicating, truth" would have been most acceptable to Miss Cather as a statement of her own conviction.

And the most satisfying technical aspect of her use of factual materials is her artistic genius in molding and individualizing their diversity into an organic totality. This is her achievement of "similitude in dissimilitude." Usually charitable in her evaluations of historical figures, she feels a tremendous bond with them and their environment. Actually, it is her consistently fostered sympathy in union with discriminated historical details which has made the *Archbishop* the greatest of her novels.

Of Willa Cather it may be said, as she herself said of Sarah Orne Jewett, that she achieved a monument noble and enduring by giving herself absolutely to her material. Her great gift is that of sympathy. The artist, she said, "fades away into the land and people of his heart, he dies of love only to be born again." The lasting accomplishment is not to be won by the spurious process of "improving on his subject matter, using his 'imagination' upon it and twisting it to suit his purpose." The best that can be gained from such writing is "a brilliant sham, which . . . looks poor and shabby in a few years." For Miss Cather the things that mattered were those to which she devoted a lifetime of love and experience and which she had to represent in their true essence as she understood it. From this came the happiness of a fulfilled promise whose best qualities she brought together in the *Archbishop*.

BERNICE SLOTE

"Willa Cather and Her First Book"

In *April Twilights* one moves in a mythic landscape. Figures
of gods and god-men perform the rituals of legend in pastoral
Arcadia, or the world of Roman glory. But the Virgilian shepherds and minstrels blend into the equally indefinite "lads" of
Housman, who had his own elegiac tone; Arcadia is also Shropshire and Provence, with life shown in allegory. The classical-
pastoral scene is overlaid with a glitter of plumes and swords
and roses from the mythical kingdom of Ruritania—a glow that
might be called "Zenda-romantic." For there is in Cather a good
deal of her much-read, much-loved *Prisoner of Zenda,* with its
far-away, heroic action and its bittersweet ending of unfulfilled
love. The poems also have some of Rossetti's medievalism. And
near by is the world of the early Yeats, minstrel poet of the Celtic
twilight and "old earth's dreamy youth."

The subjects of the poems show Cather's rich interests—literature, art, the places of the world, memories of home—and her
ready response to the particular emotional aura of the experience.
Yet the poems seldom record an encounter with immediate fact:
the real (or inner) action is usually elsewhere. Even the most
direct poems lead to other times and places. London roses are
"perfumed with a thousand years," Ludlow Castle means Sir
Philip Sidney, the express train brings home the lads who wandered. Even the boys of "Dedicatory" lie dreaming in the past.
This kind of focus does not lessen the subjects; it merely defines

the nature of the poems. They are symbolic, made of the illusion that Cather in that early poem—"Then back to ancient France"—called the greatest reality.

For poetic materials, Cather went first to the tradition of pastoral primitivism, which assumed a golden age in the past: the idealized Arcadian land of gods, shepherds, and song. She entered with Virgil, as he says in the opening lines of the *Georgics*, Book III:

> You too, great goddess of sheepfolds, I'm going to sing, and you
> Apollo, a shepherd once, and the woods and streams of Arcadia.

With Virgil she could say, "I must venture a theme will exalt me/From earth and give me wings and a triumph on every tongue." Then follows the line in the *Georgics* that has so often been identified with Cather: "I'll be the first to bring the Muse of song to my birthplace." [1]

The Arcadian metaphors were familiar to poets from Theocritus and Virgil to the Elizabethans. In the Age of Reason, the pastoral figures became more deliberately quaint, formal, and dispassionate; but with Keats (his Grecian urn has men and gods of "Tempe and the dales of Arcady"), and finally with Yeats, they took on a shadowy melancholy for that lost, bright world. "The woods of Arcady are dead," Yeats wrote in "The Song of the Happy Shepherd" (1889). So Cather used the terms of the tradition in such poems as "Arcadian Winter," "Winter at Delphi," "Lament for Marsyas," and "I Sought the Wood in Winter." The last poem, however, is a pastoral study of cyclic time (summer and winter, flowers and snow) that ends on the hard snow peaks of the mountains that lifted from the Arcadian fields: "Behind the rose the planet,/The Law behind the veil." We find in the poems all the usual figures of Arcadia—Apollo and Pan; minstrels, shepherds, huntsmen, runners of races; laurels and daffodils. In addition the troubadour's lute and the trumpets of Zenda make variations in other poems ("The Encore," "I Have No House for Love to Shelter Him," "The Poor Minstrel," "Thou Art the

[1] All quotations from the *Georgics* are from *The Georgics of Virgil*, translated by C. Day Lewis (New York: Oxford University Press, 1947).

Pearl"). "Poppies on Ludlow Castle" and "The Namesake" have a chivalric tone. All these invoke a golden age, gone with the minstrels who sang it.

Cather's deep involvement with the Arcadian theme and her identification of singer and poet are clearly demonstrated in what she wrote about Ethelbert Nevin. She had met him early in her Pittsburgh years, had delighted in his company, his music, and his family, and had altogether idealized him as a modern troubadour of remarkable beauty and genius. She wrote in 1898 (*The Courier*, Febr. 5) that the "shepherd boys who piped in the Vale of Tempe centuries agone might have looked like that, or Virgil's Menaclas, when he left his flock beneath the spreading beech tree and came joyous to the contest of song." Nevin died on February 17, 1901, a loss more poignant because of his youth (he was 39, but looked like a boy). In her article on his death (*Journal*, March 13), Cather first quoted Housman: "Lie down, lie down, young yeoman." Whom the gods love die young—"indeed it was almost impossible to conceive of his outliving his youth, or that there should ever come a winter in his Arcady." She had heard his music at a concert the preceding April. Some of the same songs were sung at his funeral, "when the snow was driving outside and 'the land was white with winter.'" It was also the world's lost youth she lamented, and the modern poet's misalliance with society. Nevin "was as incongruous here as though he had strayed out of a Greek pastoral with a flower wreathed crook, so that he seemed to the eyes of the vulgar to be always in masquerade. Out of the soot-drift of the factories and amid the roar of the mills where the battle ships are forged, he sang his songs of youth and Arcady and summertime." These contrasts of summer and winter, the artist and the world, she recapitulates in "Arcadian Winter" and "Sleep, Minstrel, Sleep."

In other modifications of the Arcadian theme, Cather followed Housman's treatment of the "lighfoot lads" in the fields of Shropshire who loved and warred, and often died while yet in summer glory. (What she did not know at the time was that Housman, himself a classical scholar, was using Arcadia in his own way.) Cather's "Lament for Marsyas" is most strongly Housman, repeating his "To an Athlete Dying Young." But here she uses Greek myth as subject—the story of the young singer Marsyas (also a shepherd in Arcady) who dueled with Apollo and lost. This poem has also a specific personal source. While she was in Arles in 1902, she saw a Latin sculpture, a triplex bas-relief, in the wall of the old Roman theater. In the center is the poet, striking his lyre. At the left is Apollo, sharpening his knife on a stone. At the right is Marsyas after his defeat, hanging by his hands from an oak tree (*Journal*, Oct. 19, 1902).

Other myths appear in the poems. "Eurydice" dramatizes insubstantial, unrealized love, and the human failure of Orpheus to fulfill the enchantment. The poem must have recalled to her the shadowy figures of Hell, lost on the river Avernus, as Virgil retells the story of Orpheus and Eurydice at the close of the *Georgics*. Both Eurydice and, in "Asphodel," the "pale shade in glorious battle slain," dreaming on the fields of Hades, are exiles from Arcadia. The invocation to Apollo in "Winter at Delphi" is to an absent god. These themes of separation and frustration turn everything a little to the dark half of the moon—the woman who cannot love, the man who cannot live, the artist who may not create.

There is always in Cather's work the sense of the rare, the beautiful, the splendid thing that is a little beyond the ordinary reach —like the note too high for the human ear. It may be captured by the instrument of art; it must be sought by desire, even odysseys of heroic effort; it was, she thought in those early years, to be found only as one reached the climates nearer to the established sources of art. *April Twilights* is turned then to Europe, to the east to which she was moving, to the old south from which she came—anywhere but to Nebraska and the West. Nothing is clearer from the poems in *April Twilights* than this almost complete orientation to the ideal of some other world. But it was the young Europe that she really meant, the April time of childhood and the youth of the world; for she had first caught through the classics the sense of glory and high adventure possible to man. Such glory came from Greece and Rome, the habitation of the gods. Splendor also shone from the medieval-romantic world of cloister, sword, and lute. So most of the poems go back, as one would search a river toward the pure water of its source.

A comment Willa Cather made twenty years after *April Twilights* suggests another association she had held in her imagination. Writing of Nebraska in the *Nation*, she said: "In this newest part of the New World autumn is the season of beauty and sentiment, as spring is in the Old World." Paradoxically, then, spring signified the beauty of the old and far away, autumn the beauty of the new and far too close (and readers of Willa Cather will find very few, or very brief, spring scenes in her novels; important scenes are in autumn or winter). No wonder that April enchantments were tenuous and bittersweet: they were part of that other beauty one did not have.

Although Willa Cather was writing short stories about the West at this time ("On the Divide" [1896], "Eric Hermannson's Soul" [1900], "A Death in the Desert" [1903]), she used the materials of her own immediate past only to dramatize the lack of that greater thing which, in her poems, hung somewhere in the bodiless world of the imagined Arcady. Other influences were of course moving like a ground swell beneath her, but at this time she could not see all ways. And here the poems are valuable as directions to the positive thing she had in view, just as the early stories show predominately the negations. I suspect that Cather's early interest in the pioneers of Nebraska was not because they came *to* the new land but because they had come *from* the old. They held the culture of that other world. In the Virginia of 1752, she wrote in an early story ("A Night at Greenway Court," *Nebraska Literary Magazine*, June, 1896), the very appearance of strangers "spoke to us of an olden world beyond the seas for which the hearts of us all still hungered." So it was in Nebraska a century later. "The early population of Nebraska was largely transatlantic," she wrote in the same *Nation* article, and she stressed the value and beauty of the character and older traditions of those people. Sometimes "cultivated, restless young men from Europe made incongruous figures among the hard-handed breakers of the soil." Literally, the world was there before her, but in her vision it was filled with those who *had* played their violins in Vienna or Prague.

The poems of *April Twilights* also show how strong in Willa Cather's imagination and habitual imagery was the archetypal figure of Apollo, god of the life-giving sun, of music and beauty. His mythic song is here the sign of creation, the invocation of magic, the perfection of beauty. In the poems, Apollo, with harp, lyre, lute, or pipe, often appears in the guise of minstrels, or shepherds, or troubadours. He is served at Delphi, the "House of Song," is the "golden harper" of "Thine Advocate," the troubadour with harp strings in "Song," the piper of "The Encore," the rhymers of "The Tavern." His broken notes are in "Arcadian Winter," an azure song in "Sleep, Minstrel, Sleep." In "Paradox," melody is combined with youth and desire, as in so many of Cather's young artists. The music of Apollo (or Orpheus, or Marsyas) is the pure and traditional symbol for the creative desire of art.

And so we can recognize the obsession with music that runs through the Cather stories and novels, heavily at first and then more lightly as she goes farther away from the direct use of the symbol. For music continues to be the Apollonian sign of that rare and spiritual thing that art may discover. The clear statement of its symbolism is in an early story, "Eric Hermannson's Soul" (*Cosmopolitan*, 1900): "In the great world beauty comes to men in many guises, and art in a hundred forms, but for Eric there was only his violin. It stood, to him, for all the manifestations of art; it was his only bridge into the kingdom of the soul."

In later works the symbol need not be explained; it simply functions. Its richest use is, of course, in *The Song of the Lark*, the story of the creation of an artist. The young Thea Kronborg begins her real encounter with art in music of mythic significance —Gluck's "Orpheus." She is involved in the primitive, intuitive force of art when, singing one evening with Spanish Johnny and his Mexican friends, music becomes the natural instrument of feeling. Finally the focus of the novel changes. We are no longer with Thea, but we observe her through the eyes of her old friend Dr. Archie. To him, hearing the mature operatic star Kronborg is like dreaming on a river of sound. There he seems to be looking "through an exalted calmness at a beautiful woman from far away." Kronborg the artist is something other than Thea the woman. She has become the realization of art, the true song of Apollo.

That to Willa Cather music meant primarily what it signified can be seen in her own dramatic rather than intellectual relationship with it. Her experiences in music were emotional and imaginative, Edith Lewis points out, the music "translating itself into parallel movements of thought and feeling." [2] Willa Cather recognized this in herself, as some of her comments before 1903 reveal. She wrote in *The Courier* (Febr. 5, 1898): "My friend Toby Rex has always accused me of too great a tendency to interpret musical compositions into literal pictures, and of caring more for the picture than for the composition in itself." Some weeks before, for example, she had written (Dec. 25, 1897) that Dvorak's "Largo" from the *New World Symphony* meant the "empty, hungry plains of the middle west. Limitless prairies, full of the peasantry of all the nations of Europe." It was a "song of homesickness, the exile song of many nations."

All of this has a direct bearing on her writing. In prose, the images of music could be diffused, transformed, and enlarged. But poetry is the traditional and direct embodiment of music in language. One passage in *The Song of the Lark* shows that Cather identified the two, but that the poem might lift out of language into pure song. When Thea learns and reads the poems of *Lieder* from Professor Wunsch, her voice changes from the sound of ordinary speech as she reads "musically, like a song. . . . It was a nature-voice, Wunsch told himself, breathed from the creature and apart from language." The poem itself can be Apollo's song, giving in short measure the larger design. This is what did happen in Cather's art. The poetry, especially that of 1903, forms in itself an epigraph for the novels which followed. And it makes a difference in our response to the prose works if we associate them with the poems and the god in Arcadia—to know that what has engrossed us in the novels with a sense of hidden power is that we are involved in the re-enactment of myth.

[2] *Willa Cather Living* (New York: Alfred A. Knopf, 1953), pp. 47-48.

JAMES SCHROETER

"Willa Cather and
The Professor's House"

If the name Willa Cather means anything at all to the young American, it is probably in connection with a college course in American literature, a name bordered on one side by Theodore Dreiser, Stephen Crane, and maybe Hamlin Garland, and on the other side by Sinclair Lewis, Fitzgerald, and Hemingway. He may recall her as the author of a story he once read in an anthology, either "Paul's Case" or "Neighbour Rosicky," and may perhaps remember that she is the author of *My Antonia* and *Death Comes for the Archbishop*, although he is not likely to have read either. An older American whose memory can go back to the 1920's and 1930's might remember her as the publicity-shy but generally acknowledged leading novelist of the time—a position in some ways parallel to that held by Salinger now, an impression formed from such ephemeral tokens of immortality as her picture on the cover of *Time* in 1931 or her "Profile" by Louise Bogan in the *New Yorker*. But the American who can remember the significant Willa Cather behind the 1920's celebrity or the embalmed textbook figure is rapidly disappearing. He is someone of her own generation, who came across her work during the era of the First World War with the excitement of genuine discovery.

It is difficult now to reconstruct the cultural and literary conditions that might have been responsible for that excitement, and impossible to outline them in a brief space, but there is one

Reprinted from the *Yale Review*, Vol. LIV, No. 4 (Summer, 1965). Copyright Yale University Press.

condition which, by itself, explains quite a bit: the indifference or hostility felt by the native-born Americans of that period toward the immigrant. This was so pronounced that only the sturdier, cruder media existing at the ragged fringes of culture— the vaudeville show, the salesman's joke—reflected it honestly. The middle-class magazines—the *Atlantic, Scribner's*, even the muck-raking *McClure's* of which Willa Cather had been managing editor—printed stories that dealt with the kind of middle-class, native-born Americans who subscribed to the magazine, or with the wealthier and more glamorous group one step higher—the automobile-owning, country-club-going set that had servants, sent their sons to Princeton, and took junkets to Europe. If there is any reference to an immigrant, it is only through the character of a maid or janitor with a Swedish accent, who is added for comic relief. There seems to be little other awareness of the tides of people who were altering American patterns of courtship, transforming the industrial economy, changing the shapes of the cities. Our literature before the First World War was for native-born Americans, about native-born Americans, and by native-born Americans, and it is probably significant that the first major American writer who was the son of an immigrant, Theodore Dreiser, was a contemporary of Willa Cather, and in some way always escaping from his past.

Only when you project the early Cather novels of immigrant life—*O Pioneers!* (1913), *The Song of the Lark* (1915), *My Ántonia* (1918)—against this kind of background is it possible to appreciate something of their freshness, and the immense courage that must have gone into the writing of them. Although "courage" is perhaps not the word to apply to someone as safe as Willa Cather, whose name had so much the right kind of old-stock American ring, and whose commerce with Bohemians and Swedes was a little like that of Jim Burden, the point-of-view character in *My Ántonia*—large-minded and tinged with *noblesse oblige*. You read in Mildred Bennett's biography that Willa sent Annie Pavelka, her model for Ántonia, money for seed wheat during the drought years. She led from a position of comparative artistic safety, too, bolstered by the authority that comes from being a teacher and editor, before attempting *O Pioneers!*; she mastered the mold before she broke it. But whatever you call the mixture of prudence and boldness that went into these books, what came out was big, independent, and original. As genteel and ladylike as these books may seem to readers brought up on Hemingway and Faulkner, they gave American literature a new landscape, a new subject matter, and they made America's best critic, Randolph Bourne, exclaim in 1918, "The stiff moral molds are broken and she writes what we can wholly understand." It was as though in telling the story of the struggle and triumph of Alexandra Bergson, Thea Kronborg, and Antonia Shimerda, Willa Cather had cut through the claptrap to the salient fact of the American experience of her time—the coming of the immigrant, his struggle, assimilation, triumph—and placed the permanent, official seal of an accomplished art on that segment of American history.

There was one immigrant group, however, and an important one, that played little part in Willa Cather's fiction, the Russian and Polish Jews who were coming to America in such large numbers in the 1890's and the early years of the twentieth century. This fact may seem surprising for a number of reasons. Generally so because of the size and importance of the immigration, because Willa's life in those years as a writer and close observer in the large Eastern cities—New York, Boston, Pittsburgh—must have brought her into close contact with it, and because the drama that so captured her imagination, the struggle and triumph of the Swedes and Bohemians, was played out in a still more dramatic way by the Eastern European Jews, who often struggled against fiercer odds and won out to a more striking success. More specifically so because the Jews Willa Cather does represent in her fiction are not viewed from the same angle as her Bohemians, Scandinavians, Germans, and French. Despite the assimilative and Whitmanesque hug with which she embraced immigrant Mexicans and stolid Norwegians in her early books, she was capable at the same time of exhibiting—in the words of Bernard Baum—"an anti-Semitism of the poolroom variety that identifies the Jew with commercial exploitation, secularization, and destruction of traditional values."

You can find examples of Willa Cather's anti-Semitism easily enough even in her essays and pieces of criticism. She complains in "Potash and Perlmutter" (1914) that New York is being taken over by Jews. The city "roars and rumbles and hoots and jangles because Potash and Perlmutter are on their way to something." One has to live in tasteless apartments because the buildings are built by Potash and Perlmutter to be lived in by Potash and Perlmutter, and one has to buy clothes designed by Potash and Perlmutter to be worn by the wives of Potash and Perlmutter. The essay is deft and the tone is light and good-natured enough, but behind it was a feeling Willa Cather held to so tenaciously it cropped up again, even though expressed in a different form, in an essay published more than twenty years later, an appreciative essay of Sarah Orne Jewett in *Not Under Forty* (1936). Mainly a defense of Miss Jewett, a writer Willa Cather had met a quarter-century earlier in the heart of Brahmin Boston when she was an impressionable beginner and Miss Jewett represented for her the purest of American cultural traditions, it launches an attack against the young "foreign" and "Jewish" critics, people "educated at New York University" and "inoculated with Freud," who are incapable of understanding the language and traditions of Miss Jewett. This essay was written in the thirties, at a time when a number of critics who happened to be urban and Jewish —Louis Kronenberger, Clifton Fadiman, William Soskin—had been publicly sticking barbs into Miss Cather's work, and it is not difficult to conclude that, in defending the Americanism of Miss Jewett, she was defending herself. Her technique is rather like the impersonal one in "Potash and Perlmutter," where she does not name herself as the victim of the tasteless apartment buildings and clothes, and one can clearly sense the same kind of fear in both essays that the Jews are taking over, the only difference being that it is the language rather than New York which is threatened in the second.

The crucial examples, though, are in the stories and novels, where feelings that could not easily be rationalized came out fairly clearly. Her first book of stories contains one, "The Marriage of Phaedra," which draws a romanticized picture of a great artist and a grotesque picture of a Jewish art dealer. The art dealer, Lichtenstein, is, in Miss Cather's words, a man of "repulsive appearance" and "innate vulgarity," who is trying to buy up the dead artist's masterpiece, and who says of it, in accents which resemble nothing so much as those Victorian imitations of Jewish talk concocted by Thackeray and Dickens: "Dot is a chem, a chem! It is wordt to gome den tousant miles for such a bainting, eh? To make Eurobe abbreciate such a work of ardt it is necessary to take it away while she is napping." She gives us another picture of a hideous Jew in a later story, "Scandal." The villain of the story, Stein, an immigrant who has made an immense fortune and bought a mansion on Fifth Avenue that used to belong to "people of a very different sort," is described as having "long white teeth; flat cheeks, yellow as a Mongolian's; tiny, black eyes, with puffy lids and no lashes; dingy, dead-looking hair." He hires a young woman to impersonate the heroine of the story, Kitty Ayrshire, an opera singer (Willa was always strangely attracted to opera singers), and lets himself be seen publicly with the double. What Miss Cather wants the reader to regard as the tragedy of the story comes from the way the victimized Kitty has her name sullied by having it linked with Stein. Another example can be found in one of her last stories, "The Old Beauty," posthumously published in 1948. One of the villains—there are several—is dark, foreign-looking, and a banker. He is not named as a Jew, but at various points in the story he is described as "repulsive," "vulgar," "pushy," "an immigrant who has made a lot of money," a man "who does not belong." Like Stein of "Scandal," he is without gallantry, and attempts to assault the heroine of the story, Lady Longstreet, intended by Miss Cather as a symbol of the graciousness and beauty of a way of life that is disappearing.

There are several striking similarities in these portraits: all show the Jew as repulsive from a physical point of view, vulgar from a social and esthetic point of view, and acquisitive from a moral. A foreigner or outsider, he is seen in the role of invader and aggressor, and he tries to use things, art objects or women (Miss Cather often identified the two), for unworthy ends.

The fullest exhibition of anti-Semitism, though, is in the novel *The Professor's House* (1925), Willa Cather's only work which contains a major, full-scale portrait of a Jew. This book is not so well known as some of her others. It has not appeared in paper, and has escaped the college vogue that has kept other books of the same era—*The Great Gatsby, The Sun Also Rises* —in the public eye. But it is an interesting, vigorous, thought-provoking book, perhaps Willa Cather's most interesting, and one of the significant American novels of the twentieth century. The Jew in the book, Louie Marcellus, does not appear to be a stereotype. Instead of being a banker or department store magnate, he is an electrical engineer. Unlike the crudely-sketched Lichtenstein, he does not speak in any identifiably Jewish way. Nor is he physically repulsive: "There was nothing Semitic about his countenance except his nose—that took the lead. It was not at all an unpleasing feature, but it grew out of his face with masterful strength, well-rooted, like a vigorous oaktree growing out of a hill-side." He is rather handsome and appeals to women. He is not even especially acquisitive or vulgar, at least not on the surface. On the contrary, he is described as "generous to a fault," and is constantly giving away expensive presents. But strangely the hero of the novel, Professor St. Peter, does not like Marcellus, and yet he can hardly put his finger on the reason. The reasons lie deeply buried in the inner patterns of the book, and they are probably the best key to untangling not only the meaning of a book which from the time of its first appearance critics have felt to be baffling and mysterious, but to Miss Cather's persistent anti-Semitism.

Willa Cather deliberately, and perhaps also unconsciously, buried these meanings deeply. This is what she meant in 1925 when she said in an interview that *The Professor's House* was the only book she had ever written in which she had tried to be "ironic." The hidden irony of the title—the "house" is, among other things, the professor's grave—has been beautifully explained by the late E. K. Brown; but no one has ever explained the irony of the epigraph, which unlocks the doors to the lower story. It functions a little like the epigraphs T. S. Eliot was coming out with at about that time, in *The Waste Land*, for instance, leading you into what is coming but refusing to give up its meaning all at once, rather like an ingenious but nasty joke which the author is playing on the readers as well as on the dramatis personae. Miss Cather's epigraph is a quotation from the Jew, Marcellus: "A turquoise set in silver wasn't it? . . . Yes, a turquoise set in dull silver."

On the more accessible level, the "turquoise set in dull silver" is a piece of jewelry, and the more accessible irony is that Marcellus, who refers to it, has no understanding whatever of its history, value, or beauty, nor do any of the people he is talking to, least of all his wife. The scene is Christmas day at a dinner party at the Professor's new house. Marcellus arrives with his wife, Rosamond, the Professor's daughter, a pretty but vain woman, who comes decked out in a gold necklace Marcellus has given her. He describes this necklace as "very old": "Rosamond doesn't like anything showy, you know, and she doesn't care about intrinsic values." Even the reader who sees that Rosamond likes only showy things and only "intrinsic" values is likely to miss that Marcellus' evaluation of the gold necklace, which is exactly opposite from the true one, is applicable only to another piece of jewelry, the "turquoise set in dull silver" which Rosamond no longer wears. Whereas the gold necklace, a present from a Jew to his wife at Christmas, is the kind of showy trinket that anyone could pick up in an antique shop if he had enough money, the "turquoise set in dull silver" which Marcellus "tolerantly" recalls (Willa Cather disliked the tolerant and affected an intolerant style) had been a gift from Tom Outland: it has never been bought or sold, it is unique, it is made by hand, it is the product of an ancient and vanished Indian civilization, and its value is of the intrinsic sort that comes from the beauty of its design and workmanship, and of the extrinsic sort conferred by its origin and the beauty of the motives behind Outland's finding it and then giving it as a gift. The basic irony, then, as those familiar with the values running all through Willa Cather's fiction will recognize, is that the half-forgotten Indian bracelet represents true beauty, while the overvalued gold necklace represents the false.

The deeper ironic levels can be seen clearly only in the light of the over-all structure of the novel. This structure is of a radical, experimental sort, in its own way a little like what some of Willa Cather's younger contemporaries—James Joyce, Virginia Woolf—had been up to. It consists of three parts, apparently quite unrelated, which compose into a surprising significance once you see the angle and distance from which you are supposed to view them. Two of these parts, Book I and Book III, deal with a single set of people, the Professor's family and colleagues, and with their depressing relationships—their petty jealousies, bickering, back-biting, greed. They are set in the present (after 1922, the year in which Willa claimed the world broke in two), in a small, dull Midwestern college town, and their general flavor, pace, and texture suggest what is small, joyless, and commonplace. Book II is in the sharpest contrast. Almost devoid of human figures and relationships, it is dominated by one character, Outland, and one relationship, Outland's friendship with Rodney Blake, a relationship opposite from those in the other books, and based like all Miss Cather's ideal relationships on disinterested friendship rather than the ties of sex, marriage, and family. Instead of telling of selfish ambition, it deals with the heroic quest of recovering a vanished civilization. Rather than being set in the joyless present, it is in the romantic past. Rather than being in the kind of dull Midwestern town excoriated so often in the fiction of the twenties, it is set on a mesa in the Southwest, a part of the country Miss Cather used in *The Song of the Lark* and *Death Comes for the Archbishop* as her symbol of ideal natural beauty.

The point is that Book II is the "turquoise" and Books I and III are the "dull silver." The whole novel, in other words, is constructed like the Indian bracelet. It is not hard to see that Willa Cather wants to draw an ironic contrast not only between two pieces of jewelry but between two civilizations, between two epochs, and between the two men, Marcellus and Outland, who symbolize these differences.

One facet of this last contrast has to do with what might be called the "traditions" of Outland and Marcellus. Like Miss Cather herself, Outland is the child of parents who moved West when he was eight. His parents "both died when they were crossing southern Kansas in a prairie schooner," and later the orphaned Tom works as a call boy on the Santa Fe and as a cowhand on a ranch. All of these details—the prairie schooner, the railway, the ranch—indicate that Tom is supposed to represent the genuine American pioneer tradition. By contrast, Marcellus, whose background is unknown or unmentioned, represents no tradition at all. He is a Jew, but seems to have dropped all of the identifying marks of one. He seems also to be of indefinite nationality; at one point he mentions that his brother is in the silk trade in China. His "tradition" is suggested by the fact that he builds a house on the "shores of Lake Michigan" designed by a "young Norwegian trained in Paris" that has "wonderful wrought iron door fittings from Chicago": "We found just the right sort of hinge and latch—and had all the others copied from it. None of your Colonial glass knobs for us."

Another facet of the contrast has to do with creativity. Willa makes Tom's creativity double, as if to drive home the point twice as hard. On the one hand, Outland is an archeologist, who discovers, explores, and preserves the artifacts of an ancient Indian civilization, driven by the desire to find the source of America's beginnings. On the other, he is a theoretical physicist, pushing the frontier of man's knowledge further through his research in the laboratory. Neither of these activities brings Tom profit, nor does he want them to. He is offered a large sum of money for the old Indian pots he digs up by people who want to carry them out of the country, but he presents them without cost to the Smithsonian. His scientific discovery has important commercial applications, a point he well understands, but he realizes nothing from it. Marcellus, by contrast, the electrical engineer, has no creative genius whatever, but knows how to make money. His talent is in getting and spending, and his money comes wholly from his application of the discovery Tom has made. The contrast, then, is that the gentile is the innovator and creator, while the Jew is the exploiter who parasitically battens off what he creates.

Willa also contrasts the men as symbols of time past and time present. Her technique and situation are a little reminiscent of Joyce's in his story "The Dead," in which there is also a contrast —between Michael Furey, who stands for creativity and true Gaelicism, and the anglicized Gabriel who betrays these things. Just as Gabriel's wife had been wooed before her marriage by the now dead and therefore romanticized figure of Michael, so Rosamond had been wooed by Outland. But the interesting parallel is in the way that the two dead men, legendary figures from a larger past giving the measure of the unheroic present, even though glimpsed briefly, overshadow their unworthy successors.

In making the free-wheeling Marcellus an electrical engineer, Miss Cather departed sharply from her model, a Canadian Jew who was a concert violinist. But she risked the temperamental improbability both to push her contrast between innovator and exploiter and to cap with a ruling symbol her picture of the ugly present. Like Robert Frost and Sherwood Anderson, she thought the threat to human values was posed by the machine, mass-production, and the substitution of the yardstick for the heart. As she saw it, the engineer was the new man. He and his machinery were pulling us relentlessly away from the past and into the future. And so she merged Jew and engineer in one.

Although worked out in terms of a vastly more subtle and comprehensive art, The Professor's House says pretty much the same thing about Jews as the shorter pieces—the Jew is a money-maker rather than a creator, a traditionless aggressor who invades from the outside; he threatens and destroys the past; and he symbolizes what is wrong with the present. But there is a still more sweeping and deplorable implication. The majority of the novel is seen through the mind of the Professor. Like Miss Cather and Outland, he came West with his parents when he was a child, and he, too, symbolizes the American tradition. Tom is the son the Professor would have liked to have; Marcellus is the son he actually gets. If the Professor can be taken as a symbol of America, then Willa's "message" is simply that America is falling into the hands of the Jews. This is what she means by having the Professor's daughter and Outland's discovery fall into the hands of Marcellus. They, the Jews, are the unworthy inheritors of that tradition and wealth which they had no share in making but which, through some unaccountable flaw in the scheme of things, they have taken over, very much as the Snopeses in Faulkner's Yoknapatawpha novels take over the glories and traditions of the old South.

A fascinating chapter in the history of the creative process could be written if it were possible for someone to get his hands on the materials showing the influences on Willa Cather in the formative months when *The Professor's House* took shape in her mind. Unfortunately what was probably the best of this material was destroyed after Jan Hambourg, the model for Marcellus, sent Willa Cather the bundle of letters, representing over thirty years of her correspondence with his wife, which Miss Cather bit by bit consigned to the incinerator. Still, it is possible to speculate about these influences, and to pull from the facts that have been made public a revealing picture.

The months in question are roughly those between May and October, 1923, when Willa Cather must have been formulating the basic characters, situations, and themes for her novel. The last serial installment of her earlier novel, *A Lost Lady*, came out in June, and appeared virtually unchanged in book form in September; so that by May she must certainly have already turned her thoughts toward her next book. And by October she was back in New York, at her flat on Bank Street in the Village, engaged in the actual writing. During this period there were, I believe, two factors that influenced her choice of theme and character.

The first was that she began to reap the tangible rewards of the success she had always dreamed of. Alfred A. Knopf, her friend as well as publisher, had pushed the sales of *One of Ours* (1922) hard, and the book was making money, as were her earlier Houghton Mifflin books. For the first time, she had all the money she wanted, and at the same time she was starting to get the recognition. In May she was awarded the Pulitzer Prize for *One of Ours,* and the reviews of *A Lost Lady* in September and October were ecstatic. Even the people back home in Nebraska, whose admiration Willa Cather may have secretly longed for most, paid her their first official homage. They raised money for Leon Bakst to paint her portrait, to be hung in the big public library in Omaha. The effect of the wealth and glory was altogether opposite from what Willa had expected. The wealth brought luxuries that seemed unimportant once they were realities, and the fame was like a cancer that ate into her privacy, obtruding into that world of memory and tranquillity which was the source of her art. The whole experience of getting the wealth and fame and then having them turn sour provided her with the major theme of *The Professor's House,* accounting for much of the contrast between Outland (effort) and Marcellus (reward), and for the "tragedy" of the Professor, whose life is split into two opposing parts, the glorious first phase in which he struggled and created, and the unworthy phase in which he wins prize money, success, and the luxury of an expensive, modern house. And it accounts, too, for an implied criticism of America, whose history parallels that of the Professor, consisting of a noble past and an ignoble present cheapened by material things.

The second factor, Willa's visit that summer with Jan and Isabelle Hambourg, had a more specific influence. Isabelle, the former Isabelle McClung, had been Willa's closest friend for fifteen or twenty years, and when she married Jan Hambourg, the Canadian Jewish violinist, in 1916, the friendship continued, apparently pretty much on the same basis. Willa would have been too proud to reveal fully what changes may have come about in her own feelings. The women continued to exchange letters regularly, and in 1920 the three of them—Jan, Isabelle, and Willa Cather—toured the battlefields of France together. After the Hambourgs acquired their home in France, in Ville-d'Avray, they outfitted a special room for Miss Cather to work in, very possibly at the urging of Jan rather than Isabelle, and invited Willa for a visit. It is impossible to say exactly what happened during that visit, but Edith Lewis, who later came more or less to supplant the position Isabelle had held, has this revealing comment to make in her book on Miss Cather:

The Hambourgs had hoped that she would make Ville-d'Avray her permanent home. But although the little study was charming, and all the surroundings were attractive, and the Hambourgs themselves devoted and solicitous, she found herself unable to work at Ville-d'Avray. She felt indeed that she would never be able to work there.

One chapter in *The Professor's House* suggests strongly what must have happened, and how this influenced the formation of the novel. This chapter, the eighth one, relates how the Professor goes to Chicago to give a lecture, engaging a room for himself and his wife in a "quiet hotel near the university," only to find that his solicitous son-in-law has cancelled the hotel room, arranged and paid for a commodious suite in the Blackstone overlooking the Lake, obtained tickets to his favorite opera, and even arranged a surprise birthday dinner at a public room in the hotel, to which he has invited all the Professor's University of Chicago colleagues. The Professor's reactions to the suite, the dinner and all the rest seem similar to Miss Cather's reactions to Ville-d'Avray: he finds everything commodious, well-arranged, luxurious, and attractive, but he is unaccountably depressed, irritated with Marcellus, and sorry he let himself in for it by accepting the hospitality. The Professor is too civilized to vent his feelings about Marcellus in anything but ironic statement or self-deprecation, a situation that seems to be a miniature version both of Willa Cather's in Ville-d'Avray, and of the larger pattern running through the book, which centers on St. Peter's reluctance to move out of his old house and his unaccountable discomfort in the new one, with its convenient study arranged by his wife and Marcellus. Clearly the visit that summer to Ville-d'Avray must have provided Willa not only with her model for Marcellus but her symbolism of houses, rooms, and studies, and the emotional furniture she put into them.

With little doubt Willa Cather's feelings toward Jan were mixed up with a good deal of hate. Plain as this is in other ways, it shows up most directly in the strange dedication, which must be one of the nastiest dedications any first-rate writer has ever appended to a first-rate book. Consistent with the ironic title and epigraph, it reads: "For Jan, because he likes narrative." Part of the nastiness comes from the fact that the book is so deliberately anti-narrative, but one suspects there may be a private joke, which no one but Jan and Willa Cather, or perhaps Willa Cather only, was in on. The hatred, I believe, can be traced to two separate roots. The deepest was a psychological root, which so far has resisted the efforts people have made to drag it into the light—although someday, if the picture of Willa Cather as a frank, hearty Westerner with a taste for French cooking is ever going to be replaced by a picture of the more complex reality, it will have to be. The second was a cultural root, which is somewhat easier to examine, and greatly more relevant to the general question of Willa's anti-Semitism.

The portrait of Marcellus must have come from both roots. Otherwise one can hardly account for the vigor of Miss Cather's hatred or the consistency with which she has worked it into the symbolic scheme. But no other portrait of a Jew Willa Cather ever did has anything like the same development or is fueled by anything resembling the same degree of creative energy. In fact, there is no other example in her novels of a major anti-Semitic strain. When one takes the balanced view, one sees that anti-Semitism, for the most part, is really a rather unimportant aspect of Willa Cather's fiction, just as it was unimportant in her personal life. The reason, I believe, is that on only one occasion did the cultural and psychological factors come together, in the portrait of Marcellus. Her other portraits of Jews, which have mainly a cultural basis, are the product of the general way of looking at things of the America of her day.

The proof of this is that the major fiction writers who were most nearly contemporaneous with Willa, the major writers born in the 1870's, Theodore Dreiser and Sherwood Anderson, are about equally anti-Semitic. One has only to recall Anderson's *Tar* or *Dark Laughter*, or the crude way both writers will refer to a character as "the Jew," without even attaching a name, content to let the stereotype stand as the total basis for the character. It is true that both writers, Dreiser especially, attach labels such as "the Swede," or "the German," or "the Irishman" in a similarly crude, unflattering, and stereotypic way, a practice Willa Cather never engaged in, but there is a similar stereotyping of the Jew in all three. Irving Howe tries to play down Anderson's anti-Semitism in his book on Anderson, claiming that "if one cared to draw up a balance sheet, it would be possible to find favorable passages about the Jews to match the disturbing passages" (a similar claim could be made for Willa Cather), but he is more nearly honest when he admits how Anderson was influenced by the "folk stereotype which regards Jews as the archetypal 'other,' alien, unknowable, and perhaps supect." Bringing out the scandalous public controversy in which Dreiser was engaged in the 1930's, F. O. Matthiessen—in his book on Dreiser —quotes the comments Dreiser made when he was trying to justify himself against charges that he was anti-Semitic—comments in which Dreiser, trying to give his sincere reaction to Jews, nonetheless comes up with the same kind of stereotype: "If you listen to Jews discuss Jews," wrote Dreiser, "you will find that they are money-minded, very pagan, very sharp in practise."

Similar attitudes can be found in the writers who came before and after. Edith Wharton, for example, born in the 1860's, creates in her portrait of Simon Rosedale most of the features Willa was to use in her portrait of Stein—the vulgarity, the money, the social pushiness—while T. S. Eliot and Ezra Pound, both born in the 1880's, concentrate nearly the ugliest stereotypes in their poems—a point that has been well enough publicized, at least in the case of Pound, to require no rehearsing here. Even Sinclair Lewis, also born in the 1880's, gives a reverse testimony to the cultural situation by his noisy insistence, for example, that Mrs. Banning and Mrs. Anneke invite Jews to their parties, or by his desire to write a play "exposing" anti-Semitism. Histories of American literature seem never to notice that the 1920's generally were dominated by this sort of thing, but there are conspicuous forms of it in Mencken, Nathan, Boyd, Hergesheimer, Cabell, and Tarkington, and even in the early work of the younger men born in the 1890's and early 1900's, who shaped the direction of the "new" American novel—F. Scott Fitzgerald, Thomas Wolfe, Hemingway, and Faulkner.

In some ways Fitzgerald uses even cruder stereotypes—for example, in his portrait of Meyer Wolfsheim in *The Great Gatsby* (1925)—than you find in Cather's work of the same vintage: for example, Wolfsheim's flat-nosed ugliness and his imitation accent (he says "gonnegtion" for "connection"), an indication that Fitzgerald like the early Willa Cather had paid more attention to the way Jews talk in British novels than in New York restaurants. But on the whole, Wolfsheim bears a curious resemblance to his 1925 literary twin, Marcellus: both characters are unpleasantly florid and sentimental; they are associated with "dirty" money in the same way; they are clever exploiters; and contact with them lowers and declasses whoever is impure enough to suffer it. Thomas Wolfe's anti-Semitism, even though it comes out sounding more pungent, is still closer to Cather's. Wolfe's physical description of Abe Jones comes from the same mold that produced Willa Cather's description of Stein, and Wolfe's picture of the rich, powerful Jews at Esther Jack's party is based on the idea of the Jew—as a rich, secretive, financially and sexually aggressive stranger—that you usually find in Willa Cather.

It is true that the younger men, especially Hemingway and Faulkner, tend to temper their anti-Semitism markedly with a two-edged irony. Hemingway, for instance, iconoclastically reverses the stereotype in his tennis-playing, expatriated, Princeton-graduated Robert Cohn in *The Sun Also Rises* (1926), and Faulkner has fun satirizing the stereotype in *The Sound and the Fury* (1929) when he makes Jason Compson rant about those "damn eastern jews," those Wall Street "fellows that sit up there in New York and trim the suckers." Yet as anti-stereotypic as Cohn may be, he still stands in the novel as the symbol of the "outsider"; and drunk as Mike Campbell may be when he calls Cohn a "kike," Hemingway leaves the reader in no doubt that the drunken Campbell is preferable to the suffering Cohn. Faulkner may satirize Jason and his anti-Semitism, but he simultaneously satirizes the cowardly Jewish drummer, a kind of earlier Sherwood Anderson type, at whom Jason's comments are directed:

> "I've known some jews that were fine citizens. You might be one yourself," I [Jason] says.
> "No," he says, "I'm an American."
> "No offense," I says. "I give every man his due, regardless of religion or anything else. I have nothing against jews as an individual," I says. "It's just the race. You'll admit that they produce nothing. They follow the pioneers into a new country and sell them clothes."
> "You're thinking af Armenians," he says, "aren't you. A pioneer wouldn't have any use for new clothes."
> "No offense," I says. "I don't hold a man's religion against him."
> "Sure," he says, "I'm an American. My folks have some French blood, why I have a nose like this. I'm an American, all right."

This kind of thing became unfashionable in the literature of the 1930's, just as pictures of watermelon-eating Negroes became unfashionable in the 1940's, but American literature before the First World War on into the 1920's has a detectable anti-Semitic strain. Furthermore, rather than being confined to any class of writers, it is characteristic of what might be called the "main tradition," the "classic" writers who practiced their craft with greatest skill, dignity, and humanity. For the most part, Willa Cather's anti-Semitism is a part of this tradition and grows from the same cultural roots.

The only significant attempt at a broad cultural explanation of Willa Cather's anti-Semitism is in a book by John Randall, *The Landscape and the Looking Glass*, a thematic study of her fiction which puts considerable emphasis, perhaps too much, on the anti-Semitism. According to Randall, it can be explained by the Populist Movement. Taking his ideas fairly directly from Richard Hofstadter, Randall explains that the Populists, who were xenophobically anti-Semitic, subscribed to an oversimplified notion of history. Written in the form of a melodrama, it cast the sturdy land-owning yeoman in the role of hero, and the Eastern capitalist, Wall Street banker, and the Jew (who was associated with the House of Rothschild and something called "the international gold ring") in the role of villain. There is much that is persuasive and even brilliant in the connection Mr. Randall makes between the Populists and Willa Cather's anti-Semitism, but to imagine the politically antipathetic Willa Cather going to William Jennings Bryan for her ethical inspiration is somewhat comparable, for different reasons, to imagining H. L. Mencken doing so. What similarities exist between Populist anti-Semitism and the literary variety are probably due to the fact that both are expressions, one political and the other artistic, of the same cultural forces.

These underlying cultural forces are too vast and complicated to pin down with any precision, but they manifested themselves in the literature by that vast, unprecedented movement westward, beginning in about 1910, of what John Macy two generations ago called the "spirit" of American literature. At the time that Sullivan and Frank Lloyd Wright were creating a new American architecture in the Midwest, Dreiser, Anderson, Willa Cather, Sandburg, and Lewis were establishing a new literature. All these writers grew up in small Midwestern villages, and their real contact with cities did not come until after their ideas and attitudes had been pretty firmly molded. Willa Cather's story is a fairly typical one: from the age of 8 to 18 in the village of Red Cloud, a tiny hamlet on the Nebraska plains; from 18 to 22 in the somewhat larger world of Lincoln and the university, punctuated by a trip or two to Chicago; and not until after that the urban worlds of Pittsburgh, New York, and the European capitals. The story makes a pattern which can be read in several ways—as the escape from the horrors of corn-belt provincialism, the tragic-hegira from pastoral innocence, or the conquest of civilization and the Bright Medusa—but however it is read, it is the story of Dreiser, Anderson, Willa Cather, and the young writers who came after them, Fitzgerald and Hemingway; and the story that they told over and over again in their novels.

There is always some image in the work of these American writers—for Hemingway it is the big, two-hearted river; for Willa Cather the plow outlined against the sun; for Fitzgerald,

Nick Carroway's memory of the wind blowing "the wet laundry stiff on the line" just before he decides to return to the Midwest; for Anderson the streets of Winesburg where George Willard walks alone and dreams; for Wolfe the trains hooting in the night—that stands out as a sharp, intensely nostalgic symbol of the lost world of youth and purity. As though the mind of the writer had frozen on some personal, private, and incommunicable childhood scene, it remains forever fixed as the pole against which the pain of life, the tragedy of change, suffering, corruption, and death are measured. Fragile and ephemeral, it is projected into one term of a terrible and beautiful metaphor, symbolizing not only the beginning of the individual conscience, but Good in its melodramatic struggle with Evil, and the birth of American history.

One wonders whether that faint hostility to the Jew in the major literature of the 1920's was due simply to the historical accident that excluded him from the Midwestern village of the 1870's, 1880's, and 1890's that was its cradle. Was it due to something as simple as the fact that he had not fished in the big, two-hearted river, or walked the streets of Winesburg as George Willard had, or plowed the red grass on the Nebraska prairies? Willa Cather said that the history of a country is always in the hearts of the men and women who pioneer it. Her country, which was only as wide as her childhood memory, was pioneered by Swedes and Bohemians, and she could not make it any larger. Her fraternity of heroes was cosmopolitan and democratic, but it was also terribly exclusive, and you were admitted only if you had shared the early years together.

A Bibliographical Note

BIBLIOGRAPHIES

The most complete bibliography to date was compiled by Phyllis Martin Hutchinson, and printed under the title "The Writings of Willa Cather" in the *Bulletin* of the New York Public Library, June 1956, July 1956, and August 1956. It gives all the known editions of Willa Cather's writings in English, including separate lists of translations, general critical evaluation, and reviews and comments about individual books. Some additions and emendations are needed to Miss Hutchinson's list of Miss Cather's pseudonymous writings, and there are other minor inaccuracies—for instance, Gilbert Seldes is listed as Selden, Newton Arvin as Norton Arvin, and Nebraska as Benraska. But the bibliography is by far the most thorough and valuable to date.

A judicious selective bibliography is included in E. K. Brown and Leon Edel, *Willa Cather: A Critical Biography* (New York, 1953), pp. 446–451. Frederick B. Adams includes bibliographical information available in no other printed source in "Willa Cather Early Years: Trial and Error," *Colophon*, I, no. 3 (1939), and in "Willa Cather Middle Years: The Right Road Taken," *Colophon*, I, no. 4 (1940). E. K. Brown describes the Benjamin D. Hitz collection of early Willa Cather material, owned by the Newberry Library, in "Willa Cather: The Benjamin D. Hitz Collection," *Newberry Library Bulletin*, December 1950.

The most recent bibliography appears in *Willa Cather: Collected Short Fiction 1892–1912* (Lincoln, Nebraska, 1965), pp. 583–594. Besides listing a few critical and biographical works about Miss Cather, it lists, by year of publication, the titles of Miss

Cather's short stories, including pseudonymous stories, along with the date and place of publication. The list, which corrects a number of erroneous attributions made in the past, is the most complete and accurate bibliography of the short fiction to date.

BIOGRAPHICAL MATERIAL

A fairly detailed biographical treatment is included in the "official" biography of E. K. Brown and Leon Edel, *Willa Cather: A Critical Biography*. Mildred Bennett, *The World of Willa Cather* (New York, 1951), presents a good deal of information concerning the people and places that went into the Nebraska portions of Miss Cather's writing. The book was improved with notes and an index in the 1961 edition issued by the University of Nebraska Press. Elizabeth Sergeant has two biographical accounts, a sketch included in *Fire Under the Andes* (New York, 1927), and a book-length reminiscence, *Willa Cather: A Memoir* (Philadelphia, 1953). The last is the most personal and interpretative of the biographies, although it does not strive for factual completeness. Edith Lewis provides fresh and valuable information based on her close association with Miss Cather in *Willa Cather Living: A Personal Record* (New York, 1953).

A number of short interviews and reminiscences can be consulted for additional biographical sidelights: Stephen Vincent and Rosemary Benet, "Willa Cather: Civilized and Very American," New York *Herald Tribune,* December 15, 1940; George Siebel, "Miss Willa Cather from Nebraska," *New Colophon*, II, part 7 (1949); a collection of sometimes unintentionally comic letters solicited by James Shively from Miss Cather's college classmates in *Writings from Willa Cather's Campus Years*, ed. James Shively (Lincoln, 1950); and Phyllis Martin Hutchinson, "Reminiscence of Willa Cather as a Teacher," *Bulletin* of the New York Public Library (June, 1956).

CRITICISM

Books

Critical books about Willa Cather include René Rapin, *Willa Cather* (New York, 1930); David Daiches, *Willa Cather* (Ithaca,

1951); E. K. Brown and Leon Edel, *Willa Cather* (New York, 1953); John H. Randall, III, *The Landscape and the Looking Glass* (Boston, 1960); Edward and Lillian Bloom, *Willa Cather's Gift of Sympathy* (Southern Illinois University, 1962); Dorothy Van Ghent, *Willa Cather* (University of Minnesota pamphlet, 1964). Rapin's book, reminiscent of an earlier fashion in criticism, is interested almost wholly in extolling Miss Cather's "native" and "regional" qualities. Daiches' book might be described as a "reading," a book-by-book and story-by-story textual examination. Brown and Edel present a too one-sidedly appreciative assessment, but it is informed by an unusually seasoned critical judgment. Their book remains the most reliable single critical source. John Randall and the Blooms are concerned with the fiction mainly as "idea" and "value," especially Randall, who treats it from the standpoint of cultural historian rather than literary critic.

Articles

There are a large number (several hundred) of critical articles and brief commentaries, some of which deserve special mention. Two interesting assessments from the twenties are Lloyd Morris, "Willa Cather," *North American Review* (May, 1924); and Thomas Beer, "Willa Cather," *The Borzoi* (New York, 1925). Morris' is a rounded estimate, one of the earliest of the general estimates; Beer's is a witty, iconoclastic, sometimes brittle appreciation, written as though by one sophisticate in praise of another.

Interesting comment from the thirties includes Louis Kronenberger, "Willa Cather," *Bookman* (October, 1931); Ludwig Lewisohn, *Expression in America* (New York, 1932), pp. 538–543; Dorothy Canfield Fisher, "Daughter of the Frontier," New York *Herald Tribune*, May 28, 1933; Harry Hartwick, *The Foreground of American Fiction* (New York, 1934), pp. 389–404; Arthur Hobson Quinn, *American Fiction* (New York, 1936), pp. 683–697. Kronenberger's comment, like Hicks's or Trilling's, reflects the decline of Willa Cather's reputation in the thirties. Mrs. Fisher's, although not well written, is of interest because it comes from a Nebraska friend of Miss Cather's, and because it explains in an original way the author's choice of Nebraska subject. Harry Hartwick, one of the first to classify Willa Cather as a "humanist" and traditionalist, is also one of the first to attempt to deal in a broad way with her political, moral, and philosophical values.

Later comment includes H. S. Canby, "Willa Cather: 1876 to 1947," *Saturday Review of Literature* (May 10, 1947), later revised and included in *The Literary History of the United States* (New York, 1948), a wise summing-up; Bernard Baum, "Willa Cather's Waste Land," *South Atlantic Quarterly* (October, 1949), a discussion of Willa Cather's anti-Semitism; Katherine Anne Porter, *The Days Before* (New York, 1952), interesting because it comes from Miss Porter; Curtis Bradford, "Willa Cather's Uncollected Short Stories," *American Literature* (January, 1955), the soundest piece on this subject; Van Wyck Brooks, *The Confident Years: 1885–1915* (New York, 1955), pp. 527–533; Frederick Hoffman, *The Twenties* (New York, 1955), which contains an excellent discussion of *The Professor's House*, pp. 184–190; and Quentin Anderson, "Willa Cather: Her Masquerade," *New Republic* (November 27, 1965), a provocative general statement.

REVIEWS

In addition to the reviews included in this book, the following should be consulted by anyone who wants to trace in more detail the development of Willa Cather's critical reputation: an unsigned review of *O Pioneers!*, in *Nation* (September 4, 1923); an unsigned review, almost certainly by Randolph Bourne, of *The Song of the Lark*, in *New Republic* (December 11, 1915); Randolph Bourne, review of *My Ántonia*, in *Dial* (December 14, 1918); Sydney Howard, review of *One of Ours*, in *Bookman* (October, 1922); Gilbert Seldes, review of *One of Ours*, in *Dial* (October, 1922); Eunice Tietjen, review of *April Twilights*, in *Poetry* (July, 1923); Stuart P. Sherman, review of *The Professor's House*, in New York *Herald Tribune Books* (September 13, 1925); H. S. Canby, review of *The Professor's House*, in *Saturday Review of Literature* (September 26, 1925); Robert Morss Lovett, review of *Death Comes for the Archbishop*, in *New Republic* (October 26, 1927); Carl Van Doren, review of *Shadows on the Rock*, New York *Herald Tribune Books*

(August 2, 1931); Newton Arvin, review of *Shadows on the Rock*, in *New Republic* (August 12, 1931); Lloyd Morris, review of *The Old Beauty*, in New York *Herald Tribune Books* (September 12, 1948).

Index